THE LITERATURE OF SCOTLAND
II

The Literature of Scotland
Scotland

The Twentieth Century

SECOND EDITION

Roderick Watson

palgrave
macmillan

First edition published in one volume 1984
Second edition published in two volumes 2007
PALGRAVE MACMILLAN
Houndmills, Basingstoke, Hampshire RG21 6XS and
175 Fifth Avenue, New York, N.Y. 10010
Companies and representatives throughout the world

PALGRAVE MACMILLAN is the global academic imprint of the Palgrave Macmillan division of St. Martin's Press, LLC and of Palgrave Macmillan Ltd. Macmillan® is a registered trademark in the United States, United Kingdom and other countries. Palgrave is a registered trademark in the European Union and other countries.

ISBN-13: 978-0-230-00037-7
ISBN-10: 0-230-00037-1

This book is printed on paper suitable for recycling and made from fully managed and sustained forest sources.

A catalogue record for this book is available from the British Library.

A catalog record for this book is available from the Library of Congress.

10 9 8 7 6 5 4 3 2 1
16 15 14 13 12 11 10 09 08 07

Printed and bound in CPD (Wales) Ltd, Ebbw Vale.

In memory of my mother and father

Contents

Preface

What is 'Scottish literature'? Is it writing *about* Scotland by anybody, or writing from authors currently living *in* Scotland, or is it literary production about anything by people born in Scotland or of Scottish descent living anywhere?

The critical and theoretical exploration of what we have understood 'Scotland' and 'Scottish identity' to mean, now and in the past, is the topic for a study in itself, but I have called this book *The Literature of Scotland*, rather than use the phrase 'Scottish Literature', in order to signal something of how I have chosen to understand these issues. The 'literature of Scotland' is intended to echo 'the matter of Scotland' in so far as the two volumes which constitute this study seek to trace the various versions of Scotland and engagements with Scotland that Scots-born writers have undertaken over more than 700 years, during some of which time, of course, the very concept of 'Scotland' was either a new idea or under discussion in a debate that has continued until the present day.

National identity is a cultural and a political construction and 'the matter of Scotland' (after the Arthurian legends of 'the Matter of Britain') may well recall Barbour, or Blind Harry, or those medieval historians who constructed their own grandiose national genealogies, to insist on Scotland's sovereign difference from whatever territories lay to the south. So it is no surprise that linguistic difference and literary production should have played key roles in this arena from the very start. Nor have such productions been slow to achieve cultural and then socio-political and historical impact, for *representations* of reality (whatever their verisimilitude) quickly become a material factor in their own right. So the prejudices and passions of our poets and novelists in the supreme fiction of literature have contributed greatly to 'the matter of Scotland'.

There have been truly remarkable developments in the critical examination of Scottish literature and culture and in the number of specialist studies available since this book, originally published as a single volume, first appeared in 1984. There has been an equally remarkable and enormously exciting growth in creative output and achievement in the field of contemporary Scottish writing. In this revised and expanded study, as with the first edition of *The Literature of Scotland*, the aim is to offer students and the general reader an introductory overview of the whole field of Scottish literature along with something of the biographical and historical background to the works at issue and the circumstances under which they arose.

The first volume of this new edition covers medieval to Victorian times and notable periods of great creative activity. This second volume recognises that the twentieth century has witnessed the richest and most diverse literary production in Scotland's long history. In the light of this wealth, and a growing international critical interest in Scottish studies, we have allocated this whole second volume to the writing and writers of the modern period. The separation is an artificial one, of course, for we can trace the immediately 'modern' back to at least the nineteenth century and have only to reflect, for example, on the continuing impact of James Hogg's *Justified Sinner* (1824) among contemporary authors to prove the point. Nevertheless, it seems appropriate – and hopefully both timely and useful – to allow more space in this book for a critical overview of current Scottish literature in order to put contemporary writing into a wider and more detailed set of contexts and connections.

We know where we are by knowing where we came from, and it is hoped that readers will understand the present in the light of the past, and the past in the light of the present, by way of the narrative and chronological approach of these two volumes, each of which stands alone as a text but should be best and most fully understood in the light of the other.

Of course no author's life can ever fully explain a work, and literary texts are inexhaustible in ways that transcend context and biography. But then again, no literary work can stand entirely apart from the conditions of its production and the political, philosophical, economic, and cultural forces of the times. What were the literary conventions of the day? Does a writer's work accept or reject them, and how should we place it against the other arts of the period at home and abroad? Where does an author stand in relation to fellow authors, or the politics and cultural mores of the time? What are the circumstances that may or may not have shaped their imagination? How does their work fit, or not fit, the necessarily changing canon of Scottish literature? Which books have stayed the course in our collective memory, and which have disappeared, and why?

No true analysis or understanding can take place without this initial locating process, and it is hoped that these volumes with their timeline will provide just such a basic contextual grounding in advance of more specialised studies. Having said that, I have also sought to signal the links and affinities between creative artists by grouping writers and topics together in ways that reflect their generic, thematic and not just their chronological connections, while still staying close to the developing story decade by decade. Then again, I hope to offer descriptive, but also specifically critical and analytical responses to key works from key writers in each century, with an indication of the various critical debates that have arisen around those texts from one century, or even one decade, to the next.

While the book deals with a place called 'Scotland' we must not lose sight of the fact that the geographical boundaries of this small country have sustained many different histories and many authors writing in several different languages. And yet, however various these writers have undoubtedly been, part of what this book will end up describing is their own engagement with this fascinating country and a series of understandings, growing and also changing, of what 'Scotland' might mean to them. So part of what this book traces is the slow growth of a Scottish canon, as writers and critics have perceived it over the ages. Nor can I pretend to stand outside my own times – or even my own preferences – in many of the critical assessments made in the following pages.

Beyond the tricky questions of canon formation, historical reception and current critical evaluation, a particular point of emphasis and acknowledgment should be declared here. I have been determined that literature in Gaelic – so often neglected in past literary histories – should take an uncontested place in the unfolding of Scotland's many different cultural expressions across the centuries. The Gaidhealtachd has been influential at every turn in Scotland's story and in how we have come to see ourselves. More detailed research into Gaelic literature and culture – and its many points of contact with and divergence from Irish, European, Classical and Lowland culture – is finally beginning in Scottish Studies today. Much work still remains to be done, but I owe a special debt to the translators who have made this work available to a much wider audience. Since many older translations of Gaelic poems adopted a rather tired poetic diction, I have used the most contemporary available English versions whenever possible. In this respect my thanks go to translations made by the late Iain Crichton Smith and the late Ian Grimble, and especially to Professor Derick Thomson and his book *An Introduction to Gaelic Poetry* (London:

Gollancz, 1974). The exigencies of space argue against dual text quotation in a study such as this, so for a fuller access to the originals readers are directed to my anthology *The Poetry of Scotland* (Edinburgh: Edinburgh University Press, 1995); or more specifically to the following anthologies: Colm O Baoill's anthology of seventeenth-century Gaelic poems *The Harp's Cry / Gàir nan Clàrsach* (Edinburgh: Birlinn, 1994); Derick Thomson's *Gaelic Poetry in the Eighteenth Century* (Aberdeen: Association of Scottish Literary Studies, 1993); Donald Meek's edition of nineteenth-century Scottish Gaelic poetry *The Wiles of the World / Caran An T-Saoghail* (West Lothian: Barbour Books, 2003); or Ronald Black's collection of twentieth-century Scottish Gaelic verse *An Tuil* (Edinburgh: Polygon, 1999).

The four literary languages of Scotland – Gaelic, Latin, Scots and English – speak for a strongly polyphonic heritage whose implications are still with us, and indeed growing, as Scotland's citizens become more ethnically and culturally diverse. It is most certainly not this volume's intention to reduce these many different voices to a single narrative of a single national identity. On the contrary, the plurality of Scottish culture – and indeed of all cultures – has been widely recognised in scholarly and theoretical circles in modern times, and has at last become a part of popular awareness. At the same time, I have sought to bring the many sides of Scotland's complex story together, while also leaving room for readers to draw their own conclusions. With this in mind I hope that this account of 'the literature of Scotland' will be found to be reliably informative and critically stimulating, as well as coherent, readable and entertaining.

Roderick Watson

Acknowledgements

Thanks are due to the Trustees of the National Library of Scotland for permission to quote from William Soutar's 'Song'; appreciation is also due to Margaret Snow for permission to quote from the poems of W. S. Graham: to Felicity Henderson for permission to quote from the poems of Hamish Henderson; to the late Ian Hamilton Finlay for permission to quote 'The Cloud's Anchor' and 'One (Orange) Arm of the World's Oldest Windmill', to Tom Leonard for extracts from 'this is the six o'clock news', to Kate Wood for permission to quote from Alastair Mackie's poems, to Kevin MacNeil for permission to quote 'Words, seahorses'. My thanks also go to Carol Ann Duffy; to Douglas Dunn and Lynda Mamy for his US rights; to Fearghas MacFhionnlaigh for permission to quote from an article published on the website of Rutherford House; to Carcanet for the use of interviews on their websites with David Kinloch and Carol Ann Duffy; and the Poetry Society for an interview on their website. My special thanks also go to Hugh Andrew of Polygon and to Michael Schmidt of Carcanet for their generosity, and warm appreciation to Ronald Black, Ian Grimble, Donald MacAulay, Donald Meek, William Neill, Iain Crichton Smith, and especially Derick Thomson for their translations of Gaelic poetry into English.

The author and publishers wish to thank the following publishers who have kindly given permission for the use of copyright material:

Anvil Press Poetry for Carol Ann Duffy: 'Originally' is taken from *The Other Country* (1990); 'Warming Her Pearls' is taken from *Selling Manhattan* (1987); 'Prayer' is taken from *Mean Time* (1993).
ARC Publications for W. N. Herbert, *The Testament of the Revd. Thomas Dick.*
Birlinn/Polygon for Robert Garioch, *Collected Poems*; *The Poems of Norman MacCaig*; Iain Crichton Smith, *The Life and Works of Murdo*; Kenneth White, *Open World Collected Poems, 1960–2000*; Liz Lochhead, *Dreaming Frankenstein*; *The Colour of Black and White*; Robert Crawford and W. N. Herbert, *Sharawaggi*; Aonghas MacNeacail, *A Proper Schooling*; *Rock and Water*; Rody Gorman, *Fax and Other Poems*; Ronald Black (ed.), *An Tuil*; Donald Meek (ed.), *The Wiles of the World / Caran An T-Saoghail.*
Bloodaxe for W. N. Herbert, *Forked Tongue*; *Cabaret McGonagall*; Kathleen Jamie, *The Autonomous Region*; *The Queen of Sheba*; Jackie Kay, *Other Lovers.*
Calder Publications for Sydney Goodsir Smith, *Collected Poems.*
Canongate Books for Derick Thomson, *Creachadh na Clàrsaich / Plundering the Harp*; Kevin MacNeil, *Love and Zen in the Outer Hebrides.*

Carcanet Press for Hugh MacDiarmid, *Complete Poems*; Iain Crichton Smith, *Collected Poems*; Sorley MacLean, *From Wood to Ridge*; Edwin Morgan, *Collected Poems*; Frank Kuppner, *The Intelligent Observation of Naked Women*; *Everything is Strange*.

Edinburgh University Press for *The Collected Poems and Songs of George Campbell Hay*.

Etruscan Books for Tom Leonard, *Access to the Silence*.

Faber & Faber for Edwin Muir, *Collected Poems*; W. S. Graham, *New Collected Poems*; Douglas Dunn, *Terry Street*; *Barbarians*; *Elegies*; *Northlight*; Don Paterson, *Nil Nil*; *God's Gift to Women*; *Landing Light*.

Fountain Publishing for Angus Peter Campbell, *One Road*.

John Murray for *The Collected Poems of George Mackay Brown*.

Mercat Press for Alastair Mackie, *At the Heich Kirkyaird*.

Oxford University Press, NY, for the US rights to quote from the poems of Edwin Muir.

Picador for Kate Clanchy, *Slattern*; *Samarkand*; Kathleen Jamie, *Jizzen*.

The Random House Group: John Burnside, extracts from 'Home', 'Annunciation', 'Suburbs' and 'Domestic' from *Common Knowledge*, published by Secker and Warburg; extract from 'A Theory of Everything' from *The Light Trap*, published by Jonathan Cape. Robert Crawford, extracts from 'The Land o' Cakes' and 'Hostilities' from *Scottish Assembly*, published by Chatto & Windus; extracts from 'Chaps' from *Masculinity*, published by Jonathan Cape. Tom Leonard, extract from 'Poetry, Schools, Place' from *Reports from the Present*, published by Jonathan Cape. All reprinted by permission of the Random House Group Ltd.

Vennel Press for David Kinloch, *Dustie-Fute*.

Every effort has been made to trace the copyright holders but if any have been inadvertently overlooked the publishers will be pleased to make the necessary arrangements at the first opportunity.

I must conclude by acknowledging the many scholars in Scottish history and literature whose researches continue to illuminate and to realign our understanding of Scotland's cultural history, never more so than in the last twenty years which have seen an explosion of critical, historical and biographical analysis in the matter of Scotland and a flood of first-rate theoretical and literary-critical analysis. And finally, special thanks are due to my many colleagues and students; to the late Derry Jeffares who first brought this project to me; to the University of Stirling for its generous sabbatical provision; to all at Palgrave Macmillan for their enthusiasm and patience; to my wife Celia for her unfailing support.

Scotland

Introduction:
into the twentieth century

In Volume I of *The Literature of Scotland* it is proposed that there have been three periods of outstandingly rich achievement in the long narrative of Scottish writing. The first two of these, which are the concern of the first volume *The Middle Ages to the Nineteenth Century*, would include the poetry of the makars from the fifteenth century and then the extraordinary period of renewal and revival that saw the Enlightenment – an outpouring of vernacular literature in Scots and Gaelic; and a major engagement with Scottish history and identity in the eighteenth and the nineteenth centuries. The third and in some ways the most striking of these developments takes us to the 'Modern. Scottish Literary Renaissance' and the later productions of the twentieth century. Such is the remit of this second volume. The division, however, is no more than a formal device, for we never really throw off the ghosts and the books of the past, and their traces are more than evident in the work of many modern Scottish authors. Thus James Robertson's novel *The Fanatic* is haunted by Hogg's *Confessions* – nor is he the only contemporary writer to be so visited. Andrew Greig's fiction refers to John Buchan and the Scottish ballads; novels by Neil Gunn and Iain Crichton Smith revisit the Clearances, while Sir Walter Scott is re-imagined by Allan Massie. Thus Edwin Muir, Fionn Mac Colla, Liz Lochhead and many more try to come to terms with the ghost of John Knox.

This volume begins with the diverse literary, political and cultural tendencies that have come to be known as the modern Scottish Renaissance. The roots of these tendencies go back to the previous century, but the term came into its own in the later 1920s as a way of describing the political and critical efforts to re-envisage a country that too many politicians, university professors and popular newspapers were coming to regard as merely 'North Britain'. And this period also marks the beginning of a wider recognition that global economic forces and the rise of the mass media were eroding everything that was most distinctive and hence of most value in *all* minority cultures in the modern world. Thus although the literary renaissance of twentieth-century Scotland began with vernacular Scots, it soon came to recognise that the country's Gaelic inheritance was still more seriously in decline than the Scots one – neglected and undervalued even by the Lowland Scots themselves. From such insights an understanding of hegemonic cultural forces and a sense of common purpose began to dawn. Nor was this analysis of relevance to Scotland only. (MacDiarmid's essay from 1931, 'English Ascendancy in British Literature', is a key early document in what would now be understood as postcolonial literary theory.)

So it was that many of the writers of the early twentieth-century Renaissance aimed to re-imagine a Scotland that could contribute something unique and valuable to the world at large. In the first half of the century this agenda gave rise to works that sought to combine the personal, the national and even the global. MacDiarmid spoke for the rights of small nations and 'minority' languages along with a universalising vision of political and scientific materialism. Edwin Muir, Neil Gunn and George Mackay Brown turned to myth-building symbolism in their poetry and prose, while Lewis Grassic Gibbon, Sorley MacLean and George Campbell Hay made a specific identification between the fate of their own people and that of oppressed cultures and individuals throughout the world. All sought in their different ways to bring together the local and the universal.

Thirty years later the socio-political focus of Alasdair Gray and James Kelman can be seen to belong to the same tradition, even if Kelman has no truck with questions of Scottish national identity as such. As a general rule, indeed, the Scottish writers of the second half of the century have been less inclined to pursue their precursor's large-scale system-building ambitions. In their place have come the exploration of personal identity and works of psychological interrogation, or works that dare to confront the modern realities of economic oppression, cultural hegemony, environmental exploitation or urban breakdown. For others, the question of what it means to be 'Scottish' is more intimately related to issues of class, race, sexuality and gender, as can be seen in the work of fine contemporary authors such as Liz Lochhead, Janice Galloway, A. L. Kennedy, Kathleen Jamie, Jackie Kay and Ali Smith. Nor is it an accident that this shift of focus should come from women, for the explosion of new female writing in the second half of the twentieth century is one of the period's most striking features. Whether they have been inspired by or merely irritated by the founding fathers of the literary renaissance of the twenties is scarcely relevant any more, for in either case they are certainly and definitively free of those often patriarchal shadows.

Of course the modern revival would have been stillborn without the talents of its remarkable writers, but scholars and academics have played a small part as well. To give a brief account of their production is to trace how Scotland's history and cultural identity have been subject to major revaluation in our times, and also to recognise the expansion of critical interest and scholarly study, which was particularly marked in the last twenty years of the twentieth century.

T. F. Henderson showed the way with his *Scottish Vernacular Literature* (1898), just as the Revd Nigel Macneill had dealt with Gaelic in *The Literature of the Highlanders*, (1892) followed by the Revd Magnus Maclean with *The Literature of the Highlands* in 1903, updated in the 1920s. J. H. Millar ignored Gaelic but his exhaustive *Literary History of Scotland* (1903) is still a valuable (and acerbic) study. More recently, in 1977 and again in 1992, Maurice Lindsay's *History of Scottish Literature* has taken a similarly inclusive approach (but still without Gaelic) from a modern point of view. By comparison with Millar's encyclopaedic book, Gregory Smith's *Scottish Literature: Character and Influence* (1919), was much briefer but much more influential, too. Smith tried to define what might be called a national psychology, or at least national habits of expression, as manifested in Scottish literature over the centuries. Hugh MacDiarmid was much impressed and promptly incorporated some of these ideas into his own poetry to use as propaganda against the English cultural establishment. Following Gregory Smith (and similarly prone to essentialism) he proposed that the Scottish sensibility was characteristically extreme, containing a combination of opposite tendencies, a 'Caledonian anti-syzygy', that manifests itself in a delight in domestic realism and the accumulation of many small details on the one hand, and a love of excess and wild flights of fancy on the other. These were 'the polar twins of the Scottish muse' and MacDiarmid welcomed them as allies against the Victorian conception of the Scotsman as a dull, canny, parsi-monious peasant. By 1936, however, Edwin Muir's *Scott and Scotland* was suggesting that the 'Caledonian antisyzygy' was exactly what was *wrong* with the national psyche, for it would swing frantically from one extreme to the other without ever reaching rest or resolution. For better or for worse, Smith's new diagnosis of 'Scottishness' had entered the critical vocabulary and the creative resources of the nation.

The natural inheritor of Gregory Smith's thesis was Kurt Wittig, a German scholar whose work *The Scottish Tradition in Literature* (1958) pursued still further what he took to be the most unique and persistent features to be found in writing from Scotland. Twentieth-century accounts of the Scottish tradition have owed much to this and two further books, both from 1961. George Elder Davie's *The Democratic Intellect* stressed the philosophical and egalitarian ideals of traditional Scottish education, and David Craig's *Scottish Literature and the Scottish People, 1680–1830* makes a vigorous materialist analysis of the social conditions and assumptions that influenced Scottish writers and readers during a crucial period of their history. David Daiches also explored the special contradictions of eighteenth-century Scotland in his seminal study *The Paradox of Scottish Culture* (1964). Ten years later, on the Gaelic front, Derick Thomson offered his invaluable *Introduction to Gaelic Poetry* (1974).

In the years since *The Literature of Scotland* first appeared in 1984, there has been an explosion of writing on Scottish literary history. Between 1987 and 1988 Aberdeen University Press produced its four-volume *History of Scottish Literature* under the general editorship of Cairns Craig. With eighty essays from distinguished scholars and critics, this produced excellent accounts of specific authors. Its new insights into various areas of study and its specified further reading make it an indispensable reference, although the collected-essay method can also leave historical and cultural *lacunae*. (As I write, another such scholarly project is forthcoming from Edinburgh University Press.) More recent accounts of Scottish literary and cultural history have also followed this format, most notably in Paul Scott's editing of *Scotland: A Concise Cultural History* (Mainstream, 1993) with illuminating essays on literature, art, music, philosophy, sport, cinema, medicine, law, mathematics, education et al. Christopher Whyte's editing of the essays in *Gendering the Nation* (Edinburgh University Press, 1995) made a crucial intervention in the debate about national identity from the point of view of the politics of gender, while *A History of Scottish Womens's Writing*, edited by Douglas Gifford and Dorothy McMillan (Edinburgh University Press, 1997), has done a very great deal to reclaim cultural and critical territory for many writers whose contributions have been undervalued or just neglected in previous studies. In similar fashion, territory was reclaimed for Scottish Drama in the essays included in *A History of Scottish Theatre* (Polygon, 1998) edited by Bill Findlay, and in *Scottish Theatre Since the Seventies*, edited by Randall Stevenson and Gavin Wallace (Edinburgh University Press, 1996). (The same editors also produced *The Scottish Novel since the Seventies* in 1993.) Marshall Walker's *Scottish Literature since 1707* (Longman, 1996) takes a more singular view, governed by a set of critical propositions and themes that allow him to analyse and compare the work of individual authors in their period. Finally, there is *Scottish Literature in English and Scots*, edited by Douglas Gifford, Sarah Dunnigan and

Alan MacGillivray (Edinburgh 2002). This mammoth volume draws on the collective teaching skills of the department of Scottish Literature at Glasgow University to operate as a combination literary history, encyclopaedia and literary companion with a wealth of suggested further reading.

Recent anthologies such as Catherine Kerrigan's *Scottish Women Poets* (Edinburgh University Press, 1991), Dorothy McMillan's *Modern Scottish Women Poets* (Canongate, 2003), and my own *The Poetry of Scotland: Gaelic, Scots, English 1380–1980* (Edinburgh University Press, 1995) have helped to develop our understanding of the literary canon. Perhaps the most striking of these is Thomas Clancy's *The Triumph Tree. Scotland's Earliest Poetry AD 530–1350* (Canongate, 1998), which speaks for a period rarely anthologised in such terms (not least because the concept of 'Scotland' had yet to be born), in the languages of Latin, Welsh, Gaelic, Old English and Norse. In the introduction to his anthology of *Early Scottish Literature 1375–1707* (Mercat Press, 1997), R. D. S. Jack makes a passionate plea for a continuity in Scottish literary history, most especially in the Renaissance period via the rules of rhetoric and the poetic profession-alism of verse production which prevailed from late medieval times to the seventeenth century. His interest in Scottish literature's polymath origins and its early propensity for multi-vocal expression is entirely in keeping with the emphasis on these factors in much contemporary crit-ical writing. Finally, the foundation of the Canongate Classics series in 1987, with support from the Scottish Arts Council, facilitated the re-publication and dissemination of over a hundred titles for both students and the general reader, in a conscious strategy to make avail-able, to rethink, and even to change the Scottish literary canon.

Recent studies and essays have understood canonicity and the constructed nature of literary history much more clearly than earlier generations, and they have theorised the pressures of linguistic and cultural hegemony and the counter-narratives of national identity. Among the most influential of these is Robert Crawford's *Devolving English Literature* (Clarendon Press, 1992), which argues that Scotland has played a key part in the development of literary study in Britain, and also sees the Scottish experience in the wider perspective of American, Australian, Irish and Caribbean writing. Cairns Craig's *Out of History* (1996) and especially his study of *The Modern Scottish Novel: Narrative and the National Imagination* (Edinburgh University Press, 1999) make a related case for the fictional techniques and innovations that have been born out of Scottish writers' awareness of the tensions between their Calvinist inheritance and the dominance of English-language culture. For my own part, I have often argued for the modern Scottish literary renaissance as only one of many such devolutionary movements across the field of 'literatures in English' as opposed to the now contested hegemony of 'English Literature'. And I have argued, too, for the role played by Scottish literature, especially in its texts in Gaelic and its many varieties of Scots, as a significantly energetic, plural and polyphonic counterpole to the monological discourses of linguistic imperialism and 'high' culture.

In the last analysis, however, the present volume is not intended to present a selective thesis in the vein of Wittig, Davie, David Craig, Daiches, Cairns Craig or Crawford; nor can it quite lay claim to the detail of the four-volume *History of Scottish Literature*, or the study of *Scottish Women's Writing* edited by Gifford and McMillan. But there is still a need, as far as the student and the general reader are concerned, for a path somewhere between these two approaches – a critical and contextualised account of the lives, times and major works of Scotland's writers. The brief and selective historical summaries at the start of each chapter have been chosen to reflect those aspects of Scottish history that feature most frequently, or contentiously, in Scottish literature. Whenever appropriate, I have tried to recognise the relevance of critical concepts such as the 'democratic intellect', the 'vernacular revival' or the 'Caledonian antisyzygy' without proposing these as necessary or exclusive analytical tools. Having said this, however, it seems to me that there are at least two aspects of Scottish culture that have only occasionally received a proper recognition – although there are signs that this is changing. First, I would point once again to the co-presence of the Gaelic tradition and the mutual inter-actions between Highland and Lowland society and their conceptions and misconceptions of each other. And secondly, I believe that the best of what might be called the Presbyterian intellectual inheritance in Scotland has been undeservedly obscured or denied, because the popular imagination has been so easily distracted (and understandably repelled) by the worst excesses of Calvinism. Thus many Scots will tell enquiring visitors that the Reformation was the worst thing to happen in Scotland and that John Knox cast a permanent shadow on the Scottish face. This is a misleading myth not least because, for better or worse, it allows Scots to hide from the truth about themselves, and is just as sentimental in the end as that other mythical Scotland where the wicked English are perpetually chasing Flora MacDonald and Bonnie Prince Charlie across the heather.

Yet literature and history have always made lively and unscholarly bedfellows. And some of Scotland's most enduring images, myths and misconceptions have been created by her greatest writers – which brings us back to the consideration of how authors choose their subject, why they choose to see it in a certain light and, from multiple reflections of such works, how *we* choose to see ourselves.

1
The twentieth century: the Modern Scottish Renaissance

WHEN THE French critic and philosopher Denis Saurat wrote the influential essay 'Le groupe de "la Renaissance Écossaise"' in 1924, he was thinking mainly of the writers associated with Hugh MacDiarmid's *Northern Numbers* anthologies and his magazine *Scottish Chapbook*, started in 1922. Yet the notion of a renaissance was not a new one: signs of a revival in culture and politics can be traced to the beginning of the century, and indeed the term was first coined in modern times by Patrick Geddes, writing of a 'Celtic Renascence' in his periodical *The Evergreen* from the Outlook Tower in 1895, with a vision of Edinburgh as 'not only a National and Imperial, but a European city – the larger view of Scotland'. But it was Hugh MacDiarmid's creative example, not to mention his political nationalism and his indefatigable propaganda, that was to make the most impact, and if he shared Geddes's insistence on a European outlook it was his satirical attacks on his own countrymen that gave the movement a necessary critical dimension.

Today 'the Modern Scottish Renaissance' is still a useful term to describe the remarkable outpouring of cultural activity that went towards making the twentieth century without question the third period of major literary achievement in Scotland's history. It has become convenient to refer to a 'second wave' in the Renaissance to describe those writers who came to prominence in the forties and fifties, and after that one might even talk of a third generation as well, although some of the younger writers discussed in the next chapter would deny any direct literary debt to MacDiarmid, Gibbon, Gunn, Muir or MacLean, or, indeed, any significant connection with each other. Thus, for example, some of the writers in the sixties looked to Europe, America or England for their models while others, especially in Glasgow and the west a few years later, were openly critical of the nationalist agenda, making a primarily socialist commitment to working-class Scottish speech and topics instead.

These three 'waves' of literary activity can also be found in the country's periodicals, with MacDiarmid's *Scottish Chapbook* leading the way from 1922. In the thirties and forties J. H. Whyte's *Modern Scot* and Maurice Lindsay's *Poetry Scotland* were among the more influential publications, with the *Saltire Review* and then the *New Saltire* taking over between 1954 and 1964. Among the little magazines mostly dedicated to poetry, *Lines Review*, which started in 1952, Duncan Glen's *Akros* (1965), and *Chapman* (1970) have all been particularly constructive. Glen's *Autobiography of a Poet* (1986) gives an account of how he started the Akros Press whose creative and critical publications were equally important in the 1960s and 1970s. As a periodical *Akros* ended its distinguished record in 1983 and *Lines* concluded in 1998 but *Chapman* remains a vital presence to this day with a commitment to poetry, prose and articles. The 'third generation' was especially marked by the publication of critical magazines such as Bob Tait's *Scottish International* (1968–74), with a broad outlook and a commitment to the arts and politics in an international arena. *Scottish International* also published early work by Alasdair Gray (extracts from *Lanark* in progress) and Alan Spence, heralding what was to be the explosion of new Scottish prose fiction in the 1980s. *Cencrastus* took a similar route from 1979 as did the quarterly *New Edinburgh Review*, started in 1969, developed by Peter Kravitz in the 1980s with an interdisciplinary interest as *The Edinburgh Review* and refreshed again in 2000 as a forum for 'the best new writing and critical thought', supported by occasional *Edinburgh Review* editions disseminating both creative and critical work. Kravitz also had a strong influence in publishing new writers when he worked for the Polygon Press in the 1980s – at that time an offshoot of undergraduate publishing at Edinburgh University.

Whether these periodicals (and the many still smaller 'small magazines' that accompanied them) speak for a single literary renaissance, or for several stages of it, or for a succession of independent initiatives, there is no doubt that the creative and critical output that started in the 1920s marks an extraordinary revival of cultural confidence in Scottish literary productivity that has continued and indeed notably accelerated right up to the present day.

Stirrings

The century began with the popular success of Charles Murray's vernacular verse in *Hamewith*, while Professor H. J. C. Grierson had begun to teach Scots Literature and Language at the University of Aberdeen. Literary histories by J. H. Millar and T. F. Henderson followed in the next ten years, while Gregory Smith's *Scottish Literature, Character and Influence* (1919) provided MacDiarmid with just the argument he needed to propose a dynamic and contradictory spirit in the Scottish sensibility – a psychology worthy of Dostoevsky himself – specifically opposed to the sentimental dilutions of the Kailyard. MacDiarmid tried to align even the vernacular tradition with the swift collisions of imagery in modernist verse and claimed that Scots was well suited to the spirit of D. H. Lawrence's prose. The Irish literary revival had impressed Scotsmen at the turn of the century and by the 1920s James Joyce was being cited as an example of a writer who could achieve international status and universal significance for books that were still deeply rooted in Ireland and his native Dublin. The local need not be parochial, and MacDiarmid stressed the point by insisting that true internationalism could not even exist without small nations. The unique identity of such countries and the need to resist their slide into the anonymity of larger political and economic bodies became an early concern of Scottish nationalism and was to be revived in the seventies, after the spirit of E. F. Schumacher's *Small is Beautiful* (1973) – a 'study of economics as if people mattered'. The First World War had played a part in this understanding, for it was fought – so the population was told – 'to preserve the right of small nations', and yet many servicemen returned to a Scotland whose cultural and economic identity seemed to be at a very low ebb indeed. MacDiarmid and Saurat were not slow to adopt the motto of the Belgian literary revival – 'Soyons nous-mêmes' – although, surprisingly, the Irish example was seldom used. For the 'Renaissance group' at least, cultural and political identity were inseparable.

In fact political nationalism and the demand for 'Home Rule' go back to the Liberal politics of the previous century, and also featured in the thinking of the Scottish Left in the Independent Labour Party (ILP) and the trade unions. Labour tensions had come to a head in Clydeside during and immediately after the First World War – under the influence of internationally minded socialists on the shop floor, and the ordinary workers' recognition that the ailing heavy industries of the central belt had been ruthlessly expanded to meet the war-effort only to face severe decline in the years of peace. The anti-war speeches of John Maclean, strikes, mass meetings, and his imprisonment with James Maxton on charges of sedition all led to real fears of revolution and 'Red Clydeside' on the part of the establishment, especially during the famous mass strike for a forty-hour week in 1919, when armoured cars and troops policed the streets of Glasgow. Maclean's hopes for a form of Scottish republican communism (free of Moscow) were not to be realised, but his many trials and his early death in 1923 made him a martyr for the cause and a potent symbol of it ever since. Sorley MacLean, Hugh MacDiarmid, Edwin Morgan, Hamish Henderson and Sydney Goodsir Smith were all to write verses about him. The old Covenanting independent spirit had not lost its power to move and this is especially clearly reflected in the secular but evangelically socialist intensities of Sorley MacLean's political poems.

After the initial euphoria at the coming of peace, the post-war slump took hold with particular force in the heavy industries and coalmines of Scotland, Tyneside and South Wales, and these areas suffered disproportionate hardships in the Depression years to come. By 1922 the Left and the ILP had made major advances in Scotland, sending twenty-nine Labour MPs to Westminster, with ten 'Red Clydesiders' headed by John Wheatley and including Maxton, Mannie Shinwell, Tom Johnston and one Communist – Willie Gallacher. The Labour movement continued to grow during the years around the General Strike in 1926, and many figures from Scotland's radical tradition played leading parts on the national stage. After all, social conditions in the post-Victorian Scottish cities and especially in the industrial west were truly appalling. Yet internal strife, dispute between the ILP and the Labour Party, widespread fears of communism, and simple dread at the prospect of the Depression getting worse, all helped to put Ramsay MacDonald's essentially conservative National Government into power in the 1930s. The radical 'Red Clyde' entered the realms of legend, although Glasgow and the west continue to be a heartland of left-wing politics in Britain.

Meanwhile a more culturally centred drive for nationalism had led to the foundation of the National Party of Scotland at Stirling in 1928, with R. E. Muirhead and John MacCormick as chairman and secretary (both from the ILP), and a spectrum of support from workers, liberals, students and radical intellectuals such as MacDiarmid and their president, Cunninghame Graham. In the 1930s the National Party amalgamated with the more liberal Scottish Party to form the Scottish National Party, and the movement began to gain strength during and after the Second World War, when the tendency once again had been to submerge Scotland's economic and social problems for the sake of Britain as a whole. It was popularly believed that, for as long as power was centralised in Westminster and in the massive population of the

Home Counties, government would never come to grips with matters in Scotland and the north of England, which continued to suffer from unemployment, industrial decline, inadequate housing and high emigration. By the more prosperous sixties the case for 'devolution' had attracted widespread interest, and after the winning of Hamilton by Winnie Ewing in 1967 the SNP began to influence Westminster, if only because its presence as an electoral threat stimulated both Labour and Conservative parties to accommodate themselves to Scottish needs. (The Liberal Party had continued to support decentralisation but made less of a threat to the status quo in parliament.)

The discovery of oil in the North Sea heralded a boom for the SNP as well, typified by the opportunistic slogan 'It's Scotland's Oil'. The widespread success of John McGrath's play *The Cheviot, the Stag and the Black, Black Oil* in 1973 had as much to do with sentimental nationalism as it had with his own brand of republican socialism but, even so, it seemed that a devolved socialist Scotland was just around the corner. Had not Scotland voted Labour since the war? Was there not a bill before parliament for moderate devolution? The bill passed at the close of 1976 only to die the death of a thousand cuts in committee stage. Then Westminster decreed that no referendum result on this topic could be valid unless 40 per cent of all registered Scottish voters voted 'yes', and when this failed to transpire in 1979 the bill died. These matters from the twenties and the seventies are worth recounting, for to many at that time it seemed as if the 'auld sang' had been heard again – in two different keys – only to be lost again, twice in one century. This was not to be the last of it, however.

If MacDiarmid's hopes for a Scottish republic never bore fruit, his vision of a broader cultural revival fared better. His own poems were set to music by his friends F. G. Scott (1880–1958) and Ronald Stevenson (b.1928), both of whom played leading parts in the Renaissance by developing modern music from aspects of traditional Scottish sources. At a less academic level – although MacDiarmid himself hated 'folk music' – there was a notable revival in traditional playing, singing and song-writing, while the School of Scottish Studies, since 1951, has developed the field of folk-life studies and promoted a new and wider appreciation of traditional and oral culture. Of course, institutions do not make art, but the foundation of the two major Scottish-language dictionaries and the Scottish Gaelic Text Society in the years between 1929 and 1937 helped to make up for past neglect. The publications of the Porpoise Press and William MacLellan, and then the popularity of public poetry-reading in the sixties, the rise of small presses, the growth of interest in Gaelic and the availability of the Traverse Theatre in Edinburgh and the Third Eye Centre in Glasgow – all these helped to bring new Scottish creative work to a wider audience.

Among painters the 'Scottish Colourists' at the beginning of the century had looked to Europe and the 'Fauves', most notably J. D. Fergusson (1874–1961), who had lived abroad until the outbreak of the Second World War. These painters shared an interest in colour via the compositional advances made by Cézanne and Matisse, and the work of Fergusson, Peploe (1871–1935), Hunter (1877–1931) and Cadell (1883–1937) has gained a steadily growing international reputation ever since. The later 'Edinburgh School' also remained true to the expressive and poetic use of colour and pattern – from its formation in 1922, with William Gillies (1898–1973) and William MacTaggart (1903–81), into the post-war years, and the appearance of Anne Redpath (1895–1965), John Maxwell (1905–62) and Robin Philipson (1916–92). These painters represent what was to be the mainstream of Scottish art in the mid-century period, as opposed to the strangely immanent draughtsmanship of James Cowie (1886–1956) and the abstraction of William Johnstone (1897–1981). The brilliant work of Joan Eardley (1921–63) combined an eye for colour, landscape and abstracted textures with an equal commitment to the social surface of the cities, especially in her studies of slum children in Glasgow, based on the work of local photographer Oscar Marzaroli (1933–88). Elizabeth Blackadder (b. 1931), James Morrison (b. 1932), John Knox (b. 1936) and Willie Rodger (b. 1930) all have established reputations. Scottish artists of this generation to have made a significant international impact include Eduardo Paolozzi (1924–2005), often cited as one of the founders of pop art, but in fact a challenging and influential modern artist in every medium, including sculpture; and Alan Davie (b. 1920), whose abstract expressionism echoes American influences along with his own interest in jazz, Zen and native American art and symbol systems. The elusive symbolism of John Bellany (b. 1942) has moved from stark evocations akin to German expressionism, to celebratory canvases exploding with colour. Bellany's contemporary Alexander Moffat (b. 1943) shares something of his colour palette and has painted many portraits of Scottish writers in a stylised realism that was to be very influential with a future generation of young painters.

If an early modern Renaissance exists at all, however, its most developed expression has been achieved in literature as writers have sought to express themselves in a modern Scotland where more than ever before they have felt the need to evaluate and remake an understanding of their own present nature and past history. No two writers have taken the same route, but the polarity between MacDiarmid and Muir is usefully suggestive of two broadly different responses, in which the materialist and extrovert energy of the one contrasts with the more inward and mythopoeic response to life from the other. The same distinction can be seen between the dynamic poetry of Edwin Morgan and the much more static muse of George Mackay Brown. Neil Gunn, Sorley MacLean, Iain Crichton Smith and most especially Lewis Grassic Gibbon tried to bring both modes together with varying degrees of success although, as always, their work speaks best for itself. The modern period really begins with a young journalist who wrote one good, terrifyingly bleak, novel before he died.

George Douglas Brown (1869–1902)

George Douglas Brown is remembered on the strength of only one novel – his second attempt at the form – and he died of pneumonia at the age of thirty-three within a year of its publication. *The House with the Green Shutters* (1901) was greeted by many critics and readers as a savage attack on the Kailyard genre, and while Brown did not disagree he also maintained that he had wanted to picture small-town Scottish life as it really was, and then to 'get inside the heads' of old John Gourlay and his son. The book does show a community undergoing social and economic changes – quite unlike the static nostalgia of Thrums, Drumtochty and the Kailyard, and in this, as with his desire to catch the humour and strength of Scots speech, Brown follows his admired John Galt. Yet he also explores several personally sensitive and autobiographical themes.

Brown must have known small communities well enough, not to mention their propensity for gossip, for he was born as an illegitimate child in the little village of Ochiltree – in the heart of Burns and Galt country near Mauchline in Ayrshire. His mother was the unlettered daughter of an Irish labourer and his father, a local farmer renowned for his dour independence and his colourful Scots speech, never did marry her. Young George moved from the village school to Ayr Academy, with the help of the rector there – and William Maybin's confidence in his new pupil was rewarded when the boy excelled in English and Classics and won a bursary entrance to Glasgow University, where he became a favourite student, and later the assistant, of young Professor Gilbert Murray. Brown's mixed feelings about his father appear in the matriculation forms from those days, in which he sometimes listed him as a farmer and at other times claimed he was dead. Artistic rather than scholarly, Brown's temperament was given to bursts of energy and vivid intuitive insights, but he graduated with first-class honours and won the Snell Exhibition Scholarship, which took him to Balliol College, Oxford. Brown's years as a student in the south were fruitful, and he took a lively part in college life, but his studies were erratic with periods of intensive activity followed by spells of depression and poor health – a familiar pattern in his later life. He read Balzac, Tolstoy and Dostoevsky – without liking the Russian giants – and began to think of writing a novel that would say something about his own background and the Scottish character. Perhaps such themes were in his mind because he had finally confronted his father before leaving for England, only to find a tired and peppery old man in place of the hardhearted tyrant he must have imagined in his youth. Whatever the reasons, Brown's classical studies began to suffer, and when his mother's health collapsed – she had been ill for years – he returned home to nurse her. She died in 1895 and he graduated later in the year with a third-class degree and a certain sense of failure, despite his recognition that such matters were no longer so important to him. He was later to modify these experiences in his portrait of young John Gourlay as a boy who finds himself out of his depth at university – a disappointment to his domineering father and a dying mother.

Set on a literary career, Brown took up freelance journalism in London, using the pen names 'William Douglas' and 'Kennedy King' for short stories and a boy's adventure novel called *Love and a Sword: A tale of the Afridi War* (1899). He became involved in a small publishing-scheme with friends and continued to produce what he regarded as hackwork. He was more serious, however, about a long story written in June 1900 that featured a powerful character named Gourlay in a village to be called Barbie. His friends encouraged him to develop the theme, so at the end of the year he retreated to a cottage in Haslemere, bought a supply of exercise books and began to write his novel.

The House with the Green Shutters, by 'George Douglas', appeared in October 1901 and was widely and well reviewed. Andrew Lang – himself a distinguished Snell Scholarship man before Brown's time – likened Gourlay to Stevenson's Weir of Hermiston and compared Brown to a Scottish Balzac or Flaubert 'with a bitter sense of humour'. Other reviews invoked Galt, as well as the power of Greek tragedy, and indeed Brown had drawn on his classical education for the 'bodies' –

the common folk of Barbie, whose gossip responds like a Greek chorus to the doings and the sufferings of the Gourlay family. Most of the gossip is malicious, and the grimness of Brown's picture of village life derives from the fact that the few decent voices are seldom heard against the spiteful and cowardly backbiting of the majority, led in especially loathsome fashion by the lisping hypocrite Deacon Allardyce. Compared with these uncharitable nonentities, John Gourlay – the self-made carter – stubborn, brutal and tyrannical though he is, strides like a tiger among worms. Like Stevenson's Adam Weir, old Gourlay is imbued with all the absolutist paternal authority of Calvinism, although he is a more limited and stupid man than the judge. Thus Brown's study of a mother's son in conflict with such a father follows the psychological symbolism of Stevenson's novel, as if the Scottish sensibility were torn between broadly feminine and masculine outlooks, between what it owes to the muse and what to Jehovah. Stevenson, Brown and Lewis Grassic Gibbon and McIlvanney all make use of the struggle between fathers and sons (or a daughter, in the case of Chris Guthrie) and exactly the same late Victorian battle with puritanical authority motivated Edmund Gosse's powerful study *Father and Son* (1907). Brown's sympathies are not easily given, however, for, although he paints Barbie and Gourlay in hellish colours, young John is little better – ending up as a weakling and a drunk.

Old Gourlay, like the house of which he is so proud, dominates the little town on the brae below, but times are changing because of the railway and the coalmines nearby, and he begins to lose commercial supremacy to a wilier businessman called Wilson who diversifies from a general store to take over Gourlay's monopoly as a goods-carrier – the only trade the older man knows. Like his business, Gourlay's personality is monolithic and inflexible, and when his rival's son is sent to university he insists that young John should go as well – as a 'lad o' pairts' whose success will reflect credit on his father. But John's weak and sensitive character cannot cope, and he fails, just as his father's business is failing, and returns home to sulk in disgrace. He takes to drink, kills his father in a drunken fit and then commits suicide, only to be followed into death by his tubercular sister and his mother – an abused creature who has nursed a fear of Gourlay all her life just as she nurses the secret cancer gnawing at her breast. Before they take poison, Mrs Gourlay and her daughter turn to the Bible and read the famous passage on charity from I Corinthians.

The conclusion is excessively unrelenting – not formal enough for Greek tragedy and too melodramatic for realism. Yet the earlier parts of the novel are well controlled, with a forensic detachment in the narrative style that makes an effective contrast to vivid descriptive passages that might have been written with the nervous excitation of young John Gourlay himself. Brown's prose is frequently criticised for a tendency to analyse his creatures, pontificating on them and on Scottish failings in general; but this is a deliberate device against the cosy familiarity of Scots speech and the Kailyard setting. Contemporary readers familiar with postmodernist fiction may find this authorial position less intrusive than did earlier critics:

> When we think of what Gourlay did that day, we must remember that he was soaked in alcohol – not merely with his morning's potation, but with the dregs of previous carousals. And the dregs of drink, a thorough toper will tell you, never leave him. He is drunk on Monday with his Saturday's debauch. As 'Drucken Wabster' of Barbie put it once, 'When a body's hard up, his braith's a consolation.' If that be so – and Wabster, remember, was an expert whose opinion on this matter is entitled to the highest credence – if that be so, it proves the strength and persistence of a thorough alcoholic impregnation, or, as Wabster called it, of 'a good soak'. In young Gourlay's case, at any rate, the impregnation was enduring and complete. He was like a rag steeped in fusel oil.

Brown defended such ironic objectivity in his notes for *The Novelist* – a study he never completed – and in the 'Rules for Writing' collected during 1901, in which he described the artist as an 'Observer of Humanity *from the outside*'. Thus he aspired to be philosophically aloof, as if *sub specie aeternitatis*, and even 'callous', for '´tis the weakling-artist who invites his lachrymose readers to a petty whine over the merited sorrows of the human race'. If there is a young man's arrogance to such a programme, it is not so very different from Stephen Dedalus's theory that the writer should be like God – indifferent and beyond his handiwork. The device is not always successful, but it was an original effort to bring a crystal-clear, hard-edged definition to the flattering mists of the 'Scotch' settings and sentiments that characterised so many popular novels of the day. It is especially fitting that his forensic tones – reminiscent of a pedantically precise Scots advocate – should be used to reinforce an equally Scottish taste for Old Testament retribution as it came to be visited on the Gourlays at the end. Without Brown's ironically inhumane distance, *The House with the Green Shutters* would be a more predictable book, and certainly less disturbing in its effect – at least until he relaxes his steely grip and melodrama takes over in the final scenes.

At the age of thirty-three George Douglas Brown was delighted with the success of his first serious novel. He visited friends in Ayrshire, assembled notes on his theories of writing and contemplated another novel, to be called 'The Incompatibles'. But pneumonia, left untreated for too long, killed him in August 1902. His novel became a special milestone in Scottish letters because it used the Kailyard's own ingredients to blight the bonnie brier-bush itself. Hay's *Gillespie* followed in 1914, but it was overtaken by the Great War and, despite enthusiastic reviews, it never became as well known as *The House with the Green Shutters* and it was 1963 before it was published again.

John MacDougall Hay (1881–1919)

Hay was born and brought up in Tarbert at the mouth of Loch Fyne to the west of Glasgow. It was a community with Highland roots, but he did not speak Gaelic. He graduated with an ordinary MA at Glasgow University, where he had begun, even as student, to write creatively and to earn money as a freelance journalist. He worked as a teacher in the west until a severe attack of rheumatic fever changed his plans and he determined to train as a minister for the Church of Scotland, returning to university in 1905 and graduating five years later. He supported himself during this time and kept up his writing with a succession of reviews and articles for various Glasgow newspapers and London magazines. He made friends with Neil Munro, already an established novelist, and he started to think of the book that was to become *Gillespie*. In 1909, after a probationary period, Hay became minister at Elderslie, a largely urban parish on the outskirts of Glasgow, between Paisley and Johnstone. He married and settled down to a reticent life as minister and author, working late into the night on his bulky and intractable manuscript.

Hay had few pastimes beyond reading and fishing, but his imaginative life must have been dramatic enough, for he said in a later interview that the intense sensations experienced by his character young Eoghan were based on his own visions and on memories of childhood. Certainly *Gillespie* is remarkable for the hallucinatory richness of its style, and it caused a sensation when it appeared in 1914, being highly praised by Hardy and particularly well received by American critics. A second novel, *Barnacles*, followed in 1916 and a collection of free verse called *Their Dead Sons* was published in 1918, but neither volume recaptured the impact of the first book, and *Gillespie*'s unrelenting grimness must have seemed less and less palatable after the war. Hay's health had never been very strong since his early illness, and he succumbed to TB in the winter of 1919. His son, only four when his father died, was to become well known as the Gaelic poet George Campbell Hay.

There are obvious similarities between the stories of Gillespie Strang and John Gourlay. Both novels paint a savage picture of Scots community life and Hay's Brieston is also based on his home town – namely Tarbert. Both books have a tyrannical father who dominates all those around him, including his suffering wife and a fey and sensitive son. Both end with death and destruction. Clearly Hay had read Brown, but his literary tastes owe nothing to his predecessor, nor does he attempt the embryo modernism of a detached prose style. In this respect it is significant that Hay liked Dostoevsky – a writer Brown considered exaggerated and obscure. There is an extravagant symbolic richness to Hay's outlook and on every page he elevates the Scottish penchant for descriptive detail to overpowering heights – like a development of Mannerism in prose. Consider this description of herring-gutters at work:

> Those beautiful fish, silk-shot with a greenish-blue through the scales, are the strongest hostages against penury. From the cold deep they have come to brighten the hearth; fashioned in silver in the dark, as diamonds in the bowels of the earth. The burnishing of knives was a labour of love in the Back Street. What a sight it was to see again the big fishing-boats laced with scales and the shining pile in the Square. The women sat on empty herring boxes by the pile, their arms bared and dappled with blood. . . . When the dusk came the work was continued within the store, whose interior, lit with torches, presented a weird spectacle. Beneath the glare of the torches mingled with smoke, the gutters with blood-stained hands sat around, their faces starting out of the reek in the murky light and falling again into shadow. The pile of herring smouldered in pools of dull gold. . . . The big guttings of former days were recalled when the splendid fishing lured gutters from Stornoway and Peterhead to Brieston. Old times were restored; the old dead were resurrected; the aged were seen as young.
>
> 'Many's the guttin' ye hae sang at noo, Flory'; and as the torches flicker and the knives grow idle, and the weary hands are at rest a moment, a sweet treble voice sings the Scottish ballad:
>
> > 'Last night there were four Maries,
> > To-night they'll be but three',
>
> and fifty women take up the haunting air, making it swell beyond the rafters and the roof to the night and the stars. In that song the hungry days are ended, and the sorrows of the sea.

Scene after scene is illuminated in this expressionist and portentous light, rising to moments of apocalyptic intensity, for Hay's outlook is genuinely metaphysical or theological, and he conceives Gillespie

Strang as a demonic force whose very birth was heralded, in unashamedly Shakespearean fashion, by evil omens. Gillespie's soul is like an iceberg, and yet he wears the outward guise of a hearty self-made businessman. Unlike John Gourlay, Hay's clever protagonist turns the law, technical progress and other people's cupidity all to his own advantage, destroying everything around him (and finally himself) in the successfully calculated pursuit of profit and self-interest. Hay reported that his target was the growing spirit of materialism in Scotland, and in true Evangelical fashion he gave its spokesman a Mephistophelian stature, a capitalist convinced that 'the stars were fighting for him in their courses', a figure who even seems to have chance and natural disaster on his side. Overcharged with physical detail and portents, *Gillespie* looks back to the Gothic Romanticism and the folk energy of Hogg's visions of evil and uses this spirit to give a uniquely eldritch animation to the nineteenth-century world of commerce and bourgeois materialism.

Neil Munro (1864–1930)

Like his young friend Hay, Neil Munro came from the Central Highlands lying to the west of Glasgow. Following a spell in a lawyer's office he turned to journalism and for two years after the First World War he was editor of the *Glasgow Evening Times*, where George Blake also came to know him. Although Gaelic was in decline in Inverary, where Munro was born, his own familiarity with the language and its speech-patterns is clearly reflected in the spare English prose of his early stories. In a sense the bittersweet short stories of *The Lost Pibroch* (1896) belong with the Celtic twilight, except that Munro looks to Highland culture and the romantic pull of its old loyalties to the chief and the clan with an awareness of how destructive these have been in both past and present experience. Beyond the Stevensonian romance of his historical novels, Munro shows an ironic fatalism that recognises that the love of 'romance' is dangerous, just as the melancholy narrator of *John Splendid* (1898) looks back to the tragic futility of Montrose's bitter campaign in Argyll, and recalls how he was caught up in it by an adventurer in the mould of Alan Breck. *Doom Castle* (1901) is an ironically Gothic tale set in the years after the Forty-five, while Munro's excellent sense of landscape and the excitements of eighteenth-century travel make *The New Road* (1914) an adventure not at all unworthy of following in the footsteps of *Kidnapped*. The young hero is harried across Scotland only to discover that the story of his father's distant death in the Jacobite cause is a lie – a lie concocted to conceal a sordid murder for simple gain at home.

As a journalist Munro wrote short stories and newspaper sketches calling himself 'Hugh Foulis', and it was under this name that he created the droll characters 'Archie' and 'Jimmy Swann'; but his most famous comic achievement was 'Para Handy', the skipper of a puffer called *Vital Spark*. The 'puffers' were tiny tramp steamers – like sea-going trucks – which used to operate out of the Clyde estuary, and the adventures of Para Handy and his eccentric crew are full of sly humour and delight in the manners and affairs of small townships up and down the west coast. Munro was reluctant to own up to these tales, but their popularity has quite overshadowed his more serious ambitions as a poet and they inspired a television comedy series in the 1970s.

John Buchan (1875–1940)

If Munro's historical fiction followed Stevenson's example, then the novels of John Buchan brought the same approach to contemporary settings. Buchan spent his teenage years in Glasgow, where his father – a Free Kirk minister – had his parish in the Gorbals. From Glasgow University Buchan won a classical scholarship to Oxford, where he arrived just as George Douglas Brown left for London. By the end of his student days he had produced a first-class degree, two historical novels and three other volumes, making a splash, too, as a Union president who made contributions to *The Yellow Book*. *John Burnet of Barns* (1898) looks to Covenanting times with lovingly detailed descriptions of Buchan's favourite Tweedside, where the holidays of his youth were spent, and this use of landscape set the pattern for most of his later fiction. After Oxford, Buchan turned to the Law in London and managed another couple of novels before going to South Africa for two years to work for the British High Commission at the end of the Boer War. He returned to London and the Law in 1903, accepted the post of literary advisor to Nelson's publishing-house and eventually became a director in 1915.

The novelist drew on his African experience for *Prester John* (1910) – a boys' adventure (not without a good deal of implicit and explicit racism) which begins on the Fife coast and takes its protagonist to a veritable 'heart of darkness' where rebelling tribesmen rise up against the white man to follow a charismatic black leader – a cross between Charles Edward Stuart and a passionate Covenanter – who invokes the legend of 'Prester John', the Christian ruler of a united African

kingdom in the distant past. The rebellion is suppressed and the imperial status quo restored. Unlike Scott in *Waverley*, Buchan does not
seem to have been ambivalent about this outcome, although the text
itself is haunted by unrecognised political and sexual ambiguities.

Buchan's enthusiasm for the original ideals of Presbyterianism and his
hatred of its latent fanaticism illuminates his historical study of *The
Marquis of Montrose* (1913), a subject he returned to with *Montrose* in
1928. The marquis's lightning campaigns over wild country particularly
appealed to him and confirmed his belief that every man should be
prepared to support his convictions or his social privileges by direct
action. A simplified version of this creed motivates the exploits of
Richard Hannay, who first appeared in 1915 with *The Thirty-nine Steps*.
Indeed, Buchan's 'shockers', as he called them, show a strongly Calvinist
sense of the presence of evil and savagery just beneath the 'civilised'
surface of the everyday world, and they are equally alert to the dangers
of fanaticism – just as extreme Calvinism was prone to what he saw as
'dark and vehement emotions'. Against such forces Buchan, like his
heroes, values success born of hard effort, a simple clarity of purpose and
a stubborn unwillingness to give up, rather than subtlety of insight or
any more profound philosophical motivation. Such was the Presbyterian
work ethic of a Scottish gentleman conservative – and there were thousands like him in the colonial service. If these values seem naive in the
face of the terrible sophistication of contemporary dilemmas, at least
they made for grand adventure tales, as another Scot, Ian Fleming, was
to discover, although his James Bond is an altogether more cynical
creation reflecting the consumerism and sexism of the sixties.

By the early twenties Buchan was living in Oxford and commuting to
London to work for Reuters and Nelson, for whom he had written a
huge history of the war. He took an interest, too, in the new stirrings in
Scottish poetry and contributed to Grieve's *Northern Numbers*, much
to its editor's delight. Although Buchan's own verse rarely strays from
the ordinary, his taste was sound, and in 1924 he compiled an excellent
anthology of old and new Scots poems which he called *The Northern
Muse*, prefaced with an essay on how Scots vernacular literature had
sunk to a provincial genre. Fond of walking and fishing, Buchan took
regular holidays in Scotland and these settings feature in many of the
thrillers he produced – one a year – between 1922 and 1936.

Perhaps the fictional protagonist who reflects Buchan's beliefs most
closely is Sir Edward Leithen, a Tory MP and barrister who features in
a sequence of novels beginning with *The Power-House* in 1913 and
ending with *Sick Heart River* published posthumously in 1941. One of

Buchan's most famous passages comes from *The Power-House* when a character explains to Leithen how precarious the rule of law actually is: 'You think that a wall as solid as the earth separates civilisation from barbarism. I tell you the division is a thread, a sheet of glass.' In reply Leithen invokes what he sees as the 'goodwill' of decent, practical people – people like himself and his creator– but the debate still reveals something of his own doubts and fears. And indeed Buchan's last novel is in a different and more sombre vein, set in the Canadian north, where a mythically Edenic valley (Sick Heart River) is supposed to be located; a dying Sir Edward becomes engaged with the fate of a tribe of native people for whom civilisation, industrialisation and the imperial project have not come as a blessing. Buchan's sense of these tensions was undoubtedly derived from the last five years of his life, which he spent as Governor General of Canada with the title of Baron Tweedsmuir. As a confidant of Franklin D. Roosevelt, he tried to mobilise American opinion to support Britain against Hitler and hence to forestall the outbreak of war. He failed, and in 1940 – when civilisation must indeed have seemed most at risk – he died of a cerebral stroke. During the course of his life he had produced over a hundred books.

As far as his 'shockers' were concerned, Buchan was content to entertain, and, although they lack the historical or psychological depth of Scott and Stevenson, their approach, like Buchan's own craft, is honourably descended from that line. The historical novel itself, infused with the glamour of Scottish history and landscape, has continued to thrive. Its later exponents include Nigel Tranter (1909–2000), a professional writer for most of his life who used his enthusiasm for Scottish history and architecture to give authentic detail to his fictionalised biographies, scholarly publications and local guides. Dorothy Dunnett (1923–2001) developed character and atmosphere as well as pages of dense and arcane historical detail in a sequence of six books beginning with *The Game of Kings* (1961), featuring a charismatically Byronic Scottish soldier of fortune called Francis Crawford of Lymond. These long novels (and a further *House of Niccolo* series with eight volumes about a hero from Bruges) use the most densely realised dialogue and settings to evoke the cruel and glittering brilliance of Renaissance Europe and the north.

R. B. Cunninghame Graham (1852–1936)

Among the remaining prose writers from the first twenty years of the century, the fiery, dandyish and Quixotic Graham might have been invented by some unlikely collusion between Oscar Wilde, John Buchan and Hugh MacDiarmid. With Spanish blood on his mother's side and remote connections with Robert the Bruce, Robert Bontine Cunninghame Graham came from a privileged background and got an early taste for foreign parts by going to Argentina at the age of eighteen to spend most of the next seven years living as a rancher, dressed like a gaucho and known as 'Don Roberto'. He returned to London, eloped with a Chilean girl whom he met in Paris, and roamed around Texas and Mexico before returning to Scotland to become a radical Liberal MP. This did not prevent him from being imprisoned after the riots in Trafalgar Square in 1887 and suspended from Parliament more than once for his support of nationalisation, socialism or communism on a platform which demanded free education, a better deal for women, stronger trade unions and more wages for a shorter day's work. A friend of Keir Hardie, Graham became the first president of the Scottish Labour Party when it was founded in 1888. During the 1890s he began to write and came to know literary figures such as Conrad – whom he helped with *Nostromo* – Edward Garnett, Henry James, Oscar Wilde, John Masefield, Thomas Hardy and George Bernard Shaw. (He was the model for Saranoff in *Arms and the Man*, although Shaw felt that he was so much larger than life that a full account would never be believed on stage.) Don Roberto cultivated his own piratical and idealistic personality to an unusual degree. His horsemanship, his South American background and fresh adventures as a latter-day explorer and gold-prospector in Morocco and Spain gave him material for his first travel books in the 1890s and then in the 1920s and 1930s he published biographies and historical studies of the *conquistadores*.

Several of Graham's first short stories and sketches were set in Scotland, for he was proud of his nationality but contemptuous of the vogue for Kailyard parochialism: 'Today a Scotsman stands confessed a sentimental fool . . .', he wrote in *The Ipané* (1899), 'oppressed with the tremendous difficulties of the jargon he is bound to speak, and above all weighed down with the responsibility of being Scotch.' Never afraid to put his spurs to sacred cows, Graham was equally scathing about the Kirk and all its doings. English imperialism fared little better, for he had a natural sympathy with foreign peoples, however distant their mores were from his own. His prose is succinctly and vigorously set down with telling and original details. Often hovering somewhere between sketch, free reminiscence and fiction, it is usually controlled by his own alert and astringent sense of irony – a style admired by many of his more famous writer friends. Further stories were collected in *Faith* (1909), *Hope* (1910), *Charity* (1912) and *Scottish Stories* (1914), which includes one of his best known tales 'Beattock for Moffat' about a Scotsman on the train from London, travelling north to die. In the post-war years Graham became critical of the Labour Party and renounced his socialism to campaign as a Liberal. He became president of the National Party in 1928 and of the Scottish National Party (SNP) when it was brought together in 1934. In these circles he met with Hugh MacDiarmid, who criticised his retreat from the radical Left but shared his delight in slashing artistic mediocrity and bourgeois values whenever possible. Writing in the *Scots Independent* in 1931 Graham reminded his fellow Scots that 'our real enemies are those among us, born without imagination, bound in fetters of their own conceit.' Sometime called the 'uncrowned king of Scotland' he is buried in the family plot at Inchmahome Priory on the Lake of Menteith.

Norman Douglas (1868–1952)

As a cultivator of personality, a 'writer's writer' and an iconoclast in his own way, George Norman Douglas was as cosmopolitan as Graham. He became famous for his loving evocation of the southern tip of Italy in *Old Calabria* (1915) and for the sardonic zest of his first novel, *South Wind* (1917), which is replete with the hedonistic spirit of Capri – fictionalised as 'Nepenthe' – and full of the author's favourite topics and disquisitions. Douglas's family came from Tilquhillie Castle to the west of Aberdeen, but his father managed cotton-mills in Austria and Norman was born there, with German as his first language. Young Douglas disliked the damp castle on Deeside and hated his English public school even more, regarding himself as a sophisticated European. At the age of twenty-eight he abandoned his short-lived career in the Foreign Service and settled in Italy as an amateur enthusiast – producing short stories with his wife Elizabeth Fitzgibbon (*Unprofessional Tales*, 1901) before their marriage broke up. He had early fallen in love with Capri and the civilised ease of the Mediterranean, where he felt that his classical hedonism, and a growing and cheerfully pagan interest in adolescent boys, was validated by past cultural history and the unsentimental brilliance of the light – all very far away from the puritanism of the North or the stuffiness of English society. Douglas became a professional writer relatively late in life, and was forty-eight before *South Wind* brought him fame by speaking for wit and sophisticated freedoms against the greyness that was post-war

Europe. Two further books of fiction – both mythological fantasies – appeared during the twenties, but Douglas's real talent was for the evocation of place in the celebration of a sun-drenched world and his own spiky nature – defined again in the travel books *Alone* (1921) and *Together* (1923) and in the autobiography *Looking Back* (1933).

Urban writing in the early twentieth century

Nothing could be further from the spirit of Cunninghame Graham or Douglas's Mediterranean than the popular literature that still prevailed on the home front in Scotland. George Douglas Brown's savage detachment may have shaken the Kailyard's more serious pretensions, but he did not dent the market for parochial light comedy – the literary equivalent, as MacDiarmid put it, of cold haggis and ginger beer. Neil Munro's friend J. J. Bell (1871–1934) was among the best of these pawky humorists and his work is not without charm. His *enfant terrible* 'Wee Macgreegor' made his debut in the *Glasgow Evening Times* at the beginning of the century, but Bell mined the same vein of working-class character comedy for over thirty years. This 'urban kailyard' lived on through the forties and fifties with Helen W. Pryde's 'McFlannels' series on Scottish Radio, and D. C. Thomson of Dundee had already founded a considerable publishing empire on dozens of periodicals aimed at a working-class and lower middle-class market for conservative values, sentiment, piety, true-love romances and droll Scots humour. MacDiarmid and other writers of the early Renaissance came to regard the comedian Harry Lauder as the patron saint of this version of Scottishness – a music-hall figure of fun, swathed in surrealistic tartans, sporting bare knees and a knobbly walking stick. Yet Lauder and the other 'Scotch comics' were undeniably popular with their audiences, representing an absurd stereotype that had come to be loved for its own sake.

Some writers, however, particularly in Glasgow, did attempt a more realistic picture of Scottish city life. John Blair gave an unusually direct account of the life of a factory girl in *Jean* (1906) which is striking, as Moira Burgess notes, for its lively and unpatronising treatment of slum life in a tale otherwise engaged with the seduction, fall, redemption and tubercular death of its heroine. Burgess's study of 'the Glasgow novel', now in its third edition, is an invaluable catalogue of fiction from this and later periods. The erstwhile Irish navvy, journalist and poet Patrick MacGill (1890–1963) drew on his own life to write two novels about the Irish immigrant experience. *Children of the Dead End* (1914) traces Dermod Flynn's search for work in Scotland and Glasgow, while *The Rat-pit* (1915), which focuses on his lover Norah Ryan, gives a particularly grim account of the slums and lodging-houses of the city. As the son of a Glasgow manufacturer, Frederick Niven (1878–1944) came from a completely different social class and had early ambitions to become a painter. He led a restless life between Scotland, Canada and London before finally settling in British Columbia shortly after the First World War. Several of his many novels – most notably *The Justice of the Peace* (1914) and *The Staff at Simson's* (1937) – give a detailed account of bourgeois and commercial Glasgow society in the first years of the century.

Catherine Carswell (1879–1946)

Catherine MacFarlane came from just such a commercial background in Glasgow, for her father was an agent for the shipping and purchase of textiles. Not untypical of their class, her family was deeply religious with Free Kirk roots and evangelical leanings. Nevertheless young Catherine grew up in a liberal spirit, visiting Italy in her teens and studying music, for which she had a lifelong passion, at the Conservatorium in Frankfurt. (Her visits to Italy and Germany were to provide material for her first and second novels.) Back in Glasgow again in 1901, she attended classes in English at Glasgow University, although as a woman she could not be admitted for the degree, and studied at Glasgow School of Art. (Charles Rennie Mackintosh's fine building was in its first phase of construction at this time.) An early marriage to Herbert Jackson went badly wrong when his mental health collapsed and he tried to kill her when she told him she was pregnant. As a reviewer of fiction and drama for the *Glasgow Herald*, she moved to London where she became a friend and confidante of D. H. Lawrence and renewed her acquaintance with Donald Carswell, whom she had first met at Glasgow University. The couple were married in 1915, the very year she lost her job with the *Glasgow Herald* for reviewing *The Rainbow* against the editor's wishes. Undaunted she continued to make her living in journalism and theatre reviewing while also working on her first novel – discussing it with Lawrence while she in turn read and reported on the manuscript of *The Rainbow*.

Open the Door! (1920) is a development novel drawing on Carswell's own life and experiences with men as it charts Joanna Bannerman's progress towards self-discovery and personal fulfilment. While Joanna feels that she must break away from Edwardian Glasgow, it is not an entirely unsympathetic portrait of family and social life there before the Great War, and the difficult relationship between mothers and daughters is described with tact. Joanna's alert and sensual nature is caught by Carswell's detailed and observant prose as it reflects her character's vivid responses to nature and the world around her as the novel takes her from Glasgow to Italy and on to London. Her journey is an emotional and sexual one, too, as she learns about herself and others in the arms of three different men before returning to Scotland to marry Lawrence Urquhart, a man who will finally allow her to be herself. The sexual freedom that the book describes and its use of symbolic details in its land- and cityscapes serve to counter this rather conventional ending. Joanna's encounters with different men can be seen as a precursor to Willa Muir's and Nan Shepherd's novels of female experience and emancipation, not to mention the tough life of Grassic Gibbon's Chris Guthrie. Unlike these sisters, however, Joanna's life remains resolutely middle class. The protagonist of Carswell's second – much shorter – novel *The Camomile* (1922) is middle class as well, but as a musician and a would-be writer Ellen is given more creative authority in challenging the accepted roles for women as she recounts her struggles in Glasgow in a series of letters to a friend in London. *Open the Door!* was reviewed favourably by both Rebecca West and Katherine Mansfield, both at the start of their own careers, both equally concerned in their fiction to explore and to expand the intellectual, social and sexual constraints of their class.

Carswell and Lawrence were to correspond prolifically until his death in 1930. Offended by what she took to be a distorted version of Lawrence painted in Middleton Murray's biography *Son of Woman* (1931) she produced her own personal portrait of him, *Savage Pilgrimage*, in the following year. Her enthusiasm for Lawrence's vision also marks the biography she produced as *The Life of Robert Burns* in 1930. Her account of the national poet as a dynamic, free-thinking and sexual being antagonised the Burns Federation and sentimental Burns cultists throughout Scotland. She was sent a bullet in the post by someone signing himself (apparently without irony) as 'Holy Willie' and moves were made to ban the book. William Power and Hugh MacDiarmid flew to its defence and its freely written almost fictionalised style remains an excellently perceptive psychological study to this day. The furore brought her into contact with these young writers in the north and she continued to correspond with MacDiarmid, the Muirs, Neil Gunn and Helen Cruickshank. She produced a biography of Boccaccio, *The Tranquil Heart* (1937), and worked on a volume of essays in memory of John Buchan (1947) but Carswell never finished her own autobiography, published as a fragment by her son John in 1950 as *Lying Awake*.

The renaissance of poetry in Scots: MacDiarmid's precursors

As far as poetry in Scots was concerned, the Kailyard strain went back at least as far as the *Whistle-Binkie* anthologies, fifty years before the new century. Stevenson's Scots poems were much better, but still tended to link the language with nostalgia or bairn rhymes. As for the rest, the sentimental rustification of Scots had left it frozen in time and place as a language apparently reserved for the 'poetry corners' of local newspapers and hundreds of talentless imitators of Burns. Even James Logie Robertson (1846–1922), who had edited many valuable popular collections of the works of Ramsay, Scott, Dunbar and Burns, could produce little more than pastoral pastiche when he wrote as 'Hugh Haliburton', with titles such as *Horace in Hamespun* (1882) and *Ochil Idylls* (1891). The language seemed lost to serious contemporary use. Yet it did retain some credibility in the hands of authentic dialect poets, and in this respect it was Charles Murray, Violet Jacob and several other North-East poets who showed what could be done in Scots in the years before MacDiarmid took up Lallans for himself.

Charles Murray (1864–1941)

Born in Alford, trained as an engineer in Aberdeen, and working in South Africa for most of his life, Charles Murray was completely at home with North-East speech and his poems move with the easy flow of oral expression – often as dramatic monologues. His taste for pithy epigrams, like his eye for landscape, weather and the trappings of country life, all stem from a folk tradition that had remained particularly rich in Aberdeenshire and Angus. William Alexander's *Johnny Gibb of Gushetneuk* was first published as a serial in the Aberdeen newspaper, and Gavin Greig (1856–1914), with the help of the Revd J. B. Duncan, had spent the last ten years of his life making a monumental collection of oral lore and ballads from the region. To this day North-East Scots has retained an unforced linguistic confidence. *Hamewith* (1900) made Murray's reputation, and it was enlarged, reprinted three times and then collated with two later collections to make the complete works of 1927. After a distinguished career in South Africa the poet returned home to a considerable degree of local fame. 'Gin I were God' and 'The Whistle' ('He cut a sappy sooker from a muckle rodden tree') are widely anthologised and much memorised recital pieces, but poems such as 'Dockens afore his Peers', 'The Three Craws' and 'A Green Yule' give a better sense of Murray's sardonic wit, while the lyrical conclusion to the last-named poem goes beyond dialect verse to the voice of the ballads infused with the grim weight of Dunbar:

Bring them alang, the young, the strang,	
The weary an' the auld;	
Feed as they will on haugh or hill,	low meadow
This is the only fauld.	fold
Dibble them doon, the laird, the loon,	Plant; boy
King an' the cadgin' caird,	travelling tinker
The lady fine beside the queyn,	girl
A' in the same kirkyard	

Violet Jacob (1863–1946)

Violet Jacob came from the Kennedy-Erskine family, who had held the lands near Montrose since the fifteenth century. In 1894 she married Arthur Jacob, an Irish officer in the British army, and she travelled to India with him when he was stationed there. Her fascinating *Diaries and Letters from India (1895–1900)* were only published in 1990. Jacob's first books were historical novels, *The Sheepstealers* (1902) telling of rural protest in the Welsh borders where her mother came from, while *The Interloper* (1904) deals with small-town conflicts in a version of her native Montrose. Her finest historical novel, *Flemington* (1911), draws on local and family history in a tragedy of loyalty and betrayal at the time of the 1745 uprising and was reckoned by John Buchan to be 'the best Scots romance since *The Master of Ballantrae*'. She also wrote short stories including the late collection *Tales of My Own Country* (1922), which looked back to the land and the Scots language of her youth, as did her three main collections of poems – *Songs of Angus* (1915), which was introduced by John Buchan, *Bonnie Joann* (1921) and *Northern Lights* (1927). She is more prone to sentimentality than Murray, partly because her focus is on the pains of love, the fears of children, or the onset of old age. Even so, her Scots is rarely coy and her sense of muted sexual shame, like her sympathy with landscape or the supernatural, is often illuminated by particularly effective small-scale images – a broken stone and black nettles ('The Jaud') or brambles and toadstools among dark fir-trees ('Craigo Woods') or a thistle going to seed on a river-bank ('The End o't'). It is in such illuminated details that MacDiarmid's debt to her might be traced. Indeed Jacob contributed to MacDiarmid's *Northern Numbers* anthologies at a time when he himself was still writing in English, and she was generously represented in Buchan's *Northern Muse*.

Marion Angus (1866–1946) and Helen Cruickshank (1886–1975)

Marion Angus and Helen Cruikshank also had their roots in the North-East, and, although most of Cruickshank's poems were not published until after MacDiarmid had shown what the Scots lyric could achieve, they qualify as forerunners along with Violet Jacob. Cruickshank also appeared in *Northern Numbers*, and Angus's *The Lilt and Other Poems* dates from 1922, followed by *The Tinker's Road* (1924) and four further collections during the twenties and thirties. Within her chosen range Marion Angus is technically the most accomplished of her generation, and a later English piece on Mary Stuart – 'Alas! Poor Queen' – might have been constructed by a young Ezra Pound. She also learned from the ballads and, although the lilting sadness of her lines can become excessively fey, her best lyrics are terse and genuinely disquieting – 'The Can'el', 'Ann Gilchrist' and 'The Blue Jacket'. Angus lived most of her life in Aberdeen, away from the storms and the teapots of literary Edinburgh. Helen Cruickshank's poems, by comparison, are nearer once more to a vernacular muse with its interest in landscape and reminiscence, although she uses this to make political points, too. She succeeded MacDiarmid as secretary of the Scottish PEN Club and proved to be a loyal supporter of most of the younger renaissance poets and a particularly good friend to MacDiarmid and his family during their difficult years in the thirties, sending blankets and supplies to them when they were struggling to set up home on the Shetland island of Whalsay.

Mary Symon (1863–1938), Pittendrigh MacGillivray (1856–1938), Alexander Gray (1882–1968) and Lewis Spence (1874–1955)

The North East connection was continued with Mary Symon from Banffshire, another contributor to *Northern Numbers*, who published her work in *Deveron Days* (1933), and with Pittendrigh MacGillivray, the sculptor who made the statues of John Knox in St Giles' and of Byron at Aberdeen Grammar School. Born near Inverurie, MacGillivray was an enthusiast for eighteenth-century Scots verse, but for the most part it is his own native voice that controls poems such as 'Observances' – drawing on folk-customs for greeting a new baby – or 'Mercy o' Gode', a finely sardonic account of two old men sitting in a churchyard. His first publication was *Pro Patria* (1915), but his best Scots work appeared in *Bog Myrtle and Peat Reek* (1922) – a privately produced and expensive little book. Alexander Gray was born in Dundee and worked for the Civil Service before becoming professor of political economy in Aberdeen and Edinburgh. He too drew on North-East Scots for his poems, and used a modified version of it to translate pieces from Danish and German, including *Songs and Ballads Chiefly from Heine* (1920), and German ballads and folksongs done into an efficient Scots verse for *Arrows* (1932). Lewis Spence also came from Dundee, working for the *Scotsman*, the *Edinburgh Magazine* and the *British Weekly* before becoming a full-time writer. In forty years he produced almost as many books on legends and mythology, from studies of the Celts to accounts of Egypt and the civilisations of Mexico and South America. He was a Fellow of the Royal Anthropological Institute of Great Britain and Ireland, and Vice-President of the Scottish Anthropological and Folklore Society. He produced a major *Encyclopaedia of Occultism* in 1920 and was especially interested in the 'Atlantis' legend, editing the *Atlantis Quarterly* in 1932 and producing five books on that subject alone. Spence championed Scottish nationalism and the cause of new writing in Scots and, although most of his own poems use a rather poetical diction in English, he chose an archaic Scots for some of them. 'The Queen's Bath-house, Holyrood', 'The Prows o' Reekie' and 'The Firth' catch the dour strength he was seeking, even if they are mainly descriptive and historically located.

Most of the above-mentioned poets using Scots were featured in three anthologies called *Northern Numbers*, which appeared between 1920 and 1922. Edited by a writer in his late twenties called C. M. Grieve, these planned to do for contemporary Scottish poets what Edward Marsh's *Georgian Poetry* collections had already achieved in England. Indeed, these little books from Montrose do mark the first stirrings of what was to be a renaissance in Scottish poetry, as well as the first significant appearance of its most energetic proponent. At this stage, however, Grieve's own poems were all in English and for his part he doubted if Scots would ever be an effective medium for modern poetry. 'Hugh MacDiarmid' was soon to change all that.

Poets and novelists of the literary renaissance

Christopher Murray Grieve, 'Hugh MacDiarmid' (1892–1978)

C. M. Grieve launched *Northern Numbers* when he was twenty-eight years old. Married and recently demobilised from the Army Medical Corps, he was a self-confessed 'late ripener'. Now that he was working as a journalist in Montrose he set about taking the first serious steps towards a literary career planned during the long watches as a quarter-master-sergeant in military hospitals in Salonika and near Marseilles. He had shown creative promise from the start, and during and after the war he kept up a correspondence with George Ogilvie, his English-master from Broughton Student Centre in Edinburgh, pouring out his doubts and ambitions and sending him examples of the many sonnets which he was writing at the time. These poems in English tended to deal with death, eternity and God in a rather studiously crystalline poetic diction.

Grieve was working in prose too, and since 1919 he had been assembling material written or planned during the war, to be called *Annals of the Five Senses* – a series of psychological studies or sketches, each of them laying bare, under various *personae*, the author's sense of his own enthusiastic mental life. The collection was ready by 1921, but could not be published until 1923, and although it is not about the war, *Annals* does relate to some of Grieve's experiences in Greece and France. He contracted cerebral malaria in Salonika and had been invalided home as a chronic case in 1918 (it was during this leave that he married Margaret – Peggy – Skinner) and it is possible that the positively feverish intensity of the consciousness described in *Annals* stems at least in part from this illness. Every character in each of the six stories has a 'brain like a hall of mirrors in which he caught countless reflections of every theme in as many shapes and sizes', and those themes are evoked in long and lovingly elaborated lists of the most esoteric details culled from his own sensations or from the world of books and newspapers to make 'a swift, beautiful catalogue of the most delightful and unexpected of interests'. (Grieve had been a compulsively omnivorous reader since his early boyhood, when the family lived in rooms beneath the Langholm public library, where his mother worked as a caretaker.) The *Annals* stories mix a furious sense of physical detail with unacknowledged quotations from dozens of writers and a tendency to abstruse or metaphysical speculation – a striking combination, even when the young man's prose style cannot quite support the strain. In view of the long catalogue-like poems that he was to write in the late thirties (and the controversy about his use of unacknowledged sources) these first studies are of critical interest and revealingly prophetic.

The Montrose years were among the most productive in Grieve's life, despite his commitments to many other fields. Apart from working for the *Montrose Review*, he sat on the town council as an Independent Socialist, becoming a parish councillor and, in 1926, a justice of the peace. After *Northern Numbers* his next project was to found a literary monthly called the *Scottish Chapbook*, which appeared in August 1922 and managed fourteen issues before the end of 1923. By then he was also publishing and editing the *Scottish Nation*, a weekly dedicated to Scottish nationalism, and the *Northern Review*, which appeared for four months in the summer of 1924. These short-lived periodicals mark the beginning of the 'Scottish Renaissance' as a self-defined modern literary movement, and for the next twenty years Grieve promoted the cause of literary and political self-awareness with a constant stream of newspaper articles, books, reviews, essays, letters and public speeches, all of which made him one of the most vociferous and best known cultural figures in Scotland. Some of his more influential and contentious essays, from a regular series in the *Scottish Educational Journal*, were collected as *Contemporary Scottish Studies* in 1926, to be followed by *Albyn, or Scotland and the Future* in 1927.

The first *Chapbook* contained a play script by Grieve and a visionary poem called 'A Moment in Eternity' dedicated to George Ogilvie. Subsequent numbers embarked on 'A Theory of Scots Letters', much influenced by Gregory Smith's 1919 study *Scottish Literature: Character and Influence*, described as 'a most searching and stimulating book'. Smith had set out to define what made Scottish literature 'Scottish' and settled on a number of features that could be traced from medieval to modern times. Chief among these was a tendency to combine opposites such as realism and fantasy ('the polar twins of the Scottish muse'), to which he gave the general term (not entirely seriously) of 'the Caledonian antisyzygy'. (A syzygy is a conjunction or a coming-together of things.) Grieve was much taken with this notion and quickly made it his own, citing the principle of 'antisyzygy' to show what Scots could offer to the modern poet – especially its 'reconciliation of the base and the beautiful' and its potential for creating images drawn from physical and psychological states no longer available, so

Grieve claimed, to an urbane and over-sophisticated English tradition. The term has become critically notorious ever since and a dispute over its efficacy as a model for writers was one of the causes of a later split between Grieve and Edwin Muir. Unlike Muir, Grieve saw a modernist dynamic at work in antisyzygy and became fond of quoting Walt Whitman from 'Song of Myself': 'Do I contradict myself? / Very well then I contradict myself, / I am large, I contain multitudes.'

Grieve found Smith's 'base and beautiful' effects along with unutilised psychological states particularly evident in *Jamieson's Scottish Dictionary* and he listed many words and phrases from its pages to make his point. He cited Dostoevsky, Lawrence and Joyce as writers who had felt the need to overthrow the old modes in order to express their new psychological insights, and went on to claim that Scots should be equally capable of contributing to the modernist movement. He had no time, therefore, for Scots as an exercise in nostalgia, nor for the Victorian stereotype of Scottish 'dourness'. Indeed, he preferred to redefine the 'true Scot' as a figure possessed by Gregory Smith's combination of opposites – 'dominated by the conception of infinity, of the unattainable, and hence ever questioning, never satisfied, rationalistic in religion and politics, romantic in art and literature' – as a figure not unlike 'Hugh MacDiarmid', in other words. Grieve's desire to follow Pound and to 'make it new' is central to his conception of the Renaissance, and from the start his periodicals and essays looked outwards to Europe and beyond. The *Chapbook*'s motto was 'Not Traditions – Precedents', and if its editor cried 'Back to Dunbar!', it was because he hoped that Dunbar's scathing spirit and complex technique would be a salutary antidote to the bucolic sentimentality of the post-Burns tradition. Yet all this activity and theorizing would have come to nothing from a literary point of view were it not for the poems that Grieve produced in four extraordinary years from 1922 to 1926.

Grieve published his first poems in Scots in the *Dunfermline Press* in September 1922, but pretended that they were written by a friend – later named as 'Hugh M'Diarmid'. He now admitted an interest in the poetic potential of 'obsolete' or 'distinctively local' words and opined that his friend's verses had a 'descriptive potency otherwise unobtainable'. One of the poems was 'The Watergaw' and Grieve was right. It was as if the vocabulary and idiom of Scots with its long tradition of colloquial utterance and domestic detail added a special and much needed physical body to the more abstract metaphysical inspiration of his early verses in English. This was a voice that could express both the sublime and the vulgar, moving from one to the other with speed, wit and the appearance of ease. Gregory Smith had described this 'medieval . . . freedom in passing from one mood to another', and it turned out to be exactly right for the author of *Annals of the Five Senses* and his volatile sensibility, so wildly idealistic and materialistic by turns. Struck by this insight, Grieve immediately explained it in his 'Theory of Scots Letters', and acknowledged the debt by adopting the name Hugh MacDiarmid for all his poems thereafter. Yet, as his 'Theory of Scots Letters' insisted at every turn, 'whatever the potentialities of the Doric may be . . . there cannot be a revival in the real sense of the word – a revival of the spirit as distinct from a mere renewed vogue by the letter – unless these potentialities are in accord with newest and truest tendencies of human thought.' He claimed that the vivid earthiness of the Scots language, as he found it in Jamieson's *Dictionary* (and indeed in the mouths of the people around him when he was growing up in Langholm), was exactly what modern writers such as Joyce and Lawrence were seeking in their technique and in the sexual and psychological frankness of their work:

> We have been enormously struck by the resemblance – the moral resemblance – between Jamieson's Etymological Dictionary of the Scottish language and James Joyce's *Ulysses*. A *vis comica* that has not yet been liberated lies bound by desuetude and misappreciation in the recesses of the Doric: and its potential uprising would be no less prodigious, uncontrollable, and utterly at variance with conventional morality than was Joyce's tremendous outpouring.

The fluidity of this language, with its ability to use Scots and English words alike, a language where neologisms might seem no less strange than the other words around them, all this was to be a liberating experience for the poet. In writing of this capacity Douglas Young was later to coin the phrase 'Plastic Scots', referring not to its artificial nature but to its protean qualities, although most people preferred to call it Doric or Lallans. (Strictly speaking, 'Doric' is usually reserved for the dialects of North-East Scotland.)

MacDiarmid's first two collections of Scots poems were called *Sangschaw* (1925) and *Penny Wheep* (1926) and both were enthusiastically received. Edwin Muir admired 'a crazy economy' in the language, 'which has the effect of humour and yet conveys a kind of horror', and he saw this as 'truly Scottish', just as distinct from the English ethos as the prose of George Douglas Brown or Carlyle. The reviewer for *The Times Literary Supplement* (*TLS*) praised 'an unusual sense of the movement and changing aspects of the earth in its diurnal round', and Professor Denis Saurat of the University of Bordeaux, who had taken an early critical interest in the Scots revival, translated many of them into French. Danish versions were made, and the poet's former schoolteacher from Langholm, a composer called Francis George (F. G.) Scott (1880–1958), set several of the lyrics, and ultimately about seventy of MacDiarmid's poems, to music. *La renaissance écossaise* was off to a properly international start. Scott and MacDiarmid renewed their old acquaintance and became close friends. In fact 'F. G.' helped the poet assemble the long sequence that became *A Drunk Man Looks at the Thistle* and that book was dedicated to him.

Some of the early lyrics use a familiar vernacular voice – 'Crowdieknowe' and 'Focherty', for example, might have been conceived by Charles Murray – but for the rest the domestic realism of the Scots is astonishingly transformed, as if their landscapes have become charged with a strange energy, like Expressionist paintings by Munch or Soutine. MacDiarmid creates a world of vivid contrasts, of 'Cloudburst and Soarin' Mune', or of wind and light where the trees fatten and thin themselves like turkeys screaming ('Sunny Gale'). Even the filthy gutter in the cowshed is transmuted – 'The aidle-pool is a glory o' gowd' – and we seem to cling to the surface of the planet with an exhilarating sense of the vastness of time and infinite distance:

> The moonbeams kelter i' the lift,   waver in the sky
> An' Earth, the bare auld stane,
> Glitters beneath the seas o' Space,
> White as a mammoth's bane.
> ('Au Clair de la Lune')

Other poems in this vein include 'Ex Vermibus', 'Country Life' and 'Farmer's Death', and their hallucinatory intensity is charged again by MacDiarmid's choice of not-quite-familiar Scots words or by the succinct and subtle breaks which he makes from what would otherwise be fairly predictable ballad-like stresses. (In this respect his handling of rhythm is reminiscent of Wordsworth's 'Lucy' poems, or some of Hardy's pieces on his wife.) A sense of cosmic scale also characterises 'Au Clair de la Lune', 'The Innumerable Christ', 'Servant Girl's Bed' and 'Empty Vessel'. 'The Eemis Stane' is rightly famous:

> I' the how-dumb-deid o' the cauld hairst night   harvest
> The warl' like an eemis stane   insecure, wobbling stone
> Wags i' the lift;   sky
> An' my eerie memories fa'

Like a yowdendrift.   blizzard with snow rising
                                                 from ground

Like a yowdendrift so's I couldna read
The words cut oot i' the stane
Had the fug o' fame   moss
An' history's hazelraw   lichen
No' yirdit thaim.   buried

The specific earthiness of Scots words such as 'fug' and 'hazelraw'
contrasts with the more English abstractions 'fame' and 'history', while
the planet teeters like a rocking boulder in the sky. If there is some
primal message or meaning to be found inscribed on the world, the
poet cannot read it because it has been hidden by his own memories
and by all the experience of the planet itself – like moss and lichen on
the surface of a gravestone.

The lyric 'Gairmscoile', written in the densest Scots, takes up the
psychological aspects of the 'Theory of Scots Letters' (indeed it was
first published in the *Chapbook*) by arguing that the old Scots words
have special access to worlds of primal instinct and Lawrentian experience and can act as 'keys to senses lockit to us yet', because –

It's soon', no sense, that faddoms the herts o' men,   sound
And by my sangs the rouch auld Scots I ken
E'en herts that ha'e nae Scots'll dirl richt thro'   thrill
As nocht else could – for here's a language rings
Wi' datchie sesames, and names for nameless things.   secret

Of course this is a poetic rather than a fully argued linguistic case, and
yet poetry in any language has always drawn on the same assumption.
Rather in the spirit of Blok's apocalyptic poem *The Twelve*, or the essays
in Hermann Hesse's *Blick ins Chaos*, MacDiarmid hopes that the
'camsteerie cast-offs' of his Scots verses will pour out of the hills to
invade the towns and interrupt 'canny civilisation's canty [cheerful]
dance'. (W. N. Herbert was to attempt a similarly alienating and liberating force in the equally dense Scots poems he was writing in the
1990s.)

MacDiarmid's Scots lyrics, and others such as 'Moonstruck', 'The
Watergaw' and 'The Bonnie Broukit Bairn', reach a truly extraordinary
imaginative compression of image, language and ideation. They meet
the requirements of Imagism and Imagist verse more effectively than
any of the poems written by Pound, HD, or T. E. Hulme, and in this
respect MacDiarmid took the Scots tradition to a new and truly

modern expression. Even so, the poet's mercurial sensibility, his polemical humour and his enthusiasm for metaphysical flights, had still further to go and he turned his energies to a much more ambitious project.

A Drunk Man Looks at the Thistle (1926) is MacDiarmid's most famous single book and one of the great poems of modernist literature – a testament to creative energy and optimism at a time when Yeats, Pound and Eliot could see only cultural decline and spiritual failure all around them. The poem's setting is simple enough – a drunken man lies gazing at a thistle on a moonlit hillside. His intoxicated state and the fickle and deceptive light of the moon send him on an imaginative odyssey as strange as any undertaken by Tam o' Shanter or Thomas the Rhymer. Operating somewhere between dramatic monologue and stream of consciousness, the poem's actual verse technique is fairly conventional for he uses simple ballad-like rhyme schemes and the language is a lightly colloquial Scots. Yet this familiarity is deceptive, for MacDiarmid creates and juxtaposes so many startling images, and makes so many swift changes of pace and tone – from broad satire to tender lyrics, to ribaldry, metaphysical anguish and back again – that the poem is electric with energy and exhilaration. The drunk man finds that the world around him and his own thoughts seem to mix and change with alarming fluidity, and the whole universe is destabilised by whisky, moonlight and his own overheated cerebration.

The poem has little formal structure beyond its individual rhyme schemes and it can be bewilderingly garrulous and repetitious, but particular images do recur to give it a thematic coherence. Most notably the thistle is a deeply ambivalent symbol – representing some ideal beauty or fulfilment by its purple flower (the thistle's 'rose') but conjuring up sterility, failure and pain in its ugly stalks and spikes. It seems that we are fated always to be caught between the two: 'Man torn in twa / And glorious in the lift and grisly on the sod'. The drunk man finds this division within himself, his country (it is the national plant, after all) and the fate of all humankind. It should be noted, too, that this is the wild thistle – a large, multi-branched and many-headed hydra of a plant, rather than the neat single emblem later adopted by the SNP. The drunk man is obsessed with it, just as Ahab was obsessed with the mystery and menace of Moby Dick, and the thistle takes a dozen different shapes through the course of the poem – comic, vulgar or terrifying – as he wrestles with its personal, social, sexual and philosophical implications:

A black leaf owre a white leaf twirls,
A grey leaf flauchters in atween,   flutters
Sae ply my thochts aboot the stem   [thistle/penis]
O' loppert slime frae which they spring.   clotted
The thistle like a snawstorm drives,
Or like a flicht o' swallows lifts,
Or like a swarm o' midges hings,
A plague o' moths, a starry sky,
But's naething but a thistle yet,
And still the puzzle stands unsolved.
Beauty and ugliness alike,
And life and daith and God and man,
Are aspects o't but nane can tell
The secret that I'd fain find oot
O' this bricht hive, this sorry weed,
The tree that fills the universe,   (Yggdrasil, the tree of life)
Or like a reistit herrin' crines.   dried herring shrivels

In the course of this Dionysian exploration, the broadest satirical
attacks are delivered on Burns Clubs, Harry Lauder and all the conventional trappings of bourgeois 'Scottishness'. MacDiarmid also created
hundreds of the most startling poetic images, by which the abstractions of his theme are embodied in the concrete particularities of Scots
speech: 'nocht but a chowed core's left whaur Jerusalem lay / Like
aipples in a heap!' If Grierson and Eliot admired a quality of 'felt
thought' in the poetry of John Donne and the Metaphysicals, this is
no less than MacDiarmid achieves in almost every page of his long
poem:

I tae ha'e heard Eternity drip water
(Aye water, water!), drap by drap
On the a'e nerve, like lichtnin', I've become,
And heard God passin' wi' a bobby's feet   policeman's
Ootby in the lang coffin o' the street
– Seen stang by chitterin' knottit stang loup oot   paroxysm; shivering; jump
Uncrushed by th'echoes o' the thunderin' boot,
Till a' the dizzy lint-white lines o' torture made   flax-white
A monstrous thistle in the space aboot me,
A symbol o' the puzzle o' man's soul.

These lines make broad comedy collide with the most intense spiritual
longing, as if Fergusson and Shelley were united in profound grotesquerie – a new category of literary taste.

Unlike Yeats and Eliot, MacDiarmid welcomes the insignificance of
man and the vastness of the universe, just as he welcomes the myriad
conflicting sensations and impulses within himself. In this he is a truly

post-Romantic modernist with absolutely no hankering for balance or the certitudes of some idealised classical past:

> I'll hae nae hauf-way hoose, but aye be whaur
> Extremes meet – it's the only way I ken
> To dodge the curst conceit o' bein' richt
> That damns the vast majority o' men.

Thus he gives himself up to change, fluidity and perpetual opposition, and embraces – very much in the spirit of Walt Whitman – the *élan vital* of the universe itself.

If *A Drunk Man* rings with MacDiarmid's special brand of optimistic modernism, fuelled by his interests in materialism, socialism and Scottish nationhood, it also has moments of visionary intensity when he glimpses some spiritual or neo-Platonic ideal of peace and enlightenment beyond the endless whirl of the world or his own introspection.

> And O! I canna thole   endure
> Aye yabblin' o' my soul,   gabbling
> And fain I wad be free
> O' my eternal me.

This ideal is symbolised by the bride carrying a bunch of thistles, or by the 'silken leddy' who drifts into a crowded and noisy tavern to create a moment of stillness and insight. For the drunk man the mystery of existence and the challenge is 'to be yersel's – and to mak' that worth bein'' in lines that echo the motto of the Belgian literary revival 'Soyons nous-mêmes', along with Nietzsche's command to 'become what you are!' So this is an imperative that goes beyond Scottish national identity (although that is the first step), for MacDiarmid believes that human consciousness is an integrated part of universal evolution and that an outstanding effort must be made to realise it – in every sense of the word. This is what he refers to as the 'seamless garment' or the 'diamond body' in later poems. For the moment, however, the drunk man can solve nothing in a world where the only constant seems to be eternal change. But at least for one glorious, intoxicated night he has given himself up to the flux of the universe and joined the dance in his own wild and fantastical imagination. If he comes to silence in the closing lines of the poem, it is the silence of human experience, or repletion, or even exhaustion, but never the stillness of extinction, blind faith, acquiescence or despair – those common ailments of the modern spirit.

MacDiarmid's drunk caused a critical sensation in Scotland – at last a fully modern poem in Scots had appeared, bursting on the nation with all the force, in David Daiches's incomparable phrase, of a child-birth in church. Yet already some readers were regretting his move away from the lyric. The poet remained in Montrose for the next three years, as prolific as ever with reviews and innumerable articles on Scotland and all things Scottish. He worked on another long poem, to be called *To Circumjack Cencrastus* (1930), in which the puzzle of the thistle is pursued yet again in the form of 'Cencrastus', which MacDiarmid associated with the Celtic curly snake with its tail in its mouth – a symbol of eternity – and with the mythological serpent whose coils surround the world, and with his own vision of the infinitely mobile multiplicity of the material universe. But the mode had been better realised in *A Drunk Man*, and, although the theme of endless complexity is central to MacDiarmid's poetry, the new book had passages where he seems bitterly dissatisfied with his life and his job as an underpaid journalist in Montrose. By the 1930s the poet was looking for a new direction and for a way of more overtly expressing his socialist principles in verse.

When Compton Mackenzie suggested that he edit *Vox*, a recently founded arts magazine for the radio, MacDiarmid seized the chance and moved to London with his wife and two children (Christine and Walter), late in 1929. But London proved to be an unhappy experience. Towards the end of the year he fell from a bus and suffered severe concussion – experiencing headaches for some years afterwards – and *Vox* had died before he recovered. The poet's marriage was under strain and when he eventually found a job as a publicity officer in Liverpool, Peggy refused to go with him and they agreed to separate. The Liverpool appointment did not last long and MacDiarmid found himself back in London. *First Hymn to Lenin and Other Poems* appeared in 1931 with an introduction and a portrait of the author by 'AE', but it was limited to only 500 copies. Many of these poems looked back to his roots in Langholm as if seeking a new stability there. He was drinking heavily and estranged from his wife, for she had found someone else, and in the middle of an economic depression he had no job and no savings at all. (The couple were finally divorced at the beginning of 1932.) 'My story', he was to write later, 'is the story of an absolutist whose absolutes came to grief in his private life.' The one good thing that happened to him at this time was his meeting with a Cornishwoman called Valda Trevlyn, a creative person in her own right, who became his wife and an unfailing source of support and courage for the rest of his life. They lived in a cottage in Sussex and then moved back to Scotland with their new baby, Michael, who had been born in the summer.

In a long essay for T. S. Eliot's *Criterion* in 1931, MacDiarmid had produced one of his most cogent critiques of the literary establishment of the day, in terms that anticipate how postcolonial theory has come to see the inequalities of power between dominant and 'subaltern' cultures. (From what he assumed to be a superior position, Eliot himself had once expressed doubts about whether there was even such a thing as a Scottish literary tradition.) MacDiarmid's essay 'English Ascendancy in British Literature' strikes a note of modest regret (and an untypically Unionist note) when he observes that:

> It is absurd that intelligent readers of English, who would be ashamed not to know something (if only the leading names, and roughly, what they stand for) of most Continental literatures, are content to ignore Scottish Gaelic, Irish and Welsh literatures, and Scots Vernacular literature. Surely the latter are nearer to them than the former, and the language difficulty no greater. . . . Few literatures offer within themselves so rich a range of alternative values, or material for comparative criticism, as does, not English, but British. . . .

The critical and cultural challenge of these words is as trenchant today as it was over 70 years ago.

When *Scots Unbound and Other Poems* appeared in 1932, MacDiarmid explained that it was to join *First Hymn to Lenin and Other Poems* as part of an extended sequence in five books to be called 'Clann Albann' – 'the children of Scotland'. The first book, 'The Muckle Toon', would consider his years in Langholm and the influence of parents, childhood, socialism and the Church on his growing sensibility. The project was never realised, but most of the poems and some short stories of the period do indeed relate to autobiographical themes. He chose a light colloquial Scots, for pieces such as 'At my Father's Grave', 'Charisma and my Relatives', and 'Kinsfolk'; and his home town and the surrounding country feature in poems such as 'Whuchulls' and 'Tarras'. Langholm is a place where three rivers meet, and MacDiarmid's fascination with water in all its changes appears as a symbol of life, itself in 'Prayer for a Second Flood', 'Water of Life', 'Excelsior' and 'The Oon Olympian', reaching a climax with 'Water Music', a Joycean extravaganza that uses a plethora of the most obscure Scots words to imitate the sound and the movements of his favourite rivers. It is not the life-*giving* properties of water that make it a symbol of life for MacDiarmid, but rather its life-*demonstrating* qualities as it ripples on its way and keeps changing its form between vapour, water, ice or steam.

Socialism was a further theme in MacDiarmid's poems of the early thirties, and in this, of course, he was in line with many other left-wing writers of the day. Yet his political roots are earlier, deeper and narrower than those of Auden, Spender, MacNeice and Day Lewis, and his idealism is more far-reaching. His father was a country postman and a socialist (as well as an elder in the United Free Kirk) and MacDiarmid had joined the Fabian Society and the ILP when he was sixteen. As a young journalist in South Wales in 1911 he had worked for a miners' newspaper, witnessed police baton charges, and made speeches in support of the Labour cause. Thus in later years he took a hardliner's delight in opposing 'bourgeois liberalism', and his overtly political poems often adopt a harshly polemical stance. The three 'Hymns to Lenin' celebrate Lenin's heroic ruthlessness, as if he were one of Carlyle's heroes who represents 'the flower and iron of the truth' and has the courage to stand apart from 'the majority will that accepts the result'. Even so, MacDiarmid's brand of millennial socialism has little to do with 'bread and butter problems', for he regards all political goals and structures as merely the first steps towards a far more radical – evolutionary – reorganisation of man's physical and spiritual resources. 'The Seamless Garment', set in a Langholm woollen-mill, makes just this point in a good-humoured way, using a low-key colloquial Scots to explain it to a 'cousin' who works there:

> The haill shop's dumfoonderin'
>   To a stranger like me.
> Second nature to you; you're perfectly able
>   To think, speak and see
> Apairt frae the looms, tho' to some
> That doesna sae easily come.
>
> Lenin was like that wi' workin' class life,
>   At hame wi't a'.
> His fause movements couldna been fewer,
>   The best weaver Earth ever saw.
> A' he'd to dae wi' moved intact
>   Clean, clear, and exact.
>
> A poet like Rilke, did the same
>   In a different sphere,,
> Made a single reality – a' a'e 'oo' –   all one wool
>   O' his love and pity and fear;
> A seamless garment o' music and thought
> But you're ower thrang wi' puirer to tak' tent o't.   too caught up with
>   poverty to heed it
>
> What's life or God or what you may ca't
>   But something at ane, like this?

In Christian doctrine the seamless garment represents the unity between Christ's life and his divine being, but 'Second Hymn to Lenin' recognises the practical difficulties of reaching that state ourselves without being 'Unremittin', relentless, / Organised to the last degree'. Thus he extols the ruthless concentration of Lenin's vision – those 'lizard eyes' – and the cold and granite-hard creed that will be necessary to realise 'The Skeleton of the Future'. In the meantime the poet could not earn enough to support his family and they were practically destitute until friends rallied to their support in the spring of 1933 and found them a cottage in the Shetlands. At last MacDiarmid had made a break with his problems in Scotland and London, and for the next nine years he committed himself to living and writing on the remote – and tee-total – island of Whalsay.

The Shetlands stunned MacDiarmid. His health was poor and they were living at little more than subsistence level, but the remote beauty of this treeless landscape, caught between the sea and the vast northern skies, offered an austere peace and a return to fundamentals. Letters to William Soutar and Neil Gunn, and a chapter in *The Islands of Scotland* (1939), all testify to this new inspiration:

> the vivifying element of water breaking up the land everywhere, and the strange glories of the displays of the Aurora Borealis; and beautiful when these are absent, in an awe-inspiring way, like a foreglimpse of the end of the world – bedrock indeed! – Earth's final state to which all else has been tending under all the veils of Maya – a world of stone, water, and light. . . .

The family ate seagull eggs and mackerel, cut peat for their fire, and MacDiarmid began to write longer poems, 'valuable new departures' he thought, in a cool and icily controlled English diction. He undertook prose too, in order to earn a living, and in 1934 his literary essays appeared in *At the Sign of the Thistle*, as well as a collaboration with Lewis Grassic Gibbon that resulted in an irreverent and entertaining book called *Scottish Scene or The Intelligent Man's Guide to Albyn*. In 1938 he founded the *Voice of Scotland*, a quarterly dedicated to 'Scottish Workers' Republicanism à la John Maclean', which published work by several of the younger poets – the 'second wave' of the Renaissance – including Norman MacCaig, George Bruce, Sorley MacLean and George Campbell Hay. The magazine reached five issues before the outbreak of war stopped it.

The isolation of the Shetlands led the poet to still further perspectives, and *Stony Limits and Other Poems* (1934) was his most substantial and challenging collection for years. It contained fine work in Scots, including a set of 'Shetland Lyrics', 'Harry Semen' (censored from the first edition, however) and 'Ode to All Rebels'. But he was also using English for political poems such as 'The Belly Grip' and 'John Maclean', and most especially for those 'new departures'. These turned out to be long meditations on scientific, geological and philosophical themes, full of obscure technical terms and a deliberately intellectu-alised diction – verses as austere and hard as the Shetland coast itself. There are poems in memory of Rilke and Charles Doughty (of *Arabia Deserta*), whose visions had also taken them into remote and desert landscapes of the spirit. And in the same vein 'Lament for the Great Music' welcomes pibroch, the classical music of the Highland bagpipe, as the sternest and loveliest art of all – 'like the metaphysics of light . . . in the grey life of these islands'. The most outstanding of these productions is 'On a Raised Beach', a meditation on death, truth and the 'bedrock' of the world, and one of the finest existential poems in modern literature.

If one can compare MacDiarmid's career with that of T. S. Eliot, then the energy of *A Drunk Man* would correspond to *The Waste Land*, and the philosophical restraint of 'On a Raised Beach' would stand on equal terms with *Four Quartets*, except that the Scot, unlike Eliot, gives himself up to the absolute and unrelenting materiality of the world:

> What happens to us
> Is irrelevant to the world's geology
> But what happens to the world's geology
> Is not irrelevant to us.
> We must reconcile ourselves to the stones,
> Not the stones to us.
> Here a man must shed the encumbrances that muffle
> Contact with elemental things, the subtleties
> That seem inseparable from a humane life, and go apart
> Into a simpler and sterner, more beautiful and oppressive world,
> Austerely intoxicating; the first draught is over-powering;
> Few survive it . . .

The 'raised beach' in question is an ancient shoreline left far from the movements of any contemporary tide, and the 'otherness' of this strange world is literally conjured up in the poem's opening lines with an incantation of magically unapproachable words, for after all, as the poet observes – 'Deep conviction or preference can seldom / Find direct terms in which to express itself':

All is lithogenesis – or lochia,
Carpolite fruit of the forbidden tree,
Stones blacker than any in the Caaba,
Cream-coloured caen-stone, chatoyant pieces,
Celadon and corbeau, bistre and beige,
Glaucous, hoar, enfouldered, cyathiform,
Making mere faculae of the sun and moon,
I study you glout and gloss. . . .

'These stones are one with the stars' writes MacDiarmid, with the same imaginative leap from domestic to cosmic that characterised the early lyrics. He insists too that 'This is no heap of broken images', and if the phrase reminds us of *The Waste Land*'s spiritual despair, it serves to emphasise MacDiarmid's refusal to submit to the comfort of organised religion – 'Let men find the faith that builds mountains / Before they seek the faith that moves them.' In place of faith the poet asks only that we 'Be ourselves without interruption/ Adamantine and inexorable', although the task may well require that men become like stones themselves by some 'immense exercise of will, / Inconceivable discipline, courage, and endurance, / Self purification and anti-humanity'. MacDiarmid celebrates the 'deadly clarity' of this materialism throughout, even if his tone is unmistakably reminiscent of Knox and the rock-hard inheritance of Scottish Calvinism: 'Listen to me – Truth is not crushed; / It crushes, gorgonises all else into itself. . . . Do not argue with me. Argue with these stones.' The poem ends with a call to 'participate' in material life – which 'is nearest of all and easiest to grasp'; except that man may have to come face to face with the inevitability of his own death before he sees that 'barren but beautiful reality' clearly enough: 'I lift a stone; it is the meaning of life I clasp / Which is death.'

It seems likely that his philosophical confrontation with a universe of stones, not to mention years of strain and the hardships of life on the island, took a considerable toll on MacDiarmid's health, and he suffered a complete nervous and physical collapse in the summer of 1935. His condition was serious and friends arranged for him to enter hospital in Perth, where he spent seven weeks in care. Recovery was slow and a photograph of the time shows an emaciated and exhausted figure, like a prisoner of war who has just been released from some frightful camp. Back on Whalsay, he soon picked up the threads of his indefatigable correspondence and renewed contacts with the outside world. But he had not lost his sense of literary and political isolation, and his contentious absolutism, which had an air of desperation about it, led him to break with many old friends and fellow writers.

Edwin Muir had been a friend since the twenties, when they both contributed to A. R. Orage's *New Age*, but now that Muir had come to live in St Andrews he was reassessing his views on the future of literature in Scots. Despite his early enthusiasm for the language (and a few ballad-like poems of his own), he had come to believe that the use of Scots only encouraged a split between thinking and feeling, and offered no hope of a national literature for as long as writers had to turn to English as well – especially in prose. Muir believed that mature cultures demand a single 'homogenous' language and that those who clung to Scots were demonstrating a preference for feeling over thought and an unwillingness to enter the adult world. There are echoes here of Eliot's theories about a 'dissociation of sensibility' and Muir argued that Scots poets would do better to use English, and (worse still, from the point of view of MacDiarmid's hopes for creative contradiction) he held that the 'Caledonian antisyzygy' could only result in a sterile cultural impasse. When Muir expressed these views in *Scott and Scotland* (1936), MacDiarmid felt betrayed and launched a bitter personal attack which ended their friendship and emphasised his own isolation as a John Maclean socialist at odds with what he took to be liberal or reactionary tendencies in Scottish culture and politics. On these grounds too he parted company with Neil Gunn, whose success as a novelist was about to be confirmed with *Highland River* (1937).

More prose projects were planned, and although some fell by the wayside others, such as *Scottish Eccentrics* (1936) and *The Islands of Scotland* (1939), brought in much-needed royalties. He also wrote *Lucky Poet: A Self-Study in Literature and Political Ideas* (1943), in which he set out to explain himself by way of an infuriating and entertainingly wayward chronicle of his multitudinous interests and opinions. The book also contained passages from unpublished long poems and a new assessment of the Gaelic spirit. MacDiarmid had already produced 'Lament for the Great Music', and a translation of MacMhaighstir Alasdair's *Birlinn Chlann Raghnaill* had followed from his meeting with Sorley MacLean in 1934; now the 'Gaelic Muse' and three 'Direadh' poems appeared in *Lucky Poet*. In these and other verses, MacDiarmid invoked the Celtic spirit, and an 'East–West synthesis' with Russia, as necessary opposition to what he saw as the commercial values and the cultural imperialism of an English-speaking ascendancy in the Western world. The same resistance to received values and literary modes inspired his plans for an epic poetry that would cast off the 'irresponsible lyricism in which sense impressions / Are employed to substitute ecstasy for information' ('The Kind of

Poetry I Want'). In the cause of that 'information' MacDiarmid redefined Celtic complexity and developed Duncan Bàn Macintyre's penchant for lengthy objective description, until his own verses became vast extended catalogues, full of borrowings from a host of unacknowledged prose sources, as if he were determined to list everything and anything that had ever caught his magpie attention in the material universe. MacDiarmid spent the rest of his life working over these epic poems from the late thirties and early forties. They were supposed to come together in a *magnum opus* to be called 'Mature Art', only sections of which – such as *In Memoriam James Joyce* (1955) – have ever appeared.

Even if 'Mature Art' did not materialise, the poems that were written under its influence offer an extraordinary 'vision of world language', as if the poet has decided to relinquish his creative and image-making power in favour of merely listening to the details of the world as it 'speaks' itself, choosing only to select examples, perhaps, from that fascinating monologue:

> They are not endless these variations of form
> Though it is perhaps impossible to see them all.
> It is certainly impossible to conceive one that doesn't exist.
> But I keep trying in our forest to do both of these. . . .
> ('In Memoriam James Joyce'; also
> 'In the Caledonian Forest', from *Stony Limits*)

The principle behind these catalogue poems was anticipated by one of the characters in *Annals of the Five Senses*, who observed that, 'if every opinion is equally insignificant in itself, humanity's bewilderment of thought is a mighty net which somehow holds the whole truth'. So these 'world language' poems were MacDiarmid's mightiest 'net' ever in the attempt to match the thistle, to capture Cencrastus, or to achieve 'the diamond body'. Scientific detail and detachment has not dimmed the poet's sense of sudden wonder at the unity of all things when 'time whuds like a flee' and microcosm and macrocosm come together before his eyes:

> What after all do we know of this terrible 'matter',
> Save as a name for the unknown and hypothetical cause
> Of states of our own consciousness? There are not two worlds,
> A world of nature, and a world of human consciousness,
> Standing over against one another, but one world of nature
> Whereof human consciousness is an evolution,
> I reminded myself again as I caught that sudden breathless glimpse,
> Under my microscope, of unexpected beauty and dynamic living

In the world of life on a sliver of kelp
Quite as much as the harpooning of a forty-two foot whale shark.
                                                    ('Diamond Body', 1939)

MacDiarmid called such works a 'poetry of fact'. Truly he had abandoned lyricism in favour of what he saw as a new kind of 'epic' dense
with information, frequently culled from other sources. Perhaps he had
abandoned poetry altogether. Or perhaps these vast intertextual
constructions were a new kind of poetry. The literary status of these
works still provokes controversy, and analogies might be made with
Ezra Pound, who devoted the latter half of his life to the *Cantos* only
to question their worth in the end. MacDiarmid managed to sustain
faith in his project, but it did get increasingly unrealisable and perhaps
more and more unreadable as the years went by.

The Second World War imposed its own priorities on the poet and
MacDiarmid was conscripted in 1941, leaving Whalsay to become a
fitter in a munitions factory in Glasgow. Life on the shop floor was hard
and after he was injured in an accident he transferred to operate as first
engineer on a Norwegian vessel servicing ships in the Clyde estuary.
When the war ended, MacDiarmid found himself at the age of fifty-
three without regular work, and with poems too long and too abstruse
for easy publication. Undaunted, he threw himself back into public life
by standing as an independent Nationalist candidate for Kelvingrove
during the 1945 general election. He lost his deposit and parted
company once again with the SNP. Few political parties could satisfy or
tolerate his contentious, contradictory and idealistic nature for long.
He himself saw no necessary conflict between his communism and his
Scottish nationalism, but neither of the two parties concerned was very
happy about his affiliations with the other and he continued to fluctu-
ate between them.

MacDiarmid revived the *Voice of Scotland* and renewed his friendship
with the younger writers on the literary scene. In 1950 he was awarded
a Civil List pension and visited Russia – the first of several visits to
Eastern European countries, where his status was high. In 1951 a small
farm cottage became available at Brownsbank, near Biggar, some
twenty-six miles from Edinburgh, and the Grieve family moved in.
Edinburgh University students helped to modernise it and Valda and
Chris Grieve spent the rest of their lives in this comfortable little house,
lined with books and portraits of the poet.

As the last of the early modern giants in the generation of Eliot,
Pound, Yeats, Carlos Williams and Joyce, MacDiarmid enjoyed the
stimulation of controversy to the end, and his spirit, intellect and

courage were unimpaired until in September 1978 cancer killed him at the age of eighty-six. He is buried in a hillside cemetery above Langholm. He was the first Scottish poet for generations to draw on the full canon of his country's literary tradition and to add a substantial contribution of his own. Thus his poetry embraces lyrical subtlety and the simple force of the ballads, the goliardic glee of Dunbar and the bitter polemic of Iain Lom. He unites Duncan Bàn's loving catalogue of the familiar landscapes of Scotland with John Davidson's scientific and philosophical abstractions, just as his poetic voice moves from colloquial Scots to the elitist and passionately didactic tones of Carlyle. Whatever the outward style, however, his work always shows a Blakean delight in the movement of the spirit and a materialistic delight in the physical universe, as he tries to show us 'the fundamental similarity of all activities', or the mystery to be found in the chemistry of water – 'aye, and ilka drap a world / Bigger than a' Mankind has yet unfurled'.

Edwin Muir (1887–1959)

As if to satisfy the principle of 'Caledonian antisyzygy', MacDiarmid's position as the major poet of the Renaissance movement is balanced by the life and work of Edwin Muir, a quiet, shy man, five years his senior, who came from the Orkney Isles. For a time, in fact, Muir was better known to English and American readers than his friend from the Borders. MacDiarmid's rejection of him in the 1930s had to do with Muir's political and cultural opinions, but the two men always did possess radically different poetic sensibilities. MacDiarmid's work is charged with lyrical, linguistic, intellectual or polemical energy, while Muir adopts an English verse of calm and neutral tone to meditate on time and the timeless by way of classical allusions or images drawn from the realms of childhood, mythology or dreams.

Muir's first book of poetry appeared in the same year as *Sangschaw*. He was living in London at the time and had already made a small reputation as a journalist and literary critic, writing as 'Edward Moore', for Orage's *New Age* – an idiosyncratically radical journal which numbered Pound and MacDiarmid among its contributors. Muir arrived at the capital in 1919 with his new wife, a woman called Willa Anderson, whose parents came from Shetland and who was to become a novelist in her own right. As a way of making a living the couple started to translate German literature, with Willa taking the leading part. They began with plays by Gerhart Hauptmann, going on to work on Lion Feuchtwanger, Heinrich Mann and Hermann Broch among others, but they are particularly remembered – and influential – for their English versions of Kafka. At first Muir was oppressed by London, and his already insecure psychological state was made worse by the size and anonymity of the city. His marriage was a happy one, however. He made friends and began to adjust; and Orage encouraged him to undertake Jungian analysis. This experience led to the unlocking of his creative capacity, as he kept a dream diary and began to reconstruct the meaning of his life with the help of images and archetypes from his unconscious. Such insights were to become central to his poetry, with its neo-Platonic sense of some timeless pattern beyond the contingent everyday. The couple moved to Europe in 1921 and lived and travelled there for three years before returning to England. Muir remembered Prague, Italy and Austria with gratitude – 'everyone should live his life twice', he wrote, and indeed he went over his old life and exorcised old griefs during that happy time abroad. Free at last, he began to write poetry at the age of thirty-five.

First Poems (1925) shows the influence of the Scots ballads and Heine, with the adoption of ballad stanzas (he experimented with Scots only briefly) to convey a childlike sense of simplicity and suspended wonder. Time seems to stand still and the world shrinks to a toy in 'Childhood':

> Grey tiny rocks slept round him where he lay,
> 　Moveless as they, more still as evening came,
> The grasses threw straight shadows far away,
> 　And from the house his mother called his name.

The mood is characteristic, and further insight can be gained into Muir's mature work from his account of how the 'Ballad of Hector in Hades' came to him:

> I must have been influenced by something, since we all are, but when I try to find out what it was that influenced me, I can only think of the years of childhood. . . . These years had come alive, after being forgotten for so long, and when I wrote about horses they were my father's plough horses as I saw them when I was four or five, and a poem on Achilles pursuing Hector round the walls of Troy was really a resuscitation of the afternoon when I ran away, in real terror from another boy as I returned from school. The bare landscape of the little island became, without my knowing it, a universal landscape over which Abraham and Moses and Achilles and Ulysses and Tristram and all sorts of pilgrims passed; and Troy was associated with the Castle, a mere green mound, near my father's house.
>
> 　　　　　　　　　　　　　　　　　　(*An Autobiography*, 1954)

It is not difficult to understand the origins of Muir's unhappiness as a young man, nor the sense of mythopoeic timelessness that haunts his verse. They both go back to his childhood on Orkney, and in a sense all his poems, although they never speak directly about himself, stem from a single biographical and metaphysical insight that he rediscovered there. As the youngest of six children, the poet was raised in the loving shelter of his father's farm on Orkney, and from his sixth to his eighth year the family lived on the little island of Wyre. He never forgot this idyllic experience of freedom and innocence, and in later life he came to see his childhood as a dream of Eden itself. The dream was all the more vivid when it stopped, for his father was evicted when Muir was fourteen, and the family had to move to Glasgow in 1901.

It was as if they had travelled forward in time from a place whose seasonal and communal pattern of life went back to earliest days:

> I as born before the Industrial Revolution, and am now about two hundred years old. But I have skipped a hundred and fifty of them. I was really born in 1737, and till I was fourteen no time-accidents happened to me. Then in 1751 I set out from Orkney for Glasgow. When I arrived I found that it was not 1751, but 1901, and that a hundred and fifty years had been burned up in my two days' journey. But I myself was still in 1751, and remained there for a long time. All my life I have been trying to overhaul that invisible leeway. No wonder I am obsessed with Time. ('Extracts from a Diary, "Summer 1939"', in *The Story and the Fable*, 1940)

Glasgow in 1901 came as a grim shock. Within four years both his parents died and two of his brothers as well, from consumption and a tumour in the brain. Muir was on his own at the age of nineteen. He earned his living as a clerk in a variety of offices, and in his own time he taught himself German, read Nietzsche, joined the ILP and educated himself as best he could. Latterly he spent two years in the office of a factory at Fairport where rotting bones were rendered down to make charcoal and fat. Already nervous and in poor health, he conceived a lasting dread of the place, and it seemed the very image of his unhappiness. Things improved towards the end of the war when he began to write for the *New Age*, and in Glasgow he made friends with Denis Saurat and the musician F. G. Scott. Then he met and married Willa – 'the most fortunate event in my life' – and the pair of them set off for London. He did exorcise the bone factory in the end, for he used his poetry as a means of personal reintegration: to discover a glimpse of Eden beyond the stench, and the stray dogs fighting over railway trucks of rancid bones.

In the late twenties the Muirs translated Kafka's *The Castle* and began to write novels themselves. Edwin produced *The Marionette* (1927); then a historical piece set in Reformation times called *The Three Brothers* (1931). In that same year Willa published her first novel *Imagined Corners*. Muir's unhappy life in Glasgow are reflected in his third, last and best novel, *Poor Tom* (1932), in which the painful relationship between alcoholic Tom, who is dying of a brain tumour, and his brother Mansie, is used to convey all Muir's distaste for the slums and the cultural and political shallowness of lower middle-class life in the city, not least the polite virtues of Christianity and the ultimately empty promises of well-meaning sentimental socialism. His best work remains in his poetry, yet his prose fiction shows that he was not afraid to confront the horrors of the social condition of the times, and the honest pains of his ambivalent feelings about such suffering – a suffering that his poetry preferred to translate into largely symbolic and mythically distanced terms.

A rather diffuse poem sequence called *Variations on a Time Theme* (1934) did not escape echoes of T. S. Eliot's style. By 1935 the Muirs and their son Gavin were in St Andrews, and Edwin made a sympathetic but curiously detached analysis of the often grim state of his country in *Scottish Journey* (1935): 'the Scottish nationalist movement at its present stage is mainly a movement to rouse Scotland from its indifference, and attempt to quicken national life and bring about an internal regeneration. . . . [The Scots] are quick to resent any insult to Scotland, but do not see the necessity of taking any action to stop their country's decline, for, being already half denationalised, they are almost unconscious of the danger.' The following year Muir offered his controversial reassessment of Scottish culture in *Scott and Scotland* (1936). He diagnosed something like Eliot's 'dissociation of sensibility', in which the Scots had long been divided between Lallans and English without a 'homogenous language' that was capable of conveying thought as well as feeling. In this respect he follows T. S. Eliot in his opinion that the polyphonic nature of Scottish literature (with work in Gaelic, Scots and English) must by definition deny it a truly 'organic' tradition, compared with what Eliot saw as the linguistically singular and mature splendour of English. (Eliot's review of Gregory Smith's study in 1919 was published under the title 'Was there a Scottish Literature?') Thus Muir saw Scots as only a dialect, 'which is to a homogenous language what the babbling of children is to the speech of grown men and women'. Postcolonial theorists have since laid bare the imperial agenda behind such judgements of 'immaturity', by which other voices and cultures are marginalised or inferiorised. Muir admired MacDiarmid as an exception, but his general opinion was that Scots writers should simply settle for English. The fact that MacDiarmid was beginning to write in English himself at just this time did not save Muir from his fury.

The poet was fifty years old when his second collection, *Journeys and Places* (1937), developed its imagery of time and fate as a 'stationary journey' endlessly repeated by poets, heroes, lovers or Trojan slaves. These poems reflect the distinction that he liked to make between the 'story' and the 'fable' (this was to be the title of the first version of his autobiography in 1940) to show how the archetypal pattern of a fable can be discerned within the everyday, historical details of the story. So his symbols become emblems, or heraldic devices on a shield (one of his favourite images), and 'Merlin' and 'The Enchanted Knight' share the same road with 'Ibsen' and 'Mary Stuart', all somehow on a journey back in search of some 'Solitary' or 'Unattained' or 'Dreamt of Place' before, or beyond, man's fall from grace. Muir uses simple ballad forms and a dispassionately plain diction for this elusive metaphysical theme and a lightly and skilfully measured lyricism:

> There is a road that turning always
> Cuts off the country of Again,
> Archers stand there on every side
> And as it runs time's deer is slain,
> And lies where it has lain.
> ('The Road')

In St Andrews the poet felt frustrated and isolated and began once again to review his life, having come to realise that his creative vision was essentially religious. When war broke out, he and Willa made ends meet as best they could until 1942, when Edwin was offered a post in Edinburgh with the British Council. In 1946 he went to Prague for three years as Director of the British Institute, but post-war Czechoslovakia was an unhappy place in the throes of a Communist take-over, and Muir felt that one kind of oppression had merely been supplanted by another. The couple were glad to return to London, and took another British Council post in Rome, where Edwin found himself deeply moved by the Catholic Church's emphasis on incarnation and mystery. Muir's *Essays on Literature and Society* (1949) confirmed his reputation as a literary theorist and critic, and in 1950 he returned to Scotland to become the much admired warden of Newbattle, an unconventionally creative college for adult education just outside Edinburgh.

The three volumes of poems from these years – and especially *The Labyrinth* (1949) – contain most of Muir's finest work, and his last collection, called *One Foot in Eden*, followed in 1956. The inwardly metaphysical themes of 'The Journey Back' – age, guilt, redemption, mystery and sweetness – are still pursued, but the grimmer historical experience of the forties, and his own frustrations with Scotland, gave a needed edge to other poems. 'Scotland 1941' rises to rage at what he saw as the pernicious influence of Knox and Presbyterianism on his country and its long history of futile internal strife – 'Such wasted bravery idle as a song, / Such hard-won ill . . .'. (He had taken a similar line in the study of Knox which he wrote in 1929.) 'The Incarnate One' and 'Scotland's Winter', from the last collection, offer a vision of his homeland crippled by 'the fleshless word' where 'all the kings before / This land was king-less, / And all the singers before / This land was songless' lie locked under ice – 'content / With their poor frozen life and shallow banishment'. Muir also drew on his post-war European experience in poems such as 'The Refugees', 'The Good Town' and 'The Interrogation', and gains a typically understated power – not unlike the spirit of Kafka in places – by refusing to be specifically biographical or documentary:

> My old friends
> (Friends ere these great disasters) are dispersed
> In parties, armies, camps, conspiracies.
> We avoid each other. If you see a man
> Who smiles good-day or waves a lordly greeting
> Be sure he's a policeman or a spy.
> We know them by their free and candid air.
> ('The Good Town')

Stranger images of dread, confusion or loss appear in 'The Combat', which was directly based on a dream; or 'The Horses', which describes the symbolic return of the old ways after some future holocaust; or 'The Return', which develops his understanding of our life as if it were a strange voyage to reconsider childhood. Muir's vision reached one of its most evocatively mysterious expressions in 'The Labyrinth', in which his theme is mirrored by the Kafkaesque and labyrinthine extension of his syntax in an opening sentence that unwinds for thirty-five lines without a break. Theseus-like, the narrator seems to have emerged from the Minotaur's maze, but nothing is certain, and he still sees the mark of the labyrinth in the landscape all around him:

> all the roads
> That run through the noisy world, deceiving streets

That meet and part and meet, and rooms that open
Into each other – and never a final room –
Stairways and corridors and antechambers
That vacantly wait for some great audience,
The smooth sea-tracks that open and close again,
Tracks undiscoverable, indecipherable,
Paths on the earth and tunnels underground,
And bird-tracks in the air – all seemed a part
Of the great labyrinth.

He is haunted by a vision of a perfect, toy-like world, or perhaps it was
the truly real world – a Platonic ideal beyond the shadows of the cave
– but, then again, nothing is certain. The difficult double negatives of
lines such as 'I could not live if this were not illusion', and the poem's
brooding last lines, epitomise the tale that precedes them (and the
experience of trying to read it) so that by implying a familiar context
which we cannot place, they throw everything into doubt again:

Oh these deceits are strong almost as life.
Last night I dreamt I was in the labyrinth,
And woke far on. I did not know the place.

In a bid to know the place more fully, Muir published a revised and
updated version of *The Story and the Fable*, this time called *An
Autobiography*, in 1954. Like Wordsworth's *Prelude*, or Neil Gunn's
Atom of Delight, the autobiographical insights in this book are deeply
coloured by the spirit of the writer's own creative achievement, much
infused – as they all are – with a longing for childhood's unmediated
access to a physical world become almost spiritual under younger eyes.

After a year as Norton Professor at Harvard in 1955, Muir retired to
Swaffham Prior near Cambridge, where he died in the first week of
1959. His *Autobiography* gives a memorably sensitive and unegocentric
account of the poet's many travels and his absorption with his inner
vision, while Willa Muir's memoir *Belonging* (1968) adds further
details of their life together and many insights into her own talents as
a writer – unfairly overshadowed by her husband's reputation.

Muir's concern to find the 'fable' as a state of grace beyond the
circumstance of history is absolutely contrary to MacDiarmid's furious
dedication to the specific material details of the world. Yet the Orcadian
does have affinities with other Scottish writers, and most notably with
the mythopoeic patterns that Grassic Gibbon and Neil Gunn sought to
establish in their novels during the thirties. Perhaps the impulse to seek
a place outside time was an attempt to escape the pressure of past

history on the Scottish psyche, or to evade the problems of present politics; or perhaps it was an attempt to reassess that history and to align it towards more creative developments in the future. In all cases the impact of J. G. Frazer's *Golden Bough* can be discerned, as the monumental work that influenced so many poets of the early modern generation to see or to seek mythic archetypes beneath the surface of the everyday. Yet Gibbon and Gunn embraced socialism as well, and in this respect they are closer to MacDiarmid and Sorley MacLean than they are to Edwin Muir.

Willa Muir (1890–1970)

Willa Muir reckoned that her first novel *Imagined Corners* (1931) was 'pre-Marxian' in its understanding of society, yet there is no doubting the critical force of its portrayal of the stifling conditions of middle class life in a small Scottish town. ('Calderwick' is based on Willa's own memories of Montrose, where she was born to Shetland parents and grew up.) The novel's focus is as much psychological as political – although Muir's understanding of the damage inflicted on the national psyche by the very Scottish combination of Presbyterianism and patriarchy lets us see that the two modes might well be one and the same. Her acute, precise and unsentimental prose style adopts a scientific discourse to convey how people affect one another:

> Human life is so intricate in its relationships that newcomers, whether native or not, cannot be dropped into a town like glass balls into plain water; there are too many elements already suspended in the liquid, and newcomers are at least partly soluble. What they may precipitate remains to be seen.

The novel traces the intertwined lives of local families, with special focus on the Shands and the Murrays in a world of respectability circumscribed by business, schoolteaching, golf and the church. Young Elizabeth is the first to change the chemical mix as she marries Hector Shand, only to understand that she has been misled by her own physical desires as she begins to see him more clearly for what he is: an incompetent businessman, a handsome, spoiled, unhappy and trivial boy with the name of a Greek hero. The second 'precipitation' takes place when her widowed sister-in-law Lizzie Shand returns to Calderwick having scandalised the town years before by eloping to Europe with a German teacher from the local Academy. Elise Mütze, as she now is, finds a special affinity with young Elizabeth and the novel ends with them leaving Scotland for a life together in the south of France.

Despite its occasionally forensic tones, *Imagined Corners* is no *House with the Green Shutters*, for it offers hope and freedom at the end, although it does not underestimate what that freedom will cost. Muir understands that men, as well as women, can know entrapment, frustration and anxiety in small-town life, but she never loses sight of the fact that it is most often the women close to them who have to pay the full cost of such unhappiness. Like Chris Guthrie at the end of the *Scots Quair* trilogy, or Martha Ironside in Nan Shepherd's 1928 novel *The Quarry Wood*, Elise and Lizzie have the courage to realise themselves –if only as a first step – by leaving men behind, and in their case, this means leaving Scotland as well. The country's 'corners' are no less claustrophobic for being 'imagined', but then again, the title's reference to Donne's Holy Sonnet VII foresees a glorious resurrection.

Muir's second novel, *Mrs Ritchie* (1933), is an altogether grimmer account of women, society and marriage in 'Calderwick', as the life of Annie Rattray is dissected stage by stage as child, girl, woman, and finally as a wife and mother. The making of 'Mrs Ritchie' reads like a case study in the growth of a domestic tyrant – a 'she-devil' to match John Gourlay forged in the furnace of will, piety and rectitude, and Muir's own hatred for these elements in Scottish life makes the book much darker than *Imagined Corners*, less compassionate, closer to melodrama and much more programmatic.

As a student at St Andrews, where she took a first-class degree in Classics, Willa had been active in the cause of women's suffrage. She was equally interested in child psychology and education, doing research on this topic in London with the help of a Carnegie grant. She lectured on Education, Psychology and English at a teacher training college until she resigned in 1919 over the Principal's objections to Edwin's freethinking in the essays contained in *We Moderns*. It is not difficult to trace the reasons for her hatred of cant. Her concern with sexual politics developed from an early study, *Women: An Inquiry* (1925), which implicitly supports traditional roles for women, to the more radical social and historical analysis and the acerbic satire of *Mrs Grundy in Scotland* (1936):

> One thing Mrs Grundy was able to achieve: she could not prevent Scottish girls from receiving an 'unwomanly' education, but she could support Mrs MacGrundy in discouraging them from expecting to be treated as full individuals once they quitted school. Your Scottish girl who profited from her education and desired to enter a profession had it made quite clear to her . . . that she need not expect to rise to the top of it.

Willa Muir knew all too well what it was like to be condescended to by men who were her intellectual inferiors and had to resist being characterised as 'the wife of the poet' for many years. She had wry comments to make on C. M. Grieve's unthinking male chauvinism when they met, and he in turn was uncomfortable with her independence and her influence on Edwin. Two further novels were written, but never published, possibly because their references to real people were too thinly disguised. *Imagined Corners* still provides the best balance of Willa Muir's analytical and creative capacities. Along with the fiction of George Douglas Brown, Catherine Carswell, Nan Shepherd and Grassic Gibbon, it remains a key contribution to that analysis of modern Scottish society which (looking back to Stevenson's *Weir of Hermiston*) recognises how central the too often unexamined issues of patriarchy and gender have been to the Scottish condition and cultural experience.

In the late 1950s Willa began a study of the oral tradition (a contract originally offered to Edwin) and *Living with Ballads* was well received when it appeared in 1965. Her memoir of her life with Edwin was published as *Belonging* in 1968 – a title with a certain poignancy to it when the couple's peripatetic life in Britain, Europe and the United States is recalled, along with Willa's sense of her Shetland roots in Montrose and Edwin's never quite lost vision of Eden in Orkney.

Compton Mackenzie (1883–1972)

Among the first to support the new political feeling in the north was Edward Montague Anthony Compton Mackenzie, who moved from London to Barra in 1928. Born in England and educated at London and Oxford, Mackenzie abandoned his studies in Law to write for the stage – his father was an actor and his sister Fay Compton was a star in Barrie's plays in the 1920s. Mackenzie's youthful milieu was Edwardian literary London, in which he cultivated a romantic and dashing personality. Success did not come, however, until he turned to prose fiction and embarked on a long and prolific career. Life behind the scenes of a variety theatre provided him with the best-selling material for *Carnival* (1912), followed by *Sinister Street* (1913), which was particularly admired by Henry James and Ford Madox Ford. The book is a lengthy semi-autobiographical 'development novel' which tells of Michael Fane's growth to maturity, from childhood to Oxford, and from there to London and experiences in the shadier parts of society. It is a long novel with atmospheric settings, and its approach to sexual frankness made it something of a *cause célèbre* when circulating libraries tried to restrict access to it. Mackenzie developed the scenario by carrying his characters over into four further books.

The First World War took Mackenzie – now in his thirties – to the campaign in the Dardanelles (*Gallipoli Memories*, 1928) and thence to a leading role in British Intelligence in Greece and the Aegean, recounted in *Extremes Meet* (1928). He delighted in the Mediterranean and continued to produce novels after the war, visiting Norman Douglas at Capri, where he renewed a friendly acquaintance with D. H. Lawrence. The Englishman could not quite approve of Mackenzie's theatrical manner, and satirised him later in 'The Man who Loved Islands'. Certainly the Scot was a flamboyant and patrician figure, and it was typical of his romantic nature that he should express his commitment to Scotland in the post-war years by setting up home in the remote island of Barra. He was a founder member of the National Party, and in those early years Mackenzie, MacDiarmid and the party's first president, Cunninghame Graham, made a formidably eclectic trio on political platforms throughout the country. Mackenzie remained an enthusiastic nationalist to the end of his life, but up to this point he had not dealt with questions of Scottish character or politics in any of his novels. These issues finally appear, if indirectly, in *The Four Winds of Love*, a series of six volumes published between 1937 and 1945.

With a truly Scottish didactic exhaustiveness, Mackenzie's *magnum opus* is a lengthy romance of travel, ideas and, once again, semi-autobiographical character-development. The hero of the sequence is Juan Pendarves Ogilvie – public-schoolboy, playwright, traveller, lover, philosopher, politician and pedagogue – and each book adds a few more years to his odyssey, from the beginning of the century to the outbreak of the Second World War. Mackenzie explained that his plan was to equate the four winds with 'four love stories and four philosophies of love and four decades of a man's life', and he associated different seasons, political motifs and different countries from his own travels with each 'wind' in turn. The action starts with early life and love in England from 1900 to 1911 and moves to Poland (*The East Wind of Love*); then it shifts to love and war under the *South Wind* of the Mediterranean from 1912 to 1917; thence to the post-war years in America and the plight of Ireland, and Ogilvie's hopes for nationalism in the rise of Mussolini (*The West Wind of Love* and *West to North*); finally the sequence comes round to the *North Wind*, with Ogilvie's home on a Hebridean island and his (and Mackenzie's) hopes for a Catholic Christian confederation of small Celtic nations. The hero renews his travels in Europe until Hitler's increasingly grandiose vision of Nordic nationalism makes him flee from the coming of a new winter to seek the sunshine of the Greek isles. *The Four Winds of Love* offers over three thousand pages of travel, complicated love affairs and political, personal and philosophical discourse, and in the end the tireless eloquence of its hero-spokesman may overwhelm all but the most dedicated reader.

As the founder and editor of the short-lived journal *Vox* (1926) and of *The Gramophone* (1923–61) Mackenzie was particularly alert to the impact of technology in the arts and he became a well-known and popular broadcaster. But he is best known and best loved perhaps for the popular fiction he produced after the 1940s, in a light-hearted series of Highland farces featuring a cantankerous, English-educated laird called 'Ben Nevis' (*The Monarch of the Glen*, 1941), or the natives of the island of 'Todday', most famous in *Whisky Galore* (1947). The author was knighted in 1952, an honour entirely in keeping with his colourful role as a literary personality, dividing his time between Edinburgh and the south of France. *Thin Ice* (1956), his last serious novel, was a sympathetic treatment of public scandal in the life of a homosexual. In later years Mackenzie dedicated himself to ten volumes ('Octaves') of exhaustively detailed personal reminiscence in *My Life and Times* (1963–71).

Eric Linklater (1899–1974)

Less directly involved with Scottish nationalism, Eric Linklater still shared Mackenzie's view that democracy and culture were best served by preserving the identity of small nations in the face of larger and more anonymous forces. He outlined these theories, very much in the spirit of the times, in *The Lion and The Unicorn* (1935) and Mackenzie dedicated the first volume of the *Four Winds* sequence to Linklater as his 'junior contemporary'. Linklater's father was a master mariner, and the novelist was actually born in Wales, but they were an Orkney family and he spent his childhood in the islands and later returned to live there for a number of years, before settling in the North-East. Educated at Aberdeen Grammar School, Linklater joined the Black Watch in the last years of the First World War to serve as a private soldier in the trenches of France, where he nearly died from a bullet wound in the head. He went on to take a degree at Aberdeen University, changing from medicine to English literature, before going to Bombay for two years as a journalist on *The Times of India*; 1927 saw him back in the

Granite City as an English assistant at the university, where he began his first novel and gained a Commonwealth Fellowship that allowed him to travel through America from 1928 to 1930.

White-Maa's Saga, published in 1929, drew on the author's own background in Aberdeen and Orkney to tell of his student hero's growth to maturity and love, while *Poet's Pub* (1929), a light comedy in Chestertonian vein, was conceived as 'sheer . . . invention', an exercise in the craft of fiction. With its acceptance Linklater determined to earn his living as a writer, and his presence in America had already given him the material for what was to be his most successful and possibly his best book. He later described *Juan in America* (1931) as a 'historical novel' about the United States during Prohibition – 'a country and a society which were vanishing even as I left them'. Juan Motley, descended from Byron's Don Juan, is Linklater's picaresque foil for a series of grotesque and hilarious adventures through the length and breadth of a nation apparently given over to college football, gangsterdom, bootlegging, movie making and West Coast cults. Everywhere he goes Juan creates disorder, like a Byronically amorous but still innocent Candide. Linklater moves with linguistic precision from an ironically classical detachment, through straight-faced lampoon, to episodes of wild, chaotic farce, and this preference for absurdity and irreverent laughter was to become essential to his conception of satire.

Linklater took pride in his professional ability to suit style to subject matter, and his next book was radically different, for *The Men of Ness* (1932) adopted a stripped and austere prose as the most appropriate voice for the epic Norse past and a stark saga of Viking fate – although it is significant that it is the 'little man', Gauk, who survives when all the grim heroes die at the end. The author returned to live in Scotland, and a short-lived involvement with the National Party saw him adopted as their candidate for an East Fife by-election in 1933. He was 'resoundingly defeated' and *Magnus Merriman* (1934) gives a satirical account of the affair from the point of view of its hero. Magnus is a sexual and political adventurer who moves from the ambitious social circles of London to end up as an inefficient crofter on his native Orkney, where he is trapped in marriage by the shy guiles of a young, beautiful and pragmatically unimaginative farm girl. She may be either his punishment or the making of him, but it is difficult to tell, for he is a romantic chameleon who changes his stripes to suit his situation whatever it may be – city sophisticate, nationalist politician or island poet. Linklater himself seems unsure, as if he, too, were divided between his plain love of Orkney and a delight in travel and smart company. In later years he liked to describe himself as a 'peasant with a pen', but his sharp talent for society farce is very far from the worlds of Grassic Gibbon or George Mackay Brown. In this sense the impasse of Magnus Merriman's fate may be revealingly honest about Linklater's position in Scotland, and even his own careless brush with politics. Given the satirical portraits in his novel, it is not surprising that he soon broke with the Nationalists, although MacDiarmid remained delighted with his incarnation as 'Hugh Skene' and liked to quote it with approval. ('He had a smooth white face, dwarfed by a great bush of hair, and in brisk, delicate, rather terrier-like features his eyes shone bright and steady. His hands were beautifully shaped and somewhat dirty.')

More novels followed, including an exuberant comedy of upper-class manners exploded by gross farce in *Ripeness is All* (1935), and *Juan in China* (1937), which did not match the success of his American adventures, despite Linklater's actual visit to China. Long aware of the brutality of fascism in Germany, Linklater displayed a liberal imperialism equally critical of communist ideology, and his essays and novels from the late thirties and early forties reflect a concern to oppose oppression and find values worth fighting for. The outbreak of war found him in uniform again, helping to establish land defences for the fleet at Scapa Flow. He renewed his regard for what he saw as the simple decency of ordinary men in the ranks and helped to run a service newspaper for the Orkneys. Later he travelled widely as a freelance correspondent for the War Office, ending up with the campaign in Italy, for which he wrote the official history. Among his autobiographical books, *The Man on my Back* (1941) records his early life as a writer, and the travails of two wars are described in *Fanfare for a Tin Hat* (1970).

Linklater's Italian experiences produced *Private Angelo* (1946) in celebration of a peasant soldier's good sense in knowing when to run away. This is his most gently controlled statement in favour of the fallible individual, innocent of ideology and the 'serious' abstractions by which large organisations seek to control him. The novelist shows compassion for those who are fated to be maimed by life, and Angelo has to lose a hand before the war is done with him. *Private Angelo* is a quietly significant novel about the pain and absurdity of war – without the raw satire of *The Good Soldier Svejk* and the zany force of *Catch 22*, it can still stand in their company. 'Without irony history would be intolerable,' a character remarks in a later novel, and to some extent Linklater's stance does depend on a rather precarious balancing-act between grotesque farce and melodrama, and sometimes his irony seems to slip into a rather heartless and mechanical process without final commitment. His later works include *Laxdale Hall* (1951), *The House of Gair* (1953) and *The Dark of Summer* (1956), in which he returns to the experience of war that so characterises the twentieth century in a book that begins on the Shetland Islands to trace a tale of memory, war, family history, guilt and betrayal. Linklater considered *Position at Noon* (1958) to be his wittiest novel and certainly, along with *A Man Over Forty* (1963), it recovers the wilder satirical exuberance of his earlier work.

By comparison with Linklater and Mackenzie, who wrote many entertaining bestsellers, the few works of David Lindsay and Fionn Mac Colla take a darker and more metaphysical twist. Lindsay's fantasy novels have affinities with the painful world of John Davidson or the strange landscapes of Margaret Oliphant or George MacDonald; while Mac Colla's angry muse has a vision of Scotland inherited from Douglas Brown or John MacDougall Hay.

David Lindsay (1878–1945)

David Lindsay is best known for *A Voyage to Arcturus*, a philosophical fantasy novel of considerable power, yet his writing career ended in obscurity and for years he enjoyed only an 'underground' reputation. Born in London, Lindsay lived most of his life in the south but took regular holidays with his father's relatives near Jedburgh, for it pleased him to maintain the connection despite the fact that his Scottish father had abandoned his wife and children without support, thus forcing his youngest son to give up hopes of university in order to earn a living as an insurance-broker. Lindsay became a shy and puritanical person, deeply interested in music and philosophy but largely self-educated in these fields. It is difficult not to identify the marks of this early history in his mature work and thought, with its almost Calvinistic distrust of pleasure and its urge to confront the face of God, and then to unmask and go beyond that ultimate figure of paternal authority. Lindsay's books are haunted by the need to identify a reality beyond reality, and the metaphysical fantasies of George MacDonald were a potent early influence on him. His rather unbending and cerebral nature responded equally to the writings of Schopenhauer and Nietzsche, who seemed to support his convictions about the importance of will in the universe and of the need for the individual to adopt a lonely and prophetic stance in the quest for a truth beyond the mob. In this respect his affinities also lie with the unhappy spirits of James Thomson and John Davidson.

Lindsay led a life of bachelor routine in his city office for over twenty years. When he was finally conscripted to help the war-effort, at the age of thirty-eight, he managed to find an administrative post with his regiment in yet another London office. The move led to a meeting with a vivacious eighteen-year-old, and within two months they were married. Spurred by his bride's enthusiasm, Lindsay determined to take up full-time writing. The couple found a house in Cornwall and by 1919 Lindsay had embarked on his first novel – derived from the notes and reflections of many years. His practical inexperience as a writer betrays itself in a clumsy pedantic prose, and he never did perfect his style or the ability to handle plot and character smoothly. Nevertheless, *A Voyage to Arcturus* (1920) is a work of such conceptual originality that it was accepted by the first publisher to read it.

Usually referred to as a fantasy, and sometimes mistaken for crude science fiction, Lindsay's book is more properly an allegory of spiritual and philosophical search. The opening chapters depend on contrivances to do with a séance in Hampstead, and a crystal torpedo that takes off from a tower on the North-East shores of Scotland to fly its passengers to the planet Tormance under the double star of Arcturus. Once there, the protagonist Maskull begins his quest to confront the nature of the universe. He has already received premonitions of his fate back on Earth, where he knew Nightspore, who will later be revealed as the alter ego of his own spirit, and Krag, their mysterious guide on the voyage. After landing, Maskull is separated from his friends and sets out to look for them, like Bunyan's pilgrim in some nightmarishly precise but undecipherable allegory. He finds new colours on Tormance and grows extra organs for his senses. He meets people whose names – Joiwind, Crimtyphon, Panawe and Spadevil – might have come from one of Blake's more obscure prophetic books. Nothing will turn out to be quite what it seems in this world under its double star – the very image of duality. Tormance is a stark place of strange sexuality bound up with kindness, pain, nameless sensations, beauty, shame, terror and successive deaths. Its ultimate nature is only gradually and indirectly revealed to the reader as Maskull journeys through grim landscapes and makes ambiguous encounters with various semi-human creatures. When Maskull finally arrives at the end of his quest it is only to meet death to the sound of the eerie drumbeats, or heartbeats, which he had first heard on the Scottish coast before he set out on his voyage. Yet through death he rejoins his 'double', Nightspore, and moves to a confrontation with Muspel, the source of all light. He finds that Muspel is locked in Manichean conflict – like some eternal symbiosis – with Crystalman, the shaping-force of worlds, whose advocacy of pleasure, art and beauty turns out to be a deceitful masquerade covering a shameful, vulgar, leering grin. This, the true aspect of the material universe, has haunted the novel from the start, for it has appeared on the face of every creature in the moment after death. When Nightspore realises this, he almost despairs, but Krag is there to assure him that they will continue the moral combat, and that Crystalman will not prevail. Maskull's journey is over. Nightspore's has only begun. The book ends at this point, and Krag reveals that his true name on Earth is 'pain'.

C. S. Lewis acknowledged the influence of *Arcturus* on his own Perelandra novels, and successive readers and critics have testified to the disturbing power of Lindsay's universe, suffused with its symbols of music, repressed sexuality, shape-changing, death, pain and moral effort. Against such a vision even his awkward prose comes to seem curiously apposite and artistically effective. It is Lindsay's finest book and, although reviews were mixed and sales small, it achieved a serious critical reputation. Lindsay was encouraged and in the next three years he produced two further metaphysical fantasies, this time set in the contemporary everyday world. *The Haunted Woman* (1922) evokes the proximity of other times and realms of being just beyond the borders of our own, with some brilliantly memorable and ambiguous images. *The Sphinx* (1923) is less effective, however, and neither book did very well commercially. Lindsay immediately wrote *The Adventures of M. de Mailly* as a historical-romance potboiler, but it was not published until 1926. For the next five years he struggled with the drafts and revisions of another novel, *Devil's Tor* (1932), but most readers found it humourless and wordy. The family moved to Sussex and eventually to Hove, near Brighton, where Mrs Lindsay ran a boarding-house to help support them. Her husband persevered with his writing and his philosophical notes, but his publishing career was over and he died in 1945, in great pain from an abscess in the jaw for which he refused treatment. *The Violet Apple* (1976) did not find a publisher in Lindsay's lifetime, and his last book, *The Witch* (1976), was left unfinished. In the light of more recent studies, however, the later books still offer valuable insights into the unique and underrated imagination that produced *A Voyage to Arcturus*.

Tom Macdonald, 'Fionn Mac Colla' (1906–75)

Tom Macdonald had only a little more luck with publishers during his career, and he shares something of Lindsay's austere and philosophical bias. A native of Montrose (although his father was a Gaelic-speaking Highlander), Macdonald trained and worked as a teacher in the North-East before going to Palestine to teach in the United Free Church of Scotland's college at Safed. He had a happy childhood, brought up as a member of the Plymouth Brethren – an extremely severe Presbyterian sect – but he later came to reject everything to do with the Reformed Church and eventually joined the Catholic faith. His critique of Protestantism is one of the themes of his first novel, *The Albannach* ('The Highlander'), which he began when he returned to Scotland in 1929. The condition of his country at the height of the Depression made him an active member of the National Party, and he went to Glasgow University to study Gaelic. Henceforth 'Fionn Mac Colla' dedicated himself to a vision of a transcendent Highland culture, which would be utterly opposed to the Kirk and the bourgeois interests of the Scottish establishment and English imperialism alike. He defined Protestantism as the historical expression of a desire to control mankind by negating individuality and creativity, and hence he saw Knox as the first in a line of dictators leading to Lenin and Hitler. For Macdonald, history was the by-product of malign or benevolent forces in the human spirit, and as an imaginative writer he possessed a powerfully empathetic understanding of the negative pleasures to be gained from the Calvinistic exercise of the will.

The Albannach (1932) describes how Murdo Anderson grows away from the repressive faith of his home, only to be recalled from Glasgow University when his father dies. Returned to the narrow confines of life in a Highland village, he succumbs to an unwise marriage and comes close to alcoholism and suicide before he learns compassion and rediscovers his creative balance and a place in the community, too, by way of crofting, piping and traditional poetry. In typical style, Macdonald's prose adopts Murdo's point of view, and the physical details of local places and faces are brilliantly charged with his subjective intensity. The same effect characterises *And the Cock Crew* (1945), a novel of the Clearances whose central scene is a long debate between an old Gaelic bard and the local minister, Zachary Wiseman. 'Maighstir Sachairi' is the protagonist, who first defends and then betrays his parishioners by encouraging them to submit to the most brutal of evictions as 'the will of God'. (The novel's title refers to Peter's betrayal of Christ.) The minister's tortured moments of certainty and doubt and his melodramatic death dominate the tale; and, although the quieter tones of the poet Fearchar imply a kinder vision, there is no sign of kindness at the end. If Gunn's *Butcher's Broom* is a poetically controlled protest against the Clearances, *And the Cock Crew* is a Gothic cry of philosophical anger.

The descriptive intensities of Macdonald's prose, and his occasional melodrama, recall aspects of *Gillespie* and *The House with the Green Shutters*, and his fiction gains further force through his fascinated and polemical hatred of Protestantism as part of a more universal 'nay-saying'. In this sense Macdonald's case against the Presbyterian conscience goes further than Hogg did, or Lockhart's *Adam Blair*. His theories were published in *At the Sign of the Clenched Fist* (1967), and a short autobiography, *Too Long in this Condition*, appeared posthumously in 1975. Macdonald worked as a head teacher in the Highlands in later years, but came to believe bitterly that fate, critics and other writers had been less than kind to his creative development, especially during his hard times in the 1930s. His case is complex, for he was a flamboyant and unhappy personality whose real gift for vivid writing was fuelled and ultimately overwhelmed by his own philosophical obsessions. *Scottish Nöel* (1958) and the debate *Ane Tryall of Heretiks* (1962) were potent fragments from what was to be a larger historical novel. After his death several other unpublished manuscripts were found among Macdonald's papers, including a novel written in the late 1950s. Not without a certain dry humour, *The Ministers* (1979) is still deeply and angrily engaged with the Kirk and its doings, and is much given to lengthy monologues revealing or excoriating the narrowness of Highland society.

Lindsay and Macdonald had a long struggle to find an audience for a few brilliantly flawed books, and their writing was much marked – one way or another – by the inheritance of Scottish Calvinism. Nan Shepherd's fiction offers a much kinder outlook, for although her humour has a particularly North-East cast to it – mindful of the poor fates that await us in the end, unsentimentally dry and even ferocious – she has compassion, too, and a never failing but entirely material sense of how the spiritual is never far from the physical world.

Anna (Nan) Shepherd (1893–1981)

Nan Shepherd was born and educated in Aberdeen, where she worked as a lecturer at the Teacher Training College all her professional life.

She wrote three novels, all produced in the five years before her 40th birthday – taking up the pen, as she said, 'only when I feel that there's something that simply must be written'. Set in North-East Scotland, these books explore questions of identity, freedom, duty and metaphysical being with particular reference to the lives and experience of young girls and older women. This remarkable body of work has a strong interest in questions of gender in society, but it is as much philosophical as it is feminist in its implications.

The Quarry Wood (1928) is a *bildungsroman*, tracing the development of Martha Ironside, from humble beginnings in a country croft to her time at Aberdeen University and her first experiences of love and responsibility. If this makes it sound like a modest Kailyard novel, nothing could be further from the truth, for the novel is written with sharp intelligence, wry humour and a penetrating psychological insight, not least into the vanities of men. Shepherd's work has a strong sense of the tensions, insecurities and class differences that operate in society and she is particularly sympathetic to that hidden network of female connections and allegiances – a web of sisters, sisters-in-law, maiden aunts, widows and grandmothers that flourishes beneath the surface of patriarchy. It is Shepherd's achievement, in all three of her books, to chart the workings of this web with a sense of humour and appreciation as well as a poignant sense of the courage, the sadness and the lost potential that are to be found there as well. *The Quarry Wood* ends with Martha Ironside determined to live her own life free of men – after a dangerously idealised and idealising encounter with her best friend's husband: 'Am I such a slave as that? Dependent on a man to complete me! I thought I couldn't be anything without him – I can be my own creator.' The story is illuminated throughout by Shepherd's wit, her totally uncondescending appreciation of uneducated country folk, a Lawrentian sense of how people are motivated by sexual and emotional tides they scarcely realise, and an extraordinary eye for the Scottish landscape under its ever-changing weather. Among other things, the book pays tribute to Shepherd's home university, giving a vivid picture of student life in Aberdeen in the years just before the Great War.

The Quarry Wood was followed by *The Weatherhouse* (1930), in which Shepherd's acute sense of the inner dynamics of human motivation is most closely allied to her metaphysical vision of the mystery and beauty of place, identity and being. This is Shepherd's masterpiece, with a truly Chekhovian spirit in which there are no 'heroes' and no subsidiary characters, but everyone is given the right to their own place on the stage, their own inner life, their own joys and failures. On the surface the plot seems to concern nothing but a minor scandal in 'Fetter-Rothnie' and one character's determination to expose a small lie. The 1914–18 war is raging and Garry Forbes has been injured and invalided home. He discovers that a local woman, Louise Morgan, has been claiming to be the secret fiancée of his best friend David Grey, who has died of TB. Before the war Garry was an engineer, used to seeing the world as a material and wholly calculable thing, a place of black and white distinctions. Louisa is telling a lie, and Garry (engaged to be married to young Lindsay Lorimer) is outraged at what he sees to be both an untruth and a slur on his friend's memory. He thinks that his duty is to deliver a blow 'against falsehood' in 'a small but definite engagement in the war against evil'. Of course he is factually correct, but what Garry learns (just as Martha of *The Quarry Wood* did when she realised that wisdom is not be found in books alone) is that the human realm – and indeed the realm of his own mind and senses – is much less clear-cut than he has imagined.

By the end of the novel Garry has come to a final vision of what Fetter-Rothnie has to tell him:

> Life pulsed in the clods of earth that the ploughshares were breaking, in the shares, the men. Substance, no matter what its form, was rare and fine.
>   The moment of perception passed. He had learned all that in college. But only now had it become real. Every substance had its own secret nature, exquisite, mysterious. Twice already this country sweeping out before him had ceased to be the agglomeration of woods, fields, roads, farms; mysterious as a star at dusk, with the same ease and thoroughness, had become visible as an entity: once when he had seen it taking form from the dark, solid, crass, mere bulk; once irradiated by the light until its substance all but vanished. Now in the cold April dawn, he saw it neither crass nor rare, but both in one.

This is precisely the vision that infuses Shepherd's book on the Cairngorm mountains, written during the Second World War, but not published until much later. A lifelong hill walker, she wrote *The Living Mountain* (1977) as a Zen-like meditation on how we approach the world and how it approaches us, in a strange marriage of spirit and matter. Her poetry shows the same impulse, both sensual and intellectual in its response to experience, and Shepherd was famous for expecting her students, on their hikes and expeditions together, to know and to care for the flowers, plants and rocks they encountered. In this respect she is wholly in sympathy with MacDiarmid's claim that the universal could best be found – and perhaps only be found – in the specific and the truly local.

Shepherd's third novel *A Pass in the Grampians* (1933) is another development novel, in which Jenny Kilgour, at the age of sixteen, decides (unlike Martha Ironside in *The Quarry Wood*) to leave her home and her beloved grandfather's remote hill farm in order to seek the bright lights of London and an entirely different society. The spirit that leads Jenny to her decision arrives in the unlikely form of Bella Cassie, a local girl, supposedly orphaned, who couldn't stand the rural life and left the farm to seek her fortune when she, too, was sixteen. Now, eighteen years later, she has come back as 'Dorabel Cassidy', a noted singer, determined to liven up the neighbourhood with parties and motorcars and her own gloriously egocentric character – much to the scandal of the locals. Bella is shamelessly vulgar, and wonderfully life-affirming. She breezes through the novel like a circus parade down the main street of Barbie, and her own version of a house with green shutters is a bright new bungalow among the old hills.

Conscious of a similar 'fury of being' within herself, Jenny longs to go beyond the pass in the Grampian mountains to reach the ocean beyond. Almost unbeknownst to herself, Jenny is in the grip of a physical infatuation with Bella, and in fact Nan Shepherd's writing is remarkable in its time for its recognition of the world of physical sensation and female sexuality. (Martha's passion for Luke in *The Quarry Wood*, and the elderly Ellen Falconer's infatuation with young Garry in *The Weatherhouse*, are treated with similar perception and tact.) But this has not been a choice of either/or for Jenny, nor an abandonment of her roots, because she comes to realise that the very spirit that leads her to her decision has also been born in that same remote community.

Nan Shepherd never married (though there are hints of a special male friend) and it seems that, like Martha and a significant number of her other female characters, she decided to live on her own terms. Certainly she had a full and vigorously active life, travelling to Norway, Switzerland, Italy, Greece, South Africa and France, with regular climbing and walking trips in Scotland and visits to her many friends. She knew most of the other writers of her time, particularly those of her native North-East; she made friends with Neil Gunn, William Soutar and Willa Muir and kept up with Rebecca Mitchell, Lewis Grassic Gibbon's widow in Welwyn Garden City. She was responsible, too, for encouraging Jessie Kesson to take up writing, having met her on the Inverurie–Elgin train in 1941. Jessie gave her the news that Charles Murray had just died, without realising at that time how close a friendship there was between Nan and Murray, whom she had first met in her father's house. Impressed by her conversation with Jessie Kesson, Nan encouraged her to enter a short-story competition, which she subsequently won.

All three of Shepherd's novels were well reviewed on both sides of the Atlantic, and it is worth noting that the New York critics were enthusiastic about her use of North-East dialect and that even the literary pages of the *New Statesman*, the *TLS* and the *Manchester Guardian* found no difficulty and much to praise in her use of Scots. It is a sad reflection on the vagaries of publication and critical reputation that Shepherd's novels were allowed to drop from sight until they were reprinted in 1987 – a fate not unlike that which befell Willa Muir's *Imagined Corners* (1931). Both authors made highly significant contributions to the literary renaissance only to find themselves overshadowed in later years by their male counterparts. Even so, it is interesting to speculate on Shepherd's most immediate influence in that two of her three books appeared well in advance of Lewis Grassic Gibbon's own *Scots Quair* trilogy – with *Sunset Song* in 1932 followed by *Cloud Howe* and *Grey Granite* in 1933 and 1934. As a precursor to *Sunset Song*, *The Quarry Wood* shows us what might have happened had Chris Guthrie gone to university, instead of staying on her croft. Gibbon's work is more politicised and darker, of course, and over the span of his trilogy he shows us a woman increasingly battered and beset by the world around her. Shepherd's vision is no less intense, but she finds redemption and humour in the human world when all that Gibbon's Ewan Tavendale can find is a parade of endless torture. All six books make up an extraordinary body of work from North-East Scotland. Indeed, *A Scots Quair* can claim to be the single most sustained and innovative achievement in modern Scottish fiction. It was made by a man who died when he was thirty-four, after only seven years as a serious writer.

James Leslie Mitchell, 'Lewis Grassic Gibbon' (1901–35)

The three books in *A Scots Quair* were Mitchell's last and finest work. They give a powerful account of history and social change in Scotland between 1911 and 1932, and at the same time they explore the fate of a particular spirit, ancient, free and intuitive, in the face of the modern world. Mitchell found this spirit in the enduringly feminine psyche of his heroine Chris Guthrie, as she grows up in the rural North-East, and he associated it with his own mythopoeic vision of Scotland's past. Neil Gunn and Edwin Muir shared a similar understanding of how timeless values were to be found within the tradition – for Gunn they were Celtic, because he himself came from the Highlands, while Muir looked to the Eden of his childhood in Orkney. Mitchell is unique, however, in bringing his poetic vision into contact with life in the modern city and in confronting it with his own fiercely socialist principles – a conflict that led to difficult tensions which made the elegiac note of his art all the more poignant.

The author's sense of place could not have been more authentic, for *A Scots Quair* sprang from his own upbringing on crofts in the Howe of the Mearns, especially at Bloomfield above Inverbervie, later fictionalised as 'Blawearie' in the parish of 'Kinraddie'. Here is the heart of the rich farmland that lies to the south of Stonehaven between the Grampians and the coast. The author liked to recall that he was 'of peasant rearing and peasant stock', and expressed pride 'that the land was so closely and intimately mine (my mother used to hap me in a plaid in harvest time and leave me in the lee of a stook while she harvested)'. Yet he was not fitted for farm work, and grew to be a sensitive and bookish boy, interested in archaeology and astronomy, with thoughts of becoming a journalist or an editor. Mitchell's village schoolmaster – a friend in later years – preserved his brightest pupil's early compositions and encouraged him to take secondary education at Mackie Academy in Stonehaven. But he was not to be a 'lad o' pairts', for Mitchell's teenage years were disturbed and unhappy and he walked out of school at the age of sixteen, to work as a junior reporter for the *Aberdeen Journal*. Stirred by the promise of the Russian Revolution in 1917 he became an enthusiastic communist; and when he went to work for the *Scottish Farmer* in Glasgow in 1919 his experiences of the unrest on Clydeside, and the terrible urban poverty which he found there, reinforced his commitment to revolutionary socialism. His career in journalism was cut short, however, when a minor scandal over the padding of expenses led to his dismissal without references. Greatly disturbed by the experience, he made a clumsy attempt at suicide and had to return home – under something of a cloud – to recover his bearings.

All too aware that his parents could not support him, and driven by the need to escape from his home background, he decided to join the army. He enlisted in August 1919 and spent the next three and a half years working for the Service Corps in Persia, India and Egypt; and his letters to Rebecca Middleton – who came from the croft next to Bloomfield – are full of a young man's enthusiasm for the romance of these distant countries and their ancient ruins. When Mitchell left the army in 1923, Hugh MacDiarmid had just started his own literary campaign from Montrose, but they were not to meet until later and the younger man's own efforts brought him no success at all. After six months during which he 'nearly starved to death', Mitchell settled once again for the security of enlistment, joining the Royal Air Force this time, in which he served as a clerk on various stations in England until 1929. He tried his hand at poetry without finding a publisher, but one of his short stories won a magazine competition and, although it was to be another four years before he saw himself in print again, Mitchell was duly encouraged. He renewed contact with Rebecca Middleton – she was a civil servant in London – and the couple took a holiday together in the Mearns and married in the summer of 1925. Rebecca, or Ray as he called her, had to leave her job and times were hard for them during the next few years.

Mitchell persevered with more stories, planned a book on exploration, and worked on a novel to be called *Stained Radiance*, closely based on his ideas and experiences. Its heroine foreshadows the later Chris Guthrie and his own ambivalent feelings of pride in and distaste for peasant life in Scotland, but it is an ironic and often an angry work, and many publishers rejected it. He continued to work at the manuscript while pursuing his interests in archaeology, anthropology and the culture of the Mayans and the Incas in America. He was particularly keen on 'Diffusionism', a theory which held that 'civilisation' began with the discovery of agriculture in ancient Egypt and spread throughout the world, sweeping away a golden age of primitive nomadic hunters in the process and bringing all the ills of property, nationalism, war and the slavery of labour in its place. The theory appealed to Mitchell's communist ideals and he associated the golden age in Scotland with the lost era of the aboriginal and matriarchal Picts, whose remote descendants were still, he felt sure, to be found among the peasants of his native North-East – far from the slums and factories of 'progress'. (He summarised this idiosyncratic account of prehistory and Scottish culture – including his regard for the Reformation as a people's cause – in a later essay called 'The Antique Scene' written for *Scottish Scene* in 1934.)

Mitchell's fortunes began to change when his speculative book *Hanno, or the Future of Exploration* was published in 1928. Early next year another of his Middle East stories was accepted for *Cornhill Magazine* – after the recommendation of H. G. Wells – and this led to the publication of twelve more in a cycle of tales later collected as *The Calends of Cairo* (1931). Mitchell could now leave the RAF with some hopes at last for his future as a writer. Articles on the Mayans had appeared in *Antiquity* and he already had a small reputation in this field. *Stained Radiance* came out in 1930, and Jarrold's, who were to publish nearly all his work, accepted his next novel too. *The Thirteenth Disciple* (1931) is another thinly disguised autobiographical book, filled with his interest in Diffusionism and particularly frank about his unhappy schooldays and his troubles in Glasgow. A daughter, Rhea, was born to the couple, and in 1931 they all moved to Welwyn Garden City, a genteel new town outside London. Leslie Mitchell poured his energies into more and more work, composing straight onto the type-writer, as was his habit, with few revisions. Within a year he produced two novels on the romance of Diffusionism – *Three Go Back* (1932), which was a time-travel fantasy about prehistoric life on Atlantis, and *The Lost Trumpet* (1932). Both were well received by writers such as Compton Mackenzie and H. G. Wells – one of Mitchell's boyhood heroes. But Leslie's thoughts had already turned back to his native Mearns, enhanced by a sense of perspective gained in the south, and encouraged, perhaps, by the critical success being accorded at home to Neil Gunn's *Morning Tide* (1930), or possibly by the example of Nan Shepherd's first two novels.

Mitchell wrote *Sunset Song* (1932) in a single and remarkably sustained creative effort that lasted less than two months. It was published under his mother's name as the first in a planned trilogy of novels on the life of a girl called Chris Guthrie. These books were to give the definitive account of the land he loved and hated, with Chris as its spokesperson and the vessel for his own imaginative spirit. The second volume, *Cloud Howe*, appeared in 1933 and the series ended with *Grey Granite* in 1934. Early in the following year Mitchell suffered a perforated ulcer, and after an emergency operation he died on 7 February. He was a man of vivacious and unusually intense energy, but not even he could sustain the pressure of work to which he committed himself at the end. In those last two years he had produced seven more books, including *Image and Superscription* (1933) and the historical novel *Spartacus* (1933), which is the best of the 'Mitchell' books. *Spartacus* (a version of which was later filmed with Kirk Douglas) shows Mitchell's sympathy for the oppressed and the exploited and his interest in the transition from his hero's initial idealism to the necessity for ruthless command and revolutionary action – a theme he would return to in *Grey Granite*. Then in 1934 there appeared a life of Mungo Park; *The Conquest of the Maya*; another time-travel adventure, *Gay Hunter*; the collaboration (as Grassic Gibbon) with Hugh MacDiarmid in *Scottish Scene*; and, finally, nine short biographies of famous explorers published as *Nine Against the Unknown.* Part of a further novel on North-East life was left unfinished when he died, and this was published in 1982 as *The Speak of the Mearns.* The trilogy remains his finest achievement, however, widely popular among Scottish readers and broadcast as a major television serial.

The voice and personality of Chris Guthrie lies at the heart of all three books in *A Scots Quair*, but it is felt most strongly in *Sunset Song*, which deals with her upbringing and young womanhood. For all its failings and the occasional brutality of country folk, her home parish of Kinraddie still offers the security of an extended family circle. It stands for 'the Scots countryside itself', as the minister remarks wryly, 'fathered between a kailyard and a bonny brier bush in the lee of a house with green shutters', but the spell of the sunset will not last and all the kailyard securities will be swept away. In fact Gibbon had few illusions about country life: Chris's mother commits suicide, worn out by childbirth and terrified of another pregnancy, while her father, brutalised by toil and made still more severe by his religion, drives his son to emigrate and eventually suffers a paralysing stroke which leaves his daughter to struggle with the farm and to ward off his commanding sexual advances. In such circumstances Chris comes to physical and intellectual maturity, determined to be her own woman, yet divided between the two Chrisses 'that fought for her heart and tormented her':

> You hated the land and the coarse speak of the folk and learning was brave and fine one day and the next you'd waken with the peewits crying across the hills, deep and deep, crying in the heart of you and the smell of the earth in your face, almost you'd cry for that, the beauty of it and the sweetness of the Scottish land and skies.

This passage is typical of Gibbon's internalised colloquial narrative method, in which the impersonal but familiar 'you' encloses Chris, the community and the reader in an easy assumption of shared experience. To the same end, the novelist italicises speech and includes it in the narrative without breaking the flow of description or reported thought. In this way the whole book is integrated within Chris's sensibility as she recalls the key events of what passed before, advancing the story chapter by chapter, like a retrospective diary which returns to the 'present' at the end of each section. Chris carries out these acts of recollection while resting among standing stones beside a loch on the hill above her home. As her favourite private spot, this place sets her experiences against the passage of epochs, and allows Gibbon to express his

Diffusionist feelings for the timeless value and innocence that once prevailed when the world was young. She has an affinity with these mysterious perspectives, and is haunted, in all three novels, by a sense that nothing endures but change itself, and beyond it, the land which made her:

> The wet fields squelched below her feet, oozing up their smell of red clay from under the sodden grasses, and up in the hills she saw the trail of the mist, great sailing shapes of it, going south on the wind into Forfar, past Laurencekirk they would sail, down the wide Howe with its sheltered glens and its late, drenched harvests, past Brechin smoking against its hill, with its ancient tower that the Pictish folk had reared, out of the Mearns, sailing and passing, sailing and passing, she minded Greek words of forgotten lessons, (Παντα ρει): *Nothing Endures.*
>
> And then a queer thought came to her there in the drooked fields, that nothing endured at all, nothing but the land she passed across, tossed and turned and perpetually changed below the hands of the crofter folk since the oldest of them had set the Standing Stones by the loch of Blawearie and climbed there on their holy days and saw their terraced crops ride brave in the wind and sun. Sea and sky and the folk who wrote and fought and were learnéd, teaching and saving and praying, they lasted but as a breath, a mist of fog in the hills, but the land was forever, it moved and changed below you, but was forever, you were close to it and it to you, not at a bleak remove it held you and hurted you. And she had thought to leave it all!

Not surprisingly, the land and its elegiac and seductive voice feature most strongly in *Sunset Song*, for the novel deals, after all, with Chris's sexual growth from girlhood to maturity and with her decision to stay at home to work the croft with her new husband Ewan Tavendale – a boy of Highland descent with a darker and more fragile temperament than her own. In this respect the book is indeed a 'song', which combines Hardy's sense of season, place and rural custom with a Lawrentian insight into the sexual and psychological intensities between two young people making a life together. But the novel has a social dimension as well, for modern transport and city life are making their presence felt, and finally the Great War – at first so little heeded by Kinraddie – marks or destroys everyone in the little community. All the trees in the neighbourhood are felled for timber, and larger and more commercial farming takes over until the old peasant crofter class finally passes away. Ewan is brutalised by barrack-room life long before he is shot for desertion at the Front, and the fighting kills kindly Chae Strachan and even Long Rob of the Mill, who finally felt compelled to enlist, despite his socialism and the objections of his conscience.

Chris herself heralds a more peaceful social change, for Long Rob was one of the few people in Kinraddie who was her intellectual equal (he was modelled on Ray Mitchell's father), and she is distinguished by her determination to remain spiritually and mentally her own person in the face of a community which offers only the narrowest and most domestic of roles to women. But her pride and her poetic sense of change make her a solitary figure too, and she finds another love, and a father for her young son Ewan, in the new minister of the parish, an idealistic young man called Robert Colquhoun. Chris cannot promise him her old self – for that belongs to her first husband – but she offers him 'maybe the second Chris, maybe the third'. The novel ends with Colquhoun's sermon at the dedication of a memorial to those who died in the war. Set among the standing stones, and followed by the playing of 'Flowers of the Forest' on the pipes, this scene serves to recall, once again, much longer perspectives on mutability and human loss. (The tune refers to the waste of a generation on Flodden Field in 1513.)

Sunset Song is not without its sentimental side, but Gibbon shows that subtle and mature art can be achieved both within and beyond the Kailyard genre. In setting and development it has several striking similarities to a German novel called *Jörn Uhl* (1901) by Gustav Frenssen, and Gibbon may have read it in earlier years, although some similarities are inevitable in so far as both books deal with a common fund of peasant experience. Nevertheless, Gibbon's voice and his wider use of symbolism are decidedly his own, and his prose style is redolent of North-East Scots, for, although relatively few dialect words are used, his narrative rhythms remain distinctively local. Yet *Sunset Song* has no difficulty in communicating with its readers, and its evocation of the seasons and of rural life has made it by far the most popular of the three novels, even in America, where it was widely praised. Nevertheless, the full scope of Gibbon's complex and disturbing vision is lost if the novel is studied on its own, for Chris will not find happiness in the end, and the world beyond Blawearie will offer little comfort. (Gibbon followed the success of his novel with three stories in the same vein for the *Scots Magazine*, and 'Smeddum' and 'Clay' were published again, along with 'Greenden' and two others, as part of the author's contribution to *Scottish Scene*.)

Appropriately enough, perhaps, since she has left the scenes of her childhood, Chris's sensibility is less central to the town of Segget, where her husband takes her in *Cloud Howe*. The doings and the gossip of the place, and the strike among the linen-spinners there, give a more social and political focus to their life together as the new minister and his wife; and the voice of the community can be heard more often as it joins Chris's voice in the narrative flow – not unlike the spiteful reports from the 'bodies' of Barbie.

Colquhoun calls his wife 'Chris Caledonia', observing wryly that he has 'married a nation', and indeed she does have a symbolic part to play, in her progress from the setting sun of Kinraddie to the township of Segget and eventually – in *Grey Granite* – to the industrial city of 'Duncairn' at the height of the Depression, where her son will become a communist organiser. This movement towards a more immediate historical awareness is foreshadowed by her fascination with the Kaimes and the ruined castle there, which replaces the standing stones as her favourite vantage point, evoking years of bloodshed, fallen barons and the sufferings of the Covenanters. Robert Colquhoun is an idealistic liberal socialist who preaches about the thousands of Christs who died in the war, supports the miners in the General Strike of 1926, and tries to assuage the cynicism and the political violence of the linen-workers. These spinners have always been an exploited class, for they were cannon fodder in the war and are little more than that now to the owners of the mills. They are equally despised by the petty bourgeoisie, for Segget has lost men such as Long Rob and Chae – if it ever had them – and it is a community largely without wisdom, conscience or charity. Colquhoun starts well, but the struggle is too great for him. The General Strike fails and Chris's new baby dies at birth. She recovers, but her husband suffers a crisis of personal faith and terror – haunted by a vision of Christ and by the memory of an evicted worker's baby that was gnawed by rats. Finally his health collapses, for his lungs were gassed in the war, and when he dies Chris finds herself alone once again at the end of a grimmer book than *Sunset Song*.

She will survive, for beyond the social surface of the novel Gibbon shows us a woman grappling with her identity as if she were a succession of different Chrisses, each reacting to different men in her past and yet always remaining herself and, in some vital sense, untouched. This ancient spirit stands aloof from politics or her husband's religion, symbolised by the 'clouds' whose various formations are used to name the chapters of the book, just as the chapters of *Sunset Song* used the farming-seasons. Ewan and Chris's father were men of the earth, but Colquhoun's idealism has taken her beyond those fertile cycles to a more elevated and abstract point of view. Yet she cannot find substance in any of the doctrines of men, and, for her, even love itself is only another mirage in their busy world:

Once Chris and Robert came to a place, out in the open, here the wind blew and the ground was thick with the droppings of sheep, where a line of the ancient stones stood ringed, as they stood in Kinraddie far west and below, left by the men of antique time, memorial these of a dream long lost, and hopes and fears of fantastic eld.

Robert said that they came from the East, those fears, long ago, ere Pytheas came sailing the sounding coasts to Thule. Before that the hunters had roamed these hills, naked and bright, in a Golden Age, without fear or hope or hate or love, living high in the race of the wind and the race of life, mating as simple as beasts or birds, dying with a like keen simpleness, the hunting weapons of those ancient folk Ewan would find in his search of the moors. . . .

And she thought then, looking on the shadowed Howe with its stratus mists and its pillars of spume, driving west by the Leachie bents, that men had followed these pillars of cloud like lost men lost in the high, dreich hills, they followed and fought and toiled in the wake of each whirling pillar that rose from the heights, clouds by day to darken men's minds – loyalty and fealty, patriotism, love, the mumbling chants of the dead old gods that once were worshipped in the circles of stones, christianity, socialism, nationalism – all – Clouds that swept through the Howe of the world, with men that took them for gods: just clouds, they passed and finished, dissolved and were done, nothing endured but the Seeker himself, him and the everlasting Hills.

The chapters of *Grey Granite* are named after the silicates and crystals to be found in that durable rock, reflecting the hardships of the Depression years in Duncairn, a big city on the east coast, modelled on the granite of Aberdeen, with aspects of Dundee and Glasgow. Gibbon may not have been entirely at ease with an urban setting, and certainly the book, like *Cloud Howe* in places, bears the evidence of hasty work, for it came from that last and most desperate year of writing. It is a harsh and unsettling novel and many readers have found it difficult after the lyricism of the first volume. Yet it was clearly Gibbon's intention to disturb us in this way, for the granite imagery also charts young Ewan's commitment to communism as he comes to develop the same flinty dedication that MacDiarmid had admired in his poetic hymns to Lenin. In fact, the book was dedicated to MacDiarmid, and Gibbon shared the poet's convictions, but his picture of Ewan has a darker side, for he appears to be an activist who will sacrifice his girl, his friends, and the truth itself to the cause of revolution. Ewan loses his idealism when he is physically beaten by the police for his part in a labour demonstration. He experiences a vivid identification with all of suffering humanity, and from then on he has stone in his soul and the quiet and precocious child who collected flint arrow-heads in the hills around Segget has died within him. His moment of realisation is disturbing, masochistic and suffused with hatred:

He was one with them all, a long wail of sobbing mouths and wrung flesh, tortured and tormented by the world's Masters while those Masters lied about Progress through Peace, Democracy, Justice, the Heritage of Culture. . . .

And a kind of stinging bliss came over him, knowledge that he was that army itself – that army of pain and blood and torment that was yet but the raggedest van of the hordes of the last of the Classes, the ancient Lowly, trampling the ways behind it unstayable: up and up, a dark sea of faces, banners red in the blood from the prisons, torn entrails of tortured workers their banners, the enslavement and oppression of six thousand years a cry and a singing that echoes to the stars. No retreat, no safety, no escape for them, no reward, thrust up by the black, blind tide to take the first brunt of impact, first glory, first death, first life as it never yet had been lived –

Grey Granite offers no deliverance, nor could its author see an easy conclusion to the work. The city of factories, owners, shopkeepers, workers and sheer drudgery is seen through Chris's eyes as she helps to keep Ma Cleghorn's boarding-house, but the narrative is shared with Ewan and one of his worker friends, and, when the voices of various characters in the boarding-house are heard as well, the result is a comic and sometimes savage satire; but it means that the warmth of Chris's sensibility no longer infuses and controls the book. She marries again, but her husband, Ake Ogilvie – an old acquaintance from Segget – realises that he does not have her true self, and he grants her freedom by emigrating to Canada. Chris is finally alone and wholly given over to her vision of changeless change and independence in 'a world without hope or temptation, without hate or love, at last, at long last'. She moves to another cottage, in the countryside where her family lived before they moved to Blawearie, and she finds another vantage point on the site of an ancient Pictish fort on the Hill of Fare. Here she reflects on the journey of her life and on the role of change as 'Deliverer, Destroyer and Friend in one', and she seems to die away in the closing sentence of the trilogy.

It is difficult not to feel that Chris has been somehow defeated – she is only in her forties and yet her life seems over. Ewan is left planning a workers' hunger march on London and his story is still to be decided. Perhaps Gibbon could see no further, for the novel ends in virtually contemporary times, with all the issues of the thirties necessarily unresolved and a heroine already much older in experience than he was himself. On the other hand, Chris's end returns us to a vision of the land in which she is the harbinger of a fundamentally feminine and disinterested faith in existence, simply for its own sake. The vision grew from Gibbon's poignant sense of his own lost past, and it sustains the trilogy at a poetic level, more moving, profound and problematical than any of his more 'masculine' and intellectual allegiances to Diffusionism or communism. Yet Chris simply drops out of history, and, although the future must belong with Ewan, Gibbon's heart seems to stay behind with the rain and the lapwings and the eternal stasis of Scotland's empty spaces. Thus *A Scots Quair* belongs with the several great books in Scottish literature that have dealt with the theme of the divided self and the spiritual antithesis between 'masculine' authority and 'feminine' sensitivity. Most of these novels forced a confrontation and ended tragically, but Gibbon's gift seems to be suspended between the two, although it is possible that Chris's early death tells us that it is time to leave the enduring power of 'Kinraddie' and all its sister villages in the heartland of Scottish letters.

Sentimental realism

Fred Urquhart (1912–95), John Reid, 'David Toulmin' (1914–98), Cliff Hanley (1922–99), Anne Smith (b.1944) and Jessie Kesson (1916–94)

The genre survives, however, for it is derived from common Scottish experience, and, like Chris Guthrie herself, it has great strength. It appears without ambiguity in the work of Fred Urquhart, whose first and autobiographical novel, *Time Will Knit* (1938), showed his interest in the stream-of-consciousness technique. His short stories contain strong Scots speech and a particularly realistic evocation of rural life – collected in *The Dying Stallion* (1967) and *The Ploughing Match* (1968). The stories and novels of John Reid, 'David Toulmin', a farm worker from the North-East, revive the world of Grassic Gibbon in more melodramatic and emotive terms – *Hard, Shining Corn* (1972), *Blown Seed* (1976). Further novels of growth and development in the same vein include *The Taste of Too Much* (1960) by Cliff Hanley and *The Magic Glass* (1981) by Anne Smith.

Vivid sentimental realism (the term is not used pejoratively) and town and country life in the North-East can also be found in the work of Jessie Kesson. Jessie Grant McDonald was an illegitimate child born into extreme poverty in the slums of Elgin. At the age of eight she was moved to an orphanage and although she showed promise at school and had the support of a teacher who wanted her to go to university, she was thrust into domestic service at the age of sixteen. Things did not go well for her in the next few years, during which she suffered a breakdown, spending a year in a mental hospital before being boarded out again in a village to the north of Inverness. Here she met and married John Kesson and the couple set up life together as farm workers in a succession of tied houses. Pressed to support herself and her family, and encouraged by a chance meeting with Nan Shepherd, Kesson began to contribute stories, essays and poems to the *North-East Review* and the *Scots Magazine*. These pieces drew on her own rich life experiences and she began to write plays for BBC Radio Scotland from the same source. The success of these plays led the Kessons to move to London in the 1950s, where Jessie continued to write for radio while working as an office cleaner and a carer for troubled youngsters and in hostels for old people.

Kesson's first novel, *The White Bird Passes* (1958), is clearly based on her own childhood with its account of Janie, a bright girl from the slums coming to maturity in an orphanage, and the precarious world outside. Yet this is more than just a typically autobiographical first book, for Kesson has a strong sense of what it is to be always on the outside, as she explained in an interview with Isobel Murray:

> Every work I've ever written contains ae 'ootlin'. Lovely Aberdeenshire word. Somebody that never really fitted into the thing, and that is when I think o't everything . . .

Kesson's sympathy with the marginal and marginalised is evident in all her writing, but she is especially interested in those who are 'out' – and don't want to be 'in'. Janie's resilience, her refusal to be a drudge, her ambition to write 'great poetry', and the vivid characters she meets, the street prostitutes, the tinkers and carnival people all begin to undermine the authority of the orphanage, the asylum and the schoolroom with their middle-class expectations of what is 'proper' for the impoverished working class and for women in particular.

The Glitter of Mica (1963) draws once more on Kesson's experience but is focused around a male protagonist in a grim account of the brutal labour and insecure lives of farm workers under the cottering system. Hugh Riddel's family background, his frustrations and passions come to a dark conclusion in the spirit of George Douglas Brown. The novella *Where the Apple Ripens* (1978) deals with adolescence and was collected with Kesson's short stories in 1985. *Another Time, Another Place* (1983) gives a balanced and sensitive account of a young crofter's wife – Janie again – now married to a good but silent older man and frustrated by the routine and dullness of her life on the land. The novel reflects on the paradoxical nature of imprisonment and what being a prisoner means when Janie has to look after Italian prisoners of war who have been sent to work in the fields. Both *The White Bird Passes* and *Another Time, Another Place* were made into successful films, while some of Kesson's poems and radio scripts appeared as *Somewhere Beyond* (2000).

If *Another Time, Another Place* is haunted by being 'outside' and by what might have been; and if Grassic Gibbon's fiction looks through Chris Guthrie's spirit to find a golden age of free hunters long ago, Neil Gunn's origins offered him a similar ideal rather closer to home. Through a long and productive literary career he was to develop his vision of an elusive but vital saving spirit, much needed in the modern world, which he associated with the deserted landscapes and the marginalised culture of the Highlands.

History and myth

Neil M. Gunn (1891–1973)

Gunn grew up as a fisherman's son, the fifth of seven boys in a family of nine, living in Dunbeath near Helmsdale on the far north-east coast of Caithness, and, although he was not a native Gaelic speaker, he was always very aware of the Gaelic, Norse and Pictish influences in the region. He valued a Celtic inheritance in the face of the modern world and his first short stories were in the style of 'Fiona Macleod' and Neil Munro. He soon threw over their twilight fatalism, however, and his best work has a clarity of style and focus which relates to Gaelic literature's delight in the actuality of things, and then points to universals beyond them. This tendency is also evident in his treatment of character and of women in particular. The result might be called 'Celtic Platonism' if it were a philosophy, and 'symbolic realism', or even allegory at times, in fiction. Gunn shares this mythopoeic tendency with Grassic Gibbon, and both are inclined to idealise the feminine 'other', but the two writers arrive at radically different conclusions. Hence Chris and Ewan represent an impasse of irreconcilable spiritual and political values at the end of *A Scots Quair*, while Gunn's intention was to try to restore completeness to the individual and to offer Scottish culture at least the possibility of regeneration from within.

This search for self-development and wholeness motivates most of the characters in Gunn's books, and, like Wordsworth, he feels that the philosophical implications of this quest can be found in the journey to maturity from the landscapes and exploits of childhood. He was an athletic and adventurous boy who loved to go exploring, fishing and poaching in the sheltered strath of Dunbeath water. The central symbols in his later fiction come from these years when he watched the men go to sea in their little boats while the women waited at home, and he saw a wider meaning in the search for herring – 'the silver darlings' – or in clandestine expeditions after salmon – that ancient Celtic symbol of wisdom, now reserved for the gentry and protected by gamekeepers. Like Wordsworth, too, Gunn made a creative act of recollection at the end of his life in an autobiography called *The Atom of Delight* (1956), and in a key passage he remembers cracking hazelnuts as a boy, and how a sudden moment of insight and unity gave him the ideal which he sought so long in later adult experience:

> I can't remember now how I got on to the boulder in the river but I was there. It was a large flattish boulder and I was sitting on it with my legs stuck out in front at the angle which is wide enough both to give complete comfort and to crack nuts within it. I had picked a stone from the bed of the stream and was using it as a cracking hammer. . . .
>
> The shallow river flowed around and past with its variety of lulling monotonous sounds; a soft wind, warmed by the sun, came upstream and murmured in my ears as it continuously slipped from my face. As I say, how I got there I do not remember. . . .
>
> Then the next thing happened, so far as I can remember, for the first time. I have tried hard but can find no simpler way of expressing what happened than by saying: *I came upon myself sitting there.*
>
> Within the mood of content, as I have tried to recreate it, was this self and the self was me.
>
> The state of content deepened wonderfully and everything around was embraced in it.
>
> There was no 'losing' of the self in the sense that there was a blank from which I awoke or came to. The self may have thinned away – it did – but so delightfully that it also remained at the centre in a continuous and perfectly natural way. And then within this amplitude the self as it were became aware of seeing itself, not as an 'I' or an 'ego' but rather as a stranger it had come upon and was even a little shy of.
>
> Transitory, evanescent – no doubt, but the scene comes back across half a century, vivid to the crack in the boulder that held the nut.

This passage is typical of how Gunn approaches the world as a writer, for he insists on a local and scrupulous clarity and on the difficulty of describing inner experience in words. Yet in Scottish folklore hazelnuts are associated with the putting-on of wisdom or prophetic ability, and so the little scene is also invested with intimations of magical or symbolic power. Gunn's fondness for such archetypes tends to place his vision outside history and politics, just as Chris's standing stones are remote from the injustices of the factory floor that Ewan had to face. Yet Gunn would claim that his espousal of wholeness, traditional wisdom, communal care, courage and loyalty is exactly what is needed to redeem the sad vacuum of modern life, even if Gibbon would have felt that such gains were meaningless without an economic revolution too. In either case, these two novelists tackle universal questions about the human spirit, just as they draw on a poetic sense of the past to confront the central issues of modern alienation. In their books the regional setting of the 'Scottish novel' is redeemed, and Caithness and the Mearns (like Auchtermuchty in MacDiarmid's *Drunk Man*) become part of a continuing concern with the 'timeless flame'.

At Dunbeath the fishing industry was in decline and times were hard; so Gunn left home when he was twelve, to stay with his married sister in Dalry. At fifteen he went to London and worked as a bank clerk for a couple of years before coming to Edinburgh to prepare for a career as a Customs and Excise officer. He passed his Civil Service exams in 1911 and was posted to Inverness, from where he travelled as an 'unattached' junior to a variety of offices and distilleries all round the north. Gunn spent the war years working with shipping from Kinlochleven and was just about to be called up when the conflict ended. This was a considerable relief to his mother (his father had died in 1916), for, among her sons, Ben had been killed on the barbed wire, John was badly gassed (their stories are used in *Highland River*) and the twins, who had gone to Canada, also lost their lives as a result of their army service. Prompted by a posting to the south, Neil married his Dingwall girlfriend Daisy Frew in 1921 and the couple set up house in Wigan. During a year there Gunn had to assess pension claims on behalf of miners who were suffering the worst of poverty as a result of wage-cuts and lockouts by the owners – for the coalmines had been returned to private hands after the war. Such experience, so close to the sacrifices of the Front, marked him deeply and confirmed his socialist sympathies. He was glad to return to Lybster and then to Inverness, for, even if the Highland economy was in ruins too, there was always the familiar countryside and a sense of surviving community life. He settled in a permanent post as Excise officer for the Glen Mhor distillery and began to write seriously.

Gunn corresponded with MacDiarmid in Montrose and soon placed short stories in the *Scottish Chapbook* and other periodicals. The best of these pieces suggest a darker version of the Celtic twilight, or hint at themes to come, and a collection, *Hidden Doors*, appeared in 1929 from the Porpoise Press in Edinburgh – a new Scottish publisher that was to produce most of his books in the 1930s until Faber and Faber took it over. Grieve was enthusiastic about Gunn's talent and, although he criticised a predictable 'anti-Kailyard' impulse in parts of the first novel, he detected the arrival of an original vision and 'a purely Scottish use of English'. The two men became close friends. *The Grey Coast* (1926) is an account of rivalry in love set against Highland life in a small fishing and crofting community. Coloured 'grey' indeed by Gunn's hatred of poverty, avarice and lust, it offers a bitter and gloomy account of the fate of the modern Gael living in a bleak landscape, 'a land of knotted rheumatism and dead things', in the generations after the Clearances. He developed the same theme more melodramatically in his next work, *The Lost Glen* (rejected by London publishers but serialised in the *Scots Magazine* in 1928), in which a failed university student returns home – a disgrace to his family – to work as a gillie and to see his people as a depressed peasant class, slyly subservient to southern incomers with superior airs. Depressed by this bleak book, and by his inability to find a publisher for it, Gunn turned to drama for a spell, with the help of John Brandane and James Bridie. But the three-act symbolic drama *The Ancient Fire* was not well received and he settled for a lasting friendship with Bridie and a return to prose.

His hopes were greatly rekindled by the success of his third book. *Morning Tide* (1930) is a much happier thing than its predecessors. Prompted by the recollections of his brother John, Gunn turned back to the scenes of his childhood in Dunbeath – as if to recover optimism by means of the story of a growing boy, Hugh, and how he comes to terms with his parents, his sisters and the dangers of the sea. It is the first of four notable novels in Gunn's output (*Highland River*, *The Silver Darlings* and *Young Art and Old Hector* are the other three) that deal with the growth of a boy's mind, looking to childhood as an age of primitive and intuitive truths.

When *Morning Tide* was selected as a Book Society choice, Gunn followed it with a revision of *The Lost Glen* (1932), whose grimmer theme was less popular. Turning away from modern times, he plunged into a more symbolic and philosophical vision of the ancient past with *Sun Circle* (1933), the first of a set of three historical novels – *Butcher's Broom* and *The Silver Darlings* being the others. *Sun Circle* is an exploration of creativity and brutal violence imagined along racial terms in the clash of ancient peoples and their different characteristics in the

north of Scotland in the ninth century. Here another young protagonist, Aniel, has to learn about cruel Viking power and the 'civilising'
influence of Christianity, both of which will sweep away his ancient
Pictish-Celtic world; and yet Gunn imagines that its spirit will still
somehow survive in the Highlands, beyond the reach of history and
change – in the imaginative wholeness, the acceptance and timeless
affirmation symbolised by the sun circle:

> As the Sun puts a circle round the earth and all that it contained, so a man
> by his vision puts a circle round himself. At the centre of this circle his spirit
> sat, and at the centre of his spirit was a serenity for ever watchful.

Gunn's next book turned to more immediate history, and *Butcher's
Broom* (1934) describes how the values of Highland life – personified
by the healer Dark Mairi – were betrayed by the Clearances at the
beginning of the nineteenth century. The Strathnaver events were still
a matter of bitter folk-memory in Gunn's Caithness, and English-
speaking 'improvers', such as the factor 'Heller' (based on Patrick
Sellars), can see nothing but poverty and 'gibberish' in the community, because the Gaelic tongue is not available to them. In fact
Gaelic's graceful sensitivity to minute discriminations (paralleled by
Gunn's talent for subtle detail and inner states in prose) is the real
cultural and philosophical wealth of the place – uncountable, of
course, by those who can think only in material terms. *Butcher's Broom*
spoke directly to the political and nationalist issues of Scotland in the
thirties, and Gunn himself was active for the Scottish National Party
behind the scenes in Inverness. The book was a great success and
Grassic Gibbon wrote to marvel at how Gunn had managed to control
his rage at the fate of 'those people of yours'. Faber and Faber were
interested in Gunn, and T. S. Eliot and the American publisher Alfred
Harcourt came north to visit him at home. Up in Shetland, however,
Neil's old friend MacDiarmid was becoming rather cool, and naming
the intransigent Fionn Mac Colla as the true Gaelic novelist of the
future.

Gunn's next book was one of his finest. *Highland River* (1937)
returns once more to Dunbeath and the river strath where the author
spent his childhood – a simple landscape in which a boy's struggle to
land a poached salmon with his bare hands becomes an initiation into
life's mystery, wisdom, fear and secret delight. Gunn dedicated the
book to his brother John, for it encapsulated their youthful adventures
together, and his hero, Kenn, becomes a scientist as John had done and
shares his experiences of gas and a brother's death at the Front. Gunn

found unexpectedly deep resonances in this book, and his imagination was profoundly stirred. The story is told in a series of overlapping presents that annihilate the apparent passage of time, so that Kenn's childhood and his wartime and adult experiences coexist and reflect on each other through a series of witty and moving associative links. Finally, he revisits the river of his boyhood in order to trace it, and the nature of his own being, back to the source. The river-mouth and its shallows are associated with infancy, just as he frequented the middle reaches when he was an older boy. But he never did find the source before he left home, and indeed he could not truly have attained it or understood its nature then, which is what he does at the end of the book, when he returns as a mature and solitary man. The theme is very evocative, with traditional overtones of the 'river' of life and time; and yet its style imitates the scientific precision of Kenn's trained intellect, and this dispassionate and analytical enquiry is very different from the poetic surrender to mood and the flow of dialect that Grassic Gibbon chose to use for his Chris:

> The heath fire and the primrose: the two scents jotted down by Kenn as simple facts of experience, without any idea of a relationship between them.
> And then suddenly, while the mind was lifting to the cold bright light of spring, to the blue of birds' eggs and the silver of the first salmon run, there came out of the tangle in a soft waft of air the scent of primroses.
> An instant, and it was gone, leaving a restlessness in the breast, an urgency that defeats itself, an apprehension, almost agonising, of the ineffectiveness of the recording machine. Finally nothing is jotted down and the mind is left exhausted. . . .
> But the grown Kenn knows quite exactly one quality in the scent of the primrose for which he has an adjective. The adjective is innocent. The innocency of dawn on a strath on a far back morning of creation. The freshness of dawn wind down a green glen where no human foot has trod. If the words sound vague, the pictures they conjure up for Kenn's inner eye are quite vivid. The grasses and green leaves in the clear morning light have a quality of alertness like pointed ears. And they sway alive and dancing-cool and deliciously happy.

As a scientist, Kenn – whose very name suggests the act of knowing – also finds this elusive delight in art and good action. It is the very spirit of Duncan Bàn's 'Ben Dorain' – a pagan realism quite removed from the strictures of organised religion or politics or official dogma of any kind. He remembers when he first found it in science, too, in an exam question on how 'the principal forms of energy are traceable to the sun':

Forests of dead trees turn into coal. . . . Sun takes up water into clouds; clouds fall and form rivers and waterfalls; falling water directly used for making electricity. . . . The cycles of action were cosmic wheels, opening fanlike, each spoke glittering in Kenn's mind. The excitement of apprehension made his brain extraordinarily clear; his sentences were factual and precisely written.

Here the 'sun circle' has been rescued from the Celtic twilight to be redefined as the 'energy cycle' with a scientific clarity that actually enhances its symbolic force.

The 'salmon of knowledge' and this 'excitement of apprehension' (in both senses of the word) lie at the heart of Gunn's novels, and Kenn emerges into the sunlight as a new kind of sensibility – a solitary atheist, ready for laughter at the unexpectedness of the universe, and yet coolly detached, too, for his war experiences have marked him with a ferocious sense of irony:

> The blowing of gaps in the advancing Germans on that early morning towards the end of 1917 on the Somme was coarse unskilled work, though its sheer devastating efficacy had its fascination, because – apart from the joyous potting of church steeples and such – even observers saw little of the actual results of the gun-teams' labours. On this particular morning, however, precision in its trigonometrical sense was almost entirely confined to the exquisite narrowness of the shaves by which death passed them by or the instant arid annihilating manner in which it got them. Escape was a matter of pure chance.

After his brush with death and a near blinding by gas, Kenn goes back to memories of the river and eventually, years later, at the age of thirty-seven, he reaches the source and comes to understand the humour and the beautiful indifference of being:

> Bow to it, giving nothing away, and pass on the moor like sunlight, like shadow, with thoughts hesitant and swift as a herd of hinds. In this way one is undefeatable – until death comes. And as death is inevitable, its victory is no great triumph.

Yet beyond the watershed he sees a mountain; and, beyond that, 'the grey planetary light that reveals the earth as a ball turning slowly in the immense chasm of space'. In the end, there is no end and no goal – only the quality of the moment.

Gunn's prose achieves a memorably cool expression of the elusive, considering nature of the human mind, where symbolic insights meet the Gaelic poetic genius for impersonal and detailed actuality. This is a

Scottish novel that is entirely free from 'Celtic' twilight, not to mention the old penchant for rural sentiment. For this reason *Highland River* has a claim to be Gunn's finest book: it was awarded the James Tait Black Memorial Prize for 1937, widely acclaimed and frequently reprinted; and as a novel of individual development it bears comparison with Joyce's *Portrait of the Artist*. Encouraged by Eliot and the directors of Faber, Gunn committed himself to full-time writing by resigning from his job at the age of forty-six and taking his wife to live at Braefarm House near Dingwall, to the north of Inverness. *Off in a Boat* (1938) gives an autobiographical account of that summer of freedom. Essays, plays and two more novels followed in the next two years, but they seem to be marking time somewhat before the appearance of his most popular book.

The Silver Darlings (1941) links the theme of personal development in *Highland River* with an account of the growth of the herring-industry after the Highland Clearances in the early nineteenth century. It is Gunn's most fully researched historical novel. Based on his own Dunbeath, now fictionalised as 'Dunster', it is founded on two generations of economic and social change and filled with fine descriptions of local character, landscape and the thrill and danger of the sea. Against this densely realised setting, Gunn relates the inner odyssey of the boy Finn, growing up without a father, coming to terms with his mother's affection for another man, finding a girlfriend himself and eventually a boat of his own and a place in the working community of men. These simple themes are filtered through the Lawrentian intensity of young Finn's pride and innocence, but the book begins with his mother Catrine, who was forced to the shore by the Clearances. Her inexperienced young husband is press-ganged by the navy while he is fishing in his little boat, and eventually he dies abroad. In later years Catrine's suitor Roddy is one of the most successful skippers on this dangerous coast, but she fears and hates the sea, to which he, and now her son, is so inevitably drawn. Thus Finn comes to realise that his home embraces polarities beyond the obvious truths of every day, just as Gunn himself describes his own background as 'the boy' in *The Atom of Delight*:

> As his existence had two parents, so it had the earth and the sea. If his mother was the earth, his father was the sea. In fact he could hardly think of his father without thinking of the sea. Out of the sea came the livelihood of the household. They depended on the sea, and of all the elements in nature it was the least dependable. You could never be sure of it as you could be sure of the earth.

Here the presence and authority of all those Scottish fathers – Weir, Gillespie, Gourlay or Guthrie – has come down to its most elemental role. Yet, despite the terrors of the waves, a man at peace with himself can approach them and work in harmony, although he must never take anything for granted. On the other hand, the land is always there, comforting, stable and feminine. In figurative terms, Finn's achievement is to reach maturity by bridging the gap between the empathetic and land-oriented spirit of Chris Guthrie and the unrelentingly harsh universe of Adam Weir, symbolised by the capricious sea. More conventionally, Gunn likens the sea to a mistress and the land to a wife, and Finn has to learn to share the sea, and his mother too, with Roddy, whom he greets at first with jealousy and suspicion. Finn's rite of passage is made during a voyage to Stornoway when the crew of Roddy's boat comes close to shipwreck and starvation until the boy makes a courageous ascent of an impossible cliff to fetch water and raw food to sustain them all. When the tale is retold it is as if it has become a part of folk history, linking Finn with Finn MacCoul, his heroic namesake in an epic past. But Finn's real victory comes later in the book, in the quiet moment when he finds peace within the circle of his own heart and a place within the circle of the community. Only now can he enter the bustle of history, and the book ends by recognising that Finn is at last truly ready to begin: a properly whole person with a part to play in the world and plans for a family of his own. The novel's closing words are 'Life had come for him', and the optimism of this conclusion makes a marked contrast with the melancholy diffusion that overtakes Chris Guthrie at the end of *Grey Granite*.

The popularity of *The Silver Darlings* is not unrelated to its foundation in social history and realistic detail, but later novels would seek an increasingly symbolic exploration of his favourite themes. At first *The Serpent* (1943) marked time with another plea for the whole individual in the face of a narrow-minded, Kirk-ridden village, but Gunn's new direction is particularly clear in the development from *Young Art and Old Hector* (1942) to *The Green Isle of the Great Deep* (1944). These are two separate but linked narratives that move from the gently light-hearted and instructive vignettes of the first to an anti-utopian fantasy novel that casts reflections on the nature of totalitarian rule. As a wilful eight-year-old, young Art gains 'instruction' and exasperation in the company of Hector, an old poacher with his best years behind him but still wise in the insights of folklore and tradition. Their first book together has a grave whimsy that can stray dangerously close to sentimental 'philosophy'. Naomi Mitchison suggested as much in a letter to the author, which initiated a friendly debate over the years, in which Gunn stubbornly defended his case for simplicity and individual self-realisation in the face of her more conventionally socialist enthusiasm for collective action and political involvement. The indirect result of their wrangle was *The Green Isle of the Great Deep* – a different kind of book altogether

In *The Green Isle* . . . Art and Hector fall into a salmon-pool and find themselves in a version of Tir nan Og (the Celtic isle of the ever-young), that is run like an enlightened totalitarian state. An early reference to Nazi concentration camps reminds us of the date when the two protagonists 'drown', but the main target of this anti-utopian allegory is the rational arrogance of faceless 'scientific' authority, which presumes to know best and attempts to tranquillise and control us for our own good. Gunn had read Arthur Koestler's *Darkness at Noon* (1940) and been dismayed by recent reports of 'brainwashing' in Stalin's Russia. At an imaginative level he saw the materialistic assumptions of corporate decision-makers as a more real menace to the future than the Gothic horror of Nazi fascism, approaching its end in the ruins of Europe. The question was: How would the quiet, interior wisdom of his two unlikely Highland heroes fare against these 'Administrators'? The answer is worked out through humour, surprise and Art's anarchic boyish spirit, which his captors seem to be incapable of suppressing or trapping. He becomes a 'legend', until God returns to investigate and put things right in the domain he left long ago. In the end it is Art's understanding that beyond 'knowledge' there is 'wisdom', and beyond that 'magic', which returns them to the real and imperfect world where they are fished out of the salmon-pool, dripping wet and alive. It may be debatable whether 'magic' is enough in the face of the power of the corporate state, but Gunn's defence of what MacDiarmid called 'the shy spirit that like a laich wind moves' would be to say, as anarchists do, that if every individual had such quality within them, then external coercion would indeed wither away. The *Green Isle of the Great Deep* deserves to be much better known than it is, for it is a key dystopian novel in the spirit of Huxley's *Brave New World* (1932) and Orwell's *Nineteen Eighty-Four* (1949) and a good deal more relevant to today's managerial climate and corporate culture than either.

In the last six years of his writing career, Gunn's novels tried to realise the quest for intuitive wholeness in more contemporary settings, for he was determined to avoid a return to the 'chronicle novel' and he could do little more with the overt allegory of *The*

Green Isle. Besides, he was sensitive to accusations that his spiritual outlook was mystical or escapist. Thus, in a realistic setting the symbolism of *The Drinking Well* (1947) relates to earlier work, looking back to the paternal conflicts in *The Serpent* and *The Lost Glen*, as does the more melodramatic psychological thriller *The Key of the Chest* (1945).

The post-war years were difficult ones in Gunn's personal life, and, like many of his friends, he had become increasingly pessimistic about the future of socialism in the light of Stalin's tyranny. The novels of this period – *The Shadow* (1948), *The Lost Chart* (1949) and *Bloodhunt* (1952) – take a darker look at the split between the rational intellect and the wholeness of feeling, with symbols which often relate in too familiar terms, perhaps, to the intuitive power of women as opposed to the reductive habits of the masculine mind, and images which conjure up the atavistic thrills of violence and the hunt. A lighter-hearted book, *The Silver Bough* (1948), had been well received – Edwin Muir particularly admired it – but Gunn had not recaptured his earlier successes and he began to feel a sense of literary and geographical isolation in his beloved north. He was fifty-nine years old and his career as a writer was nearly at an end; yet, if his last novels tend to echo themes and books that had gone before, they were still to be transmuted in significant ways.

The Well at the World's End (1951) follows the spirit of *The Silver Bough* to make a triumphant return to the archetypal innocence and humour of the world of *Highland River*, but this time it is experienced by a middle-aged academic, a man who already knows the wider world and the horrors of history. He comes to moments of comedy, mystery and near death in the course of a picaresque camping holiday in the everyday Highlands, and the world is renewed by his experience of delight and laughter, even laughter at himself, just as his own inner being and his relationship with his wife are refreshed. The protagonists are not unlike Gunn and Daisy themselves, and the novel is the sweetest of the late works, for it manages to catch the ineffable 'nothingness' of interior insight – clear as water in a well, transparent as the Caithness light itself. There is a stranger humour and affirmation too in *The Other Landscape* (1954), in which an anthropologist narrator struggles to understand the archetypally mischievous nature of existence in the vision of a gifted and eccentric musician who has lived as a recluse ever since his wife died in childbirth, cut off from help. This novel, as 'metaphysical' as any by David Lindsay, was followed by Gunn's autobiography – his last book.

The Atom of Delight (1956) is the author's defence of a lifelong preference for personal unity and insight in the face of fashionable pessimism, collectivism and the aesthetic and political violences of the 'modern' world. In retrospect he found affinities between the pagan spirit of freedom in his boyhood and the irreverent teachings of the Zen masters who demonstrate a letting-go of self in moments of intuitively integrated action. This was the single vision that Gunn had pursued in various forms through all his novels:

> Without consciously thinking or striving, 'It' is achieved, spontaneity comes into its own, the arrow lands in the bull. Musical composers, scientists, painters, writers, know how in the midst of their striving 'It' takes charge, strife ceases, and the 'marked passage' is born. In that moment of delight freedom is known; as, not to be high falutin, its rare moment is known in archery, cricket and putting the shot, not to mention the way a rosebush looked at the boy when he had landed his fish.
> The future remains open to this kind of freedom.

Neil Gunn lived for another seventeen years, actively engaged in local affairs, literary magazines and broadcasting, until he died after a short illness in January 1973. The Neil Gunn International Fellowship has since been awarded to many distinguished overseas novelists, including Heinrich Böll, Chinua Achebe, Saul Bellow, Ruth Prawer Jhabvala, Mario Vargas Llosa, and Nadine Gordimer.

Naomi Mitchison (1897–1999)

The work of Andrew Lang and J. G. Frazer had been hugely influential in generating an international wave of interest in the myths and rituals of primitive societies, and a sense of the mythopoeic and historically ancient patterns to be found in rural life had characterised the writing of Edwin Muir, Lewis Grassic Gibbon and Neil Gunn. This interest in ancient and mythic ways of seeing the world was shared by Naomi Mitchison. It is evident in early work such as *The Conquered* (1923), which imagines a Celt indentured to a Roman master in the first century, and especially in her twelfth book, over 600 pages long, *The Corn King and the Spring Queen* (1931), which is set in the second century BC. Following her own interests in ancient history and anthropology after the manner of Frazer, in what she called her 'dear old *Golden Bough*', the later novel revolves around the rituals of kingship and fertility in the ancient world of Scythia and the Mediterranean yet, as with much of her historical fiction, she uses the events of the past to illuminate contemporary issues of power, sexuality and resistance to tyranny. The novel charts a journey made by Erif Der, a girl witch from the shores of the Black Sea – a world of ritual and magic – to what was becoming the modern world on the shores of the Mediterranean. She made a conscious connection between the rise of the Spartan state in this novel and what was happening in Mussolini's Italy. H. G. Wells wrote to tell her that he considered this 'one of the greatest historical novels ever done. . . . I really believe it is something like it really was.' Linklater's *Men of Ness* and Gunn's *Sun Circle* followed within two years. *The Blood of the Martyrs* (1939) linked the persecution of the early Christians under Nero to the plight of the Jews in Hitler's Germany. Closer to home, *The Bull Calves* (1947) drew on her own family history – she was a member of the distinguished Haldanes – to tell a tale set in Perthshire after 1745. A free-spirited Fabian free-thinker, Oxford educated, from an upper-class background, Mitchison played a leading part in left-wing politics and women's rights, travelled widely and was adopted as advisor, 'mother' and honorary chief of the Bakgatla tribe in Botswana. Her early work was often thought to be sexually daring in treating with rape and homosexuality set in the past, but there was something more of a critical scandal when she treated such subjects in a contemporary novel, *We Have Been Warned* (1935). With scenes set in the Soviet Union (based on Mitchison's visit in 1932), the novel deals with politics as well as sex, but it was the treatment of abortion and contraception that led to a break with Cape and the end of her friendship with D. H. Lawrence's great supporter Edward Garnett. Looking back on the furore Mitchison noted philosophically, 'I don't suppose any reputable writers before my time had mentioned the unpleasantness of the touch of rubber.'

Naomi Mitchison met and corresponded with Neil Gunn and Hugh MacDiarmid as well as, among many others, H. G. Wells, Arnold Bennett, E. M. Forster, Robert Graves, W. H. Auden and Stevie Smith. A noted beauty, she co-authored a book with and had her portrait painted by Wyndham Lewis. In a long and full life she published over 80 titles including social studies, fiction, historical fiction, science fiction in the remarkable *Memoirs of a Spacewoman* (1962), children's fiction, plays, poems and short stories, as well as a series of personal memoirs that offer tantalising glimpses into her privileged literary and social circles from an Edwardian childhood to modern days. These were published as *Small Talk* (1973), *All Change Here* (1975) and, in a title typical of her wit, *You May Well Ask* (1979).

Other novelists of the early twentieth century

Ian Macpherson (1905–44)

Ian Macpherson anticipated aspects of *Sunset Song* in his first novel, *Shepherd's Calendar* (1931), based on his own youth and education in the rural North-East. Occasionally overwritten, the book charts an adolescent's painful farewell to the farm he loves in order to satisfy his mother's desire to see him 'succeed' at university. Macpherson's next two novels took the Clearances for their theme, but his last and best work, *Wild Harbour* (1936), was a more original tale about a young married couple trying to live in the Highlands away from the universal future war which has broken out in '1944'. Their love for each other, the summer wilderness of remote Speyside, and the skills of stalking and lonely survival are all economically recounted before the anarchic world catches up with their idyll and sweeps them to random and meaningless deaths. The author himself was killed in a motorcycle accident in 1944.

A. J. Cronin (1896–1981), Dot Allan (1892–1964) and George Blake (1893–1961)

A. J. Cronin began a long career as a popular author with *Hatter's Castle* (1931), re-creating some of the themes of *The House with the Green Shutters* in a vein of sentimental realism. His own medical expertise and his interest in politics and social problems enlivened several of his books and made *The Citadel* (1937) a best-seller. Based on his own experiences as a doctor in the mining towns of Wales, it was successfully translated into a TV serial, like the rather looser adaptations that went to make the series *Dr Finlay's Casebook*.

Other novelists at this time looked to modern city life for their material, in what might be called a 'Glasgow school'; and, although there was no formal movement as such, their devotion to urban realism in the west of Scotland makes a significant counterbalance to the more mythic symbolism of Gibbon and Gunn. In the later 1920s, Dot Allan had placed several stories of family life in a Glasgow setting from the First World War or during the Depression, and a later novel called *Hunger March* (1934) dealt with the plight of the city's unemployed workers. Chief among these urban writers was George Blake, a Law graduate who turned to journalism after the war, becoming a colleague of Neil Munro at the *Glasgow Evening News* and later the editor of *Strand Magazine* in London. He returned to Scotland in the 1930s to

join George Malcolm Thomson at the Porpoise Press when it amalgamated with Faber. Throughout his career, Blake made a sustained
effort to write about Scotland's mercantile and working classes in the
face of industrial decline in the Clyde and Greenock from the 1920s to
the Second World War. His first book, *Mince Collop Close* (1925), was
a melodramatic tale about a female gang-leader in the slums, but *The
Wild Men* (1925) and *Young Malcolm* (1926) – dealing with revolutionary politics and the education of a young man – were less sensational, if still in the vein of sentimental realism. Blake is best known for
The Shipbuilders (1935), a major attempt to evoke Glasgow during the
Depression by following the problems, the family-ties and the different
fortunes of two men who formed a friendship during the Great War.
Ex-soldier and officer's batman Danny Shields is now a riveter at
Pagan's shipyard, working for his admired 'Major' – the owner's son
and manager, Leslie Pagan. But the yard has taken its last order. Pagan
bows to economic forces, although he keeps his wealth, and before he
leaves for England he offers the riveter a job on his estate there.
Danny's proud nature decides to 'stick to his trade' and seek work
among the other yards on the Clyde. He does not know it, but his skills
are already made obsolete by the new electric welding.

The Shipbuilders is notable for its evocation of a grimy and beloved
city, with its lively culture of tenements and trams, street gangs, pubs
and football matches. But Danny is sentimentalised as a loyal and stalwart type-figure, as if the author himself saw the workers from the
point of view of Pagan's officer-class. The human interest of the friendship with Pagan, like the latter's fatalism, is neither developed nor
shaken by circumstances, and this draws the centre of the novel well
away from any more crucial psychological, political or economic understanding. Even so, Blake handles the urban scene well. *David and
Joanna* (1936) and *Late Harvest* (1938) developed his understanding
of the strength and the plight of women tied to frailer men folk, and
the resignations of life in a declining industrial town. The latter book
painted a particularly detailed picture of shabby respectable existence in
a fictionalised Greenock, and this paved the way for a series of later
works set in 'Garvel'. These include *The Constant Star* (1945) and *The
Westering Sun* (1946), which follow the dynastic history of the shipbuilding Oliphant family, from the early nineteenth century to the fate
of the last daughter of the line, who struggles through the Depression
in Glasgow to die in a wartime air raid. Blake's personal commitment
to the history of his home region led him to produce several books on
ships, shipbuilding and the lighthouses of the Clyde – a fascination

which also featured in his autobiographical study *Down to the Sea* (1937).

James Barke (1905–58), Edward Gaitens (1897–1966) and Guy McCrone (1898–1977)

Among the novels of James Barke, *The Land of the Leal* (1939) tells the epic story of a peasant family's progress through various jobs in nineteenth-century rural Scotland, to finish in Glasgow during the Depression. The book draws on Barke's own background and socialist sympathies to make popular fiction out of social history – full of humour, dialect, and admiration for the indomitable strength of his heroine, Jean Ramsay. This is another novel to recognise the cultural and personal force of strong female characters in Scottish society, an understanding shared by Catherine Carswell, Nan Shepherd, Grassic Gibbon, Naomi Mitchison, Jessie Kesson and Willa Muir. Barke's *Major Operation* (1936), which was also produced as a play, explored the dialectics of labour and capital by placing a union-organiser and a businessman in the same hospital ward. Barke also edited the poems of Burns, and from the late forties he produced five popular novels based on the life of the poet. Alexander McArthur and H. Kingsley Long became famous for their collaboration on *No Mean City* (1935), a lurid semi-documentary novel on slum life and gang-warfare in the Gorbals of the 1920s. Edward Gaitens was born in that once-notorious district and with the support of James Bridie he sought publication for stories based on his life there before the First World War. Some of these were collected as *Growing Up and Other Stories* (1942), and six of them appeared again re-set as chapters of a novel called *Dance of the Apprentices* (1948). These books are notable for handling domestic realism and working-class vitality without the usual pitfalls of melo-drama or sentimentality. By comparison the novels of Guy McCrone belong to a more popular mode of domestic history and family chron-icle. His second novel, *Antimacassar City* (1940), introduced readers to the middle-class Moorhouse family in Victorian Glasgow, and the title indicates something of McCrone's ironic view of the merchant classes with their mixture of philistine gentility, commercial vision and sly self-interest. This was followed by two further instalments, *The Philistines* and *The Puritans,* finally published as the best-selling *Wax Fruit* trilogy in 1947, and then extended by two sequels, *Aunt Bel* (1949) and *The Hayburn Family* (1952). As a talented singer McCrone was deeply interested in opera and as a cousin of James Bridie he became involved in 1943 with the founding and then the running of Glasgow Citizens' Theatre, which was to play such an influential part in modern Scottish drama.

Theatre, plays and playwrights

J. M. Barrie's successes on the London stage did not offer much of a model for the revival of drama in the north, nor were there to be any truly outstanding Scottish playwrights in the early modern period. Nevertheless, new growth did appear in a field that had lain fallow for a long time. Fallow, perhaps, but not unfertile, for in fact there *was* a long-standing and very popular theatrical tradition in Scotland in the form of pantomime and music hall, especially as working-class entertainment in the large cities. These popular roots were rediscovered by directors in the 1970s when theatre companies such as 7:84 and Wildcat married the music hall tradition to the proletarian social realism that had done so well in the twenties. Nevertheless, from the start of the century right up to the 1970s, the prevailing mode in Scottish drama remained a form of realism whose stagecraft would not have been in any way unfamiliar to Ibsen in the 1880s.

Dr John McIntyre ('John Brandane', 1869–1947) and Joe Corrie (1894–1968)

Actually, it was the example of the Irish National Theatre that first stirred theatre lovers north of the Border. If the Abbey Theatre in Dublin had managed to nurture a native Irish drama, might not the same be accomplished in Scotland? The formation of the Glasgow Repertory Theatre in 1909 marked one of the first steps, and, if it lacked a fully Scottish programme, at least it provided a stage for northern actors that lasted until the outbreak of war. In the 1920s Dr John McIntyre ('John Brandane') started the Scottish National Players and wrote their first production, which was a piece called *Glenforsa* (1921), set on a Hebridean island and suffused, rather like Synge's plays, with the rhythms of Gaelic speech. The Scottish National Theatre Society followed and for the next twenty-five years the National Players provided a forum for a succession of writers, including George Blake, George Reston Malloch, Donald Carswell and the plays of Robert Kemp. 'If anything becomes of the Scottish Drama,' wrote Bridie, 'John Brandane is its begetter. He spent more time . . . on raw young

dramatists than he spent on work that might have made him famous.'
Brandane's best known play was *The Glen Is Mine* (1923), set once
again in the Hebrides, where the old ways have to meet with the new
– not without sentiment – while his one-act comedy *Rory Aforesaid*
(1928) is still a regular favourite with amateur companies. Yorkshire-
born Dr Gordon Bottomley was equally committed to theatre in
Scotland and became a leading light in the Community Drama
Association, which started in the thirties. His rather antique verse play
Gruach – a prequel to *Macbeth*, no less – made a hit in 1923 and shared
the bill with *The Glen Is Mine*. In complete contrast, the plays of Joe
Corrie introduced urban domestic realism and political issues to the
National Players' repertoire. Corrie was a coal miner, hailed as 'the
Scottish Zola', who gradually turned to full-time writing, and his best
play, *In Time of Strife* (1928), deals with the fate of a mining family
during the General Strike. He wrote poems too, and dozens of one-act
plays for amateur productions, such as the Bowhill players, later the
fully professional Fife Miner Players – actual miners and their wives
who toured with these productions. Corrie's stylised working-class
speech was a brave new experience on stage in the 1920s, although it
can seem rather stilted when asked to bear the full literary burden of
dramatic description and evocation.

Osborne Henry Mavor, 'James Bridie' (1888–1951) and the Glasgow theatre

Osborne Henry Mavor was a young friend of Brandane's and a fellow
doctor, who joined the board of the Scottish National Theatre Society
in 1923 and played a generous role himself in helping young playwrights, including Neil Gunn. Mavor's interest in writing went back to
his student days at Glasgow, for he had enjoyed them enormously and
taken a long time to graduate. He had served in the Royal Army
Medical Corps (as he did again in the Second World War) and when he
returned to general practice and hospital work he resumed his enthusiasm for the stage as well. Brandane and a brilliant young producer
called Tyrone Guthrie helped Mavor with *The Sunlight Sonata* (written
by 'Mary Henderson') at the Lyric Theatre, Glasgow, in 1928. This
was the first of over forty plays by Mavor, who became much better
known as 'James Bridie' and gave up practising medicine in 1938. He
was a popular and witty character with a droll sense of humour, who
liked to conceal considerable energy and commitment behind a
pretence of laziness and irreverent frivolity. One of the best early plays

and his first London success was *The Anatomist* (1930), a study of the egocentric Dr Knox's involvement with the Burke and Hare body-snatching scandal in Edinburgh in the 1820s. In *Tobias and the Angel* (1930) Bridie's use of colloquial speech and his experience of the Middle East during the First World War help to transform the story in the Apocrypha of an archangel's visitation into a lively comedy of modern attitudes. *A Sleeping Clergyman* (1933) was a more innovative play: it follows the sorry family history of a medical researcher back through three generations in order to refute the suggestion that we are slaves to heredity. The tale is told by means of flashbacks from a chat between medical men in a respectable Glasgow club in the 1930s, but the clergyman of the title – like God, perhaps, in the modern world – sleeps throughout the whole play.

Bridie has a very Shavian delight in the excitement of debate, and his talent for this and for novel conceptions and confrontations on stage helps to make up for the structural imbalances in many pieces. Thus *Mr Bolfry* (1943) – one of his wittiest works – draws on the Scottish penchant for religious dualism and diabolerie to conjure up the Devil on a dull Sunday evening in a Free Kirk manse in the contemporary Highlands. When 'Mr Bolfry' appears, he is dressed like the minister himself and the two engage in a ferocious debate, before the man of God finally suspects that he is confronting an aspect of himself and learns to find strength in simple faith rather than disputation. Bridie's plays were regularly produced in the West End but he kept in touch with the arts in Scotland, helping to establish the Glasgow Citizens' Theatre in 1943 and involving himself with the Edinburgh International Festival, and in particular with the Robert Kemp and Tyrone Guthrie production of Lindsay's *Satire of the Three Estates* in 1948. In 1950, the year before he died, he helped to establish a College of Drama at the Academy of Music in Edinburgh. Bridie's best later plays include a telling study of the hopes and despairs of a middle-aged teacher (*Mr Gillie*, 1950), while *The Queen's Comedy*, from the same year, is set among the gods and mortals assembled around Troy. It is given a modern bias, however, and its satire on war and power is contemporary enough. The author called *The Baikie Charivari* (1952) a 'miracle play', mixing together fantasy and symbolism with the stories of Punch and Judy and Pontius Pilate in a contemporary setting, to make his most experimental work.

Although Bridie was the most notable and successful playwright of his day, there were to be few successors to his style. He founded the Glasgow Citizens' Theatre with the hopes that it would develop into a national theatre and, after a rather sticky start in 1943, it had some success in its second season with plays by John Brandane, Joe Corrie and Bridie himself. It can be argued, however, that the formation of the Unity Theatre in Glasgow in 1946 was more influential, not least because its radical programme was to be picked up again by writers like Bill Bryden and Roddy McMillan (who started his acting career with Unity) and companies such as John McGrath's 7:84 group in the 1970s.

The Unity brought together a number of smaller theatre groups whose 'actors, playwrights and technicians have been drawn from the ranks of ordinary working people, whose background and everyday life is identical with the masses who form its audiences'. And indeed the plays they produced took the lives of 'ordinary working people' for their subject, too, with dramas such as *The Gorbals Story* (1946), a passionate exposé of the city's terrible housing conditions by Robert McLeish (b. 1912), which proved to be one of the company's most successful productions, being frequently revived, and made into a film in 1950. In keeping with the spirit of the Unity group, many of the actors contributed to the development of their characters in *The Gorbals Story* – a method of collective engagement that John McGrath would also adopt in later years. Other working-class dramas from the Unity were *Gold in his Boots* (1947) by George Munro (1901–68), about a young man's hopes to be a professional footballer; and, most notably, the plays of Ena Lamont Stewart (b. 1912), who took a woman's perspective to look at the realities of nursing in *Starched Aprons* (1946), and of working-class domestic life in her best known play, *Men Should Weep* (1947). Stewart summed up much of what the Unity stood for when she recalled what spurred her to write: 'One evening in the winter of 1942 I went to the theatre. I came home in a mood of red-hot revolt against cocktail time, glamorous gowns and underworked, about-to-be-deceived husbands. I asked myself what I wanted to see on the stage and the answer was Life. Real life. Ordinary people.' Set in Glasgow in the 1930s, *Men Should Weep* is literally a kitchen-sink drama dealing with the heavy weight that so many women had to carry at home under the burden of male unemployment and the social, sexual and economic inequalities of the time. The play struck many chords with its audience, not least with women, and went on to make successful tours in Edinburgh and London. It was rather forgotten in later years until successfully revived (in revised form) by the 7:84 company in 1982. Lamont Stewart remained modern Scotland's only female playwright until much more contemporary times.

In keeping with their political commitment to socialism and realism the Unity plays used working-class urban speech with considerable force, but they had little interest in the revival of the Scots language as such. The most prominent names in this endeavour – from the 'second wave' of the literary Renaissance – were Robert McLellan and Alexander Reid. Not surprisingly, historical themes tended to prevail in a drama that sought to use broad Scots, while at the same time the reductive spirit of the language delighted in bringing great men and great events down to earth.

Robert McLellan (1907–85)

Robert McLellan grew up among Scots-speaking farm people in Lanarkshire, and his book *Linmill and Other Stories* (1977) evokes that milieu with considerable linguistic and personal sensitivity. His first play, the one-acter *Jeddart Justice* (1934), was a comedy based on Border feuds in the sixteenth century, as were *The Changeling* (1935) and his first full-length play, *Toom Byres* (1936). His best and most popular work was the 'historical comedy' *Jamie the Saxt* (1937), distinguished by the pace and humour with which it recounts the struggle between the scheming Earl of Bothwell and King James, 'the wisest fool in Christendom' – harried on all sides, weak, wily and finally triumphant. McLellan's Scots is vividly concrete in its idioms, colloquial, versatile and unstrained – the perfect vehicle for a comedy of character and deflation. Such free and vernacular skill is more than a passing delight in McLellan's plays, for it encapsulates a literary tradition and a habit of mind which in themselves make an indirect critique of affairs of state and fallible human beings, however lordly their dress. Other plays followed, including *Torwatletie* (1946) and *The Flouers o Edinburgh* (1948), which are set in the eighteenth century. The latter play deals with the then contemporary question of whether 'gentlemen' should speak Scots or not, and makes great comic play with the affected English of one of the characters. McLellan has three volumes of collected plays to his credit, but he stopped writing for the stage in the 1950s. Given the fluency of his Scots and the importance of its spirit to his meaning, he became understandably depressed at the difficulties that arose in finding enough native actors who could speak it well and theatre managers who would stage the plays. *Jamie the Saxt*, however, has enjoyed frequent revivals, and the late Duncan Macrae is particularly remembered for his brilliance in the leading role, although McLellan disliked the liberties he would take with the script.

Alexander Reid (1914–82) and Robert Kemp (1908–67)

The two Scots comedies of Alexander Reid placed legendary medieval figures in humble settings among the common folk of the Borders. *The Lass wi' the Muckle Mou'* (1950) features Thomas the Rhymer returned from fairyland, while *The Warld's Wonder* (1953) became another hilarious vehicle for Duncan Macrae, as the wizard Michael Scott. It was the skill of actors such as Andrew Keir and Roddy McMillan at the Glasgow Citizens' that first inspired Reid to write in Scots, and he made a sturdy defence of it in the Foreword to the 1958 edition of his plays. Yet, to meet a wider audience, he anglicised the texts of that edition and sadly diluted the spirit of his work. (On the other hand Sydney Goodsir Smith used an entirely stiff and rhetorical Scots for *The Wallace* in 1960, and this tended to make it more of a political pageant than a play.) Robert Kemp also used Scots for his stage and radio drama, while the poet Alexander Scott followed his flair for the language in three rumbustuous verse plays in the 1950s. In more recent years, however, broad Scots has declined in favour of the wit and violence of colloquial urban speech in a notable resurgence of proletarian drama.

The 'second wave' of the Scottish Renaissance

It remains now to turn back to those writers after MacDiarmid, Gibbon, Shepherd and Gunn who made up the 'second wave' of the Renaissance. One man in particular – the poet William Soutar – properly belongs to the first group, but he is included here to re-introduce some of the debates about using Scots that marked the language revival of the time. By the same token the Gaelic poet Sorley MacLean – might be ranked with the first generation, but his poetry did not reach a wider audience until relatively late in his lifetime and so he joins the many fine poets in Scots, English and Gaelic who came to prominence between 1940 and 1960. Quite apart from MacDiarmid's propaganda for a renaissance, the number of writers who achieved a high literary standard in this period speaks for itself.

Poetry in Scots

William Soutar (1898–1943)

Poets were not slow to follow the example of MacDiarmid's early lyrics, as Albert D. Mackie (1904–85) acknowledged in *Poems in Two Tongues*

(1928). Even William Soutar, whose first three collections were all in English and who was not to return to Scots until the 1930s, sent four 'Triolets in the Doric' to be published in *Scottish Chapbook* in 1923. Soutar's health had started to deteriorate during his service in the navy, and when he graduated after the war he had to live at home in Perth because of recurring pain in his feet, legs and back. He turned to private study and writing poetry, influenced by Romantic and Georgian models. Initially opposed to MacDiarmid's polyglot energy (he produced a satire called 'The Thistle Looks at a Drunk Man'), Soutar's nationalist sympathies were aroused and he began to formulate his own theories about making Scots available to children. By 1928 he was writing 'bairn rhymes' for Evelyn, the little girl his parents had adopted, for he was more or less housebound and much in her company. He had contracted a progressive disease of the spine and by 1930 he found himself confined to bed in a ground-floor room that he was not to leave for the rest of his life. His journals and dream-books are a testament to the courage with which he faced a painful fate. Resettling his life around books and visits from friends and fellow writers, he developed an eye for detail and a love of nature from what he could see of the world beyond his window. A selection from his journals was published as *Diaries of a Dying Man* (1954), edited by Alexander Scott and revised and reprinted in 1991. Four further collections of his English poems were published in his lifetime, and his socialist and pacifist beliefs illuminate verses such as 'Beyond Country', 'The Children' and 'The Permanence of the Young Men'. But Soutar is chiefly remembered as a poet in Scots, for he found a colloquial ease, humour and pathos there that escaped the precision of his English work. The first Scots poems were for children, and *Seeds in the Wind: Poems for Children in Scots* (1933) was dedicated to young Evelyn. 'If the Doric is to come back alive,' he wrote to MacDiarmid, 'it will come back on a cock horse,' and he based the rhythms of his animal fables and rhymes on playground chants and dance games. He had discovered the ballads, too, and learned a lot from them, as in 'The Whale', which spins a fantastic tale in ballad stanzas, or 'The Lanely Mune', which catches a moment of uncanny simplicity in only six lines.

Soutar came to believe that it was in the ballads 'that we hear the voice of Scotland most distinctly' and he hoped for a 'new age in which the people shall regain their articulateness and art has an anonymous character'. At times his own ballad poems can seem rather too 'anonymous', but the best of them rediscover the true eerie note, and then add a powerful sense of anguish that never states its personal origin.

'Song' and 'The Tryst' from his second collection of *Poems in Scots* (1935) are rightly famous:

> Whaur yon broken brig hings owre;
> Whaur yon water maks nae soun';
> Babylon blaws by in stour: dust
> Gang doun wi' a sang, gang doun . . .
>   ('Song')

A collection of riddles followed in 1937, but the rest of Soutar's work in Scots comes from manuscripts, which were first published posthumously in an otherwise unsatisfactory *Collected Poems*, edited by MacDiarmid in 1948. He has been better served in more recent editions. The poems in 'Theme and Variation' move away from bairn rhymes to offer a sequence of variations and imitations of English poems and translations from European literature, while the 'Whigmaleeries' contain some of his most humorous verses, such as 'Ae Nicht at Amulree' and 'The Philosophic Taed' – deceptively small pieces infused with an irreverent philosophical glee that refused to submit to his illness. The poet's house in Perth has been kept as he left it and is now a listed building, 'Soutar House', available to writers in residence.

Soutar's example lived after him in the work of J. K. Annand, a teacher whose delightful bairn rhymes are widely used in Scottish schools. *Sing it Aince for Pleisure* first appeared in 1965; two further collections followed suit; and *Poems and Translations* (1975) covers the work of nearly fifty years, going back to his early contacts with MacDiarmid. The Scots of the next poet, however, is far removed from the simpler tongue of Annand and Soutar, or the more colloquial language of his other contemporaries.

Sydney Goodsir Smith (1915–75)

Born in New Zealand of a Scottish mother, Smith did not arrive in Edinburgh – where his father had been appointed professor of Forensic Medicine – until his late teens. After an unsuccessful start as a medical student, he completed his education at Oxford before returning to Auld Reekie, the city he loved and was to celebrate for the rest of his life. *Skail Wind* (1941) contains poems in English and his first awkward verses in Scots, but by the time his third book appeared – *The Deevil's Waltz* (1946) – he had attained a characteristic literary voice. Indeed, he launched himself into the world of the middle-Scots makars as if he had found his own spirit and enthusiastic appetites reflected there. Beginning with obvious debts to Dunbar, Montgomerie and Douglas, Smith created a modern poetry of his own, just as Pound had done with the echoes from his interest in Provençal, Old English and Chinese poets. Smith's vocabulary and his cultural references can be arcane enough, but the energy of his expression becomes increasingly colloquial as the years go by. *The Deevil's Waltz* placed poems to John Maclean alongside a hymn to Venus, while its allusions link Prometheus, Beethoven, Pompeii, Tchaikovsky, Delacroix and the Declaration of Arbroath to the fall of Warsaw and the struggle at El Alamein. The whole war-torn world has become a 'Devil's waltz' in the poet's eyes. The breadth of Smith's references, and the many snatches of different languages that he incorporates into his poetry, give some clue as to what it was that Smith discovered when he chose to write in Scots, a language, after all, that had not been his native tongue. It is the already 'plastic' heteroglossial capacities of Scots, and yet its strong association with the immediacy and fluidity of spoken language, that gave Smith permission to produce such extraordinarily polyphonic, multi-voiced verses.

Most of Smith's best poetry was written in the post-war period, although his main collections did not appear until the fifties, with *So Late into the Night* (1952) and *Figs and Thistles* (1959). At the heart of his work at this time there are two outstanding books. The first is *Carotid Cornucopius* (1947), a prose extravaganza that reads as if Sir Thomas Urquhart had persuaded Rabelais to describe the joys of drink and fornication in Edinburgh after the style of *Finnegans Wake*. Begun in 1945 – 'Anno Dambomini' – it is an ultimately exhausting tour de force of scatological and creative etymology, with the author himself – known as 'the Auk' to his friends – as the thinly disguised hero of the title page:

> Caird of the Cannon Gait and Voyeur of the Outlook Touer, his splores, cantraips, wisdoms, houghmagandies, peribibulatiouns and all kinna abstrapulous junketings and ongoings abowt the high toun of Edenberg, capitula of Boney Scotland.
> A drammantick, backside, bogbide, bedride or badside buik . . .

Smith's undoubted masterpiece, however, is *Under the Eildon Tree* (1948), a linked series of twenty-four love-poems, meditations, satires and elegies, and the only other long Scots poem of the movement to match *A Drunk Man*. By now his poetry, and his life too, had come to celebrate a Villonesque vision of man's fate, with himself cast as a bard

at the mercy of love and drink, swinging between exaltation and fornication as if to drive home the glorious fallibility of a human condition
utterly opposed to Presbyterian respectability, material possession and
industrial progress. His setting was Auld Reekie in the spirit of
Fergusson, except that for Smith it becomes a timeless place where
Diana and Eurydice haunt the streets along with Bothwell and Huntly
and 'fair Montrose and a the lave / Wi silken leddies doun til the grave'
– not to forget sixteen-year-old 'Sandra', picked up in a pub, 'drinkan
like a bluidie whaul' with her 'wee paps, round and ticht and fou / Like
sweet Pomona in the oranger grove' (xiii: 'The Black Bull o
Norroway').

This ribald, goliardic spirit is constantly qualified by the poet's sense
of that moment when all the merry music 'turns to sleep' and 'The
endmaist ultimate white silence faas / Frae whilk for bards is nae
retour' (i: 'Bards Hae Sung'). In the meantime, as he sees it, there is
only love, whose spiritual or carnal delights bind us to our physical
natures and undermine the 'serious' world of politics and public affairs.
Yet even so, in post-coital sadness or romantic partings, the ties of love
bring us to a sense of death again. Hence the title of the poem
sequence refers to Thomas the Rhymer's eerie encounter with the
Queen of Elfland, and Smith's elegies reflect on the unhappy fates of
Burns's Highland Mary, Orpheus, Cuchulainn, Dido, Tristram, and
Antony. Elegy xii, for Orpheus, is a particularly fine example of the
poet's capacity to move between mockery, pain, rage and tenderness in
the space of a few lines. Such pace is reminiscent of the 'jostling of
contraries' in MacDiarmid's *Drunk Man*, but Smith has more confidence in handling free verse in Scots and a Poundian breadth of reference:

– Euridicie stummelt.	stumbled
(Lauchter cracked abune, Jupiter leuch;	above; laughed
– And richtlie sae!	
Och, gie the gods their due,	
They ken what they're about.	
– The sleekans!)	crafty ones

She stummelt. I heard her cry. And hert ruled heid again.
    – What hert could eer refuse, then, siccan a plea?   such a
        I turned –
            And wi neer a word,
                    In silence,
Her een aye, bricht wi the joy o' resurrectioun,
She soomed awa afore my een intil a skimmeran wraith

And for a second and last time was tint for aye   lost
Amang the gloams and haars o Hell   shadows and mist
  – Throu my ain twafauld treacherie!

'Quhar art thou gane, my luf Euridices!'

iv

Sinsyne I haena plucked a note   Since then
  Nor made a word o a sang . . .

The same dramatic and technical confidence appeared in *Figs and Thistles* in the unlikely form of a poem written 'To Li Po . . . in memoriam Robert Fergusson', and in 'The Twal', which is the liveliest available translation of Alexander Blok's long visionary poem in which the dispossessed of the earth drive towards revolution through the snowstorm of history with Christ in the lead. The play *The Wallace* (1960), however, was less successful and *Kynd Kittock's Land* (1965), written for television, and *Gowdspink in Reekie* (1974) were longer poems that covered already familiar ground without refreshing it. Smith also wrote for radio and edited a number of Scottish literary texts. Among his last poems there are several fine lyrics as well as 'Three', 'The Riggins of Chelsea' and 'Spring in the Botanic Gardens', which recaptured the ironical swagger and the brave melancholy of a generous, comic and genuinely anarchic spirit who chose to live like someone reincarnated from the vulgar and scholarly howffs of eighteenth-century Edinburgh.

Douglas Young (1913–73)

More scholarly still, and almost as unconventional, Douglas Young was one of several of the new makars (including Smith) who met in Edinburgh in 1947 to formulate rules for the spelling of modern literary Scots. (Their recommendations were well intended, but poets soon went their own way again.) A polyglot enthusiast and Oxford scholar, Young taught classics at the universities of Aberdeen, Dundee and St Andrews before accepting a chair in North America in 1968. Over six feet tall, with a large black beard, he was a notably extrovert figure in Scottish Nationalist circles, and during the war he refused conscription from any but a Scottish government on a point of law going back to what he took to be broken terms in the Treaty of Union. This was legally subtle and even true perhaps, but unlikely to be received with much sympathy while the Luftwaffe were bombing Clydeside, and he duly served a term in prison. (He said his incarceration was not unlike a return to his old public school at Merchiston Castle.) Young produced two volumes of his own poems in the mid-forties and, although his Scots is not always smooth, it included verses taken from Russian, German, French, Italian and Latin originals, as well as translations of Gaelic poems by Sorley MacLean and George Campbell Hay. Young played a very important role in the early renaissance by bringing people together in this way and infecting them with his own enthusiasm for European culture. In particular he presided over the friendship between MacLean and Hugh MacDiarmid, helped MacLean publish his first collection, and was a friend and confidant to George Campbell Hay. Young's own *Selected Poems* appeared in 1950, while *The Puddocks* (1957) and *The Burdies* (1959) were Scots versions of the comedies by Aristophanes: a merging of the colloquial and the classical on stage that Liz Lochhead and Edwin Morgan were to return to twenty years later. Young gave a lively account of his classical travels and his political and cultural commitments in the autobiographical *Chasing an Ancient Greek* (1950).

Robert Garioch (1909–81)

A quieter and more retiring personality than his friend the Auk, Robert Garioch Sutherland had family roots in the North-East but graduated from the University of Edinburgh with a degree in English to spend the next thirty years as a schoolteacher – unhappy with the drudgery of the task and the constant need to keep discipline. He first appeared on the literary scene in 1933, with a column in the *Scots Observer* and 'The Masque of Edinburgh' – a satirical scenario of life in his native city, complete with famous figures from past and present. (An expanded version was published in 1954.) Garioch (he rarely used his last name) committed himself to his main subject and to what he called 'artisan Scots' from the very start, and declared in 'The Masque' that 'a man who'd write in Edinboro / maun seek his language in a pub'. It was to be many years, however, before he found a publisher for his work, and his first two slim pamphlets were printed by himself. During the war Garioch served in the Royal Signals and was captured in North Africa in 1942. His prose memoir *Two Men and a Blanket* (1975) gives an anti-heroic account of his time as a prisoner of war in Italy and Germany, cold, bored and obsessed with food, like all the other prisoners. When peace came, he lived in London for thirteen years before returning to Edinburgh. Thenceforth Garioch adopted the position of a sceptical bystander in all his poetry. He felt a strong affinity with

Robert Fergusson's outcast fate, making his own tribute to him in the fine sonnet 'At Robert Fergusson's Grave' and imitating his manner in a light-hearted satire on the Edinburgh Festival, called 'Embro to the Ploy'.

Garioch had a wholly scholarly grasp of literature, for he translated George Buchanan's *Jephthah* and *The Baptist* from Latin into Scots in 1959, as well as poems from Apollinaire and many sonnets from the nineteenth-century Roman dialect of Giuseppe Belli. Nevertheless, the most frequent voice in his own poetry is that of the disaffected common man. Thus a brilliant sequence of 'Saxteen Edinburgh Sonnets' deflates the Athens of the North and its International Festival by describing it from the sidelines:

Some dignitaries in the cawrs, gey posh	cars
in queer, auld-farrant uniforms, were haean	old-fashioned; having
a rare auld time, it looked a lot of tosh	
to me, a beadle of some sort displayin	
frae ilk front sait a muckle siller cosh:	each; seat; great silver
shame on them aa, whativer they were daean!	doing
('Queer Ongauns')	

If the speaker in 'Heard in the Gairdens' is newly unemployed, he is also free at last, for 'nae gaffer, boss nor beak / can touch me ferder . . . And nou I drop my guaird, / bide still in my ain neuk, lift up my heid'. The poet's own experience as a schoolteacher is never very far away in these and other pieces, and the comedy of 'Sisyphus' shows the teacher as a man who actually *chooses* the pointless labour of heaving boulders endlessly up a hill, simply for the sake of job security – 'shair of his cheque at the month's end'. 'Repone til George Buchanan' warns any would-be poets to avoid a profession in which 'ilka weekend, month and year / his life is tined [lost] in endless steir, / grindan awa in second gear'.

At such moments there is a hint of rage and pain beyond the light comedy, and if a belief in God, work and education lies at the heart of the Scottish Presbyterian ethos, then many of Garioch's verses are quietly but profoundly subversive. 'A! Fredome is a noble thing!' quotes 'The Canny Hen', but then she adds 'and kinna scarce, to tell the truth, / for naebody has muckle rowth [much to spare] / of fredome gin [if] he warks for wages'. Another thoughtful bird, 'The Percipient Swan', has 'ideas and notions and aibstract conceptions', but is still condemned to swim round and round in its pond because its wings have been clipped by the town council 'to keep me good':

soumin roun
like a mous in a well,
glowred at by ratepayers
bored like masel.   myself

In poems such as these, Henryson's beast fables and the romantic debasement of Baudelaire's 'Le Cygne' have been redefined in typical Garioch fashion. Yet even while going through the motions 'laid doun for me / by the Parks Committee', the bird plans a 'swan-song' that 'sall rhyme the end / of your hale stupid faction'.

In the same vein, 'Brither Worm' describes the stone slabs of the New Town, whose neoclassical squares and crescents are the epitome of property and propriety; yet here the poet finds a stray worm, a messenger of lowly roots from another world:

I was abaysit wi thochts of what was gaun-on ablow my feet,
that the feued and rented grund was the soil of the naitural Drumsheuch
   Forest,
and that life gaed on thair in yon soil, and had sent out a spy . . .

The realisation brings him to philosophise on the wonders of Nature and 'the deeps of the soil, deeper nor the sea' until the mood is broken by the sudden arrival of a rat – one of nature's other faces – 'he leukit at me, and wes gane'.

Robert Garioch was very popular in public readings on the strength of his gently comic personality, and so the subversive nature of his humour and the darker vision that lies beneath it has often been under-estimated by his many admirers. His long poem 'The Wire', for example, offers a nightmare allegory of entrapment and death on some vast moor, perhaps a Scottish grouse moor, where the heather, blae-berries and gossamer spider webs are overtaken by barbed wire and guard towers – images from his own imprisonment during the war, and more clearly universal ever since. 'The Muir' is a more ambitious attempt to write a discursive verse in Scots which can describe relativity, atomic physics, gravity and light, but Garioch's final mastery of free verse in Scots came with the longer poems from slightly later in his career. Verses such as his translations from Apollinaire, or 'Lesson' or 'The Big Music', are effectively weighty but still colloquial, with his own unique voice balanced between sober judgement and a kind of sadness at what he sees as all the small limitations of life and art. 'The Big Music' (an English translation of the Gaelic *Ceòl Mhor*) describes a piping competition being held in a draughty drill hall in London:

The piobaireachd comes til an end, gin we my cry it end,
the grund naukit again, as tho it had aye been sae.   naked
Gin it werenae a competition, wi international rules,
there seems nae reason why it sudnae stert owre again,
gin the piper has braith eneuch, and there's nae dout about that,
but he neatly thraws the thrapple of the deil in his pipes,   rings the throat
that dees decently, wi nae unseemly scrauch.
He taks leave of us wi dignity, turns, and is gane.
The judges rate him heich, but no in the first three.

('The Big Music)

The last line may have been a wryly elliptical comment on his own poetic reputation, but if so, he was unnecessarily modest.

Alexander Scott (1920–89)

The poetry of Alexander Scott is equally colloquial – he grew up speaking Scots in his native Aberdeen – but his own bold and vigorous nature, and a preference for alliterative effects, gives his work a rough-hewn formality – a paradoxical combination which suits his resolutely physical and anti-sentimental stance. This began with an early translation of the Anglo-Saxon 'Seafarer' and it characterises poems such as 'Haar in Princes Street' and 'Heart of Stone', a notable long poem on his native city. Scott championed Lallans and the teaching of Scots throughout his long career at the Department of Scottish Literature at Glasgow University, and as a well-known critic and editor his opinions were as forthright as his verse. His own writing in both English and Scots had remained consistent ever since *The Latest in Elegies* appeared in 1949, but his best work is in Scots. Poems such as 'Dear Deid Dancer' and 'To Mourn Jayne Mansfield', from *Cantrips* (1968), show his extrovert and sometimes cruelly sardonic outlook – 'Cauld is thon corp that fleered sae muckle heat, / Thae Babylon breists. . . .' Yet he shows a kind of brutal sympathy for the fate of such 'beautiful people', as if his real topic were to rage against mortality itself – a theme first raised in 'Coronach', a fine poem for the dead of the Gordon Highlanders with whom he served in the war. His *Collected Poems* were published in 1994.

Tom Scott (1918–95)

The earliest poems of Tom Scott were in English after the style of the New Apocalypse, which brought him into contact with Dylan Thomas and W. S. Graham. He came to write Scots in the 1950s, especially as a mature student at Newbattle Abbey (under Edwin Muir) and later at the University of Edinburgh. His work reflects his scholarly involvement with the European cultural world of Villon, Dante and especially Dunbar – the subject of a book by him published in 1966. Scott's *Seevin Poems o Maister Francis Villon* (1953) manage an effective balance between the colloquial and a sense of the originals' medieval nature. In *The Ship and Ither Poems* (1963) he produced verses on Ahab, Orpheus, Adam and Ulysses ('Ithaka'), all of which pursue the theme of freedom and renewal through pain and worldly experience. As a poet and a self-styled 'old fashioned utopian socialist' Scott deplored the egocentricity of modern so-called confessional verse and argued for the older and more culturally stable literary forms of allegory and epic. Thus 'The Ship' is a long symbolic piece on the plight of our materialistic culture, using the Titanic as the model for a modern ship of fools. His didactic impulse and the poetic problems of describing actions and speech eventually overburden the poem, but Scott persevered with what he called 'symphonic verse' in *The Tree* (1977). The moments of excitement in this massive verse meditation on evolution do not offset duller pages of scientific and moral philosophising in English, and much the same is true of his long anti-war poem *This Dirty Business* (1986). Nevertheless, Scott was determined to produce what he called a poetry of 'polysemous veritism' after the example of the later poems of MacDiarmid and John Davidson, and he did this with a lonely and acerbic integrity, at odds with academic criticism and often frustrated by what he took to be a lack of recognition, rather like his friend Fionn Mac Colla. Most critics have preferred the colloquial Scots in 'Brand the Builder', from a series of St Andrew's studies that he began in the 1950s.

Alastair Mackie (1925–95)

The publication of *Clytach* (1972) and *Back-Green Odyssey and Other Poems* (1980) came relatively late in life for Alastair Mackie but they show a sensitive use of conversationally unforced Scots in his wry and humane reflections on family history, the nature of parenthood and middle age, or nostalgia for a boyhood in Aberdeen. His sequence *At the Heich Kirk-Yaird* (1974) uses a highland journey to reflect on the balance between the personal and the national landscapes, while *Ingaitherins: Selected Poems* (1987) was produced after he retired from teaching in 1983. Mackie's work makes the ordinary world new again with a plain dignity and a craft free from sentiment or bombast:

Inside us we maun hae a clock that tells
the cheenge o season to oor haill body,
hair-thin its motions and aa but hidden
as now when the first sma whirrs
inside the blood begin, till the 'oor striks
and Aatumn is the time your body tells.
                        ('At the Heich Kirk-Yaird 12')

The Scots pronunciation of the season in the last line can also sound
like 'aa toom' – all empty.

Duncan Glen (b. 1933)

Duncan Glen seeks a similar end with a low-key Scots in deliberately
prosaic and transparent lines, at its best in the poems of personal recollection from *In Appearances* (1971) and *Realities* (1980) and the
Selected Poems, 1965–1990 (1991) or *Selected New Poems, 1987–1996*
(1998). Glen founded and edited the poetry magazine *Akros* from
1965 to 1983, and through many books from the Akros Press and his
extensive work on Hugh MacDiarmid he has made a direct and invaluable contribution to Scottish letters for over thirty years. Glen worked
all his life in typography and graphic design in colleges and universities
in England, and so his Akros books were mostly published from
Preston in Lancashire and many young poets owe their first publication
to this imprint and to Glen's unfailing commitment to writing in Scots.
He himself has produced dozens of small volumes of poetry, often in
the form of poem sequences, whose loose structure follows the turns
of his own thought: 'A twistit road. / Again I face the white sheet of
paper, / the pathless wey upwards / and think o surface and symbol'
('Frae Heich Touer'). He gives an account of these years and his own
ambitions in *The Autobiography of a Poet* (1986).

William Neill (b. 1922)

A more fiery exponent of Scots, English and Gaelic verse is William
Neill, a poet motivated by a strong sense of Scottish political and
cultural identity, who taught himself Gaelic and turned his considerable
technical skill and a scathing, fleering wit in Scots to defend the cause.
His main collections include *Despatches Home* (1972), *Making Tracks
and Other Poems* (1988), *Straight Lines* (1992) with a *Selected Poems*
published in 1994. Neill continues what is by now the well established

tradition set by Alexander Gray, Douglas Young, Robert Garioch, Tom Scott, Alex Scott *et al.* of translating European texts into Scots. (Duncan Glen and Peter France edited an anthology of just such translations, *European Poetry in Scotland*, in 1989.)

Robert Garioch's move towards the use of a looser and more colloquial form of Scots in poetry, followed by Alexander Scott, Neill, and especially Glen and Mackie, would prove to be the literary norm in the years to come, at least until the new and academically inspired generation of Crawford and Herbert, who deliberately returned to the dictionary density of early MacDiarmid.

Poetry in English

The works of Linklater, Gunn, Muir, Goodsir Smith and Sorley MacLean all testify to the fact that the 1940s were a productive period, despite the exigencies of war, and many new poets writing in English made their mark during these years. Figures such as J. F. Hendry, Maurice Lindsay, G. S. Fraser and Norman MacCaig had all had early contacts with the 'New Apocalypse' movement in the south. The very early work of George Mackay Brown – when he was still at Newbattle Abbey – also shared something of that movement's sense of the world as a physically animate and energised realm of almost hallucinatory intensity – an intensity that poetic language would have to struggle to describe. The work of these poets also featured in *Poetry Scotland* – an influential set of magazine-format anthologies founded and edited by Maurice Lindsay over four issues between 1943 and 1949. Also included in these volumes were poems by William Soutar, MacDiarmid, Muir, MacLean, Alexander Scott, George Bruce and Douglas Young. The *Poetry Scotland* series was published by William MacLellan, whose fine press produced some of the best poetry books of the period. MacLellan also published five issues of *Scottish Art and Letters* from 1945 to 1950, edited by R. Crombie Saunders and the painter J. D. Fergusson. Among the other poets whose works appeared in the MacLellan volumes were William Jeffrey (1896–1946) and R. Crombie Saunders (1914–91), both of whom wrote in Scots as well, and Joseph Macleod ('Adam Drinan', 1903–84), who worked in theatre and wrote poems for broadcasting before retiring to live in Florence. Ruthven Todd (1914–78) was educated in Scotland and spent the war years in London before moving to America where he wrote adventure novels and edited the work of William Blake. Many of his verses reflect toughly or tenderly on his own northern inheritance and the Scottish landscape. Like Todd and Macleod, William Montgomerie (1904–94) spent many years abroad, and he and his wife Norah followed Soutar's lead by collecting and editing Scottish nursery rhymes (1946) and *Sandy Candy* (1948). Norman Cameron (1905–53) lived mostly abroad and in London, and he is especially remembered for his poems on the war in the desert.

Hamish Henderson (1919–2002)

The same campaign gave Hamish Henderson his best and most remarkable book of verse, which was granted the Somerset Maugham award. *Elegies for the Dead in Cyrenaica* (1948) was based on his service in the desert with the Highland Division. As an intelligence officer he played a role in the subsequent invasion of Italy, and his love for the country and his socialist convictions later led him to translate Antonio Gramsci's *Letters from Prison*. The *Elegies* offer an effective documentary picture, poetic and sometimes rhetorical, of the desert war, but Henderson takes in a larger perspective too. In his Foreword he notes how frequently vehicles would change hands in the 'deceptive distances' of the desert, and how the landscape and dust seemed to turn their enemies into mirror images of themselves. Thus he sees the ordinary soldiers of both sides united in death, and united against death – a metaphysical and egalitarian theme for which he uses colloquial slang as well as more austere passages coloured by Gaelic speech patterns:

> There were our own, there were the others.
> Therefore, minding the great word of Glencoe's
> son, that we should not disfigure ourselves
> with villainy of hatred; and seeing that all
> have gone down like curs into anonymous silence,
> I will bear witness for I knew the others.
> Seeing that littoral and interior are alike indifferent
> and the birds are drawn again to our welcoming north
> why should I not sing *them*, the dead, the innocent?
> (First Elegy, 'End of a Campaign')

Henderson joined the School of Scottish Studies in 1951 as a researcher and became widely known and respected among traditional musicians. One of his mentors at the school was Calum MacLean (1915–60), brother of the poet and a distinguished ethnologist and folk-life scholar. Henderson gained a permanent post in the School in 1954 and has entered the tradition with his own songs, such as the wartime 'Ballad of the D-Day Dodgers', 'The Banks o Sicily', 'The Freedom Come All Ye', 'The John Maclean March' and 'Free Mandela'. Henderson was accepted and moved freely among the Travellers in the North-East of Scotland and the berry-pickers of Blairgowrie (his birthplace), recognising that it was they who were keeping the old ballad traditions alive. (He had served an early apprenticeship with Alan Lomax when Lomax visited Scotland with a primitive recording machine in 1951.) Henderson is credited with bringing the work of Jeannie Robertson, one of the finest tradition bearers and singers, to a wider audience and is often cited as the father of the folksong revival in Scotland in the great enthusiasm for traditional music that sprang up from the 1950s to the 1970s. His own 'Writings on Song, Folk and Literature' were published as *Alias MacAlias* in 1992, which includes memoirs of war service and his horror when he saw what Allied bombers had done to Berlin, a city he knew from before the war. The *Collected Poems and Songs* were published in 2000, while *The Armstrong Nose* (1996), a selection of his letters from the 1940s to the 1990s, speaks for an extraordinarily rich and lively life, reprinting the details of his hilarious public flyting match with MacDiarmid in the 1960s over the latter's contempt for what he could only see as 'the boring doggerel of analphabetic and ineducable farm labourers, tinkers and the like'. Henderson saw something else. His care for folksong, like his lifelong socialism, was based on his preference for the underdog (not that he would have seen it in those terms) for he was on the side of minority dialects and languages, just as Gramsci had supported Sardinian against Italian, and again like Gramsci, he saw the folk tradition as something more vital than mainstream culture and forever opposed to 'official society'. Henderson turned down an OBE from the Thatcher government in 1983 and was impolite enough to say so in public. Morris Blythman ('Thurso Berwick', 1919–82) belongs to the same radical tradition, with songs such as 'The Scottish Breakaway', though his roots as a writer go back to the socialism of Glasgow in the thirties. The performative and challenging power in the voice of a contemporary folk-singer such as Dick Gaughan comes from the same vein and owes much to the example and the enthusiastic research of Henderson.

J. F. Hendry (1912–86) and G. S. Fraser (1915–80)

The short-lived Apocalypse movement reacted against overtly political commitment by following a programme of much more inward-looking, symbolic or surrealistic verse. One of the leading lights of this movement, along with Henry Treece and G. S. Fraser (their theorist) was J. F. Hendry (1912–86), who co-edited all three Apocalypse anthologies. His novel *Fernie Brae* (1947) describes life in Glasgow and the west from his own childhood, but his verse has a much more abstract and intellectual style, with staccato lines and a crystalline coolness, especially in the visionary title-poem, called a 'polar sonata', in *Marimarusa* (1978). G. S. Fraser (1915–80) was born in Glasgow and educated in Aberdeen, but after the war he spent most of his time in England working as a freelance journalist, a critic and then a lecturer at Leicester. His own verse had never been truly Apocalyptic and, indeed, he became an influential figure with the 'Movement' poets in London in the fifties. Some of his best early poems took the form of 'letters home' during the war, which he spent in the Middle East ('A Winter Letter'), and this mode continued to suit his relaxed, civilised and wryly self-deprecating verse. He admired the selfless mildness of Edwin Muir's poetry, but mental tensions of his own gave new urgency to the work of the late sixties – 'Speech of a Sufferer', 'The Insane Philosophers'. Fraser never truly lost his gently sceptical neoclassical balance, however, as can be seen in *Poems of G. S. Fraser* (1981), which reprints all four of his earlier collections.

Norman MacCaig (1910–96)

Although this poet wrote his first two collections in the Apocalyptic vein – *A Far Cry* (1943) and *The Inward Eye* (1946) – he took particular care to disown them in later years, having come to value clarity, compassion and a certain humane elegance of the mind above all else – fitting qualities for a Classics graduate of Edinburgh University. His refusal to take or to aid the taking of life made him a conscientious objector during the war and he served a spell in prison for his belief before being released to do work that did not support military aims. He was phlegmatic about the experience, and never wavered in his conviction that the taking of human life was utterly abhorrent. He worked as a primary school teacher and lived in Edinburgh all his life, becoming the first writer in residence at the university there in 1967. Three years later he joined the English Department at the University of Stirling, subsequently becoming Reader in Poetry until his retirement in 1978. He was a friend of Goodsir Smith's and became a well-known and gregarious figure in Edinburgh circles, along with the other 'second generation' writers in the 1950s, including Tom Scott, George

Mackay Brown, Sorley MacLean and Robert Garioch, many of whom frequented various bars in Rose Street, especially Milne's Bar, where the walls are now crowded with their fading photographs. MacCaig developed a close relationship with Hugh MacDiarmid in the older poet's later years, although they enjoyed vigorous disagreements about politics, the use of Scots and the future of the lyric, which MacDiarmid claimed was dead – at least since he stopped writing them himself. MacCaig nevertheless remained true to his lyric impulse, and true to his deep suspicion of all forms of artistic and political dogma: 'Watch him when he opens / his bulging words – justice, / fraternity, freedom, internationalism, peace, peace, peace. / . . . Nobody with such luggage / has nothing to declare' (Smuggler').

Greatly in demand at public poetry-readings, MacCaig produced a book every one or two years, from *Riding Lights* in 1955 to the ominously titled *Voice-Over* in 1988 and the revised *Collected Poems* of 1990, with a further edition of his poems in chronological order of composition in 2005. MacCaig's poetry grows from the delight with which he greets the world, but the images that he creates to describe people, animals and landscapes also reflect back on language and his own observing mind. So MacCaig is never simply a 'nature' poet, and his preference for linking precise observation with creative wit can be seen from the very start in an early poem, 'Summer Farm': 'A hen stares at nothing with one eye, / Then picks it up.' But he recognises that this is a perception which depends on his own eye too, as if he could lift the farm 'like a lid and see / Farm within farm, and in the centre, me'.

Despite his long career in Edinburgh, the spiritual fulcrum of MacCaig's work is to be found in Assynt, where he retreated from the city to spend every summer with his wife in a tiny cottage at Achmelvich to the north-west of Lochinver. 'Return to Scalpay' (on the island of Harris where his Gaelic-speaking mother was born) affirms his deep love for the people and the landscapes of the North-West, from where he derived the gaiety, the penetrating understatement and the wry modesty that characterises his work. It recognises, too, as does the poem 'Aunt Julia' and many others in similar vein, that there is a value in such communities that is often lost or undervalued in modern life:

> . . . half my blood and half my thought is Scalpay,
> against that pure, hardheaded innocence
> that shows love without shame, weeps without shame,
> whose every thought is hospitality –
> Edinburgh, Edinburgh, you're dark years away.

MacCaig's work came to full maturity of expression and technique with his move to free verse in the mid-sixties (*Surroundings*, 1966) and in a succession of poems over the years he delighted readers with his deftness in creating likenesses which seem just so, but were never there before – frogs die on the roads 'with arms across their chests . . . like Italian tenors' ('Frogs'), or a toad is told to 'stop looking like a purse' ('Toad'). In such a world the poet has cultivated his capacity for surprise ('Country Dance') or even sudden terror ('Basking Shark'), while a quiet rage at the fact of human suffering is found in 'Assisi', one of several poems that take issue with God, and the platitudes that are uttered in His name. Nevertheless, the reflective-reflexive habit of mind is not an unmixed blessing, and in other poems MacCaig has explored the more awkward implications of the relationship between himself, language and other people. 'A Man in My Position' ponders simply stated but disturbing questions about subjectivity and the nature of texts ('hear my words carefully. / Some are spoken / not by me, but / by a man in my position') that are all the more unsettling because the poem presents itself as a love poem. While 'Private' recognises that there is a popular poet and a 'comfortable MacCaig whose / small predictions were predictable', hiding 'ugly wounds' under the 'clean white bandages' of language. 'Equilibrist' tells how the radio can be switched from tortures in foreign prisons 'to a sonata of Schubert (that foreigner)' and the poet draws his own conclusions from the juxtaposition with typical reserve: 'Noticing you can do nothing about. / It's the balancing that shakes my mind'. Since, as a self-declared atheist he does not accede to Christian or political dogma of any kind, he has to achieve that balance on his own, just as he had to reconcile himself to the death of MacDiarmid and to that of his close friend A. K. Macleod from Inverkirkaig. That effort led to a collection called *The Equal Skies* (1980), which contains some of his most moving and finely controlled poems in the elegiac sequence 'Poems for Angus'. Thus the poem 'A month after his death' says something – beyond personal mourning – about MacCaig's understanding of all human life:

Out there are the dregs of history. Out there
mindlessness lashes the sea against the sea-wall:
and a bird flies screaming over the roof.

We laugh and we sing, but we all know we are thinking
of the one who isn't here.

The laughter and the singing are paper flowers
laid in a wet grave in an empty darkness.

Never an overtly political poet, MacCaig's care for the people of the Highlands and his own Gaelic ancestry nevertheless led him to write a number of poems about what depopulation and less than sympathetic landowners had done to the North-West. 'Two thieves' meditates on the Clearances and on the cultural losses that leave Gaelic place names bereft of meaning, while 'Old Sarah' and 'That Journey' reflect on an ageing population and a fading culture, and the uncharacteristically long poem 'A Man in Assynt' (written for a TV film of that remote and beautiful region) asks a number of telling questions:

> Who owns this landscape? –
> The millionaire who bought it or
> the poacher staggering downhill on the early morning
> with a deer on his back?
>
> Who possesses this landscape? –
> The man who bought it or
> I who am possessed by it?

MacCaig's later poems, especially those in his last collection *Voice-Over*, return to these darker reflections on meaning and the purpose of art as he deals with the death of friends and the illness and death of his wife Isabel. But that sense of potential loss had always been there in his work and indeed it is the chief source of the constant joy he took in observing the minutiae of the everyday world in poem after poem, in a celebration of how art combats transience throughout a long and distinguished creative career: 'A tattery rosebush at a road corner / makes jubilant / a surly morning' ('A sort of physics'); 'A butterfly crazy with wings, / is trying to go in every direction / at once' ('Seen in the City'); 'The ten minutes are up, except they aren't. / I leave the village, except I don't. / The jig fades to silence, except it doesn't' ('Notations of ten summer minutes').

W. S. Graham (1918–86)

A more theoretical involvement with the problems of creative language can be found in the poetry of W. S. Graham, a Greenock man who lived in Cornwall for much of his adult life. As a friend of Dylan Thomas and George Barker, Graham showed affinities with the Apocalyptic writers in his early work, although verses such as 'The Children of Greenock' are more autobiographical, if still characteristically energised in the 'apocalyptic' manner as he remembers 'a high tenement at Spring's sill / Over the street and chalked lawland / Peevered and lined and fancy-manned // On a pavement shouting games and faces.' Graham made his reputation with *The Nightfishing* (1955), a long poem that makes fishing and the sea (which features in much of his work) a symbol for the creative process. (Like MacCaig, he is ever alert to the physicality of the moment and the formal trickiness of trying to catch it.) The poem has vivid passages of action at sea – worthy of the Anglo-Saxon *Seafarer*, or of MacMhaighstir Alasdair's *Birlinn Chlann Raghnaill*; and it also has moments of more abstract reflection – in beautifully realised free verse – on what makes us what we are:

Within all the dead of
All my life I hear
My name spoken out
On the break of the surf.
I, in Time's grace,
The grace of change, am
Cast into memory.
What a restless grace
To trace stillness on.

The making of poetry and the nature of language itself have been consistent themes in Graham's work ever since. Thus the cerebral wit of 'Malcolm Mooney's Land' associated the awful spaces of arctic exploration with the terrifying whiteness (for a writer) of blank paper, and 'The Dark Dialogues' brought this more abstract concern with the place 'where I am, between / This word and the next' into closer touch with his childhood in Greenock:

This is no other place
Than where I am, between
This word and the next.
Maybe I should expect
To find myself only
Saying that again
Here now at the end.
Yet over the great
Gantries and cantilevers
Of love, a sky, real and
Particular is slowly
Startled into light.

This welcome biographical directness returns in such fine poems as 'Loch Thom' and 'To Alexander Graham', from *Implements in their Places* (1977). In the same collection 'Joachim Quantz's Five Lessons' uses a well-realised historical setting and a musical metaphor to consider the disciplines of art and (indirectly) his own position as author, ours as readers, and the altogether peculiar nature of poetry:

> So that each person may quickly find that
> Which particularly concerns him, certain metaphors
> Convenient to us within the compass of this
> Lesson are to be allowed. It is best I sit
> Here where I am to speak on the other side
> Of language. You, of course, in your own time
> And incident (I speak in the small hours)
> Will listen from your side.
>
> ('The First Lesson')

Graham's work in this vein is strikingly prophetic of the insights offered by writers such Roland Barthes in post-structuralist critical theory, but his poetry is driven first and foremost by a deeply personal need to communicate at a level of linguistic honesty, integrity and urgency that is more than merely theoretical but yet has nothing at all in common with the 1960s vogue for 'confessional' verse. Graham reintroduces 'Malcolm Mooney' to ask 'What is the Language Using Us For?' in a witty sequence on the elusive, illusive, nature of syntax and sentences.

> What is the language using us for?
> From the prevailing weather of words
> Each object hides in a metaphor.
>
> This is the morning. I am out
> On a kind of Vlaminck blue-rutted   [a Fauvist painter]
> Road. Willie Wagtail is about.
>
> In from the West a fine smirr
> Of rain drifts across the hedge.
> I am only out here to walk or
>
> Make this poem up. The hill is
> A shining blue macadam top.
> I lean my back to the telegraph pole
>
> And the messages hum through my spine.

Supported by T. S. Eliot in his early years and perhaps better appreciated by American critics than readers closer to home, Graham has a spare and elliptical beauty of voice that has produced very fine late modernist verse whose concerns are still strikingly contemporary:

> This morning I am ready if you are,

To hear you speaking in your new language.
I think I am beginning to have nearly
A way of writing down what it is I think
You say. You enunciate very clearly
Terrible words always just beyond me.
                    ('A Note to the Difficult One')

James Hyman Singer, 'Burns Singer' (1928–64)

A less well-known poet, with as fine an ear, was James Hyman Singer ('Burns Singer'), who was born in New York of a second generation Polish Jewish father (himself born in Manchester) and a Scottish mother. The family came to live in Scotland and Singer abandoned an early start as a student at Glasgow to seek his living as a writer. He got to know MacDiarmid and moved to Cornwall, where he pitched his tent in W. S. Graham's back garden in order to be near the poet he so admired. He eventually returned to university to study zoology, although his studies were cut short again by lack of funds and his mother's suicide, after which he worked as a scientific assistant at a marine research laboratory in Aberdeen. He wrote a popular book on the fishing industry in 1957 and his poems were published as *Still and All* in the same year. His critical reputation was on the rise but his intense personality left him prone to depression and bouts of drinking. He married and moved to Cambridge, but died of a heart attack in his mid-thirties. The title-poem 'Still and All' is a beautifully intellectual lyric, reminiscent of Graham: ' I give my word on it. There is no way / Other than this. There is no other way / Of speaking. I am my name. I find my place / Empty without a word, and my word is / Given again.' His finest work, and one of the most moving poems to come out of the Second World War, is the long poem 'The Transparent Prisoner', which is based on a story told to him by an ex-soldier and prisoner of war, who in the extremity of his forced labour, frozen and starved in a coalmine, began to see his own body and the world above him reduced to a strange transparency: 'I saw the moments and the seasons swim / precisely through me. . . .' Singer's verse had always had a strongly metaphysical vein, and perhaps his own unsettled nature and family history gave him a special affinity for this extinguishing vision of a world become transcendently clear: 'Splendour descending, splitting tenderly / Skin, skull, and atom, till, though merely man, / I recognised a reason for all pain.' In this spirit, although his voice is different, he can be seen to have affinities with John Davidson and the later MacDiarmid.

George Bruce (1909–2002)

The bare and telling verses of George Bruce, on the other hand, see the word and the world as inescapable and deeply stable verities, set against the weaknesses, both endearing and awful, of humankind. Bruce, like MacCaig, was a conscientious objector during the war. He grew up in the fishing town of Fraserburgh to the north of Aberdeen and the stern religious faith of the place, its clear light and its harsh coast are all reflected in the linguistic austerity which he chose for his first collection, *Sea Talk* (1944). 'Inheritance' maintains that 'This which I write now / Was written years ago. . . . It was stamped / In the rock formations / West of my home town.' The longer lines of the title-poem describe the culture of the place, using the sand-blown fields, the bony-faced fishermen and a beach of stones, crabs, bones and splinters of shell for his images and setting them against the terrors of the sea and the shapelessness of salt fog. This is as much a philosophical position as one of personal experience, for Bruce came from an educated, lively and artistic family, much given to debate around the table, and he was a skilled footballer in his teens before going to study English at Aberdeen University.

'A Man of Inconsequent Build' remembers his father as a cooper in Fraserburgh, while a set of four poems on 'Tom' mixes the pathos of childhood playing among the rock pools of the North-East coast with more chilly premonitions of the future – 'We hold out our hands to History / Then ask not to be taken.' Bruce has used Scots in his own work, but wrote mostly in English and was no proponent for the revival of Scots as his friend Hugh MacDiarmid had been. Bruce's later poems take many of their themes from the occasional world around him. Some are visions of horror from television news ('Laotian Peasant Shot') while others reflect fondly on children, friends or loved ones, as in the poem on his wife 'Elizabeth Polishing an Agate'. But his best work has always seemed to come from the same mould as the original themes of *Sea Talk*. 'Cliff Face Erosion', from 1988, which he considered a key poem, shares something of MacDiarmid's late poetry and his determination to embrace the world of irreducible facts, science and knowledge almost as an act of faith. Unlike MacDiarmid, however, Bruce's response is simpler, sweeter and uncomplicatedly romantic in the end:

> no more are you the bastion that you were,
> resisting and denying access to the sea's force,
> the great wave falling from you, and you

remained yourself. Now to the gnawing salt,
the flux of waters, cross-fire of elements,
you concede. Ravaged, penetrated, scuffed,
deep-graven – your face is witness,
as is the human face, to the years.
I look upon your face and it is mine.
I look upon you and marvel.

George Bruce's first volume of *Collected Poems* appeared in 1971, the year he retired from a long career as talks-producer for the BBC, during which time he did much to encourage younger authors. On retiring he was even more active as a visiting writer carrying his unstoppable enthusiasm for creative work to readers and listeners in Scotland, America and Australia. His own production enjoyed an extraordinary late flowering, with another large collection, *Perspectives* (1987), a collaboration with painter John Bellany called *Woman of the North Sea* (2001), followed by *Today Tomorrow: The Collected Poems of George Bruce, 1933–2000* (2001) and a book of 'haikus' illustrated by Edinburgh painter Elizabeth Blackadder, which was published post-humously as *Through the Letterbox* (2003).

Sidney Tremayne (1912–86) also worked in the media, as a journalist, but took little active part in literary circles. His *Selected and New Poems* (1973) shows how he achieved an unselfish descriptive purity that grows from his observational delight in the countryside with its animals and the weather in all its moods. His is a genuine 'nature poetry', thoughtful, but without the metaphysical stress that Bruce or MacCaig find in their landscapes.

Maurice Lindsay (b. 1918)

All the foregoing poets appeared in *Poetry Scotland* during the forties. It is appropriate to close this particular group with the work of Maurice Lindsay, who had so much to do with that important series and who has continued an active career as journalist, editor, drama and music critic and literary historian ever since. He was among the first to anthologise the new literary movement with his *Modern Scottish Poetry, 1920–1945* (1946) and was a founder editor of the annual volumes of *Scottish Poetry*, which appeared for over ten years, starting with co-editors George Bruce and Edwin Morgan in 1966. Lindsay worked for Border Television and became director of the Scottish Civic Trust in 1967 and his contacts with television have kept him in the public eye, as have his books on Scottish literature, Burns, and the cities of

Glasgow and Edinburgh. His early experiments with Scots (*Hurlygush*, 1948) did little new with the medium, tending to favour ballad-like verse forms, or rhythmic patterns that would have been familiar to Burns. By the 1960s, however, his own polished responses to the social scene had come into their own. Conservative structures of rhyme and rhythm give a Georgian ease to Lindsay's work that is not found in many of his Scottish contemporaries, and his occasional verses, light satires and love poems show a companionable enjoyment of the world – an enjoyment a little ironically recognised in the urbane titles he has chosen for his various collections, such as *This Business of Living* (1969), *Walking Without an Overcoat* (1977), and a personal memoir called *Thank You for Having Me* (1983). No slave to fashion, and certainly not a modernist, Lindsay explained in the Preface to his *Collected Poems* (1979) that he has been glad to write as 'an enjoyable poet'. This stance was further celebrated in a long autobiographical poem in ottava rima called *A Net to Catch the Winds* (1981) and by further collections *On the Face of It* (1993), *News of the World* (1995) and *Speaking Likenesses* (1997).

The last four figures to be considered in the 'second wave' of poets who used English could not be more different from each other. They come from the four corners of the country and embrace literary and philosophical views almost equally far apart.

George Mackay Brown (1921–96)

Born in Orkney, Brown worked as a local journalist for the *Orkney Herald* until he was in his thirties, before becoming one of Edwin Muir's mature students at Newbattle College. It was through Muir's direct encouragement that his first major collection, *Loaves and Fishes*, was published in 1959. (An earlier collection had been published at his own expense in 1954.) Brown suffered badly from tuberculosis, which was to interrupt and curtail his studies more than once; nevertheless he persevered, gained entrance to Edinburgh University and graduated in 1960, continuing with academic research on Gerard Manley Hopkins for a couple of years before returning to Orkney where he was to live for the rest of his life, only very rarely leaving the island. From the very first, Brown's poems presented a consistent vision of Orkney life in a style derived from the sagas and reduced to its archetypal essentials, so that the little community of 'fishermen with ploughs' becomes a model for all life, and especially for the balanced life that he prized so much.

Mackay Brown was deeply opposed to the values of industrial materialism, which he saw as an inheritance from the Reformation, being influenced in these views by Muir's autobiography and the friendship he formed with the older poet. He made his feelings clear in the first chapter of his book of essays, stories, poems and folklore, *An Orkney Tapestry* (1969):

> I often think that we are not really interested in the past at all. There is a new religion, Progress, in which we all devoutly believe, and it is concerned only with material things in the present and in a vague golden-handed future. It is a rootless utilitarian faith, without beauty or mystery; a kind of blind unquestioning belief that men and their material circumstances will go on improving until some kind of nirvana is reached and everyone will be rich, free, fulfilled, well-informed, masterful.

Against such a capitalist vision of endless desire and material plenty, the poet notes, in a phrase that could have come from Gunn's *Green Isle of the Great Deep*, that 'Word and name are drained of their ancient power. Number, statistic, graph, are everything.'

While there is an undeniable justice in this position – not least after the Holocaust and Hiroshima – poets also need to live in and deal with the world as it is and Mackay Brown can be criticised for a certain escapism in seeking values that are only ever to be found in some other time or in the exclusion of modernity. Certainly he goes much further than Grassic Gibbon and Gunn as a writer seeking to evoke timeless and mythopoeic patterns in his work. Like Muir and Fionn Mac Colla before him, he found these qualities in religion and joined the Catholic Church in 1961. The very title of *Loaves and Fishes* relates to the sacramental symbols in his ideal vision of life on Orkney, while a poem such as 'Our Lady of the Waves', from his next collection, *The Year of the Whale* (1965), uses the simple ritual of labour among the holy brothers at Eynhallow in order to reflect all experience:

> Queen of Heaven, this good day
> There is a new cradle at Quoys.
> It rocks on the blue floor.
> And there is a new coffin at Hamnavoe.
> Arnor the poet lies there.
> Tired of words and wounds.
> In between, what is man?
> *A head bent over fish and bread and ale.*
> *Outside, the long furrow.*

Through a door, a board with a shape on it.

Guard the plough and the nets.

Star of the sea shine for us.

Such pure images, short sentences and terse lines are typical of Mackay Brown's lucid, gentle inspiration, and his feeling for reverence and ritual in the humble acts of life produced memorable work. His best and most innovative poems appear in *Fishermen with Ploughs* (1971), a linked 'poem cycle' which records, very obliquely, the rise and fall of the community of Rackwick on Hoy. Different sections take it through the ages from the epic days of its foundation to modern decline, and then on to a resettlement which is described in prose journals after some unknown future cataclysm. It is characteristic of Brown's historical position that he should explain that 'the same people appear and reappear through many generations . . . all are caught up in "the wheel of bread" that is at once brutal and holy'. This is not to say that he does not have a dry sense of humour in some of these verses, as also in, for example, the 'Tea Poems' from *Winterfold* (1971). Even so, after several collections, the poet's cyclical themes do tend to lead always to the 'same people', until the timeless is in danger of becoming merely static.

Brown's short stories bring him back into contact with the world, and they may yet be judged to be his finest achievement. The title-story from *A Calendar of Love* (1967) takes place in modern times, but the author calls on episodic cycles of fertility, birth, shame and forgiveness to set the stage for a succession of such tales from different eras. He is closest to contemporary life in *A Time to Keep* (1969), and his studies of alcoholism and loneliness in 'Celia' and 'The Eye of the Hurricane', and of the cruelty of fate in 'A Time to Keep', show that his prose can rise to an outstanding tact and sensitivity. 'Celia' was made into a memorable television production and Brown has written many other plays and radio plays, not least through his association with the composer Peter Maxwell Davies and their work together for the Orkney Festival. His novel *Magnus* (1973) establishes a pared-down, epic quality to the life and martyrdom of St Magnus, operating somewhere between a saga and a devotional meditation while interspersing the ancient story with parallel tales of suffering in the Nazi concentration camps. Brown's prose is effective, and if his engagement with modern history is characteristically oblique it is no less effective for that. His novels tend to take the form of epic historical sagas, such as

Vinland (1992) or of linked tales and narratives across time like his last novel, the award-winning *Beside the Ocean of Time* (1994). The same pattern can be found in his most successful novel, *Greenvoe* (1972), which describes the end of an island community on the fictional 'Hellya' in the 1960s.

Greenvoe is taken over by an unspecified military-research or government defence project called 'Black Star'. Brown assembles a picture of the community by revealing the foibles of its various inhabitants from different points of view, and the reader might be forgiven for feeling that it is rather close to the Kailyard, not least on account of the author's obvious affection for the place and its people. Yet it does deal with issues that have considerable political resonance for modern Scotland, from the anthrax island in Gruinard Bay, to the torpedo and missile ranges in the Hebrides, or the atomic reactor at Dounreay, or the nuclear submarine bases in Faslane and the Holy Loch, or the exploitation of North Sea Oil. The book weaves seventeen different narratives together with real skill, each chapter being structured to a similar descriptive pattern, starting with an account of the weather and ending with a secret and ancient ritual to do with 'the Lord of the Harvest' and the Horseman's Word. Yet Hellya is no sooner cleared of its inhabitants (an echo of earlier Scottish 'improvements') than the project closes down and the place is left derelict. In the larger perspective of Brown's mythic vision, however, the old rituals of the 'Lord of the Harvest' survive and the saga continues. Whether this is enough, is the question. There is no doubt that Brown's preference for the view *sub specie aeternitatis* tends to engender a fatalistic habit of mind that will not let his theme develop to anger, tragedy, or action. Nor, perhaps, does it always do justice to the tensions and complexities inherent in the contemporary world.

Iain Crichton Smith, 'Iain Mac a'Ghobhainn' (1928–98)

In a different sense, Crichton Smith is equally at the mercy of a metaphysical point of view, for his upbringing on Lewis brought him into contact with the absolutism of the Free Kirk and his poetry bore the marks of that meeting for the rest of his life. Smith's view of small communities is quite different from that of Edwin Muir and Mackay Brown, for although he can admire a sense of closeness and common culture, he also felt the narrowness of such places and, especially in Lewis, the stifling orthodoxy of religion. The effects of this can be seen in the titles of several of his collections, such as 'Thistles and Roses', 'The

Law and the Grace', 'Love Poems and Elegies' and 'The Leaf and the Marble', all of which suggest a dialectical struggle between contraries that is very much in the Calvinist tradition. Caught between discipline and freedom, Smith's work is divided again between Gaelic and English, for he wrote poetry and prose in his mother tongue, and translated some of it into what he called a 'foreign language'. Nevertheless, it was as an English teacher that he worked in Oban for twenty-two years. A complex, sensitive and intelligent poet, Smith was a compulsive and sometimes too prolific writer, with over twenty-four volumes of verse to his name, as well as plays, short stories and several novels.

MacDiarmid saw excitement in the thrilling clash of contraries, but Smith finds it a more personal and painful thing, closer, perhaps, to Edwin Muir's diagnosis of a Scottish division between the head and the heart – 'I am tied to the Highlands,' he wrote in the Gaelic poem 'Eight Songs for a New Ceilidh', 'that is where I learnt my wound'; and, again, 'it was the fine bareness of Lewis that made the work of my mind'. If he paraphrases Sidney's advice to poets with '"Look in your own heart and write",' then his heart is a divided place. Translations of his two main Gaelic collections can be found in *The Permanent Island* (1975). They are *Biobuill is Sanasan Reice* ('Bibles and Advertisements', 1965); and *Eadar Fealla-dha is Glaschu* ('Between Comedy and Glasgow', 1969). Smith seems able to speak more directly in his Gaelic verse, and many poems in the 1965 collection offer invaluable insights into his work as a whole – from his love of the stark landscapes of his native island and his desire for the 'bareness of the knife's blade' to the sense of desolation which he finds there, too, and an awareness of Nagasaki, Hiroshima and Belsen set against the standing stones of Callanish. He writes of division in his relationship with language, seeing himself 'In the dress of the fool, the two colours that have tormented me – English and Gaelic, black and red, the court of injustice, the reason for my anger': (from 'An t-Amadan' / 'The Fool'), and he concludes that the result is a motley 'so odd that the King himself will not understand my conversation'.

Crichton Smith is a poet haunted by images, sometimes almost beyond his capacity to comprehend them; thus, in the Gaelic poem 'Dé tha Ceàrr' ('What is Wrong'), he feels once again divided between head and heart, until a characteristic moment of insight occurs:

> But one day I saw a black pit in green earth, a gardener kissing flowers, an old woman squeaking in her loneliness, and a house sailing on the water.
> I don't know whether there is a language for that, or, if there is, whether I would be any better breaking my imagination into a thousand pieces. . . .

His many volumes of poetry in both Gaelic and English describe a continuing search to find 'a language for that' and, sometimes too, the breaking of his imagination into a thousand pieces. Thus the sequence 'Am Faigh a' Ghaidlig Bas?' ('Shall Gaelic Die?', 1969) links a passionate concern with the future of his native tongue with a more philosophical understanding of the nature of all language-systems as limited conventions standing between the real and the abstract – and yet they still encapsulate untranslatable subtleties. The sense of urgency that can be detected in such passages would turn out to have a personal component, too, for the poet suffered a mental breakdown in middle age that took the form of extreme anxiety and paranoia and led to him being hospitalised for a spell. He used this experience with remarkable frankness in his novel *In the Middle of the Wood* (1987).

The bareness of Lewis and the starkness of Calvinism come together in Smith's early work to make a complicated weave of love and hate – 'Here they have no time for the fine graces of poetry', he wrote in 'Poem of Lewis', from his first collection in 1955. His admiration for the stoic strength of such an inheritance and his equal alarm at its grim narrowness feature in his many poems about old women, who become symbols of mortality for him, as well as key figures in the daily life between hearth and Kirk. He can describe the 'thorned back' and the 'set mouth' of righteousness which 'forgives no-one, not even God's justice / perpetually drowning law with grace' ('Old Woman'); yet at the same time he understands this spirit and shares its delight in hard – even anti-poetic – certainties.

'There is no metaphor', he concludes bluntly in *Deer on the High Hills* (1962); 'The stone is stony. / The deer step out in isolated air. . . . We move at random on an innocent journey.' This long meditation in 14 sections gets close to the heart of Smith's sense of a separation between himself, the world and language and yet the urgent need for all of us, and not least the poet, to bridge that gap. If the same sense of urgency and linguistic distance can be found in the work of MacCaig and W. S. Graham, who were not native Gaelic speakers, it still speaks for a special awareness on the part of poets in Scotland, living in a culture with three mother tongues. Beyond any question of native versus dominant language use, however, *Deer on the High Hills* engages with wider aesthetic issues by playing variations on the Russian Formalist critic Viktor Shklovsky's famous line that the purpose of art is 'to make the stone *stony*' ('Art as Technique', 1917). Smith turns this insight into a lyric of repetition and defeat that is yet strangely moving and beautiful in its uncanny emptiness:

The deer step out in isolated air.
The cloud is cloudy and the word is wordy.
Winter is wintry, lonely is your journey.
. . .
for stars are starry and the rain is rainy,
the stone is stony, and the sun is sunny,
the deer step out in isolated air.

The deer are symbols for the spirit that moves him in this long poem, and also for the impossible but necessary encounter with what is irredeemably 'other', because 'A deer looks through you to the other side, / and what it is and sees is an inhuman pride'.

The same sense of one's inescapable distance from life leads Smith to know compassion and the importance of dignity in the face of death, and 'Old Woman', from *Thistles and Roses* (1961), with an almost hidden undercurrent of helpless rage, is one of the finest and most lyrically moving accounts of old age in modern literature:

And she being old, fed from a mashed plate
as an old mare might droop across a fence
to the dull pastures of its ignorance.
Her husband held her upright while he prayed

to God who is all-forgiving to send down
some angel somewhere who might land perhaps
in his foreign wings among the gradual crops.
She munched, half dead, blindly searching the spoon.

Outside, the grass was raging. There I sat
imprisoned in my pity and my shame
that men and women having suffered time
should sit in such a place, in such a state

and wished to be away. . . .

Crichton Smith chose an old woman as the protagonist of his first novel, *Consider the Lilies* (1968), giving a grim account of the Clearances through her consciousness. Difficult memories of his mother – he lived with her for many years and married relatively late – add to his insight into such themes, and he has reflected on the harshness of her youth as a fish-gutter following the herring fleet around Britain, compared with his own sheltered education at Aberdeen University (*Love Poems and Elegies*, 1972). In other poems his compassion for young girls may well grow from his awareness of the hardships that the world will probably bring to them.

While many of Smith's poems respond to the physical beauty of the hills and the islands, other verses, in *From Bourgeois Land* (1969) and in sequences such as 'By the Sea' and 'The White Air of March', convey his scathing impatience with much of Lowland Scottish life – stifled by respectability, given over to third-rate jokes and music, or cluttered with souvenirs for the tourist trade. His novels produce a similarly critical, but less savage account of bourgeois life and the limitations of a timidly intellectual middle class – especially schoolteachers. *My Last Duchess* (1971) and *An End to Autumn* (1978) make their points by exteriorising the inward states of such characters, rather than through any broader social analysis.

Despite the rather grey world of these books (sometimes rather greyly written, too, it must be admitted) it would be wrong to suppose that Crichton Smith lacks humour, for his dry wit and sometimes wild laughter can be found in English and Gaelic alike, most notably in the poems of *Eadar Fealla-dha is Glaschu*, and an entertaining series of epigrams, 'Gaelic stories' and 'haikus' in affectionate mockery of his own background. In prose, too, Smith's short stories reveal a surreal sense of humour, as in 'Napoleon and I', which has a Beckettian relish for the comedy of old age, madness and failing faculties. He shows a similar delight in the absurdities of cultural self-consciousness using the persona of 'Murdo Macrae' to pontificate on bilingual poetry translations, Scottish education, the Kailyard, Calvin, Gaelic singing competitions at the Mod, or the clichés of Gaelic broadcasting and folk-life interviews on the BBC:

How old am I? I am ninety-five years old. We used to have a black house, a dung heap, and a byre. Now we only have a microwave, a cooker and a freezer. . . .

In the early days, we had brose, oatcakes and milk: now we have weetabix and sometimes my daughter makes lasagne.
    The oral tradition? I remember that we used to sit around the fire in the ceilidh house reading *The Guns of Navarone* aloud. It took three weeks. Before that we had *Where Eagles Dare*. . . .

I had seven children. Most of them worked for the Gaelic BBC. Did you ever hear the programme 'From the *Slabhraidh*'? It was my daughter Sheila that did that. It used to be on at four in the morning.
    Of course when I was young we never locked our doors. Stealing was unknown. There was some incest, but if a man was caught stealing he would be put out of the community.
    We have funny neighbours now, *a ghraidh*. A Frenchman, a German, and a man from Portugal. They are the only ones who speak Gaelic.
                ('Seaordag's Interview with the BBC, by Murdo')

[*slabhraidh*: the chain to hang pots on over an open fire; *a ghraidh*: my dear.]

Murdo, from *Murdo and Other Stories* (1981) and *Thoughts of Murdo* (1993), is a considerable comic creation, but there is a sense of desperation in the humour as well, a desperation that Smith had explored at length in his long poem 'Shall Gaelic Die?' and again in 'Real People in a Real Place', written in 1982 and collected in his volume of essays *Towards the Human* (1986):

> For Gaelic to die would be for the islands to die a more profound death than economics could bring. The imperialism of language is the most destructive of all and indeed we can see this when we admit that a word like *cliù* ['good name'] in Gaelic is really untranslatable, implying as it does a community, and not the reputation of, say, a film star or pop star.
> . . .
> For an Englishman, secure in his own world, to study French literature does not seem to be a form of treachery: and yet because of the guilt that his conditions impose upon him . . . for the islander to be influenced by T. S. Eliot or William Carlos Williams instead of by Duncan Bàn Macintyre is almost to be a traitor. To write in English becomes a form of treachery. . . .

Of course Iain Crichton Smith was fully familiar with Eliot and Williams, as well as being an admirer of Robert Lowell, and of course much of his own poetry was written in English. But Smith's extended meditation on exile, cultural dispossession and guilt explains a lot about what Franz Fanon theorised as the internally generated sense of inferiority that comes about when a dominant culture impinges on a minority culture.

In later collections Smith reflected on the Gaelic diaspora and on the culture's widely shared experience of exile: 'sometimes I hear graves singing / their Gaelic songs to the dingos / which scrabble furiously at the clay' ('Australia', from *The Exiles*, 1984), and it is clear that his sense of exile went beyond just a matter of having to leave Lewis to seek a living – as so many have had to do. In fact for Smith the island becomes a special metaphor for a sense of existential dispossession that transcends biography, even although its roots may be found there. He recognised these roots in the collection *A Life* (1986) in which he reviewed his journey from Lewis in the 1920s to Taynuilt in the 1980s, noting that 'Our landmark is the island, complex thing . . . / It sails within us, as one poet said; / its empty shelves are resonant. A scant / religion drives us to our vague tremens. / We drag it at our heels, as iron chains.' But by the end of the sequence he comes to a wider perspective, and it is one that can be glimpsed in the background of many of his poems from the very start, as he realises that 'There is no island. / The sea unites us. / The salt in our mouth.'

Poetry in Gaelic

Although MacDiarmid's programme for the Renaissance began with Lowland Scots, it was not long before he included Gaelic in his vision of how a truly distinct Scottish culture should develop. By 1930 specifically Gaelic references were appearing in his work, and major poetic statements such as 'Lament for the Great Music' and 'Island Funeral' soon followed. Nevertheless, it was the poetry of Sorley MacLean that most truly brought the Gaelic tradition into the twentieth century, and in this respect he was as vital an example to his fellow writers as ever MacDiarmid was to poets in Scots and English. As with the Kailyard, comic Gaelic verses and sentimental 'homeland' themes had persisted into the new century, while other poets were content to stay within the traditional modes – as, for example, the Skye man Angus Robertson (Aonghas MacDhonnchaidh, 1870–1948), who also wrote a novel (*An t-Ogha Mor*, 1913) set between the Jacobite risings. All this changed when MacLean's first collection of poems appeared in 1943.

Somhairle MacGill-Eain, Sorley MacLean (1911–96)

MacLean was born on the island of Raasay, between Skye and the mainland, coming from a family with strong roots in the tales, music, songs and poems of the Gaelic tradition. Studying for a degree in English at the University of Edinburgh in the 1930s, the young man came into contact with the poems of Eliot, Pound and the seventeenth-century Metaphysicals. In his final year he came across MacDiarmid's early lyrics and the *Drunk Man*, and they left a lasting impression on him, crystallising many of his feelings about Scottish culture and how a poet could encompass both intellect and passion in his work. Writing to Douglas Young in 1941, he claimed that there is 'nothing on earth like the greatest of those lyrics . . . always a miracle and mystery to me. Of course they don't influence my own work. They are completely "magic" and unable to be emulated.' By 1934 MacLean had met the older poet and was helping him with his translations of MacMhaighstir Alasdair's *Birlinn Chlann Raghnaill* and Duncan Bàn Macintyre's 'Moladh Beinn Dòbhrain'. MacLean's pursuit of what he called 'the lyric cry' in verse took him in a completely different direction from MacDiarmid, and he was never a fully convinced Scottish nationalist; nevertheless, the two men found much in common – they were both committed socialists, after all – and they remained close friends for many years.

MacLean was one among the many writers in the thirties to be deeply concerned by the rise of fascism and the outbreak of the Spanish Civil War. Social justice at home seemed equally important, and the poem 'Calbharaigh' ('Calvary') from his student years reflects his outrage at the slums of the Depression:

> My eye is not on Calvary
> nor on Bethlehem the Blessed,
> but on a foul-smelling backland in Glasgow,
> where life rots as it grows;
> and on a room in Edinburgh,
> a room of poverty and pain,
> where the diseased infant
> writhes and wallows till death.
>
> (trans. S. MacLean)

Employment as a schoolteacher took the poet to Mull for two years, where he saw the effects of cultural decline and the Clearances on every beautiful and barren hillside. This experience led him to compose more poems and to seek publication for them. The bitterness of 'Ban-Ghàidheal' ('A Highland Woman') belongs to this period: 'Hast Thou seen her, great Jew, / who art called the One Son of God? / . . . Thy gentle church has spoken / about the lost state of her miserable soul, / and the unremitting toil has lowered / her body to a black peace in a grave.' Like Crichton Smith, or like MacCaig in 'Assisi', MacLean's rage at godhead marks the depth of the church's influence in Highland culture, even among those who have grown to repudiate it. In the later 1930s, the poet underwent an extremely intense emotional experience, caught up in complex feelings towards two women (an Irishwoman and a Scotswoman) neither of whom could fully give themselves to him. These two people, along with memories of the first stirrings of romance in the poet's youth and his current feelings of love, frustration, promise, disappointment and betrayal, all came to be personified in the figure of 'Eimhir', the name of Cuchulainn's beautiful wife in Irish legend.

The pressure of events in the world at large joined with MacLean's own heightened emotional state to produce the creative outpouring of the 'Poems to Eimhir' in his first and most famous collection. (He had already shared a little hand-printed booklet with Robert Garioch – *17 Poems for 6d*, 1940.) The new manuscript was complete by 1941, when MacLean left Scotland to serve in the desert campaign in North Africa, but the problems of wartime publishing were such that the book did not appear until 1943, by which time its author was in an English hospital, convalescing from serious wounds suffered at the battle of El Alamein. The publication of *Dàin do Eimhir agus Dàin Eile* (*Poems to Eimhir and Other Poems*, 1943) was a milestone in modern Gaelic poetry, assuring MacLean of a lasting reputation, even although it was to be twenty-seven years before his next book was published.

Among the 'other poems' in the collection there are pieces, such as 'Gleann Aoighre' ('Glen Eyre') and 'An t-Eilean' ('The Island'), which celebrate his own family history and the beloved landscapes of Skye; others focus on his political convictions. 'Cornford' is an agonised lament on the Spanish Civil War, in which John Cornford, Julian Bell and García Lorca died, and the poet feels that he should have made a more active commitment, with a sense of guilt at not having joined the International Brigade himself. The heart of the book, however, is to be found in the forty-eight lyrics to 'Eimhir', although they are not conventional love-poems at all. (The sequence left some poems out when first published and a total of sixty-one have since been traced.) It is as if MacLean's mixed feeling about the affairs, his worries about his mother's health and his father's failing business, his thoughts on his Gaelic heritage, his political awareness of the agony of Europe and a passionately spiritual idealism have all been heated and brought to almost unbearable intensities by the catalyst of love. Poem IV, 'Gaoir na h-Eorpa' ('The Cry of Europe') is terribly divided between personal desire and a more general awareness:

> Girl of the yellow, heavy-yellow, gold-yellow hair,
> the song of your mouth and Europe's shivering cry,
> fair, heavy-haired, spirited, beautiful girl,
> the disgrace of our day would not be bitter in your kiss.
>
> Would your song and splendid beauty take
> from me the dead loathsomeness of these ways,
> the brute and the brigand at the head of Europe
> and your mouth red and proud with the old song?
>
> (trans. S. MacLean)

In poem XLIII: 'Am Mùr Gorm' ('The Blue Rampart'), she becomes 'my reason and the likeness of a star', or he celebrates her as a 'dawn on the Cuillin' (LIV: 'Camhanaich'), or he muses on the pointlessness of writing anything at all:

> I do not see the sense of my toil
> putting thoughts in a lying tongue
> now when the whoredom of Europe
> is murder erect and agony;

but we have been given the million years,
a fragment of a sad growing portion,
the heroism and patience of hundreds
and the miracle of a beautiful face.

(trans. S. MacLean, LV: 'Chan Fhaic Mi . . .' / 'I Do Not See . . .')

MacLean creates an extraordinary tension in these poems, and, although they are still based on traditional Gaelic metres and modes of expression (he admired William Ross and Mary Macpherson), he brings many other elements from beyond the native canon. Thus he has been influenced by his reading of Yeats and the Metaphysicals, there are echoes of Sidney's plight in *Astrophel and Stella*, and in particular he uses musical and opaque images in the manner of European Symbolism. Driven by his own urgent socialism, mixed with feelings of desire and guilt, MacLean's verse is haunted by images of hurt and desolation, as when the 'knife' of his brain 'made incision, my dear, on the stone of my love, / and its blade examined every segment' (XLV: 'An Sgian' / 'The Knife'); or his unwritten love-poems come to seem like dogs and wolves with the spoor of their paws dappling the snows of eternity, 'their baying yell shrieking / across the hard bareness of the terrible times' (XXIX: 'Coin is Madaidhean-Allaidh' / 'Dogs and Wolves').

In the end Eimhir becomes a timeless symbol of beauty and pain, as if the poet were struggling to reach an aspect of his own ideal spirit against the world itself and the inevitability of defeat and loss. This metaphysical dimension also appears in 'Coilltean Ratharsair' ('The Woods of Raasay'), and although it is not one of the love-lyrics, this long celebration of the woods shifts from the detailed descriptive tradition of Gaelic praise-poems to a more complex and symbolic meditation on the tangles of love and idealism, concluding –

There is no knowledge of the course
of the crooked veering of the heart,
and there is no knowledge of the damage
to which its aim unwittingly comes.

There is no knowledge, no knowledge,
of the final end of each pursuit,
nor of the subtlety of the bends
with which it loses its course.
(trans. S. MacLean)

The poet's own English versions give very little sense of the beauty and complexity of the Gaelic. MacLean regarded his translations as little more than a gloss, and although they have their own dignity his English verses are a pale shadow of the original. Douglas Young and Iain Crichton Smith both attempted to give more poetic renderings of MacLean's Gaelic, but the language's densely assonantal nature is very difficult to catch in English. The endnotes and commentary of Christopher Whyte's indispensable edition of the collection go some way towards explaining the full effect for non-Gaelic speakers.

In 1939 MacLean began work on 'An Cuilithionn' ('The Cuillin'), a densely symbolic long poem in the form of a sequence inspired, perhaps, by MacDiarmid's use of the longer form in *A Drunk Man.* The Cuillin Mountains in Skye symbolise the noblest potential and aspirations of the spirit, yet all around him the poet can see only the disgrace of capitalism, the indifference of the bourgeoisie and cultural decay in the aftermath of the Clearances. (Crichton Smith was to revisit these themes thirty years later.) Although centred in Skye, McLean's concern for the human condition speaks for oppressed minorities around the world as he declares his hatred for the imperialism of Britain, France and Germany alike. At that time, when appeasement with Hitler seemed possible, MacLean felt that the only hope was to be found with communism and the Red Army. 'The Cuillin' has a starkly passionate and unrelenting air, but by the time publication became possible in the middle 1940s, the poet had begun to lose confidence in Russian communism, and in the end it was never fully revised and only selections from it have been published since.

After the war MacLean returned to teaching in Edinburgh, and from 1956 until he retired in 1972 he was headmaster at the school in Plockton on the mainland to the east of Skye. He published in *Poetry Scotland* and other periodicals from time to time, but the emotional storm of *Dàin do Eimhir* had passed and it was 1970 before a substantial selection of his work appeared again, in a book published by Gordon Wright, which also included poems by George Campbell Hay, William Neill and Stuart MacGregor. This volume, *Four Points of a Saltire*, did much to revive a wider awareness of MacLean's achievement, and Crichton Smith's translation of poems from *Dàin. . .* followed from a small press in Newcastle in 1971.

MacLean's selected poems from 1932–72 were published in two languages as *Reothairt is Contraigh / Spring Tide and Neap Tide* (1977). The poet's war experiences in the desert feature in poems such as 'Curaidhean' ('Heroes'), 'Latha Foghair' ('An Autumn Day') and 'Glac a Bhàis' ('Death Valley'), but there are no polemics against fascism here; rather, a resigned wisdom and compassion for the living and the dead of either side. He was later to acknowledge his reluctant preference for a relatively weak British Empire against the horrors of Hitler and Mussolini. From such experience, perhaps, MacLean's socialism lost something of the bitter certainty of his earlier years, and in this respect he makes better poems from the modulated and complex political insights of 'Aig Uaigh Yeats' ('At Yeats's Grave'), 'Palach', and 'Ard-Mhusaeum na h-Eireann' ('The National Museum of Ireland').

MacLean was not a prolific writer and most of his poetry dates from between the 1940s and the 1970s. He produced another sequence 'Uamha n' Oir' ('The Cave of Gold'), that draws on traditional legend, but the best of his work marries a personal intensity to historical concern in the 'lyric cry' with which he began. These poems come to have the power of a threnody or incantation, sustained through a web of historical, cultural and family references within which traditional metaphors and his own singular and haunting images take their place. The elegy for his brother Calum MacLean takes a modern form to raise the old tradition of lament (*cumha*), while 'Screapadal' reflects on a deserted township on Raasay that now overlooks a torpedo range and the passing of nuclear submarines in the sound. MacLean's most famous poem about the Clearances is 'Hallaig', which invokes the eerie beauty of a long deserted township on Raasay where his own ancestors lived before the place was emptied to make a sheep-farm in the 1850s. In this outstanding poem he reflects that 'The window is nailed and boarded / through which I saw the West'. There are no people at Hallaig now and only birch trees are to be seen there – 'straight their backs, bent their heads' – like slender girls in some vision of the past:

> and their beauty a film on my heart
> before the dimness comes on the kyles,
> and when the sun goes down behind Dun Cana
> a vehement bullet will come from the gun of Love;
>
> and will strike the deer that goes dizzily,
> sniffing at the grass-grown ruined homes;
> his eye will freeze in the wood,
> his blood will not be traced while I live.
>   (trans. S. MacLean)

The conceptual complexity and the musical beauty of these lines, with the image of Time shot like a deer in the woods, capture the best of MacLean's muse. His passionately personal and direct address in combination with politics and symbolism was something completely new in Gaelic poetry.

George Campbell Hay, Deòrsa MacIain Deòrsa (1915–84)

As the son of the author of *Gillespie*, George Campbell Hay, taught himself to speak Gaelic and wrote in English and Scots as well, which is a relatively unusual combination, although William Neill was to take a similar route in the late sixties. Not surprisingly, given his scholarly nature and his nationalistic convictions, Hay's poems in Scots and Gaelic show interest in traditional modes, metrical structure and rhymes. Many of them celebrate the natural world, as in 'Do Bheithe Boidheach' ('To a Bonny Birch Tree') or 'Oran' ('Song'), and especially the sea in all its moods ('Pleasure and Courage'). Hay also follows classical themes with a ballad-like narrative approach in 'Tilleadh Uiliseis' ('The Return of Ulysses'), or a supernatural tale of shipwreck in the Scots poem 'The Three Brothers'. This delight in formal pattern, and his patriotic care for Scotland, is evident in 'Ceithir Gaothan na h-Albann' ('The Four Winds of Scotland'), while his feeling for weather and landscape features in 'An Ciùran Ceòban Ceò', for which he also made a most musical version in Scots – worthy of Alexander Montgomerie – 'The Smoky Smirr o Rain':

A misty mornin' doon the shore wi a hushed an' caller air,   fresh
an' ne'er a breath frae East or West tae sway the rashes there,
a sweet, sweet scent frae Laggan's birks gaed breathin' on its ain,
their branches hingin' beaded in the smoky smirr o rain.

The hills aroon war silent wi the mist alang the braes.
The woods war derk an' quiet wi dewey, glintin'sprays.
The thrushes didna raise for me, as I gaed by alane,
but a wee, wee cheep at passin' in the smoky smirr o rain.

Other Gaelic poems of Hay's were translated into Scots by his friend Douglas Young. Hay himself wrote some verses in French and set out to translate work in Greek, Arabic, Italian, Welsh, Irish, Icelandic and even Finnish into poems in Scots and Gaelic, thus greatly expanding the outlook and the range of expressive possibilities in his native tongues.

Hay's peace of mind was damaged by a war he never wanted to join. Nevertheless, after an initial protest he entered the army and served in North Africa, Italy and Macedonia where, as an education sergeant, his friendship with local working-class people led to him being mistaken for a communist agitator and he was physically attacked – leading eventually to a breakdown and a war pension. The experience of conflict had been difficult for him and an agonised vision of the world characterises his work from the 1940s and 1950s, in poems such as 'Truaighe na h-Eòrpa' ('Europe's Wretchedness'), 'The finely hewn ramparts of Europe / . . . down in a heap upon her plains', and he wrote 'Esta Selva Selvaggia, This Savage Wood' in English to reflect that

The swaying landmines lingering down
between Duntochter and the moon
made Scotland and the world one.
At last we found a civilisation
common to Europe and our nation,
sirens, blast, disintegration.

The Gaelic poem 'Bisearta' was based on his unhappy experience when he saw Bizerta in flames in the distance while he stood night guard in North Africa:

What is their name tonight,
the poor streets where every window spews
its flame and smoke,
its sparks and the screaming of its inmates,
while house upon house is rent
and collapses in a gust of smoke?
And who tonight are beseeching
Death to come quickly in all their tongues,
or are struggling among stones and beams,
crying in frenzy for help, and are not heard?
Who tonight is paying
the old accustomed tax of common blood?
                                        (trans. G. C. Hay)

A similarly impassioned empathy for the underdog informs 'Atman', a poem on behalf of an Arab convicted of theft by a well-fed judge, and he further developed this concern in a distinguished long poem *Mochtàr is Dùghall* (*Mochtar and Dougal*), which parallels the experiences of Gaelic and Maghreb communities whose sons are caught up in the war. The poem was never fully finished and only published in 1982, but its concern to do justice to the folk-life and ancestral awareness of Highlanders and Arabs makes it a remarkable document from that desert conflict, very much in keeping with the compassionate vision of Hamish Henderson's *Elegies for the Dead in Cyrenaica*, except that Hay is driven to despair at man's capacity for cruelty and shame: 'Murder of the dead, murder of the children'. In later years, troubled in mind and struggling with alcoholism, Campbell Hay wrote at infrequent intervals. His late work turned once again to his love of landscape and weather with no diminution of his powers, but his greatest themes were behind him.

Ruaridh MacThómais, Derick Thomson (b. 1921)

As critic, scholar, and founder-editor of the quarterly *Gairm* since 1952, Derick Thomson has played a leading part in Scottish Gaelic studies, and most of his own poems from previous collections can be found in *Creachadh na Clàrsaich / Plundering the Harp* (1982). His language is more colloquial than MacLean's and he uses freer verse forms, although of course he still draws on Gaelic's capacity to use subtle rhymes and assonances in the vowels within a sequence of words. Over the years his work has shown a sustained engagement with his origins in Lewis in relation to the wider world beyond. As an academic educated at Aberdeen and Cambridge, and after years as a professor of Celtic at Glasgow University, Thomson cannot look back on the distant island of his boyhood without recognising that there is no longer a working place for him in it. The poem 'Cisteachan-laighe' ('Coffins'), from his second collection, describes what has happened to him and others like him by remembering his grandfather as a carpenter making coffins. He associates the process with his own education, in which English was compulsory. (In fact many Gaelic children of Thomson's generation were actively dissuaded from speaking Gaelic in the classroom at any time, and even punished for it.)

> And in the other school also,
> where the joiners of the mind were planing,
> I never noticed the coffins,
> though they were sitting all around me;
> I did not recognise the English braid,
> the Lowland varnish being applied to the wood,
> I did not read the words on the brass,
> I did not understand that my race was dying.
> Until the cold wind of this Spring came
> to plane the heart;
> until I felt the nails piercing me,
> and neither tea nor talk will help the pain.
> (trans. D. Thomson)

The same sad recognition informs the plaintive cadences of 'Triomh Uinneig a' Chithe' ('When This Fine Snow is Falling'), but there is a sharper edge to poems such as 'Cruaidh?' ('Steel?') and 'Strathnaver'

('Srath Nabhair'), which manage a bitter wit at the recollection of the Clearances:

> And throw away soft words,
> for soon you will have no words left;
> The Tuatha De Danann are underground,
> the Land of the Ever-young is in France
> and when you reach the Promised Land,
> unless you are on your toes,
> a bland Englishman will meet you
> and say to you that God, his uncle, has given him a title to the land.
> ('Cruaidh?' / 'Steel?', trans. D. Thomson)

(The Tuatha De Danann are a supernatural race in Ireland, sometimes said to be progenitors of the fairies.) 'Donegal' and 'Budapest' extend the poet's wry rage beyond Scotland's borders, while the fine movement of 'Eadar Samradh is Foghar' ('Between Summer and Autumn'), the title-poem of his second collection, shows the music of Thomson's Gaelic in a quieter mood:

> Up from the sea, in a lonely hollow
> is a patch of grass where the shoots were bruised,
> on a summer's day I can never forget;
> but when I garner both grass and corn,
> autumn stays not for me in the stacks,
> nor will summer return though I will it so.
>
> The sea below me, white and red,
> white-skinned wave-crest and dark-blue trough,
> receding and nearing,
> joy with its breath held,
> swelling and breaking,
> with healing in its hurting;
> and I grasped a moment
> to think of the mutability
> that lay below me,
> and to think of the constancy
> that I see now I utterly lacked.
> (trans. D. Thomson)

The bittersweet and intimate relationship between Thomson and his homeland became the central theme of his third volume of poems *An Rathad Cian / The Far Road* (1970), a collection of fifty-six linked lyrics in free verse. The poet's clear images seem to rise in the most unforced way from the natural landscape or from casual memories, and yet they accumulate to make the book a sustained statement as timeless as Mackay Brown's *Fishermen with Ploughs*, but more in touch with the contemporary world and with his own wry distance from the island he is visiting. Thomson does not make Lewis into Edwin Muir's remembered Eden, but there is a strongly elegiac note in many of his poems; and somewhere between the shafts of his anger and the eloquent music of memory and longing there is an acceptance and a submission to fate which MacLean, for example, refuses by turning to the more strenuous tradition of resistance through recollection. For MacLean, the evocation of dates, places and names in family or cultural history (as in the lament for his brother, or 'Screapadal') becomes an act of affirmation, with implications for community memory and an understanding of history. Thomson's, by contrast, is a more personal sense of history, with an essentially lyrical and *triste* vision. This seems to lie at the heart of his work even if he has also produced finely topical and satirical verses, or political allegories such as 'An Iolaire' ('The Eagle') or 'An Crann' ('The Plough').

Thomson's later collections include *Smeur an Dòchais / Bramble of Hope* (1991) and *Meall Garbh / The Rugged Mountain* (1995), in which he continues his characteristically reflective, cool and tender observation of the world as he glimpses the objects around him, or a chance encounter with animals or birds, or people caught passing in the city street. Thus *Smeur an Dòchais* contains a series of eighteen poems 'Air Stràdean Ghlaschu' ('On Glasgow Streets') which offer fleeting impressions of the passing urban scene, not without their own tart comments on the corruption of city councillors, or the irony of being a Gaelic speaker in an English-speaking city trying to understand the Asian voices around him: 'A delicate music my ears could not properly hear, / and I felt some kindness towards them in my heart – / I understood how difficult it is for the SED / to understand the Gael's wishes' ('Smuaintean an café an Glaschu' / 'Thoughts in a Glasgow café'). The SED mentioned is the Scottish Education Department, now much exercised by the challenges of a multi-cultural society, but less concerned with the challenge in the past when it was closer to home. Thomson's recent work has also been notable for its developing exploration of the sensuous world, where both landscape and the body can be imbued with an almost erotic charge, with what he calls, in one poem, the 'sap of joy'. That joy, and the onset of age and decay, is another theme, specifically explored in the longer poem 'Gormshuil' ('Blue Eye'), in which an old woman in an island community remembers the fires of her youth in language that leaps from the erotic to the sacred and back again in 'a world shrunk to a single room' with two or three hens outside and the potatoes lifted. It is a theme also explored in the work of Iain Crichton Smith, but Thomson's verse seeks to introduce a new sensuality almost as an act of resistance to the shadow of the Free Church.

Domhnall MacAmhlaigh, Donald MacAulay (b. 1930)

Domhnall MacAmhlaigh, Donald MacAulay is yet another man from Lewis (an island of poets) whose work looks to his origins, critically and otherwise. He is moved by traditional psalm singing and by the 'liberating, cascading melody' of Gaelic prayer, which is 'my people's access to poetry' ('Soisgeul 1955' / 'Gospel 1955'); or he deplores the narrowness of religion, as in 'Self-righteousness' ('Fein-Fhìreantachd'). A spell in Turkey led him to recognise the social intolerance of the small community that is his home ('Amasra, 1957' and 'Latha Feill' / 'Holiday'), while his poem 'Do Phasternak, mar Eiseamplair . . .' ('For Pasternak, for Example . . .') reflects on how a poet must sustain his art against the 'contrary wind'. MacAulay is professor of Celtic at Aberdeen, and his work features in an anthology edited by himself, *Nua-bhàrdachd Ghaidlig / Modern Scottish Gaelic Poems* (1976), which contains work by all the above-mentioned writers as well.

Iain Crichton Smith's Gaelic poetry has already been discussed, but the example of his Gaelic short stories and novels should not be underestimated, for this is a small but growing development in Highland publishing, to which John Murray (Iain Moireach) and the Revd Colin Mackenzie (Cailein MacCoinnich) have also contributed.

Choosing to write in Gaelic or Scots involves a significant act of cultural self-identification. This does not necessarily apply to Scottish writers using English, least of all, perhaps, to those who may live in England or Europe or whose work is set furth of Scotland. Yet many writers feel a certain gravitational attraction to the land of their own or their parents' birth, or they come to realise that their work has been marked to a greater or lesser extent by the educational and cultural influences of their early years. Some authors are content to leave it at that, while others embark on a lifelong exploration of the forces that made them what they are. And of course it is always tempting for literary critics to seek those shaping forces, too, even although the authors themselves may demur.

Scottish novelists, Scottish themes (i)

Muriel Spark was brought up in Scotland, and it is possible to trace her origins in aspects of her fiction, although she took little part in the world of Scottish letters, spent most of her life out of the country, and cannot be said to be part of the 'Renaissance' movement as such. Robin Jenkins, on the other hand, while he travelled abroad and wrote books set in the Far East, shows a sensibility deeply marked by the culture and the ethos of his native land and a determination to explore its painful imprint in novel after novel. It seems appropriate, or at least not inappropriate, to start the next chapter with Robin Jenkins and to end this one with Muriel Spark, whose mordant wit and playfully metaphysical interests make a striking contrast to the grimmer prose realism of the Scottish novelists of the 1960s and 1970s.

Muriel Spark (1918–2006)

Spark was born Muriel Camberg and spent the first eighteen years of her life in Edinburgh before moving to Rhodesia, then London and ultimately to Italy. She was educated at James Gillespie's School for Girls where she met the model for Miss Jean Brodie, her most famous literary creation, but felt herself to be a 'constitutional exile' in Edinburgh, which she found to be stiflingly if not puritanically proper. At the same time she recognised that certain habits of mind had survived from her youth, regarding herself, as she said in an interview in 1988, as 'born free, being a Scot'. She asserted her freedom early enough by marrying Oswald Spark when she was nineteen and travelling to Rhodesia to be with him. Oswald turned out to be unstable and violent, the marriage was not a happy one, and Spark returned to England in 1944 to work in London as an intelligence officer for the Foreign Office, eventually involved with 'black propaganda' against the Germans. Her son Robin was effectively brought up by Spark's parents in Edinburgh. Spark's years in London during and after the war feature in a number of her early novels, most especially *The Girls of Slender Means* (1963), while the intelligence world reappears in spectral form in *The Hothouse by the East River* (1973). In 1947 Spark became secretary of the Poetry Society, which was another rich source for her later fiction, not least 'the Autobiographical Association' of *Loitering with Intent* (1981). She also started writing poetry of her own and short literary studies of Mary Shelley – *Child of Light* (1951) – Emily Brontë (1953) and John Masefield (1953). In 1951 she entered an *Observer* short story competition and won first prize with 'The Seraph and the Zambesi', a strange story that begins like a white settler's tale about putting on a Christmas pageant at an old garage near Victoria Falls, only to have an utterly alien seraph arrive on stage, radiating heat and burning the place down before disappearing up river. The spare narrative style recounts an inexplicable metaphysical visitation in such a matter-of-fact first-person narrative tone that the whole event seems scarcely less surreal than the idea of angels and wise men and 'Good King Wenceslas' under the African sun in the first place. The effect is disconcerting, both comic and slightly sinister, with a sharp eye for the follies of middle-class colonial society and a presciently postmodern sense of the constructed nature of narrative prose. Muriel Spark had found her characteristic voice.

Spark's first novel, *The Comforters*, was published in 1957 and over the next 47 years she was to produce another 23 novels, all of them models of concision, along with radio plays, collections of short stories and some wittily idiosyncratic poems. Critics frequently claim a distinctively Scottish strain in her work and it seems likely that a grain of Edinburgh Calvinism met with the Old Testament authority of her father's Jewish faith to forge the particularly ruthless intelligence by which she lays bare the pains and petty failings of her characters. In her autobiography Spark describes herself as a 'people-watcher and a behaviourist' and her characteristic narrative position – crisp, spare and objective – could indeed be one of an amused almost scientific detachment, even when speaking in the first person. The brilliant opening page of *Loitering with Intent* gives a flavour of this narrative and emotional economy. The protagonist is Fleur Talbot, a novelist herself, whose manuscript will be stolen from her – as one of Spark's was:

> One day in the middle of the twentieth century I sat in an old graveyard which had not yet been demolished, in the Kensington area of London. . . .
> This was the last day of a whole chunk of my life but I didn't know that at the time. I sat on the stone slab of some Victorian grave writing my poem as long as the sun lasted. I lived nearby in a bed-sitting-room with a gas fire and a gas ring operated by pre-decimal pennies and shillings in the slot, whichever you preferred or had. My morale was high.

Thinking of her own upbringing, Spark recalled the influence of the Border ballads, whose 'steel and bite, so remorseless and yet so lyrical, entered my literary bloodstream, never to depart'. Her interest in the macabre and her sense of the immanence of other realms of being, not least the presence of evil, could be said to come from the same source, along with the economy of her stories' telling – almost all her novels are short – their oral ease and their fable-like plots.

Memento Mori (1959) is a dark comedy about the democracy of impending death whether one is a distinguished elder citizen like Dame Lettie Colston OBE or one of the twelve gaga grannies in the Maud Long Medical Ward for old people. Death seems to be making itself increasingly known to Dame Lettie and her circle (habitually engaged with intrigue, committee meetings and high tea in their twilight years) by way of an anonymous phone caller saying 'remember you must die'.

The Ballad of Peckham Rye (1960) introduces us to crook-backed Dougal Douglas, or Douglas Dougal, mobile, protean, amoral, Scottish and devilishly charming when he wants to be – a con man, an 'Arts man', a would-be biographer, perhaps the very father of lies himself – who sets the cat among the pigeons when he comes to Peckham to work at 'Meadows, Meade & Grindley, manufacturers of nylon textiles, a small but growing concern'. Spark's eye for shabby gentility never fails in this world of shopkeepers, pompous small businessmen, landladies and local gossip, nor her sense of the absurd as her dialogue spits and crackles and the plot unfolds in a succession of lightning quick vignettes. Douglas is hired to reduce absenteeism, but it flourishes under his care, and in fact everywhere he goes he seems to cause disruption and conflict, releasing the worst in people, before he skips off at the end of the novel to sell tape recorders to witchdoctors in Africa, and eventually to draw on his own life experiences to become an author himself. He is a sprite of malicious misrule, the negative spirit that makes things happen, like Ivan's devil in *The Brothers Karamazov*, or indeed like the sly and protean figure of Gilmartin in Hogg's *Justified Sinner*.

It is significant that Muriel Spark had converted to Catholicism in 1954 and while one cannot deny the Catholic faith's commitment to the fallibility of humankind, and the blessed release of confession, one is equally struck by the ruthless clarity of Spark's intelligence and her sense that human life and all its failings can only be absurd *sub specie aeternitatis*. The Scottish Presbyterian tradition will concede to no one in its sense of the immanence of evil in the world, but Spark's response to it is ironic, even light-hearted, as her fiction manages an extraordinary dance between the devil and the deep blue sea.

The Prime of Miss Jean Brodie (1961) relates to a clash between two different kinds of authority – indirectly Calvinist and Catholic – as played out between a schoolteacher and her disciple Sandy Stranger (the name is not insignificant), who will eventually betray her. Set in

Edinburgh in the 1930s (when young Muriel Camberg was herself at James Gillespie's) the schoolteacher Jean Brodie is both an inspiring and a pathetic figure in her self-declared 'prime' as she becomes increasingly dependent on the admiration of her chosen favourite pupils – the 'Brodie set' – at the Marcia Blaine Junior School. Yet she is dictatorial in her ways, enthusiastically recommending 'instinct', a love of art and the culture of Italy, while really seeking to mould the girls in her own image, not least in her admiration for Mussolini. After an initial flush of adoration for her assured and commanding teacher, Sandy gradually comes to see that Miss Brodie takes delight in bending her pupils to her will, living a vicarious life through the manipulation of their tastes and feelings. She will send one of her protégées to die in Spain, fighting *for* Franco; and in Sandy's class (sailing under the flags of free-thinking and D. H. Lawrence), she is shaping one of the girls, the placid Rose, to become the lover of Teddy Lloyd the art teacher, a married man she herself desires but is in the end too timid to commit herself to. She prepares Sandy, who is repeatedly described as having small staring piggy eyes, to be the go-between.

> by the time the girls were sixteen Miss Brodie was saying to her set at large: 'Sandy will make an excellent Secret Service agent, a great spy'; and to Sandy alone she had started saying 'Rose will be a great lover. She is above the common moral code, it does not apply to her. This is a fact which it is not expedient for anyone to hear about who is not endowed with insight.'

Sandy (like Spark) comes to associate this attitude, despite its less than moral position, with a feeling of power in allocating people's destiny that is positively Calvinist in its origins: 'She thinks she is Providence, thought Sandy, she thinks she is the god of Calvin, she sees the beginning and the end.' At the same time Spark gives Brodie a line that is more familiar to the Jesuit priesthood than it is in the Kirk of Scotland: 'Give me a girl at an impressionable age and she is mine for life. The gang who oppose me shall not succeed.' In this way, the novel sets out a wider and more philosophical context for the petty intrigues at Marcia Blaine's. Who has the right to influence others? How does 'influence' work and what are its hidden motives? What are the well-springs of action and what are the results of our actions on others?

Sandy does not come from Edinburgh, she is indeed a 'stranger', and the book is mostly focalised through her own unreliable, but slowly improving grasp of the world around her as she comes to realise that Brodie's claim to cultural authority with the 'crème de la crème' of her set – is nothing less than a form of emotional fascism. Sandy longs for her own agency and would rather like to possess the firm Presbyterian faith she sees around her, if only so that she can rebel against it herself. In her own way, seeking control from behind the scenes, she is not unlike Miss Brodie, and in this respect it is as if she were Brodie's double, fated to overthrow her own likeness. She does this by colluding with the school authorities to have her teacher dismissed. Brodie's views on sexual freedom are too difficult for the authorities to confront, so her political influence is the given reason:

> 'Why did she get the push?' said Rose. 'Was it sex?'
> 'No, politics.'
> 'I didn't know she bothered about politics.'
> 'It was only a side line,' Sandy said, 'but it served as an excuse.'

In the end, when they have left school, it is not Rose, but the eighteen-year-old Sandy who becomes Teddy's model and lover, although all she can see in his portraits of her is the faint but ineradicable likeness of Jean Brodie, declared on his canvases even as it is hidden in his heart. Sandy's own motives for betrayal may be clearer to the reader than they are to Sandy herself. Teddy Lloyd is a Catholic, and Sandy soon tires of him, displaying a certain ruthlessness of her own:

> By the end of the year it happened that she had quite lost interest in the man himself, but was deeply absorbed in his mind, from which she extracted, among other things, his religion as a pith from a husk. Her mind was as full of his religion as a night sky is full of things visible and invisible. She left the man and took his religion and became a nun in the course of time.

That last throw-away sentence is characteristic of how Spark tells the story, for it is not told in sequence, and in her role as omniscient novelist – omniscient as Joyce's artist 'like the God of creation' – she jumps forwards and backwards in the timeline, breaking the illusion of reality by informing us of the fates of the various characters, beyond the plot of the actual novel itself:

> 'You did well,' said Miss Brodie to the class, when Miss Mackay had gone, 'not to answer the question put to you. It is well, when in difficulties, to say never a word, neither black nor white. Speech is silver but silence is golden. Mary are you listening? What was I saying?'
> Mary Macgregor, lumpy, with merely two eyes, a nose and a mouth like a snowman, who was later famous for being stupid and always to blame and who, at the age of twenty-three, lost her life in a hotel fire, ventured, 'Golden.'

The sudden appearance of an omniscient narrator in this way serves to make us aware of the nature of fictional textuality. But there is an added – purely Sparkian – dimension to it as well, an electric metaphysical thrill: the thrill perhaps of pure power over one's invented creatures.

In later years Sandy meets the now retired Miss Brodie to find her a shadow of her former self. Her old teacher is worried about which one among her special set had betrayed her: 'Sandy replied like an enigmatic Pope: "If you did not betray us it is impossible that you could have been betrayed by us. The word betrayed does not apply . . ."' This is a response worthy of a Jesuit and indeed Sandy will soon enter the Catholic Church, 'in whose ranks she had found quite a number of Fascists much less agreeable than Miss Brodie'. In fact Sandy joins a closed order of nuns and from this seclusion writes a well-received book on psychology called the *Transfiguration of the Commonplace*. (The title might well stand for how Spark invests the banal everyday in her own fiction with grotesque, supernatural or metaphysical elements.) Now middle-aged and known as Sister Helena of the Transfiguration, Sandy is finally permitted visits because of the reputation of her book and gets talking to a man who was at school in Edinburgh about the same time as she was at Marcia Blaine's.

> 'The influences of one's teens are very important,' said the man.
> 'Oh yes,' said Sandy, 'even if they provide something to rebel against.'
> 'What was your biggest influence, then, Sister Helena? Was it political, personal? Was it Calvinism?'
> 'Oh no,' said Sandy. 'But there was a Miss Jean Brodie in her prime.' She clutched the bars of the grille as if she wanted to escape from the dim parlour beyond . . .

A characteristic of Spark's prose style – especially in this book – is to keep returning to the same descriptive phrase or phrases about people in the course of the novel – a device not unlike the patterns of oral narrative or the incremental repetition of the Scottish ballads. The effect is to stress again the author's presence and the constructed nature of all fiction (however 'realistic' it may seem) and also to cast her characters in a fixed mould – a kind of Calvinist predestination indeed. From its opening to its closing pages (in that re-cycling time-line) we are haunted by this image of feeble-eyed Sandy, the middle-aged author of a 'strange book' on transfiguration, crouching forward in the dark and clutching the bars of her grille 'more desperately than ever'.

The Prime of Miss Jean Brodie is a succinct and brilliant book, as symbolically subtle, profound, perfectly constructed and as inexhaustible in its way as *The Great Gatsby*. In the end it is not Jean Brodie, with her confusions between liberal and elitist values, that holds our imagination so much as the complex moral fate of Sandy Stranger, and the final mystery of what they are, and what they have been, to each other.

In the early 1960s Spark went to live and work in New York, where she was to stay for a few years before finally moving to Italy in 1967. *The Prime of Miss Jean Brodie* was first serialised in The *New Yorker*, as was *The Mandelbaum Gate* (1965), Spark's longest and most politically aware novel, which won the James Tait Black Memorial prize. Set in Jerusalem it explores the meeting and crossing points and the political tensions between Christian, Arab and Jew. She returned to the political arena again with *The Abbess of Crewe* (1974), which uses a fable of ecclesiastical political infighting to satirise the Watergate scandal and Nixon's obsession with secret tape recordings. *Aiding and Abetting* (2000) uses the actual events surrounding the disappearance of Lord Lucan (there are no less than two characters who claim to be him in the novel) to further pursue questions of identity. (On reflection, the real Lord Lucan's story might have been written by Muriel Spark in the first place.) The novelist started to write her own story in the autobiographical *Curriculum Vitae* (1992), which she saw as a chance to put right various facts about her life and times. It is an interesting read, not least because one can trace often unflattering links between real people and various characters in her novels, but it has a rather severe and chilly spirit and seems somehow to lack the verve and swerve of her fiction.

It is not difficult to find a Scottish flavour in Spark's 'mordant irony' nor is it an accident that Jean Brodie claimed the notorious Deacon Brodie as an ancestor, the patron saint – or at least the crooked Baillie – of the divided Scottish self. Yet Spark's complex vision of our mortal lives in all her many novels is never reducible to any simple binary set, or formula of 'doubling'. This is entirely appropriate, after all, when one recalls the instability of the subjective and objective worlds and the clashing narratives of the *Justified Sinner* itself. It is interesting to reflect for a moment on the parallels between Hogg and Muriel Spark. The latter's fiction engages with a world of middle-class privilege, while Hogg's characters are from humbler stock, yet both show a lively appreciation for the eccentric energy of humankind as a species peculiarly subject to conviction, obsession and delusion. In one sense Hogg's covenanting Presbyterianism and Spark's Catholic belief could not be further apart, yet they share a strongly eschatological sense and a mutual fascination with the interpenetration of the natural and the supernatural worlds. Spark's work is not easily reducible to a matter of her specifically Catholic faith, but what is consistent, however, is her awareness of mortality as the one last thing that faces us all, whatever our religion might be, and a serious but blackly comic vision of how we know ourselves, spend our time and impose on each other until that last moment comes. It came for her, in the spring of 2006.

2
Beyond the Renaissance: old themes, new blood, new voices

As a coherent and specifically focused movement the Scottish Literary Renaissance lasted into the late 1940s, while the writers of the 'second wave' carried that momentum into the 1960s. It follows that the contemporary scene might be said to commence between the late 1960s and early 1980s, with the appearance of two key texts, both enormously influential, namely Edwin Morgan's collection *The Second Life* (1968) and Alasdair Gray's *Lanark* (1981). These two books can be said to herald much that followed. Some critics see them as markers of a completely new start, while others talk of a 'third wave' of the Renaissance despite the fact that some younger writers would deny any connection to the original literary movement with its emphasis on political and linguistic nationalism and its various mythopoeic explorations of Scottishness. Be that as it may, the last thirty years of the twentieth century have been marked by a remarkable wealth of creative work in Scotland and it is difficult to imagine the liveliness of this contemporary scene without the foundations of cultural confidence that were first established in the 1920s.

Scottish novelists, Scottish themes (ii)

Not that such strong foundations necessarily led to any kind of optimism, at least in the first instance. In the popular imagination, the 1960s and 1970s were times of change, with youth culture, slowly rising standards of living and devolution in the air – although the setback of the 1979 referendum was still to come. Yet many of the novels and plays of these two decades are still coloured by post-war disillusion and a strongly Calvinist, if secular, sense of failure and unworthiness. For prose fiction in particular, it looks as if the 'bodies' of Barbie have moved into the city to inhabit a tenement with green shutters. Such writing is no longer a reaction against the sentimental excesses of the Kailyard, but more the response of a generation of authors who grew up in the 1950s, in the grip of post-war austerity and a sense of linguistic, cultural and class dispossession, urban decay, fraying hopes for change and growing industrial erosion. In fact Scotland had voted for a socialist government since 1945 but to generally little effect because of the demographics of Britain. The novels of disillusionment and decline that characterise the 1960s and 1970s are partly a response to that situation, partly the last rattle of Scottish cultural inferiorism and partly the metaphor for a much darker philosophical view of the human condition in general. Having said that, there is an undeniably forensic aspect to much of this writing as it analyses, in book after book, the wasteland of a specifically Scottish psyche. This is no less than the central remit of the novels of Robin Jenkins, for example, for although he was born in 1912, he did not publish until the 1950s and his work can be said to set the scene for much of the realistic fiction over the next two decades. Jenkins's vision of the aftermath of Scottish Calvinism in petty bourgeois society is not a pretty one, and yet his concern with larger moral issues, with the nature of good and evil and individual culpability is itself the historical product of an earlier and more dynamic Scottish culture linking the Reformation and the Enlightenment. Other authors, such as Williams, Friel and McIlvanney, seek to understand the Scottish condition via a sustained exploration of masculine disempowerment, and look back to the struggles between fathers and sons to be found in George Douglas Brown and Robert Louis Stevenson. If some of these themes can be said to have appeared again in the 1980s with *Lanark* and *1982 Janine*, it will have been in a different and more redemptive spirit, but not before they had run their course in a succession of grim novels of cultural scepticism, psychic damage and urban realism. In the prose fiction of the 1960s and 1970s the Zen insights of Neil Gunn's highland river or Grassic Gibbon's saving vision of the timeless land could not be further away.

Robin Jenkins (1912–2005)

Jenkins did not identify himself with the Renaissance writers, and as a schoolteacher of English in Glasgow and Argyll he was thirty-nine before his first book was published. Most of his novels are set in

Scotland, although he left the country between 1957 and 1968 to teach in Afghanistan, Spain, Borneo and Malaysia. He produced six novels from these settings, including *Dust on the Paw* (1961) set in Afghanistan and *The Holy Tree* (1969). With over 30 books to his name, the moral focus of Jenkins's work is not unlike that of Muriel Spark, but his vision, especially in the early novels, is much gloomier as he takes issue with central problems of morality and the nature of innocence, goodness and maturity in a world seemingly hostile to such qualities. He sees the central belt of Lanarkshire and the urban West of Scotland as a place of crumbling streets or stifling gentility, of brutal crowds and lonely individuals, and he sets this against the nearby Highlands as a place of remote beauty, old estates or isolated forests. Of course, good and evil can be found in either scene, but Jenkins's novels gain power from his use of such settings, where he finds the symbols that suit his vision. His third novel, *The Thistle and the Grail* (1954), describes a small Lanarkshire town, not unlike Cambuslang where he was born, where the 'holy grail' of football is to win the Scottish Junior Cup. Its account of a petty and crowded place full of narrow minds and frustrations becomes a grim comment on the state of modern Scotland and the diminished spirits of its people.

Jenkins was a conscientious objector during the war and did his war service as a forestry worker, and this undoubtedly gave him the setting for at least two of his books, particularly *The Cone Gatherers* (1955), arguably his finest novel, which won the Frederick Niven Award. It takes place on a country estate during the Second World War, as if a parable of that wider evil were being acted out among the pine trees and their cones that symbolise both present darkness and the hope of seed for the future. The action unfolds between Calum, a retarded, kindly and hunchbacked forestry worker and Duror, the obsessed and unhappy gamekeeper who comes to hate him as he hates his sick wife and his own dire nature, so used to dealing out death in the depths of the forest.

> Since childhood Duror had been repelled by anything living that had an imperfection or deformity or lack: a cat with three legs had roused pity in others, in him an ungovernable disgust. Other boys had stripped the wings off flies, he had been compelled to squash the desecrated remnants: often he had been struck for what was considered interference or conceited pity. Nobody had guessed he had been under a compulsion inexplicable then, and now in manhood, after the silent tribulation of the past twenty years, an accumulated horror, which the arrival of these cone gatherers seemed at last about to let loose.

The isolation of this estate and the narrow focus of Jenkins's plot bring us inescapably close to the barest and rawest elements of existence and the dark wellsprings of human motivation. Tall, thin, grey-haired and burdened with his charge, Calum's brother Neil resents his subservience to the aristocratic landowners, but does their bidding all the same. Duror (a name worthy of *A Voyage to Arcturus*) is burdened with a paralysed wife bed-ridden for twenty years and monstrously obese. Hunchback Calum is burdened by the death or suffering of every bird and rabbit in the wood, causing disgust and confusion when he interrupts a hunt to fling his arms around a blood-soaked dying deer. Out of his own dark nature Duror hates Calum and takes a chance to suggest to Lady Runcie-Campbell that the simpleton may have sexual desires for her young daughter – Calum has an old broken doll of hers that he has taken to mend. The poison Duror spills into his employer's ear is closer to his own urges than it is to any truth. Publicly shamed for harbouring such suspicions, he waits his chance to take revenge on the hunchback – the symbolic figure of his own pain. His opportunity comes when Lady Runcie-Campbell's young son tries to emulate the cone gatherers by climbing to the top of a pine tree. He gets stuck and she sends for the brothers to get Roderick down. Neil takes his chance to make a stand, refusing to help and observing that 'a man can surrender only so far'. On hearing of this, Duror goes off to find the brothers and in a passion of rage he ends up shooting Calum. Then, in complete despair, he kills himself.

The novel makes a very telling commentary on the cost of the war (and perhaps its roots) and on the inequalities of human fate, the complacencies of class privilege and the gangrene of class subservience – all laid equally bare in an isolated estate. The final mystery, however, is the relationship between the source of Duror's pain and the evil that he does. The novel's resolution remains as unfathomable as the darkest Greek tragedy and as primitive and atavistic as a ritual human sacrifice in ancient times.

Jenkins's combination of prose realism with an unrelentingly ethical imagination finds one of its best expressions in *The Changeling* (1958), which traces the relationship between a sanctimonious but well-meaning schoolteacher and one of his pupils, a boy from the worst slums in Glasgow, to whom he becomes a mentor. The novel explores what makes us what we are, and is never certain about the motives of those who would seek to do good. The theme is revisited in *A Would-be Saint* (1978), an understated study of the ambiguities of unforced goodness and the problems that it brings to Gavin Hamilton's life as he grows up during the Depression. When war breaks out Gavin, like his creator, becomes a conscientious objector and leaves town to work in the forests, which become the stage for his confrontation with himself and what he owes to a world that cannot understand him. The themes of 'innocence', corruption and continuing moral ambiguity are pursued yet again in *Just Duffy* (1988), in which an insignificant teenager takes up a crusade, convinced of his own rectitude – becoming 'Just' Duffy, with a vengeance – very much in the spirit of the deluded Justified Sinner. Yet his vision, however simplistic it may be, makes us question what we ourselves have learned to tolerate or accept without comment.

The novelist's most virulent and blackly comic account of cultural life and spiritual failure in Scotland is given in *Fergus Lamont* (1979), the first-person 'autobiography' of an illegitimate slum boy who becomes a soldier and poet with aristocratic and nationalistic pretensions during the modern literary renaissance. Reading like a sourer version of Linklater's *Magnus Merriman*, the novel charts the rise and fall of an egocentric, creative, self-destructive and hypocritical man in a snobbish career of repeated petty betrayals and lost love. Once again Jenkins explores a Scotland where class divisions are as deeply divided as its landscape, from the urban squalor of Central Scotland to the remote beauty of the Hebrides, and if the formula is familiar by now, it can at least be traced back to Hogg and Stevenson. A far sweeter and more light-hearted tone – and it makes a welcome change – characterises Jenkins's late fiction, which engages with old age and mortality. Written in the aftermath of his wife's death, *Willie Hogg* (1993) is a deeply compassionate account of an elderly couple's trip from Glasgow to a Navajo reservation in Arizona where Willie's wife's sister is dying of cancer. *Childish Things* (2001) returns to first-person narrative to give an ironically comic account of the adventures at home and abroad of Gregor McLeod, a golf-playing ex-schoolteacher and recent widower who is finally set free, after a lifetime of convention, by the twin angels of retirement and bereavement.

James Kennaway (1928–68)

In complete contrast to Robin Jenkins's long and productive writing career, James Kennaway died in a car crash while suffering a heart attack at the age of only forty. He wrote six novels but never quite recaptured the success of his first one, *Tunes of Glory* (1956), which was based on his experience of National Service with the Queen's Own

Cameron Highlanders and especially the Gordon Highlanders in Germany. After his time in the army, Kennaway studied philosophy, politics and economics at Oxford and began his writing career while working for a publisher in London. He married Susan Edmonds in 1951 and something of his turbulent, charming and hard-drinking personality can be found in *The Kennaway Papers* (1981), a commentary on his notebooks and a personal memoir that she published after his death.

Tunes of Glory centres on the characterisation of Colonel Jock Sinclair, a hard-drinking, hard-fighting, vain, coarse, immature, obsolete old soldier, who seems doomed to destroy himself in a clash with the educated Sandhurst officer from England who arrives to replace him as acting head of a Highland regiment. Both men are haunted by their past lives. The army saved Jock from the slums and a future in prison, but not from drink and a capacity for violence. Basil Barrow on the other hand has never recovered from his time as a prisoner of war under the Japanese. In the end it is the new commander who commits suicide, and Jock survives disgrace only to suffer a final breakdown. The novel is an extraordinarily succinct and intense exploration of masculinity and military culture at its best and worst, along with great insight into the desperate fragility of a certain Scottish style of bluster and bravado, never far removed from violence.

Kennaway's own restless emotional life was something of a struggle in between bouts of obsessively hard writing. His subsequent novels often deal with destructive marital or emotional conflicts within a family or between lovers, and he gave a specifically Scottish setting to this theme in *Household Ghosts* (1961), which explores a love triangle and the intense relationship between a brother and a sister in an aristocratic Perthshire family that has seen better days. Kennaway had begun to work on film scripts and the huge success of his own treatment of *Tunes of Glory* in the 1960 film starring Alec Guinness and John Mills confirmed him in this métier. He adapted *Household Ghosts* to both stage and film versions as *Country Dance* (1970) and went on to write film scripts for *The Shoes of the Fisherman* (1968), *The Battle of Britain* (1969) and his own 1963 thriller *The Mind Benders* (1973).

The Bells of Shoreditch (1963) and *Some Gorgeous Accident* (1967) continued to explore the topic of infidelity, much marked in the latter case by an affair that his wife had with the novelist John le Carré. *The Cost of Living Like This* was published posthumously in 1969, as was his novella *Silence* (1972). A strange, almost allegorical narrative stripped to the bone, *Silence* is set against racial tension and violence in a winter-bound New York and has a claim to be Kennaway's most striking work since *Tunes of Glory* and *Household Ghosts.*

Archie Hind (b. 1928)

One of the first novels of the contemporary period to bring together the themes of urban decay and artistic aspiration was *The Dear Green Place* (1966) by Archie Hind (b. 1928), which won both the Guardian Fiction Prize and the Frederick Niven Award. The title is a Gaelic transliteration of Glasgow as *Gles schu*, and 'the dear green place' is both a loving and an ironical reflection on the spirit of a city, once the industrial workshop of the Empire, now fallen on harder times. The novel is indirectly autobiographical as Mat Craig, a bright schoolboy from a working-class background, eventually gives up his job as a clerk to pursue his dreams of writing 'the best novel ever to have been written in Glasgow'. It is a tale of sacrifice and deprivation for both himself and his family, as his increasingly uncompromising literary ambition takes him into poverty and near despair. The novel contains an early diagnosis of a theme of linguistic insecurity, class awareness and self-hatred that would come to haunt so many of the books in this vein, until that anxiety came to be tackled head-on and put to flight in the work of Tom Leonard and James Kelman.

> Where did the failure of his work come from? Was it from some other source? Lack of courage? Fear of risk? Or the hazards of success?
> Was it in the language he spoke, the gutter patois into which his tongue fell naturally when he was moved by strong feeling? This gutter patois which had been cast by a mode of life devoid of all hope or tenderness. This self-protective, fobbing-off language which was not made to range, or explore, or express; a language cast for sneers and abuse and aggression; a language cast out of the absence of possibility. . . .

The novel ends by recalling the rhyme that describes the city's coat of arms, as if it were emblematic of all such fallen hopes:

> *This is the tree that never grew,*
> *This is the bird that never flew,*
> *This is the fish that never swam,*
> *This is the bell that never rang.*

– and a modern Scottish literary genre was born.

Gordon M. Williams (b. 1934)

The early work of Gordon M. Williams is another such vision generated by a sense of anger and shame at the nature of Scottish failings – especially in matters of drink, sexual guilt and physical violence. His second novel, *From Scenes Like These* (1968), confronts these aspects of the national inferiority complex to describe a year in the life of young Dunky Logan, creating one of the darkest pictures of Scottish life since *The House with the Green Shutters*. The title comes from Burns's poem 'The Cotter's Saturday Night', which describes a domestic idyll of family piety and notes that 'From scenes like these old Scotia's grandeur springs, / That makes her lov'd at home, rever'd abroad; / Princes and Lords are but the breath of kings, / "An honest man's the noblest work of God".' Williams takes a rather different view. The farm where Logan finds himself labouring at fifteen years old is sandwiched between a factory and a violent housing estate and Dunky comes to damaged manhood in a hard-man culture of drink, football and fighting – the symbolic wasteland of modern Scotland in the 1950s.

> It made him angry, just thinking about that love rubbish, keeping themselves pure! She was just a frigid wee bitch. Real women let you do *anything*. . . . It was like a man, to have a good laugh about other people's hard luck. Hard lines pal, as they said in Kilcaddie. . . . Well that's how it was, a hard world, laugh while you can.

From Scenes Like These was short-listed for the first Booker Prize in 1969 and was written out of Williams's conviction (like Kelman in the decade to come) that the British novel had lost touch with the reality of how life is for many people in the streets and housing schemes of the nation. At the same time, the novel is fired by rage at the poverty of expectation to be found in Scotland, and its associated inferiorism, not least in the social status of the Scots tongue compared with English:

> When the Craigs spoke broad it wasn't quite the same as common Kilcaddie – some of their expressions sounded as if they came straight out of Rabbie Burns! . . . He still spoke the school's idea of proper English, he knew that all right because every time he opened his mouth he could hear himself sounding like a real wee pan-loaf toff. . . why did they try and belt you into speaking like some English nancy boy on the wireless? . . . Was it being a guttersnipe to talk your own country's language? . . . Why teach kids that Burns was the great national poet and then tell you his old Scots words were dead common?

Williams's novel is another of those key works in the Scottish canon that raise such issues of class, language and identity, while also laying bare the symptoms of damaged masculinity in the Scottish cultural inheritance, from George Douglas Brown to the TV plays of Peter MacDougall, from *Weir of Hermiston* to *1982 Janine*, from *Gillespie* to John Byrne's *Slab Boys* trilogy, from William McIlvanney to Janice Galloway, Laura Hird and the works of Irvine Welsh. *Walk Don't Walk* (1972) is more cheerfully scathing about national limitations. Based on Williams's own experience, it tells how a Scots novelist copes with a promotion-tour of America when all his images of that country have come to him from his boyhood love of Hollywood films devoured in dark little cinemas at home during the war years. A free-verse prologue to the novel offers a more humorous version of the national inferiority complex: 'We knew our country was a smalltime dump / where nothing ever happened and / there was nothing to do. / And nobody had a name like Jelly Roll Morton.' Williams's first encounter with Hollywood came when the film rights to his 1968 novel *The Man Who Had Power Over Women* were bought for £27,000 and his work became even better known when his next novel *The Siege of Trencher's Farm* (1969) was filmed by Sam Peckinpah as the notoriously violent *Straw Dogs* (1971). Williams's text is more restrained than Peckinpah's version, but it is still a gripping tale about a visiting American academic and his wife being threatened in a remote Cornish farmhouse by violent locals. A journalist by training, Williams regards himself as a professional writer with over 20 books to his name, including a novel about professional football in the then near future, *They Used to Play on Grass* (1971), produced in collaboration with his friend Terry Venables, who also worked with him on a TV series in the late 1970s about an ex-cop cockney private eye in London called Hazell.

George Friel (1910–75)

The novels of George Friel, on the other hand, stayed in Glasgow to chronicle the lives of lonely individuals against the pressures of the city. Friel lived and worked in Glasgow all his life, and the city and his long experience as a schoolteacher in what one of his characters describes as 'one of Glasgow's wild-life reservations, a pocket of vandalism, a pool of iniquity', provided the characteristically ironic tone and subject matter for all his writing. Influenced by James Joyce's *Dubliners*, Friel sets out to describe the intellectual and spiritual paralysis at the heart of his own society, most often manifest in the uneasy relationships between adults and youngsters. What hope is there for the future, Friel seems to ask, when there is such a breach between the generations; when what one side wishes to hand on is treated with such contempt by the other? Yet this gap of understanding is seen in a bleakly humorous light in fable-like tales that illuminate the failings on both sides even as they seem to deny the possibility of any resolution.

Like many first novels, *The Banks of Time* (1959) was based on Friel's own early years. Born into poverty and brought up in a two-room flat in Maryhill, he determined that his work should tell the truth as he saw it in both his personal and professional life. Looking back on his output in 1972 he defended his pessimism by explaining:

> If I could see a lot of sweetness and light in Glasgow I would be happy to write about it: this is life. If you say what is going on then something might get done. But if you play Mr Glasgow and pretend that it's a fine warm-hearted city then you are kidding yourself, kidding the public, and pledging the future to no reform.

Once again, this credo would not be out of place in the mouth of James Kelman, who was to speak for a marginalised workforce in *The Busconductor Hines* in 1984 and again for alienated teachers in *A Disaffection* (1989). Friel's own engagement with the marginalised often takes place in the classroom, for it is here that the state and the individual meet, in a tiny theatre that might have much to reveal about the general health of the nation. What Friel sees, with dark irony, is a field of play in which the best intentions gang aft agley, ending more often than not simply in a struggle for power. In *The Boy Who Wanted Peace* (1964) a gang of schoolboys discovers the proceeds of a bank robbery in the school cellar, and Percy Phinn, older than the rest, declares himself the Moses-like leader of a cult of 'El' based on the power of money and its ability to buy leisure time, if not peace. With notions of being a poet like his namesake Shelley, Percy dreams of a cottage at Land's End and presides over the cash while trying to use it for good and to help the people around him. But Savage, a younger and greedier rival, usurps him and Percy flees, only to be arrested in London. Savage takes over the gang and in a wild ritual of his own he burns the remaining cash 'in an ecstasy of destructiveness', thrilled by the power that such an act gives him in the eyes of the others. A gangster stranger who has been tracking the loot, weeps over the ashes under the contemptuous gaze of the schoolboys, free from the nakedness of his need.

An even drier humour prevails in *Grace and Miss Partridge* (1969), whose narrative style casts a surreal light over a story of tenement life in which demented old Miss Partridge, full of religious zeal like one of the elect, tries to protect the young girl Grace from the temptations of life, even to the point of trying to kill her with a poke of poisoned sweeties. Friel takes great delight in playing with a familiar theme in the Scottish canon, as if the serious core of Robin Jenkins's vision and the tradition of Hogg were being retold by a mischievously cynical sprite. The prose style dances to its own tune, breaking into rhyme in unexpected places, and the author's admiration for Joyce shows up in his use of puns, proper names, intertextual echoes and mellifluous wordplay. The effect is relentlessly striking, and even when it seems excessive, it is an original and welcome departure from the grey prose realism of 'the Glasgow novel'. The narrator lives in the tenement too, and only at the very end of the book do we discover that he has married Grace in later years, just as we also discover that his account may contain passages that he made up or got wrong – as his mother makes clear when he shows her his manuscript. Less than impressed, she asks him if it is 'a history pretending to be fiction', or 'a fiction pretending to be history'. The reader, too, is left to ponder, while the narrator vows to do better next time: 'I still think that's how it was. And with God's grace I'll write a story one day about the tenement where I was born.' Friel's play on grace/Grace generates an intriguing tension between punning and profundity that haunts the whole novel.

Friel's short stories pursue similar themes and were collected after his death as *A Friend to Humanity* (1992), and his last novel, *An Empty House* (1974), used the decaying villa of its title, surrounded by a housing estate and a culture of vandalism, as a metaphor for the state of the country. His finest and darkest novel remains *Mr Alfred MA* (1972), which takes his preferred themes to their farthest expression in a tale about the breakdown of a failing and about to be disgraced schoolteacher. Friel's irony pervades the narrative to the point where the relentlessly anthropological and distantly amused tone in which he tells of juvenile gangs and their culture of mindless violence in the city comes to seem like a dry despair – not unlike the condition of his protagonist. Something of this distance also appears in Friel's use of obscure words as he describes a children's squabble in the Provan household in terms of 'scapular blows', 'a strabismic glare' and 'a defence of temporary kyphosis' (hunching of the back). This wryly alienating narrative position might be said to echo Mr Alfred's own weary disaffection and yet we still sympathise with him, a would-be poet on the edge of alcoholism and in the grip of an unwise attraction to his pupil Rose, surrounded by pusillanimous fellow teachers and brought down by anonymous slander from Gerry Provan, one of his pupils. The novel, and Mr Alfred's crisis, comes to a climax when, rather the worse for drink, he bumps into some of his former pupils and gets beaten up by them. Coming-to in the gutter, groggy if not delirious, he is helped by a mysterious youth, calling himself Tod (which is German for death, or Scots for a cunning fox and hence the devil), who also claims to be a former pupil and a better poet than his teacher. Tod is the poet of graffiti and the modern city, the unacknowledged legislator whose motto is 'Deride, deface and destroy'. Contemptuous of the social workers who seek to explain or excuse his every move, he finds his models in the Hitlerjugend or the Red Guard and speaks for the anarchic democracy of perpetual opposition.

> 'That's me,' said Tod. 'I say "No" to you and your likes. I'm nibbling away at the roots of your civilisation. I'll bring it down. The felt pen is mightier than the sword.'
> 'You've made my city ugly,' said Mr Alfred. 'Apart from all the stabbings and fighting in the street, this writing on the wall everywhere – it's an offence against civilisation.'
> 'Civilisation means class distinction,' said Tod. 'To hell with it. Life is more important than civilisation. Life is a comprehensive school. Every child is equal.'

Challenged by the gang graffiti all around him, Mr Alfred suffers a mental collapse and writes his own on a wall 'MENE MENE TEKEL UPHARSIN'. Appearing on the wall of Belshazzar's feast, these were the mysterious words that Daniel decoded to foretell the fall of the Babylonian empire, telling the king that he had been weighed in the balance and found wanting. – '"What lingo's that?"' says a policeman to his partner, '"No idea," said King. "He's not a Paki is he?"' Mr Alfred adds 'GLASGOW YA BASS' and is arrested, arraigned and finally committed to a mental institution. Everyone in Friel's novel has been found wanting. The reactionary fierceness of his humour is difficult to disentangle from his protagonist's habitual mindset, and the relentlessly ironic distance of his prose hovers somewhere between black comedy, anguish and rage. With this tone and their shifts between realism, romance, the fantastic and the nightmarish, Friel's books are not far from the then contemporary American style that the critic Robert Scholes would call fabulation. It's a disturbing mixture, and perhaps this is why Friel got so little credit in Scotland during his lifetime for this and his other novels, despite their brilliantly prickly variations on mony an auld Caledonian theme.

William McIlvanney (b. 1936)

William McIlvanney was also a schoolteacher. Born to a working-class family in Kilmarnock he graduated from Glasgow University and taught for seventeen years before becoming a full-time writer. His first two novels explored environmental and family tensions in the urban west of Scotland. In *Remedy is None* (1966) a student kills his stepfather in a grim retelling of the Hamlet theme caught up in class rather than dynastic conflict, while *A Gift from Nessus* (1968) deals with the experience of an adulterous businessman. The title 'Remedy is None' comes from Dunbar's 'Lament for the Makaris': 'Sen for the deid remeid is none. / Best is that we for dede dispone. / Eftir our deid that lif may we: / *Timor mortis conturbat me*.' These lines signal McIlvanney's continuing engagement with existential philosophy, especially the work of Albert Camus and its emphasis on individual choice in the face of mortality. Yet whether his third book, the Whitbread Award winning *Docherty* (1975), offers such choice to its characters is a moot point, for the heroes of McIlvanney's universe often seem fatalistically bound from the start. It is also a deeply masculinist universe, reflecting its author's fascination with violence, whether it is the social violence of an unjust class structure, or the physical violence of strong men or hard men – the products of that system, driven to react against it.

Unlike McIlvanney's other books, *Docherty* is a historical novel. It looks back to the years before the Great War and the Depression that followed it, to describe the hardship and courage of a coal-miner in fictional 'Graithnock', a sister town to the author's own Kilmarnock. Unlike Williams and Friel, McIlvanney still believes in class solidarity and the possibility that individuals can transcend their circumstances and make a difference. Tam Docherty is held up to us as the champion of the local 'High Street': punishing a peeping tom, seeking education for his youngest son, he is a stalwart family man and an exemplary worker. Yet he seems trapped by his environment, and his rough virtues avail him nothing in the end, unless it is to be remembered – sentimentally – as a local legend: 'He wis only five foot fower. But when yer hert goes fae yer heid tae yer taes, that's a lot o' hert.' Docherty dies in a mine accident while saving a fellow worker – 'diving into his own death to push Hammy out of his' – and all that can be seen of him at the end is a clenched fist protruding from the rubble. The novel leaves it up to us to decide whether this has been an act of heroism and resistance, or an almost suicidal escape from intolerable circumstances. McIlvanney's expressionist naturalism makes the point from the very start, describing the human situation in intensely deterministic terms where neighbourliness is seen as a reflex action and men crack like machines with metal fatigue:

> Behind every other trivial occurrence lay a stress-point upon which poverty or despair or a crushing sense of inferiority had played for years. Consequently, frustrations tended to explode in most of them from time to time.
>
> Sometimes men would disintegrate spectacularly, beating a wife unconscious one pellucid summer evening or going on the batter with cheap whisky for a fortnight. Such bouts of failure were not approved of, but they never earned a permanent contempt. They were too real for that.

Tam's struggle in the face of such odds is undoubtedly heroic, but he has no resources other than his own endurance and – surprisingly for a man with such class loyalty – he does not turn to political action. His story is the story of someone with a strong sense of individuality and pride who slowly begins to realise that nothing of what makes him a man in his own eyes, and earns the admiration of his fellows, can help him or save his family from eventual defeat at the hands of an unjust economic and social system. Even the working-class camaraderie of the pub at the end of a hard day (described in quasi-religious terms) turns sour in the light of this realisation:

> Now he stood at the bar, where before the company of his friends had approximated to a congregation, a confirmation in mass of his personal conviction, and he felt himself participating in a useless ritual, mechanically lifting and lowering a glass, savouring the sourness of his past. He saw Mick as a son abducted and dismembered, and he was without response save anger, without recourse not just to defence but even to understanding. Tam felt redundant to his own life. His previous authority over his own experience was a joke. He was like a gunfighter, practised to perfection, unafraid, heroically hard, and pitted against germ warfare.

Tam's three sons are the legacy of his life, and this too turns to dust in his mouth: his son Mick, who lost an arm in the trenches, has become an embittered Communist; Angus betrays his fellow workers by subcontracting his labour; and at the end of the book, Conn (the educated one who still had to go down the mine like his father), is left 'in twa minds', divided between his two brothers. When Tam Docherty finally sees the light, it is a vision so terrible that he may well have sought his own death in that mine accident.

> his own rage against himself. He had fed his children to a system that gave them back as the bread he ate every day of his life. And it wasn't until he

had eaten them that he discovered what he had done. Now that it was too late, he understood.

The theme of cannibalism will reappear in Alasdair Gray's *Lanark*. McIlvanney's writing shows a continuing fascination with the individualism of masculinity and its capacity for courage and violence. *Docherty* and some of the short stories in *Walking Wounded* (1989) pursue this strain in Scottish working-class culture, as well as a tendency to see women either as objects of romantic longing or as creatures set on taming their men in the name of convention, security and social respectability. At one level *Docherty* is the most searching analysis of the futility of just such masculinist value systems – an elegy to the defeat of the individual 'gunfighter' – and yet at another level it shares those values for, like all elegies, there is an element of love and admiration in the text as well.

The same theme, and the same ambiguity, can be found in Docherty's successor *The Big Man* (1985), set in the Thatcherite 1980s, which tells the story of unemployed Dan Scoular, a gentle hardman in his way, who is driven by need and a sense of honour to take up bare-knuckle fighting for money on behalf of a gangster. McIlvanney sees this as emblematic of how people are used and brutalised by capitalism, and yet having made this connection, the novel, as with *Docherty*, does not seem to allow any space for further analysis or collective action. Indeed Scoular has nothing but contempt for those who would theorise about changing the system, in place of living in the here and now: 'The system. Where does it live? You got an address for it?' Dan's solution is to steal money from the gangster to help his defeated opponent, and to walk into his local pub knowing that he is now a marked man. McIlvanney sees this as the supreme existential moment – choosing not to run and hide, choosing life in the face of mortality – whether death comes in its own time, as it does for us all, or tomorrow at the hands of a criminal called Matt Mason. The gunfighter ethic has a certain magnificence, and McIlvanney is honest enough to admire courage in direct physical confrontation, however unfashionable it may be in liberal circles. But it is also complicit with the violence it espouses.

Between *Docherty* and *The Big Man*, McIlvanney wrote two novels about a Glasgow Detective Inspector, and *Laidlaw* (1977) and *The Papers of Tony Veitch* (1983) were later followed by *Strange Loyalties* (1991) in a highly successful series, regarded by some critics as the author's best work. (The first two received the Crime Writers'

Association Silver Dagger Award.) Writing in his essay 'The Courage of Our Doubts' McIlvanney argues that 'Laidlaw invites us to join him in a place where there is no them and us. There is only us . . . where we may feel a little lost among the shifting borders of good and bad, or right and wrong.' So these are not quite genre novels because McIlvanney is more interested in the sensibilities of hunter and hunted and the interplay and affinities between them, than he is in 'who did it' and the twists and turns of police investigation as such. Jack Laidlaw carries his own emotional damage and often reflects on the irony of his role as the defender of a society whose bourgeois values he despises. The detective genre is an excellent vehicle for McIlvanney's existential individualism and the hard-bitten Chandleresque romanticism of a protagonist who mixes intellectual disquiet with bar-room philosophy, with his densely and richly downbeat observations: 'His face looked like an argument you couldn't win.' 'The man with the bottle stood swaying, drawing his dignity round him like an opera cloak. His irises had a furry look.' In common with Chandler's private eyes, it is as much his own inner space that Laidlaw explores as the backyards and narrow alleys of his beat.

In the end, however, McIlvanney's Laidlaw novels resist any simple classification as 'detective fiction' because their author has integrated them, along with *Docherty* and *The Big Man*, into what amounts to a linked body of work set in 'Graithnock' and Glasgow. So Matt Mason features in *Laidlaw*, just as Laidlaw is mentioned in *The Big Man*, along with many of the characters in the *Walking Wounded* short stories. *Strange Loyalties* is told by Laidlaw himself in first-person narrative and he also has a walk-on part in McIlvanney's most recent and perhaps most personal novel, *The Kiln* (1996), whose protagonist is Tom Docherty (Conn's son and Tam's grandson), now a middle-aged novelist looking back on the summer that saw him begin his career as a writer and come to maturity as a man.

McIlvanney has produced three collections of poetry, more narrative and discursive than lyrical, and the essays and journalistic pieces collected in *Surviving the Shipwreck* (1991) revisit a number of his preoccupations. In particular 'A Shield Against the Gorgon' condemns the middle-class sophists of political ideology and 'revolution', as opposed to the author's preference for 'rebellion' as something more unruly, individual, 'pragmatic and salvationary'. The same essay discusses his own novels and especially *Docherty* in the light of his admiration for Conn's refusal to leave his class roots, and yet he notes that 'the central paradox of the book' is that 'it is written for people most of whom will never read it'. This is an anxiety that James Kelman will also feel.

Ian Rankin (b. 1960)

In fact the Laidlaw books have turned out to be remarkably influential, or at least prophetic, for a growing number of younger Scottish writers have since engaged with genre fiction while maintaining high literary quality. (One thinks especially of a flourishing school of science fiction, most notably the novels of Iain M. Banks; or the work of his friend Ken MacLeod, who offers an equally left-wing vision of alternative futures; or the *noir*-ish and violent worlds of Richard Morgan.) In crime fiction especially, the Inspector Rebus novels of Ian Rankin, from *Knots and Crosses* (1987) onwards, have taken over the familiar mantle of the battered cop, and the hard-boiled police procedural novel. With settings in Edinburgh rather than Glasgow, Rankin stays closer to the convoluted plotting conventions of the crime mystery genre, although he too uses the form to explore aspects of Scottish society. In fact it has become a feature of the Rebus novels that they should reflect, directly or indirectly, the social, political or economic issues of the day in novels that have steadily grown in complexity and sophistication. At the same time, Rankin has remained true to an older tradition of internal division, as he explains in words that go back to Miss Jean Brodie's scandalous ancestor the good Deacon himself:

> Edinburgh is the perfect setting for crime writing. It has a split personality – on the one hand it is the city of history and museums and royalty, but at the same time there is this feeling that behind the thick walls of those Georgian townhouses there are all sorts of terrible things happening.

The *Literary Review* duly noted, perhaps rather worryingly for the natives, that 'Rankin captures like no one else, that strangeness that is Scotland at the end of the twentieth century.'

Edward Boyd (1916–89) and Frederic Lindsay (b. 1933)

Although less commercially successful than the Rebus books, McIlvanney's Laidlaw novels undoubtedly contributed to what is sometimes referred to as 'tartan noir', paving the way for later exponents such as Val McDermid, the wilder extravagance of Christopher Brookmyre, and Rankin himself. Nevertheless, while McIlvanney certainly made it his own, the Chandleresque spirit in a Glasgow setting spiced with romantically gritty dialogue was pioneered in the work of Edward Boyd, who wrote film scripts and many serials and plays for both radio and television, including scripts for *Z Cars* and the successful BBC TV series *The View from Daniel Pike* (1971–73), starring Roddy McMillan as a hard-nut Glasgow private eye. Boyd had been an actor, a stage manager and a director for the Glasgow Unity Theatre in the 1940s, before going on to work for broadcast media and films. The tough spirit of his Daniel Pike programmes undoubtedly paved the way for the later police series of *Taggart*, while his earlier radio serial plays such as *It's Always Sinatra* (1969), *Badger by Owl-light* (later done for television in 1982), and *Castles in Spain* (1987) show a highly literary and stylish talent at work, very much in the spirit of *film noir*. The dark thrillers of Frederic Lindsay were equally influential at this time with the pioneering urban gothic of novels such as *Brond* (1983), *Jill Rips* (1987), *A Charm Against Drowning* (1988) and *After the Stranger Came* (1992), followed by his Inspector Jim Meldrum series thereafter.

Alan Sharp (b. 1934)

Alan Sharp worked in the Clydeside shipyards when he left school before going on to university, and eventually to London and America, where he became a successful screenwriter with many original screenplays and film treatments to his name. His work has been directed by Sam Peckinpah, Arthur Penn and Robert Aldrich and he produced a memorably earthy script for *Rob Roy* directed by Michael Caton-Jones in 1995. *A Green Tree in Gedde* (1965) and *The Wind Shifts* (1976) are the first two volumes of a trilogy that was never completed. They follow the lives, thoughts and journeys of four characters in search of 'home' in an effort to understand and explore existential questions of sexuality and identity. Sharp set himself a large-scale task with these picaresque novels, and under the influence of Henry Miller and James Joyce he adopted a highly-wrought and various prose, moving from impersonal narrative to impressionism, terse dialogue and elaborately poetic evocations. It was a brilliant and ambitious debut, but Sharp seems to have left it unfinished with something of an air of relief.

Elspeth Davie (1919–95)

By comparison the novels and stories of Elspeth Davie offer a much quieter but no less sensitive account of city life within the daily setting of bourgeois existence, most usually in Edinburgh, where she herself lived, married to the distinguished philosopher George Elder Davie. Elspeth Davie wrote four novels, *Providings* (1965) on family relationships, and *Creating a Scene* (1971), which follows her interest in art (she was a skilled painter) to deal with the relationship between two art students and their teacher during a project to help to 'humanise' a housing scheme. *Climbers on a Stair* (1978) is structured around vignettes from the linked lives in an Edinburgh tenement building very similar to the one she lived in herself, while her last novel, *Coming to Light* (1989), explores the sad discrepancies between modern Edinburgh and what the city achieved in the Scottish Enlightenment. Davie's best work, however, is to be found in her short stories. She won the Catherine Mansfield short story award in 1978 and the form suits her understated Edinburgh settings and an elliptical modernist approach combined with an almost neoclassical restraint. Her collections *The Spark* (1969) and *The High Tide Talker* (1976) contain memorable images of the lonely and unique nature of ordinary people, conveyed in outstandingly clear, succinct and subtly polished prose. Subsequent collections, *The Night of the Funny Hats* (1980), *A Traveller's Room* (1985) and *Death of a Doctor* (1992), confirm a coolly descriptive observational skill with a painter's eye for the telling if oblique detail, and the quiet mysteriousness of everyday surfaces. Writing of her understanding of the artist's task, she noted the need

> to recognise and preserve the more secret side of life. The writers who chiefly interest me are those who strike in at an angle to experience rather than going along parallel to it. . . . The desolating and the unfamiliar is happening continually between our getting up and our going to bed. . . . It is of this day to day business of living, its mysteriousness and its absurdity, that I would like to write.

Such an approach explains the cool and compassionately sceptical nature of her work, which is every bit as fine and revealing as Muriel Spark's short fiction, but without the latter's fiercely ironic and impatient gaze.

New drama and new realisms: theatre, film, television

It is impossible to discuss drama, or indeed the fiction of the 1960s and 1970s, without also recognising the cultural impact of contemporary Scottish film makers and the work being done for television and radio. Thus, for example, the severe realism of the novel at this time had its counterpart in a sequence of films made by Bill Douglas, while the demotic energy to be found in the second wave of Scottish drama features equally vividly in a number of plays for television. In fact the links between literature, theatre, radio, film and television were bound to become progressively stronger, if only because so many young dramatists in recent years also make their living (have to make their living) as scriptwriters.

Bill Douglas (1934–91)

The introspective creative energies of Bill Douglas, born in Newcraighall, a failing mining village outside Edinburgh, took him directly to film making in Scotland, a path strewn with difficulties at that time, not least because his work was so uncompromisingly minimalist, not to say stark in its realisation. Douglas's later projects include *Comrades* (1987), a film on the Tolpuddle martyrs that took eight years to make, and a version of the *Justified Sinner* that was never completed; but he is best known for the autobiographical trilogy of films *My Childhood* (1972), *My Ain Folk* (1973) and *My Way Home* (1978). Set in Douglas's home town, the *My Childhood* trilogy traces the protagonist's life from a boyhood in abject poverty to his teenage years, national service abroad and the beginnings of his interest in film. This work is particularly relevant in the present context because it transcends the conventions of 'working-class realism', and despite their grim settings, the films have a stark graphic beauty to them as they move from scene to scene and image to image in an indirect and severely elliptical manner reminiscent of silent film in the early Russian cinema. Such austerity is quite different from the comparatively broad emphasis of the novels discussed above and it is equally far from the direct address and the robustly popular colloquialism of what was happening in the Scottish theatre at this time, as it rediscovered and re-energised the socialist tradition of the Glasgow Citizens' Theatre in the 1940s.

Roddy McMillan (1923–79), Stewart Conn (b. 1936) and Hector MacMillan (b. 1929)

That link with earlier days at the Glasgow Citizens' is provided by Roddy McMillan, whose first play in a naturalistic mode, *All in Good Faith*, was a success there in 1954. Stewart Conn, poet and radio-producer for the BBC, advanced the trend by writing *I Didn't Always*

Live Here (1967), evoking the humour and harshness of Glasgow life and speech from the Depression to the post-war years through a series of flashbacks from its two female protagonists. Roddy McMillan's second play, *The Bevellers* (1973), is a sympathetic study of an apprentice's initiation into life on the shop floor of a glass-bevelling works where the language is anything but polished, and it remains the most convincing of the several plays of the period that were set in places of work. Hector MacMillan used a similar linguistic freedom in exploring the internal horrors of Protestant bigotry in Glasgow with *The Sash* (1973).

Bill Bryden (b. 1942)

Bill Bryden came to the Edinburgh Lyceum in 1970 and assembled a talented company of Scottish actors. With a stellar cast, *Willie Rough* (1972) was guaranteed popular success. Set in Bryden's native Greenock, it follows the political education of a moderate shop steward on 'Red Clydeside', whose increasingly radical commitment costs him his freedom and his job, but not his spirit. It is a story of working-class life and sentiment with a naturalistic succession of scenes from 1914 to 1916. Bryden is a skilful and successful director, but the theatrical formula behind his writing became clearer with *Benny Lynch* (1974) and clearer still with *Civilians* (1981). Nevertheless, *Willie Rough* was the vanguard of a revival in urban 'sentimental realism' and a new popular interest in the Scottish stage. Bryden's later work in Scotland developed a deliberately epic scale with *The Ship* (1990), which was staged in Govan in the former engine shed of Harland and Wolff during Glasgow's year as European City of Culture. The plot engaged with family and sectarian tensions, with star-crossed lovers and prejudice from either side of Glasgow's religious divide, and climaxes in a *coup de théâtre* by which a 67-foot model of the Queen Elizabeth II was 'launched' each night. This was a theatre of spectacle, as was *The Big Picnic* (1994) in the same venue, which took its audience 'over the top' in an astonishing laser-lit climax invoking the experience of Scottish troops in the Great War. It was Bryden's remit in both plays to engage with the great myths of Scottish working-class male identity and experience at home, in the workplace and on the battlefield, and he succeeded brilliantly in doing this, using music and stage effects to the full. Yet the final effect was deeply mythical too, for in the last analysis these were epic acts of communal celebration, rather than serious attempts to throw new light on the old stereotypes, or to question or understand the historical forces that were being invoked. This outcome might be put down to the sheer scale of the productions, but the same tendency can also be traced in Bryden's earlier work. Nevertheless his impact as a director marked a new confidence in staging Scottish drama and in finding large audiences for it.

John McGrath (1935–2002)

The very name of the 7:84 Company proclaimed the radically political purpose of its founder, John McGrath, who came north in 1973 to start a Scottish branch of the theatre company he had first conceived in London. (The numbers come from a 1966 report in the *Economist* claiming that 7 per cent of the population owns 84 per cent of Britain's capital wealth.) McGrath lived in London and Liverpool from 1958 to 1965, working as a reader for the Royal Court Theatre as well as writing his own plays, doing screenplays for Hollywood and scripting and directing numerous television programmes for the BBC. His engagement with ordinary lives and regional accents, for example, was evident in the innovative police series *Z Cars*, set in Liverpool in the 1960s. As a playwright he had particular success with *Events while Guarding the Bofors Gun* (1966), a psychological drama of class warfare in the army under National Service, not unlike an 'other ranks' version of *Tunes of Glory*. Two years later the play was made into a gripping film with Nicol Williamson and David Warner.

For the 7:84 project McGrath developed a style of Brechtian propaganda drama (equally influenced by John Arden and Joan Littlewood) which mixed together documentary material, music-hall routines, folksong, jokes and satirical ditties to make fast-moving and hilarious shows, full of melodrama, pathos and didacticism. In taking inspiration from music halls and the pantomime, he was tapping into a popular Scottish tradition and a long-established audience for such entertainment. In fact the previous year had seen *The Great Northern Welly Boot Show* use sketches, songs and comic routines to tell the story of the work-in at the Upper Clyde Shipbuilders to full houses in Glasgow and the Edinburgh Festival. A young Billy Connolly, himself an ex-shipbuilder, provided material for that show and appeared on stage with Bill Paterson, John Bett and Alex Norton, all of whom were to join McGrath's new company the following year. The 7:84 actors were encouraged to help develop and produce the play, and audiences were encouraged to sing along with them on the stage.

The company's Scottish debut was *The Cheviot, the Stag and the Black, Black Oil* (1973), which argues for socialism in Scotland against the exploitation of working people by landowners and the power of capital, from the time of the Clearances to the great Victorian hunting estates and the global oil corporations of the present day. It arrived at just the moment when devolution and North Sea oil were the hottest topics in the country, and the play was taken on tour to twenty-eight community centres and remote town halls before it ever saw the major theatres. Memorably fuelled by the talent and conviction of the actors themselves and by Gaelic songs from the powerful folk-singer Dolina MacLennan, *The Cheviot* struck home with its account of the Clearances in the very places where they happened. It was an enormous popular and critical success and the tour of the Highlands was followed by a tour of Ireland and two appearances on national television. Its Brechtian engagement with history as a way of establishing a critique of the present was equally influential, as was McGrath's calculated conflation of class identity and Scottish identity within an international and socialist perspective. Subsequent plays from 7:84 adapted different themes and different social problems to the same political end and, perhaps inevitably, the message became predictable despite individually brilliant actors and the high energy of the group's demotic style. Memorable productions included *The Game's a Bogey* (1974) about John Maclean on 'Red Clydeside'; and plays that reflected women's experience of working-class life such as *Little Red Hen* (1975) and *Blood Red Roses* (1980).

In 1982, McGrath and the company acknowledged their political precursors by performing the 'Clydebuilt' season in Glasgow, with the highly successful revival of five plays originally produced by Glasgow Unity, the Fife Miner Players, the Theatre Workshop and the Glasgow Workers' Theatre Group. These were George Munro's *Gold in His Boots* (1947); Joe Corrie's play about the General Strike *In Time of Strife* (1927); documentary dramas from the 1930s in Harry Trott's *UAB Scotland* and Ewan MacColl's *Johnny Noble*; Ena Lamont Stewart's play about working-class women *Men Should Weep* (1947); and *Screw the Bobbin*, a new play by Chris Hannan, Alan Clews and the company itself. While recognising a historical debt to these earlier companies, 7:84's most vital contribution to theatrical experience and community involvement was to add the popular arts of variety theatre, folksong and protestsongs to the mix, thus allowing the Scottish theatre to move on from the realist/naturalist tradition of previous generations. However, the slow withdrawal of Scottish Arts Council funding (and many wrangles over the company's political focus and its financial management) led McGrath to resign from 7:84 Scotland in 1988. The company name was continued under the direction of David Hayman to perform more work with the same values, if less exclusively on Scottish topics.

The Cheviot paved the way for a number of other production companies. Principal among these was the Wildcat Theatre Company, founded in 1978 by three former members of 7:84 who wanted to stay true to the original formula. A similar remit was behind the establishment of the Glasgow Mayfest in the early 1980s, as a citywide celebration of working-class culture. John McGrath and Wildcat collaborated at the Tramway in Glasgow (an exciting space made from an old transport museum that had once been a repair centre for the city's trams) to produce two epic and large-scale works of historical dialectic. *Border Warfare* (1989) challenged narrowly nationalist accounts of Scottish identity, in its account of the country's long struggle with England as a major colonial and colonising power. It was later broadcast as a three-part television series. Its successor *John Brown's Body* (1990) did much the same with regard to the history and effects of industrialisation. Wildcat productions played a leading part in the Mayfest celebrations until the company was closed in 1991 when its Scottish Arts Council funding was also withdrawn. The debate over public funding for the arts in Scotland continues to this day, as does the struggle to find an audience large enough to satisfy the funding bodies or the Scottish Executive's 'entitlement' policy. In this context McGrath's determination to find a new audience for drama looks particularly prescient. How long such a drama could expect to sustain itself on the same radical political platform, and continue to fill houses, has been another question.

Donald Campbell (b. 1940)

In 1976 the Traverse Theatre presented *The Jesuit* by the poet Donald Campbell, about the trial of Catholic martyr John Ogilvie in the seventeenth century. Like much of Campbell's work, the play focuses on an historical moment of personal crisis, but the completely modern colloquial style of the common soldiers' dialogue marks what was soon to become a vogue in Scottish plays. Campbell went on to write more than twenty works for the stage, using their historical settings to explore more contemporary issues, as with *Somerville the Soldier* (1978), for example, which recounts the true case of a soldier who objected to the army being used to suppress civilian unrest in the nine-teenth century. ('Bloody Sunday', when British paratroops fired on Civil Rights protesters in Northern Ireland, had happened in Derry in 1972.) The play gives a complex account of the mixed motives and the many agendas operating on both sides of the case. *The Widows of Clyth* (1979) deals with survivor's guilt and the family cost of a fishing disas-ter in Caithness, while *Till All the Seas Run Dry* (1981) stays with a female perspective to give Jean Armour's account of Robert Burns's life.

Tom McGrath (b. 1940)

Equally notable at this time was a taste for plays with profanity and 'hard-man' attitudes, the most striking of which was indeed called *The Hard Man* (1977), by Glasgow writer Tom McGrath. The play's exploration of violence and its interest in the Nietzschean strength of will of its protagonist was based on the actual life and times of Jimmy Boyle, who worked with McGrath on the production. In keeping with the novels of Williams and McIlvanney and in anticipation of what Kelman and Welsh were to do in prose fiction, such plays are another of the ways in which the pains and horrors of damaged masculinity were tackled in Scottish writing of the late 1960s and 1970s. They also brought the demotic immediacy of Scots street speech to the stage, and to thousands of playgoers it seemed like a breath of salty fresh air.

John Byrne (b. 1940)

This is particularly the case with John Byrne, a graduate of Glasgow Art School who worked as an artist and set designer, doing the *Great Northern Welly Boot Show* among other projects, and building a set like a folding 'pop-up' book for *The Cheviot*. Byrne's paintings and graphic works are exhibited in many galleries, but he is at least as well known as a writer for stage and television. His first play, *Writer's Cramp*, appeared in 1977, but it was *The Slab Boys* (1978) that made his repu-tation. Based on Byrne's own experiences, it is set in the 'slab room' of a carpet factory in Paisley where the colours are mixed by apprentices, and, appropriately enough for teenagers in the 1950s, this is a place where 'patter' reigns supreme. The dialogue crackles between Phil and his friend Spanky as they talk about clothes and music, plan the conquest of girls and rather cruelly torment the nerdy Hector. Like Byrne himself, the character called Phil wants to go to art school and has to cope with a mentally unbalanced mother. The play is both exhilarating and disconcerting as the dialogue switches from humour to pathos with lightning speed. Byrne was encouraged to produce sequels, which eventually became the *Slab Boys Trilogy*. The second play follows the first by a matter of hours, describing the factory staff dance in *The Loveliest Night of the Year* (1979), later revised as *Threads* (1980) and revised again as *Cuttin' a Rug* (1982). The sequence ends with the reunion of the two main characters, ten years later, in *Still Life* (1982).

The essence of Byrne's work is in the sharp and sometimes convoluted wit of the repartee and its author's own undisguised affection for teenage culture of the 1950s. Subsequent revivals (including a film in 1997) have embraced an increasingly nostalgic spirit and it is also from this source that Byrne produced his comic masterpiece, *Tutti Frutti* (1987). This was a six-part BBC Scotland television serial about a middle-aged Scottish rock 'n' roll band making a disastrously final 'jubilee' tour with the younger brother of their now defunct lead singer. Produced on film with a memorable soundtrack and a cast including Maurice Roëves, not to mention Robbie Coltrane, Emma Thompson and Richard Wilson, all of whom were to become much better known in its aftermath, *Tutti Frutti* deservedly won a BAFTA award. In its transplantation of retro American rock lifestyle into an increasingly black West of Scotland humour, the work is a perfect example of cultural hybridity and has proved to be immensely influential in how Scottish culture has come to see itself. Byrne repeated the feat to equally hilarious effect with *Your Cheatin' Heart* (1989), a complex and more mannered script exploring gangster culture and Glasgow's deep love affair with Country and Western music.

Bill Forsyth (b. 1946)

Something of the same sense of hybrid celebration, along with a multicultural ease of reference and a stylistic confidence, can be seen in the films of Bill Forsyth, and it is no accident that his first feature, *That Sinking Feeling* (1979), should have been screened only a year after *The Slab Boys* appeared. These works mark a major shift in sensibility since the austerity of Bill Douglas's *My Childhood* trilogy only seven years earlier and the cultural despair of novels such as *From Scenes Like These* in the late 1960s. Forsyth left school at sixteen and found himself a job as an assistant in the film business. His first two films, *That Sinking Feeling* and *Gregory's Girl* (1982), came from scripts he had started to develop in 1977 when he was working with young actors in the

Glasgow Youth Theatre. The low-budget success of *That Sinking Feeling* allowed Forsyth to finance the more ambitious *Gregory's Girl*, kick-starting his own career and that of his leading man John Gordon Sinclair. Forsyth's most successful film in this vein was undoubtedly *Local Hero* (1983), nominated for six British Academy awards, and winning best Screenplay and a number of other film prizes in Britain and America. Here again, an appreciative awareness of transatlantic culture plays a large part, along with an ironic awareness of earlier films about Scottish identity, especially Alexander Mackendrick's *Whisky Galore* from 1949 and *The Maggie* from 1954. Forsyth's work has a characteristically gentle sense of wonder to it and an alert eye for absurdity – often in the background of a scene or in passing – that would do justice to Jacques Tati. His Scottish films, including *Comfort and Joy* (1984) set in Glasgow at Christmas time, and the less success-ful sequel *Gregory's Two Girls* (1999), all manage to find new things to say about the cinematic portrayal of the Scottish character. As with John Byrne, Forsyth's influence on subsequent productions for both film and television has been considerable, along with a welcome ability to strike a lighter note. (Ninian Dunet and Michael Hoffman's film *Restless Natives* in 1985, the TV series *Hamish MacBeth* running from 1995 to 1997, and *American Cousins* by Sergio Casci and Don Coutts in 2003 all follow in his footsteps.) While less inclined to sentiment, something of the same eclectic outlook, pace and style can be found in cinema productions like *Small Faces* (1995), the MacKinnon brothers' brilliant film about youth gangs in 1960s Glasgow; and of course the internationally successful *Trainspotting* (1995) directed by Daniel Boyle.

Peter McDougall (b. 1947)

A grimmer mixture of gallows humour, dramatic pace and violence in speech and action characterised a number of gripping films for televi-sion by Peter McDougall, some of them made for the prestigious BBC Play for Today series and all of them in depressed West of Scotland urban settings. His first script, *Just Your Luck* (1972), goes straight to the heart of religious prejudice when a Greenock teenager discovers that she is pregnant by a Catholic boy. *Just Another Saturday* (1975) deals with a young man's involvement in an Orange march in Glasgow and while the play does not shrink from portraying sectarian prejudice, drink and violence, yet there is hope, humour and a carnival atmos-phere as well, along with an uncomfortable understanding of how even a culture of bigotry can bind its members together. *Elephant's Graveyard* (1976) follows two men as they escape to the hills when they are supposed to be working; *Just a Boy's Game* (1979) is a dazzling and terrifying story of street violence when a young Greenock hard man tries to win the respect of his grandfather who was himself a razor king from Depression days. Like Tom McGrath before him, McDougall wrote his own version of the Jimmy Boyle story as *A Sense of Freedom* (1979). *Shoot for the Sun* (1986) dealt with the heroin trade in Edinburgh; *Down Where the Buffalo Go* (1988) followed the failing marriage of an American, played by Harvey Keitel, stationed at the Holy Loch; while *Down Among the Big Boys* (1993) was a more indulgent gangster caper starring Billy Connolly, who had in fact been given his first acting roles in *Just Another Saturday* and *Elephant's Graveyard*.

Sue Glover (b. 1943) and Rona Munro (b. 1959)

McDougall's plays, especially when directed by John Mackenzie, had their own considerable influence on subsequent productions for film and television, especially in the strongly masculinist bias of such work. In recent years, however, female playwrights have managed to claim back territory of their own, if still within the by now familiar historical and/or working-class genres. In this respect they are following in the footsteps of Ena Lamont Stewart, looking back to the success of her plays with a female perspective such as *Men Should Weep* in 1947. *Bondagers*, by Sue Glover achieved great success when it was first performed at the Traverse Theatre and then at the Tramway in 1991, and has been frequently revived and also filmed since then. It tells the story of women workers in Scotland who used to be hired as 'bondagers' by ploughmen, who were themselves hired to work the large farms of the time. This was a sexually and economically exploitative system that lasted until the Second World War and the play uses dance and song to convey the dauntless and vibrant spirit of six such women on a Borders farm in 1860. An earlier play for the Traverse, *The Straw Chair* (1988), looks back to the eighteenth century to tell the experience of a young woman and her minister husband when they go to live on the remote island of St Kilda. The work of Rona Munro uses more contemporary settings but she too explores female experience with scripts for a largely female cast, often dealing with present difficulties, a sense of entrapment and the revelation of trauma from the past. *Bold Girls* (1990) is set in Belfast in the 1990s following the lives of three women whose husbands have been either killed or imprisoned because of the Troubles, while *Iron* (2002) happens in a woman's prison, as Josie visits her mother Fay, a lifer she has not seen since she was sentenced fifteen years ago for a horrific murder. In more poetic and symbolic modes, Liz Lochhead's plays have also explored female experience, from the monstrous 'conception' of Mary Shelley's *Frankenstein* in *Blood and Ice* (1982, revived and revised 2003) to the theatrical *tour de force* of *Mary Queen of Scots Got Her Head Chopped Off* (1987), for the Communicado Theatre Company under the direction of Gerry Mulgrew.

In the face of so many plays that have searched the Scottish soul via politically or historically centred topics, or the stories and films that mine the seam of male violence, female grit and urban realism, experimental drama has had a more modest and erratic presence in Scottish theatres.

Robert David MacDonald (1929–2004), Stanley Eveling (b. 1925) and Gregory Burke (b. 1968)

Under the care of Giles Havergal, Philip Prowse and Robert David MacDonald, the Citizens' Theatre in Glasgow during the 1970s gained an international reputation for thrillingly innovative direction and the production of plays by a wide variety of authors from Shakespeare to Brecht, Strindberg to Noel Coward, Oscar Wilde to Edward Albee. Brilliantly individual works and adaptations were done by Robert David MacDonald with *The De Sade Show*, *Chinchilla*, *The Ice House*, *Dracula* and *No Orchids for Miss Blandish* in the 1970s and 1980s, but for the most part this theatre was no longer a venue for new Scottish writing. On the other hand, the Citizens' did develop an admirable outreach theatre project, established in 1967 and now known as the TAG touring company, bringing an eclectic selection of plays and adaptations to young people, first of all in Glasgow and then throughout Scotland.

By comparison the Traverse Theatre has done a lot over the years to premiere new work by Scottish writers, as well as plays by European and American authors. The Traverse was founded in 1963 by American Jim Haynes, who had started the Paperback Bookshop in 1960 as an outlet for modern literature with an international and eclectic scope. Haynes certainly enlivened the cultural scene in his day, as he was instrumental in helping to organise an International Writers'

Conference on the novel in 1962. This was followed in 1963 by an International Drama Conference, now notorious for the 'happening' at the McEwan hall in which a nude model was briefly glimpsed on the balcony while the general debate slipped into chaos and the local clergy fulminated the next morning against 'godlessness and dirt'. Haynes's aims for his theatre were similarly eclectic and avant-garde, with work by Arrabal, Jarry and Sartre in the opening months, as well as *Balachites* by Stanley Eveling, which was the first new piece done by the Traverse at its Lawnmarket venue. Originally from Liverpool, Eveling contributed a number of plays in what might be called an absurdist or surreal vein, including *The Lunatic, the Secret Sportsman and the Woman Next Door* (1968), *Dear Janet Rosenberg, Dear Mr Kooning* (1969), and *Caravaggio, Buddy* (1972), to make the Traverse a small corner of notably experimental drama in the North. Other notable productions included Stewart Conn's *Birds in the Wilderness* (1964) and *Thistlewood* (1975); C. P. Taylor's *Allergy* (1966), *Schippel* (1974) and a two-play set called *Walter* (1977). The promotion of new Scottish plays at the Traverse was particularly strong in the 1970s under the guidance of Chris Parr, with Hector Macmillan's *Gay Gorbals* (1976) and *The Sash* (1980); Donald Campbell's *The Jesuit* (1976), *Somerville the Soldier* (1978); and of course John Byrne's *The Slab Boys* (1978) and its sequels. The play *Gagarin Way* by Gregory Burke achieved critical acclaim at the Traverse in 2001 with a forensically searing account of Scotland and the modern world in the eyes of three different men whose workplace has been bought out by a multinational company. They kidnap a visiting executive and discuss their plans to kill him over a long night together in the factory store room. Cruel and funny by turns, described by its author as '*Waiting for Godot* with guns', *Gagarin Way* makes a striking comparison with *The Slab Boys* as a much more politically aware play from a young writer of the *Trainspotting* generation.

Chris Hannan (b. 1968) and Sharman Macdonald (b. 1951)

Recent plays from authors such as Sharman Macdonald, Simon Donald and Chris Hannan have rung the changes on West of Scotland urban realism. The early work of Chris Hannan appeared at the Traverse, with *Elizabeth Gordon Quinn* (1985) following Bill Bryden, but this time taking a woman's counter perspective on the days of 'Red Clydeside'. Later pieces such as *The Evil Doers* (1990) found comedy in its Glasgow setting while the award-winning *Shining Souls* (1996) used urban deprivation and family trauma in the city's East End to frame a story about an impending wedding that is chaotic, farcical and surreally profound by turns. *The Life of Stuff* (1992) by Simon Donald won 'most promising playwright' awards for its account of street life in and around a seedy Glasgow nightclub, yet its style was to go beyond brutal realism to a grotesque and nihilistically black humour prophetic of Welsh's *Trainspotting*, which was to appear the following year. (The film version in 1997 was much less successful than Boyle's version of *Trainspotting* from 1995, but the gangster movie that Donald wrote and produced, *Beautiful Creatures*, did much better in 2000.) *When I was a Girl, I Used to Scream and Shout* (1984) by Sharman Macdonald is a fine memory play that uses shifts in time and space to follow its author's characteristic interest in the relationship between past and present and what happens between mothers and daughters. *The Winter Guest* (1995) is a beautifully elliptical reflection on the passage of time and the processes of ageing, while *Borders of Paradise* (1995) reflects on similar issues but from the point of view of awkward adolescence. While remaining realistic in their delivery, Macdonald's scripts often generate a markedly poetic rhythm of their own and in fact all these plays from the nineties show an expressionist tendency and a welcome interest in moving beyond urban or domestic realism.

The struggle to find audiences continues, however, and one of the ways in which this has manifested itself in Scottish theatre has been to produce plays based on already established novels, such as George Douglas Brown's *House with the Green Shutters*, Grassic Gibbon's *Sunset Song*, Neil Gunn's *Silver Darlings*, Irvine Welsh's *Trainspotting*, or Janice Galloway's *The Trick is to Keep Breathing*. Many of these adaptations have been undoubtedly brilliant in theatrical terms but whether they advance the cause of playwrights and original drama may be another question. Another route has been to stage adaptations of classical texts translated into the Scots language. This had also been done in the 1940s and 1950s with productions such as Robert Kemp's version of Molière, *Let Wives Tak Tent*, and Douglas Young's translations of Aristophanes as *The Puddocks* and *The Burdies*. But Scots adaptations found a new and wider audience in the 1980s, perhaps because they chose to use urban colloquial Scots, rather than the more formal Lallans of plays from the early years of the modern Renaissance. Notable productions in this vein include Liz Lochhead's versions of *Tartuffe*, and *Medea*; Edwin Morgan's of *Cyrano de Bergerac*; the

Borderline Theatre Company's versions of plays by Dario Fo; and Martin Bowman and Bill Findlay's outstandingly successful translations of Québécois French dialect ('joual') in plays such as Michel Tremblay's *Les Belles-soeurs* (1968) done into Glaswegian demotic as *The Guid Sisters* (1989).

Changing times

Alexander Trocchi (1925–84)

In keeping with the experimentalism of the Traverse Theatre, and very much in the spirit of the International Writers' Conferences on the novel and drama in the 1960s, the writing of Alex Trocchi demonstrates a cool awareness of what was happening in European and American prose fiction at that time. Alexander Trocchi was born to middle-class parents in Glasgow, the son of a second-generation Scots-Italian father. His plans to go to university were interrupted by the war, during which he served as a seaman on the Arctic convoys. When peace came Trocchi returned to Glasgow University to study English and Philosophy. He married early and on graduation in 1950 moved to Paris where he began to make his reputation as a writer in avant-garde circles, becoming friendly with Maurice Girodias of the Olympia Press and acting as an editor or co-editor of the periodicals *Merlin* and *Paris Quarterly*, which were influential in publishing work by Sartre, Beckett, Ionesco and Genet, as well as Henry Miller, Creeley, and William Burroughs. Trocchi threw himself into the bohemian life, writing pornographic novels under a pseudonym for the Olympia Press (notorious at that time as the publisher of Henry Miller) and involving himself with the Situationist International groups, who took revolutionary surrealism into the streets as a form of 'anti-art' cultural and political action. During these Paris years he left his wife and two daughters for an American lover, worked on his first 'serious' novel *Young Adam* (1954) and began a lifelong addiction to heroin. Originally written as a book for Girodias by 'Francis Lengel', a revised version of *Young Adam* was published under Trocchi's own name in 1961. The book contains memorably erotic scenes, and yet its protagonist, Joe, is infused with an existential numbness often compared to that of the character Meursault in Camus's famous novel *L'Étranger* (1942). Joe is a drifter who works a longboat on the Edinburgh–Glasgow canal when he's not seducing the skipper's wife. The setting is significant, for this is an in-between and shoreline territory that is neither rural nor urban, a place not so much distant as dis-located from the pressures and commitments of city life. And it is a philosophical space too, as Joe is committed to satisfying the often lovelessly carnal appetites of the moment in a kind of diurnal suspension. The book explores the themes of sex and death as Joe becomes obsessed with the drowned body of a young woman that he and his skipper friend Les haul from the water. What she comes to represent for him, and what she was to him before her death, and what his responsibility might be towards her and towards the man who is charged with killing her, all this gradually unfolds as Trocchi's prose invokes the strange detachment at the heart of Joe. It is a memorable novel, adding a powerful and chillingly existential dimension to the genre of prose realism. A film version was made by director David Mackenzie in 2004.

After a spell in London, Trocchi went to America and found himself working on a barge in New York Harbour. He made friends with many of the writers of the Beat generation, married again and started work on his next novel. *Cain's Book* (1961) undoubtedly draws on Trocchi's own life at this time, exploring the condition of the 'outsider' in society. His protagonist is 'Joe' once again and he is a heroin addict and would-be writer (with an Italian father and a Glasgow background) who lives aboard a working scow in the Hudson waterways. Very much in the vein of William Burroughs, Trocchi wrote that the identity of 'junkie . . . was consciously chosen. The resulting experience is by definition that of an alien in a society of conformers, a personal cosmology of inner space.' The hip solipsism of the book hit the spirit of the times and it sold widely, becoming even more famous after an obscenity trial in Britain in 1963. But in the end there was nothing very romantic about Trocchi's addiction, which led him to drug-dealing, various arrests and scrapes, petty crime and the betrayal of friends and partners. Eventually he had to leave America to return to Britain, where he took part in the International Writers' Conference in Edinburgh in 1962 – famously crossing swords with a 70-year-old Hugh MacDiarmid who could see no merit in this younger generation of writers with their commitment to an international avant-garde. They could see little merit in his nationalism, and none in his status as revered elder statesman of Scottish letters. He in his turn, not quite the statesman yet, called them 'cosmopolitan scum'. Trocchi was proud to be cosmopolitan, however, and formed the 'Sigma Project' to promote just such international and experimental directions in the arts whenever possible. To this end he compèred the famous poetry reading at London's

Albert Hall with Ginsberg, Ferlinghetti et al. in 1965 and spent the last twenty years of his life engaged with various projects of this sort, even although his addiction had taken a severe toll on his own and his second wife's health. He published a book of poems in 1972 only to endure illness and death in his family through cancer and suicide. He was working on another book in his later years but never completed it. The left-bank counter-cultural model of hip addiction in an intellectual elite that made his reputation in the 1960s had come down to teenage junkies in the housing schemes of Edinburgh in the 1980s. The world was a different place and the times were indeed changing.

The Albert Hall reading in London, and the growth of the Festival Fringe in Edinburgh, signalled a growing appreciation for music and the public performance of poetry. In Scotland the influence of Hamish Henderson and the School of Scottish Studies played a part in a specifically Scottish folksong revival that had been growing since the 1950s, marked by the spread of folk clubs and venues in bars and hotels, and this began to merge with the rise of an international audience for protest songs, and singer-songwriters of the calibre of Leonard Cohen (who had helped Trocchi when he fled to Canada at one time), along with Joan Baez, Bob Dylan, Joni Mitchell and many others. In Scotland this led to a demand for public performance where folk-singers, poets and singer-songwriters could share a platform. One of the paradoxes of this development was that Sorley MacLean, now retired, began to appear in public much more often, reading to appreciative but largely non-Gaelic-speaking poetry lovers. The literary scene in the 1960s and 1970s saw Christopher Logue's jazz-poetry and Adrian Mitchell fêted for his poems against Vietnam. The 'Liverpool poets' (Roger McGough, Brian Patten and Adrian Henri) developed a cosier version of Beat poetry, to achieve wide popularity with a new young audience, and Scottish groups such as Bread Love and Dreams, and especially Robin Williamson and Mike Heron's Incredible String Band, pushed the boundaries of the medium with their own brand of Celtic-folk psychedelia.

Walter Perrie (b. 1949), Alan Bold (1943–98), Tom Buchan (1931–95), Alan Jackson (b. 1938) and Robin Fulton (b. 1936)

The literary scene in Edinburgh at this time saw the foundation of *Scottish International* (1968–78) edited by Bob Tait (b. 1943) and *Chapman* (1970) under the editorship of poet Walter Perrie whose

Lamentation for the Children (1977) mixed family memory with the grim history of Scottish coalmining in a long impressionistic modernist poem worthy of Ezra Pound or Basil Bunting. *Lines Review* prospered over nearly ten years with a special awareness of European literature under the editorship of Robin Fulton, while Duncan Glen's *Akros Press* continued to support new Scottish writing and especially writers in Scots from its base in Preston. Journalist, distinguished literary critic and editor Alan Bold was writing poetry collected as *This Fine Day* (1979). New poets such as Donald Campbell, Alan Jackson, William Neill and D. M. Black, four very different writers, along with English poet Pete Morgan, who was then living in Edinburgh, were in demand at poetry readings, while the 'Heretics' group, founded by novelist, poet and songwriter Stuart MacGregor, provided another forum where younger writers mixed with musicians and more established practitioners such as MacLean, Garioch and MacCaig.

One of the *Scottish International* editors, the poet Tom Buchan, also helped script *The Great Northern Welly Boot Show* and produced a lively first collection of poems, *Dolphins at Cochin* (1969), that took an ironic look at Scottishness – 'Scotland the Wee' and 'The Week-end Naturalist' ('I trip on a delinquent peat/and fall on my face') – while also being sensitive to the horrors of the war in Vietnam in 'The Flaming Man'. Donald Campbell (b. 1940) was soon to become better known as a playwright, but the poems in urban Scots collected in his *Rhymes 'n' Reasons* (1972) signal early mastery of a colloquial mode that was to serve him so well on stage. The poems in *The Grim Wayfarer* (1969) and other collections by Alan Jackson, reprinted in *Salutations: Collected Poems 1960–1989* (1990), utilise rhyme, humour and a racy epigrammatic delivery to spell out a consistent concern for the survival of the human spirit in the face of man's capacity for envy and greed. The poems of Robin Fulton seek a northern clarity and a spareness of vision and expression that is absolutely in line with his admiration for Scandinavian culture, especially the poetry of Tomas Tranströmer for whom Fulton has been an internationally acclaimed translator. Fulton's own work is marked by a lucid awareness of the spaces around us and between us, as if the world, so closely observed, were in danger of somehow fading away unless caught in the precision of the poet's bare lines. Even the titles of his books convey something of this compulsively pure attention to the details around us: *Inventories* (1969), *The Spaces Between the Stones* (1971), *Tree Lines* (1974) and *Fields of Focus* (1982). Fulton has lived and worked in Norway since 1973.

D. M. Black (b. 1941)

The work of D. M. Black is somewhat different. His is a much more elliptical voice, darkly urbane and surreal in its strange extended retelling of Grimm in 'The Hands of Felicity' or the authorial and priestly confessions of 'Notes for Joachim', or tales of the Red and the Black Judge:

> We shut the red judge in a bronze jar
>
> – By 'we', meaning myself and the black judge –
> And there was peace, for a time. You can have enough
> Of the yowling of certain justices. The jar
> We buried, (pitching and swelling like the tough
> Membrane of an unshelled egg), on the Calton Hill.
> And there was peace, for a time. . . .
>   ('The Red Judge')

Haunted by reflections on sexuality, mortality and the confining structures and strictures of society, Black's work is closer to Peter Redgrove than to most Scottish writers of his day. (He shared a volume in the Penguin Modern Poets series with Redgrove, as well as an interest in psychoanalysis.) He published *With Decorum* (1967), *The Educators* (1969) and *Gravitations* (1979), with *Collected Poems, 1964–1987* appearing in 1991. The unfashionable length of Black's deadpan poems, with their unfolding Borgesian narratives and their unique tone, make for demanding but rewarding reading. His characteristic mode anticipated what might now be called a postmodern muse, more familiar now in the writing of Alasdair Gray and Frank Kuppner.

Kenneth White (b. 1936)

Kenneth White, on the other hand, looked more towards America in the low-key translucence of his verse and especially in his conception of what he sees as a spiritual relationship between poetry, self and the more remote spaces of the world. If Trocchi had an affinity with Burroughs, White's work is closer to poets like Gary Snyder with his strongly ecological focus. The hills and shores of Scotland were an early influence on the young boy, for he spent his youth roaming the countryside of Ayrshire in the south-west, near Largs where his father worked as a railway signalman. The natural landscape and his sense of himself as a beachcomber on the shoreline of the world were to become controlling metaphors for the poetry that was to come. White took an

Honours degree in French and German at the University of Glasgow followed by postgraduate work in Munich and Paris before returning to Glasgow University to teach modern French literature. After four years he moved to France in 1967 (experiencing the *événements* in Paris the following year) and although he has since travelled widely, he has spent the rest of his professional and creative life in that country, holding a Chair in Twentieth-century Poetics at the Sorbonne from 1983 to 1996. In his early years in France he lived in an old farmhouse in the Cévennnes and renewed his boyhood love of the countryside while studying Japanese and Chinese poetry and Buddhism, as well as developing his theories about what he would come to call the 'geopoetics' of humankind's deep relationship to place. He showed an affinity with the later 'world-language' poems of Hugh MacDiarmid, with their insistence on the absolute materiality of the world, and on how science can, as MacDiarmid wrote in 'The Kind of Poetry I Want', 'replace a stupefied sense of wonder / With something more wonderful / Because natural and understandable'. The poems in his first collections *The Cold Wind of Dawn* (1966) and *The Most Difficult Area* (1968) all aspire to a Zen-like emptiness, and an insistence on our indivisible relationship with the physical and especially the natural world, and this set the tone for all his later work. To attain this at-one-ness is indeed 'the most difficult area', nor is it easy to convey in verses that aspire to a similar simplicity:

. . .
A grey heron
watching, listening
in an early morning
glitter of waters –
maybe dreaming?

Fishing in nothingness
(that is one way of putting it)
here on Loch Sunart
bright falling of the year
quiet, so quiet

It is, of course, the poet who is 'fishing in nothingness' and such lines seek an open calmness, rather than the encyclopaedic all-inclusiveness of MacDiarmid's late work, and they certainly do not share the older poet's concern for Scots and Scottish nationalism, although this poem ('Early morning light on Loch Sunart') does quote three lines from Duncan Bàn Macintyre's Gaelic poem 'Ode to Glen Orchy'.

In fact White was to become increasingly drawn to the marginalised status of 'Celtic' cultures and to what he saw as their unromantic and entirely objective closeness to nature. Living on the 'margins' of the modern world in this way became a matter of preference and principle for him, and in later years he set up house on the north coast of Brittany as just such a location 'on the edge'. One of the most productive elements in his geopoetical theory relates to what he saw as a philosophical and cultural affinity between the communities of the North Atlantic rim, from Portugal to Brittany and then on to Ireland, the west coast of Scotland, the Hebrides and across the ocean to Greenland, Newfoundland and Labrador. White sees these connections as a new kind of mapping: tracing the coordinates of a value system and a hardy outlook on life, rather than those of language, race, artificial political boundaries or (worst of all in his eyes) narrow nationalism. It is a stimulating concept and he sees it as the key to a more progressive vision of human identity that can stand against the cultural imperialism, alienation and ecological destructiveness of the modern world. Travelling 'the bird path' – realising one's self-nature off the beaten path – as a modern wanderer (his preferred term is 'nomad'), he keeps 'way books' that are part diary of the trip, part autobiography, part hip notebook, part historical and anthropological research. This is the method of *The Blue Road / La Route Bleu* (1983), which mixes prose, poems and essays to describe a journey he made to Labrador as one of the few places left 'where we can *listen to the world*'.

For White, such listening is the purpose behind the rituals of so-called primitive peoples by which a Shaman (or the poet as Shaman) calls up the spirit of the world to help us live at a deeper level than materialism and consumerism. But such invocation requires the Shaman to take centre stage, at least for a while, rather as Whitman does (he is one of White's influences) when he shows us America. Thus although White eschews Romantic subjectivity and the role of all-seeing poet, his poetry can sometimes seem to struggle with the desirable, paradoxical but perhaps unattainable goal of achieving the selfless ego. It has to be said that his critical and creative writing makes a little too much of the coincidence that makes Alba (which can also mean 'white') an ancient name for Scotland; and he frequently refers to the 'white world' as a synonym for his concept of the 'open world', 'neither old nor new', in what French critics have called 'a new mental geography'. Much of White's essay writing (including three volumes of an autobiography) has been done in French and it would be fair to say that the 'Pelagian discourse' of his theories has been better received by intellectuals in France, where he founded an International Institute of Geopoetics, than in his native country, although a small group of fellow-thinkers do sustain a centre for geopoetics in Scotland.

The selected essays in *On Scottish Ground* (1998) give some idea of the eclectic and sometimes repetitive scope of White's thinking and his preference for a model of Scottishness that draws on the lifestyle of the early Celtic Christian monks, or the wandering scholars in medieval Europe, or undervalued polymaths like Patrick Geddes. White's longer and shorter poems were finally published in Britain as *The Bird Path* (1989) and *Handbook for the Diamond Country* (1990), while a complete collection of work from 1960 to 2000 has been published as *Open World* (2003). His is a challenging vision of how cultural 'marginality' and 'Celtic' roots might be invoked to transcend the usual parameters of politics and nationalism, although he may be vulnerable to the accusation that this is just another version of Celticism at work. On the other hand, despite the obvious differences and White's avant-garde prosody, there are aspects of his work that can be related to the Zen moments in Neil Gunn's *Highland River* and the holistic communities imagined by George Mackay Brown. And if White prefers to associate himself with Whitman, Rimbaud and Gary Snyder, he can still be said to have affinities with contemporary Scottish writers engaged with the sea and coastlines, such as Stornoway poet Ian Stephen, Glasgow-born Kenneth C. Steven, and the Inverness artist Will Maclean, who produces box-construction artworks reflecting his fascination with voyages, boats, the sea and fishing.

Kenneth White was not alone in trying to make a poetry that did not depend on the English tradition or on familiar Scottish models. Chief among the avant-garde publishers in Edinburgh in the 1960s were Ian Hamilton Finlay and Jessie McGuffie with their little magazine *Poor. Old. Tired. Horse.* (*P.O.T.H.* for short), which was published from 1962 until 1968 as an outlet for the latest in European, American and Scottish experimental writing seeking to make common cause with Robert Creeley, Robert Duncan, Lorine Niedecker and Louis Zukovsky. (The magazine title comes from a line in Robert Creeley's poem 'Please'.) In an attempt to make space for his own work and a different kind of poetry, Hamilton Finlay, like Trocchi, dared to challenge the iconic status of Hugh MacDiarmid, who responded by flyting them as 'The Ugly Birds without Wings' (1962).

Ian Hamilton Finlay (1925–2006)

Finlay was a writer who went beyond the page to become known as a leading concrete poet/installation or conceptual artist, designing work that graces many sites throughout Britain and Europe. Born in Nassau he was brought up in Glasgow and then the Orkneys, where he returned to work as a shepherd after wartime service in the Royal Army Signal Corps. Moving between Edinburgh and Orkney in the 1950s, Finlay began to see ways of making art that fitted what was to become a simultaneously naive and extremely sophisticated vision of the world. He started by writing short stories, *The Sea-Bed and Other Stories* (1958), a radio play *Walking Through Seaweed*, and a collection of poems, *The Dancers Inherit the Party* (1960), whose odd humour and deliberately small scale was already original. (It includes a teasing little poem called 'Mansie Considers the Sea in the Manner of Hugh MacDiarmid'.) A collection of animal 'haikus' illustrated with cut paper shapes by John Picking followed and *Glasgow Beasts, an a Burd Haw, an Insecks, an, Aw, a Fush* (1961) was written in Glasgow urban speech as a significant forerunner of the work that was to come from Tom Leonard in later years. MacDiarmid, suffering from a certain thickening of the revolutionary arteries, declared that such language could never be suitable for poetry, and he was to find Finlay's later work even more intractable. Undaunted, Finlay founded the Wild Hawthorn Press as an outlet for his increasingly original creative vision and 1962 saw the appearance of *Poor. Old. Tired. Horse.* and his flyting with MacDiarmid. Looking back to the 1960s Edwin Morgan remembers with gratitude the excitement, the eclecticism and the international focus of *P.O.T.H.* with work from Russia, France, Italy, Finland, Poland, Hungary and Japan, varying from abstruse theory to the whimsy of a 'teapoth' issue. Scottish writers also featured, with authors as different as George Mackay Brown and D. M. Black, or J. F. Hendry and Robert Garioch or Edwin Morgan and Helen Cruickshank. Whatever *P.O.T.H.* was, it was not predictable. There were 25 issues of the magazine/pamphlet in the end, each published in a different format, but it would be true to say that it was better appreciated in the United States than it was at home. From this base Finlay soon became involved (in issue number 6) with the international movement known as 'concrete poetry'.

There are many kinds of concrete verse, but essentially it is a move away from expressive models of the poet's autobiographical subjectivity towards a work that concentrates on language itself, or even the shape of individual words and how they are spaced out on the page.

Edwin Morgan's concrete verse from the mid-60s often plays on witty shapes, puns and acrostics: for instance, his poem to Isambard Kingdom Brunel is shaped like a bridge made out of lines which ring the changes on his name – 'I am bard / I am Isobar / I am Iron Bar', etc. By comparison Finlay has taken a quieter and more classical line towards his declared goal of 'lucidity, clarity, resolved complexity'. A collection of concrete poems, *Rapel*, appeared in 1963 The title is a joke about drunken Glaswegians singing 'The Rose of Tralee, the opening lines of which are 'The pale moon (pron. *ra pell mune*) was shining above the green mountain'. This was followed by a whole series of booklet poems and card poems, beautifully produced by a number of graphic artists under Finlay's guidance and all available at very modest cost. Such productions became *in themselves* the poem or the art object, rather than simply a convenient and functional medium for the transmission of words. This was a concept of poetry, or art, that blurred the boundaries between the verbal and the visual, between the concept and the material object. Finlay's gentle meditations on his favourite themes –with an imagery of small boats and horizons– signal a profound and prophetically conceptual shift away from the mono-lithically literate and ego-bound *weltanschauung* of MacDiarmid, Eliot or Pound and the other giant system-builders of early Anglo-American modernism. Perhaps the old man was right to feel threatened, after all.

In 1966 Finlay and his wife Sue settled in a remote farmhouse, 'Stonypath' at Dunsyre in the Borders, to set up a small press and produce still more of his booklets, poem-prints and over 200 cards in his unique style. He used recurring images of fishing-boats, nets, waves, canals, sailing-ships, stars, sundials and the seasons, and his poems and constructions share a simple and beautiful integrity – a welcome alternative to the then prevailing vogue for psychodrama and agonisingly 'confessional' verse. *Poems to Hear and See* (1971) uses coloured inks and graphic effects, such as the word 'a c r o b a t s' printed over and over to fill the page as if the letters are standing on each others' shoulders. Or the word 'STAR' is repeated in a wavering column down the page until it suddenly becomes 'STEER' at the last line. In these examples the conceptual implications within and beyond what the words mean have been explored in an engagingly unpreten-tious way. He also wrote 'one-word' poems that operate rather like the Japanese haiku in that they depend on an imaginative leap between the title and the verse. Thus the poem called 'The Cloud's Anchor' consists of a single word – 'swallow', and 'One (Orange) Arm of the World's Oldest Windmill' becomes 'autumn'. The last issue of

P.O.T.H. was devoted entirely to one-word 'monostitch' poems in this style.

Finlay's work continued to evolve and much of it was now realised in stone, wood and glass, always finely constructed to his designs by different artists and craftsmen. His work has been more widely exhibited and commissioned in Europe than in Britain, but not without controversy. The artist's own prickly integrity led him to fall out with the Scottish Arts Council on more than one occasion and Stonypath was duly renamed 'Little Sparta'. The 1980s were difficult times during which he suffered a long skirmish with Strathclyde Regional Council over serious issues to do with the rateable value of his property. They retaliated by illegally seizing works of art; nevertheless he managed to turn the dispute into the wryly Situationist 'war of Little Sparta', which in itself produced more works of art. More serious was the scandal over his commission to design a garden at Versailles in honour of the two-hundredth anniversary of the Rights of Man in 1989. His fascination with St Just and the French revolutionary terror, and his equal fascination with military machinery and the iconography of German *blitzkrieg*, provided his rivals with the ammunition they needed to scupper his plans. In a snakes' nest of misrepresentation and misunderstanding – not helped by his own utterly uncompromising nature – Finlay lost the contract and won risible damages in the law case that followed.

Perhaps Finlay's greatest work, however, is located in Scotland at his home at Stonypath. Over the years he constructed a carefully landscaped garden around his house to become another kind of artistic statement, expressed through plants, sundials, sculpture and inscribed stones. The link with Roman gardens and eighteenth-century landscaping is not accidental, for Finlay took a learned and resolutely classical approach to his art, enlivened by his fondness for apparently iconoclastic but ultimately satisfying images – such as a nuclear submarine's sail (conning-tower) in black slate, which serves as a wordless *memento mori* at the edge of an ornamental pond; or a stone aircraft carrier in the garden that serves as a bird table, or his 'garden temple' thought-provokingly dedicated to 'Apollo / His Muses / His Missiles'. In another series of prints and sculptures he brought the neo-classical pastoralism of Poussin, and the classical tag '*et in arcadia ego*', to bear on the conventions of camouflage and the leaf-like traceries that were realised on the armour of German tanks from the Second World War. Here, as always, Finlay was fascinated by the balance between what is natural and what must submit to conceptual order, always with the recognition that 'nature' can be utterly savage, too. From the thunderbolts of Zeus to the 'flute' of an air-cooled machine-gun barrel, Hamilton Finlay's brilliantly metaphorical and philosophical leaps of imagination have passed beyond the conventional definitions of 'poetry', although everything he has done is indeed a profound reflection on the nature of art and its moral and aesthetic relationship to the world at large. Whatever forms he chose over the years, the subject has always been the relationship between *meaning* and *context*. Nor did he ever lose his feel for the marriage of the homely and the infinite, nor for how familiar and unlikely objects can open us to quiet surprise, illumination and delight. In a noisy world of 'challenging' novelty, fashionable theory and the commodification and institutionalisation of art. Finlay's quiet garden may be the most revolutionary of all.

New visual art

Finlay's uniquely original contribution cannot be underestimated – though it sometimes seems that he has had little honour in his own country – but he is by no means the only artist in the lively and very various creative scene that is Scottish art in the second half of the twentieth century. The present study can only hint at these riches, but one of the most significant events of the period under discussion was the exhibition 'The Vigorous Imagination', which came to be held in Edinburgh in 1987. The painters to make most impact at this widely attended and well received show were graduates of the Glasgow School of Art and had in their different ways all been influenced by the figurative realism of Alexander Moffat, who taught there. This exhibition confirmed an international reputation for the group sometimes called the 'new Glasgow boys' – whose different approaches in art can also be linked to movements in literature at that time and in the years to come. The early paintings of Ken Currie (b. 1960), for example, took the labour history of Glasgow and the icons of socialism and trade unionism as their topic in large emblematic compositions in the style of Diego Rivera and socialist realism. This is particularly the case in the murals he did for the People's Palace in the late 1980s, but since then his canvases have shown strangely spectral studies of individually isolated and damaged bodies and faces, almost like medical illustrations, that make their own comment on the objectification and the distress of the human subject. Peter Howson (b. 1958) explored another side of Glasgow's identity with his 'heroic' and 'noble dosser' paintings of the broken and brutalised faces and bodies of the city's street vagrants. His later work made equally powerful studies of skinheads and football thugs and British National Party bruisers with their baseball caps and pit bull terriers, or confused and struggling crowds in a more allegorical comment on the admass chaos of the city experience. Howson went to Bosnia as a war artist, and his vision of human life *in extremis*, not to mention his own peace of mind, was not sweetened by what he experienced there. With or without his rather ambivalent interest in human suffering, Howson's response to the human figure finds a muscular ugliness that may or may not have its own beauty. Both he and Currie can be seen to be making their own very different contributions to a view of life that can also be found in the writing of James Kelman and Irvine Welsh.

On the other hand, Steven Campbell (b. 1953) has pursued a consciously literary and playfully postmodern vision with a large and remarkable output of paintings that seem to be offering dramatic events or encounters in a narrative whose context and wider meaning must remain closed to us –or completely open to free interpretation. He enjoys teasingly pretentious titles such as 'Two Humeians Preaching Causality', and much of the effect and the enjoyment of his work depends on the balance he does or doesn't strike between the superficial and the opaque, or vice versa. Adrian Wiszniewski (b. 1958) is a more restrained and poetically indirect artist with his studies of fashionable young men in a neo-romantic graphic style. Stephen Conroy (b. 1964) shares Campbell's postmodern delight in evocatively literary titles to describe mysterious encounters often between young men dressed in formal clothes, all painted with an old-masterly grasp of light and shade. All three of these artists, but especially Campbell and Conroy, show an awareness of postmodernism's problematic attitude to narrative coherence and closure, and in their different ways they could be said to be making veiled comments on the nature of masculinity, from the scramblingly active confusion of be-suited figures in Campbell, to the languor of Wiszniewski, to the hieratic and formally impenetrable style of Conroy. Other artists of this generation, such as Calum Colvin (b. 1961) and David Mach (b. 1956), have challenged the limitations of specific media in a more radical way. Colvin, educated at the Duncan of Jordanstone College of Art in Dundee, started to exhibit in the late 1980s with work that offered a theoretically challenging meditation on the nature of representation by combining *trompe l'oeil* painted constructions with fixed-viewpoint photography (and latterly the actual constructions themselves in the gallery) to generate a complex deconstruction of how images are made coherent from only one point of view, while also reflecting on the nature of national and sexual identity – where questions of constructedness and point of view are equally crucial. Since the 1980s David Mach, another graduate of Dundee, has done internationally innovative work in figurative sculpture, especially in large public places, using rubber tyres, bricks, magazines and shipping containers as well as more intimate accounts of bodies and faces using matchheads and wire coat-hangers.

Such works in the visual arts – internationally aware and internationally successful – show how Scottish culture was opening itself up to technical innovation, new topics and a new examination of old subjects. Scotland's writers had already engaged with these new perspectives, especially in the work of Hamilton Finlay, Edwin Morgan, Alasdair Gray and James Kelman, each of whom in their turn cleared still further ground for others to follow.

New visions of old Scotland

Edwin Morgan (b. 1920)

Edwin Morgan might be said to epitomise MacDiarmid's hopes for a cosmopolitan and outward-looking culture in modern Scotland, although, as with Ian Hamilton Finlay, MacDiarmid was not especially sympathetic to the young writer's actual work. Morgan's interests range widely, turning more often to Europe and America than they do to London and the south, and he has translated verse by Mayakovsky, Montale, Voznesensky, Quasimodo, Brecht, Neruda, Weöres, Juhasz and many others. In later years he contributed to the vogue for stage adaptations of classic plays into modern demotic Scots by translating Rostand's *Cyrano de Bergerac* (1992) and Racine's *Phaedra* (2000), before going on to write *A.D.* (2000), his own dramatic trilogy on the life of Christ. His poetry is equally varied, for he is a man whose essentially private and optimistic nature is attuned to the face of the contemporary world – very often as it comes to us by way of newspapers and television. Where other writers see only confusion, decay or empty technology, Morgan discovers growth, change, flux and delight. He uses his poetry to report back on these discoveries or to push our imaginations a little further beyond them. With over 600 pages (excluding six volumes of poetic translations), Morgan's *Collected Poems* of 1990 was followed by four further substantial collections in a body of work that testifies to the poet's lifelong engagement with imaginative, dramatic and experimental verse. He has written love poetry, science fiction poetry, sound poetry and concrete verse, as well as many memorable poems on his home city of Glasgow and on Scotland. Among more than twenty volumes of poetry and many small pamphlets his major collections have been *The Second Life* (1968), *From Glasgow to Saturn* (1973), *The New Divan* (1977), *Sonnets from Scotland* (1984), *Themes on a Variation* (1988), *Collected Poems* (2nd edn, 1996) and *Cathures: New Poems, 1997–2001* (2002). Morgan has become a widely popular reader of his own work. He was appointed Glasgow's first Poet Laureate in 1999 and awarded the Queen's Gold Medal for Poetry the following year; he won the Weidenfeld Prize for Translation in 2001, and Glasgow University's Creative Writing Centre is named after him; he received a lifetime achievement award in 2003 and was commissioned to write a poem for the opening of the new parliament building in 2004.

Morgan was born and educated in Glasgow, the only son of middleclass parents. He did well in his last years at school, but considered going to Art School before finally deciding to study English at Glasgow University, starting classes in 1937 and soon contributing to the university magazine. When war broke out he registered as a conscientious objector but chose to join the Royal Army Medical Corps in 1940, serving as a quartermaster's clerk in Egypt and Palestine. His poem 'The Unspoken' was to recall 'the troopship . . . pitching round the Cape / in '41':

> . . . and there was a lull in the night uproar of seas and winds, and a
> sudden full moon
> swung huge out of the darkness like the world it is,
> and we all crowded onto the wet deck, leaning on the rail, our arms on
> each
> other's shoulders, gazing at the savage outcrop of great Africa.

It is intriguing to note how many modern Scottish poets also served in the Middle East at this time – MacLean, Campbell Hay, Garioch, G. S. Fraser and Henderson all knew something of the desert during these years.

On returning to Scotland in 1946 Morgan completed his degree, graduating with first-class Honours in 1947. He was offered a scholarship to Oxford, but chose to remain in Glasgow, starting work as an assistant lecturer in the English Department of his home university. Having taken French and Russian as a student, he developed a sustained interest in European literature, especially Russian modernism, as well as an enthusiasm for medieval Scots and Anglo-Saxon poetry. (He made a verse translation of *Beowulf* in 1952.) Something of all these influences can be seen in the dense lines of his first collection, *A Vision of Cathkin Braes* (1952), published by William MacLellan of Glasgow. A companion collection, the disturbingly dark *Dies Irae* with its apocalyptic and anguished tones, was planned by an English publisher for the same year, but never appeared because of financial difficulties. A tiny edition of a long poem *The Cape of Good Hope* (1955) shows the same densely wrought and highly mannered literary expression, like a marriage between Anglo-Saxon verse, Hart Crane and the New Apocalypse. Morgan's fascination with the sensual and intellectual force of language appears again in lighter spirits in *The Whittrick*, a 'Poem in Eight Dialogues' written in 1963 that includes a playfully imagined dialogue between MacDiarmid and James Joyce – no mean word-spinners themselves. Imagined monologues or dialogues were to be a favourite genre of Morgan's in the years to come. Equally strong was his interest in American writers such as Walt Whitman, William Carlos Williams and the Black Mountain poets; and Robert Creeley had featured, after all, in *Poor. Old. Tired. Horse.* to which Morgan also contributed. He translated poems by Montale in 1959 and published a selection of translations from modern Russian poets in *Sovpoems* (1961), as well as poems by Brecht and Neruda, both equally socialist in their outlook. (One of his most successful later projects in 1972 was to be *Wi the Haill Voice*, which translated Mayakovsky's technically and politically revolutionary poetry into broad Scots – a tongue much better suited to working-class revolutionary polemic than the more managerial tones of standard English.) At about this time, too, he discovered the international movement in concrete poetry, publishing several small pamphlets in this vein, including *Starryveldt* (1965) from the Eugen Gomringer Press in Switzerland, distributed in Britain by Hamilton Finlay's Wild Hawthorn Press.

All these elements came together in Morgan's first substantial collection, which was a beautifully designed art-format book using coloured papers, from Edinburgh University Press. The impact of *The Second Life* (1968) was considerable and immediate. Here was a contemporary poet who dared to look at the modern world and find it good, who could bring specifically Scottish topics into focus with references and influences – even avant-garde ones – from around the world. (The collection included a poem to the 1965 International Poetry Festival at the Albert Hall and a poem dedicated to Ian Hamilton Finlay.) Here was a serious poet who could be light-hearted, a poet who was undoubtedly Scottish, but without the baggage of previous genera-tions. The title-poem, with its reference to a 'second life', was especially significant to Morgan for several reasons. First of all, in his forties he had at last found his own poetic voice; and his home city was looking up, too, for after years of post-war decline Glasgow was entering into a new life of growth and urban renewal:

> But does every man feel like this at forty
> . . .
>   . . . writing as the aircraft roar
> over building sites, in this warm west light
> by the daffodil banks that were never so crowded and lavish –
> green May, and the slow great blocks rising
> under yellow tower cranes, concrete and glass and steel
> out of a dour rubble it was and barefoot children gone–
> Is it only the slow stirring, a city's renewed life
> that stirs me, could it stir me so deeply
> as May, but could May have stirred
> what I feel of desire and strength
> like an arm saluting a sun?
>
>   ('The Second Life')

Morgan is not blind to the failings of the urban industrial world and he later recognised that the tower blocks and motorways of the new Glasgow were to bring problems of their own; nevertheless he has never lost this characteristically optimistic engagement with modernity. Finally, things were also going well in his personal life, for in 1963 he had met John Scott, the man who was to be his friend and lover for most of the next fifteen years. So the final resonance of the 'second life' has to do with Morgan becoming comfortable – if still rather guarded at this point – about his homosexuality.

The poet came out publicly in 1990 (Glasgow's year as 'European City of Culture') and if he was more reticent in the 1960s, or indeed the 1940s, it is simply because he is essentially a rather private person. And of course we should not underestimate the intolerance of the law in those years, nor the homophobia of Glasgow's 'hard-man' culture. Yet the evidence was subtly present in his poetry from the start and indeed Morgan has written some very fine love-poems. The poet's early discretion meant that the gender of the person present, or having recently left, in these poems (he and Scott did not live together) is rarely specified. In such work this means that the emotional freight of the moment tends to be conveyed through the landscape around a nameless couple ('From a City Balcony'), or an empty plate with two forks ('Strawberries'), or a cigarette-end in the non-smoker's ashtray ('One Cigarette'). The effect can verge on the sentimental in one or two poems, but others offer a very powerful engagement with the sheer strangeness of love itself – as in 'Absence', 'Without It' and 'The Welcome'. In these, and especially in his later love-poems Morgan sees desire as an encounter with an almost overwhelming 'otherness' that has little to do with the sex of the couple involved, although this is not to say that there is not an extra dimension to the risk of commitment, in a same-sex partnership that is still thought by too many people to be beyond the pale. Some of Morgan's later love-poems are very perceptive about the suspended moments of physical attraction or tension between people who are not quite strangers ('After the Party'; 'At the Television-set'; 'The Divide'; 'Planets'). Others offer a vision of our desiring human selves that approaches a movingly existential meditation on presence, absence and mortality: 'Absence'; 'The Milk Cart'; 'Smoke'; 'Stanzas'; and especially in 'Dear man, my love goes out in waves':

> Dear man, my love goes out in waves
> and breaks. Whatever is, craves.
> Terrible the cage
> to see all life from, brilliantly about,
> crowds, pavements, cars, or hear the common shout
> of goals in the near park.
>   . . .
> Press close to me at midnight as
> you say goodbye; that's what it has
> to offer, life
> I mean. Into the frost with you; into
> the bed with me; and get the light out too.
> Better to shake unseen
> and let real darkness screen
> the shadows of the heart,
> the vacant part-
> ner, husband, wife.
> ('Dear man, my love goes out in waves')

The brilliant use of broken lines and split words in this poem serves to fragment certainty as it recognises how we are all trapped in the cage of our perception (and our desires), while the mortal references to darkness, night and frost go far beyond the specifics of any particular season or sexual encounter.

In the title-poem, 'The Second Life', it is new growth that moves the poet. Whether it is the city or the person viewing it that changes, or both, the poem is full of references to growth, seeds, slow stirring and undercurrents that speak for Spring, as well as sexual arousal, renewal and welcome change. Part of this change will be to be more fully articulate about both personal and cultural space:

> Many things are unspoken
> in the life of a man, and with a place
> there is an unspoken love also
> in undercurrents, drifting, waiting its time.
> A great place and its people are not renewed lightly.
> The caked layers of grime
> grow warm, like homely coats.
> But yet they will be dislodged
> and men will still be warm.
>
> ('The Second Life')

Morgan is not just speaking about Glasgow and himself in these lines, but about Scotland too, for talk of devolution and political change was in the air with the promise, perhaps, of still further renewal.

Despite the coded references to his sexuality in these early poems, Morgan is neither an introspective writer nor a poet of personal confession; nevertheless it is clear that he identifies himself closely with his native city in this and later collections. Hence many of his poems with their wide-ranging, outward-looking and eclectic interests (especially in *The Second Life*) have a personal as well as a wider cultural resonance. Thus a poem on the opening of the Forth Road Bridge in 1964, for example, asks the reader to 'make and take your crossing'. A poem in memory of Edith Piaf 'regrets nothing' and a Whitmanesque or Ginsbergian elegy on 'The Death of Marilyn Monroe' asks if the past follows us around, and what that might mean. Was soulless Los Angeles responsible for Marilyn's death, or our own voyeurism? – 'Let no one say that communication is a cantword. / They had to lift her hand from the bedside telephone' – and yet Morgan's rhetorical energy almost changes the poem into a celebration. 'To Joan Eardley' welcomes the power of the Scottish painter's work to record city urchins in the slums of Glasgow, seeing such paint on canvas (and the ragged children too) as the 'rags and streaks that master us', while also recognising the paradox that the purpose of art is to depict 'the living blur / fiercely guarding / energy that has vanished' – and then to make it live again (another kind of second life) on our walls.

The city and its past feature once more in poems such as 'King Billy' and 'Glasgow Green'. These describe a grim and sordid world of urban decay, old age, religious bigotry, and muttered threats of violence or desire, all very much in the popular image of 'No Mean City'. Yet 'King Billy', about the funeral of an old razor king from the Depression years, ends with an admonition to 'Deplore what is to be deplored, / and then find out the rest'; while 'Glasgow Green' comes to sympathise with night-time in the public park, with hunter and hunted and the violent demands of our common human flesh 'as it trembles / like driftwood through the dark'. The poem ends with an extraordinary call, voiced like a sermon from the pulpit, to recognise that the race 'shall be served by anguish / as well as by children at play. / It shall be served by loneliness / as well as by family love.' It is no less than a sermon for sexual outsiders and down-and-outs, and a call for all of us to take-in that 'harvest' too.

A much later collection, *Demon* from 1999, will revive this challenge in a more light-heartedly anarchic way by imagining the adventures of a demon (or more properly a *daemon* in the Greek sense of an inferior and in this case mischievous deity) as he escapes from the underworld to wander through the world, taking-on neds in Argyle Street and singing his cheerful song of perpetual and fruitful Blakean opposition:

> I'd rather be a demon
> Ploughing through the glaur
> Whistling to my fellows
> What against is for
> Against is not for nothing
> Against is drive a nail
> Against is draw a crown down
> Fill a quaich with hail
> . . .
> For we are merry dancers
> Through curtains of the dark
> Feel us hear us fear us
> When the dark begins to spark!
>   ('The Demon Sings')

In a city notorious for sectarian division, it is as if Morgan's Glasgow poems have set out to reconstruct religion in an entirely secular and much more charitable spirit. Thus 'Good Friday' fondly imitates the gait of a man, much the worse – or the better – for drink as he staggers off a bus to buy chocolate Easter eggs for his children. The three wise men at Christmas time are reincarnated as ordinary shoppers in Buchanan Street in 'Trio': 'Monsters of the year / go blank, are scattered back / can't bear this march of three'; while the almost unbearable, dull courage of a blind hunchback is observed in the most painstaking detail as the poet helps him to visit the toilet and wash his hands: 'Does he know how frightening he is in his strangeness / under his mountainous coat, his hands like wet leaves / stuck to his half-white stick? / His life depends on many who would evade him' ('In the Snack-Bar'). The use of 'evade', with its hint of obligation, rather than 'avoid', is a masterstroke in these lines, while the poem ends with a stunningly ambiguous and challenging cry – or is it a whispered prayer? – 'Dear Christ, to be born for this!'

There are many entertaining concrete poems in *The Second Life* with the strange noises made by a 'Chinese Cat' (ending with 'mao'), and purely verbal sound play in 'Spacepoem 1, from Laika to Gagarin', which mixes dog noises and names with Russian sounds and radio static interference; or the pom and panda sounds in a poem called, and shaped like, a 'Pomander'. A line of text is dis-integrated and repeated over and over in patchy form to make many different lesser messages, until 'Message Clear' eventually assembles itself into its presumably original form as 'I am the resurrection and the life'. This conclusion is no accident, for renewal and transformation – even if accidental – is of course the theme common to the collection as a whole and the concrete poems are no exception to this. Thus 'The Computer's First Christmas Card' has a computer churn out a manic tickertape of worthy attempts at greeting, only to fail at the last line – or perhaps to make a more original blessing by wishing the programmer:

```
m e r r y C h r i s
a m m e r r y a s a
C h r i s m e r r y
a s M E R R Y C H R
Y S A N T H E M U M
```

Like 'The Death of Marilyn Monroe', the science-fiction poem 'From the Domain of Arnheim' asks what it is from the past that we take with us, except that in this case the question is posed by time-travellers, shaken by the energy of a primitive ceremony they have witnessed, and by a simple and unpremeditated act of courage they are too sophisti-cated ever to manage or to match themselves:

> We signalled to the ship; got back;
> our lives and days returned to us, but
> haunted by deeper souvenirs than any rocks or seeds.
> From time the souvenirs are deeds.

The theme of travel and transformation appears again in the long science-fiction narrative poem 'In Sobieski's Shield', and here the science of matter transmission is conflated with information transmission so that when the travellers' bodies are rematerialised in some distant galaxy, they have been subject to subtle interferences and mutations. The poem's own text is written in one long unpunctuated sentence, as a monologue from the father of the family, and it contains its own echoes from the past with a line from an old Scots ballad – in the same way that the speaker's body seems to have picked up memories, and a tattoo from a dead soldier, in a shell hole from the Great War centuries ago. The final message is that 'we are bound to all that lived / though the barriers are unspeakable. . . . I laugh to think they thought they / could divide the indivisible the old moon's in / the young moon's arms let's take our second / like our first life out from the dome . . .' (the poem's point about our inextricable links to the past is doubly made when we recognise that the reference to the moon echoes a line from the ballad 'Sir Patrick Spens'.)

Many of Morgan's central and continuing interests had been laid out in *The Second Life,* and his fascination with messages, transformation and transmutation was to appear again in subsequent collections. This was especially evident in *From Glasgow to Saturn* (1973) with work such as the 'Interferences' sequence where the poem's often elliptical meaning is suddenly sent off course by a misspelling or a linguistic disruption as if by a sudden alien presence. Thus an arrow in the first poem flies straight to its 'targjx'; or the mother of Christ in Poem iv reassures her husband with the words '"I am your virgian bride" / with a smile worlds away'. Language is an unstable compound for this poet, but it is also unpredictably liberating and creative. 'The First Men on Mercury' is about communicating with aliens, only to wonder who the *real* aliens are, as the roles and discourses are reversed upon a planet whose name is already a byword for the delivering of messages and quicksilver slipperiness. Morgan has a deep distrust of systems and dogma and welcomes the unexpected, so 'The Fifth Gospel' offers a Nietzschean reversal of familiar Christian parables, only to demonstrate that they work just as well – if not better – when subverted:

Each of you by taking thought will someday add a foot to his height.

Give nothing to Caesar, for nothing is Caesar's.

The poem 'A Jar Revisited' makes a whole new poem out of a misprint in a poem by Norman MacCaig which described a 'fictitious spaec' [*sic*] behind the painting of a jar; while 'Boxers' imagines a misheard and hilariously mutating dialogue over an unclear phone connection.

Morgan has written many poems around similar effects, including sound-poems such as 'The Shaker Shaken' from *The New Divan* (1977), which starts with a stanza of nonsense syllables (a Shaker sound-poem from 1847) that is then repeated five times – each time with a few more actual words substituted – until the listener begins to experience a poem with comprehensible but strangely beautiful images emerging from the abstract rhythmical noise, like a slowly developing surreal photograph. Morgan called his early ventures in such modes 'Emergent Poems' and has long been fascinated by language as a system of repetition, difference and coded reference. (He shares this interest with W. S. Graham, whom he knew and admired, except that Graham's expression of it is more abstracted and less flamboyant in its manifestations.) Morgan's interest in the Scots language comes from almost the same roots, for it is its *alterity* he enjoys as much as its status as a signifier of national difference, or its place in the chain of literary tradition. In this he was to anticipate the 'Informationist' experiments of Robert Crawford and W. N. Herbert in the late 1980s with their parallel English and Scots texts, both almost equally impenetrable.

Morgan's writing on Glasgow continues to find compassion and a kind of beauty in the city, for he sees energy and a superb carelessness in the drunks of 'Saturday Night', or he celebrates the 'happy demolition men' in 'For Bonfires', who tear down an old slum: 'stacking and building / their rubbish into a total bonfire . . . they all stand round, / and cheer the tenement to smoke'. Anonymous encounters in the city can lead to fear or the thrill of sexual risk ('The Suspect', 'Christmas Eve'), while the ten 'Glasgow sonnets' reflect on the old and new faces of the city, and 'Stobhill', a long poem in different voices, tells of horrors behind the scenes of a local hospital.

Morgan's paradoxically deep engagement with the surface of the modern world appears in the collection of *Instamatic Poems* (1972), which deal with the thousand and one bizarre and painful stories that we find reported in newspapers every morning. He re-imagined these stories as if they were snapshots taken with a cheap 'instamatic' camera, and then wrote the poem as if describing those fictitious photographs in relatively neutral terms. If the futurists liked to cite the newspaper as the quintessential art-collage of modernist times, then Morgan's work in this vein is his way of catching 'the living blur' that is brought to us by the media every day – trivial and profound by turns. He developed this interest still further in his collection *From the Video Box* (1986), in which he imagines a vox-pop video booth to which people come to talk about TV programmes, towards some future broadcasting of their opinions. (This was the actual remit of Channel 4's *Right to Reply* programme at that time.) In what we would now call 'reality TV' Morgan imagines a variety of unexpected and often unintentionally humorous interventions. But other poems are more serious, and through this apparently playful conceit they offer memorable and profound reflections on the spectral and disturbing way our lives are lived (often in lonely rooms) in the middle of the media storm that is Western existence. The interlocutor in Poem 5 proposes to make a 'scratch video', with scenes moving forwards and backwards in the way that a scratch DJ manipulates music on a vinyl disc. He talks of his 'friend' beside him and his narrative is invaded by phrases from Hogg's *Justified Sinner*. Poem 6 follows the same theme by having its phrases repeat and loop back on each other to strangely moving effect. Other viewers (in Poems 7 and 8) report that they have been haunted by sudden invasions of colour or hope on their TV screens at home, just as a grieving mother (Poem 17) thinks that she caught a glimpse of her long drowned son while watching 'a blizzard of images, / a speeded mosaic of change / in the Americas':

> – oh images, images,
> corners of the world seen
> out of the corner of an eye –
> subversive, subliminal –
> where have you taken my son
> into your terrible machine
> and why have you peeled off
> my grief like a decal
> and left me a nobody
> staring out to sea?

That closing image has a classical severity, and Morgan is one of the very few modern poets (in any country) to have found and made such lyrical beauty out of the technological clutter of our times.

Morgan has always been sensitive to that moment when the world of matter and the world of words are suddenly found to be mutable, frightening, beautiful, surprising or insecure. This understanding lies at the core of all his art. It links the Glasgow poems to the science-fiction verses, just as it runs through the computer and the concrete poems to go back to language itself and the world that language creates, whether it be talking about Glasgow or Saturn or simply about itself, as when he ran through 14 variations of 14 words from John Cage's 'I have nothing to say and I am saying it and that is poetry':

> I have to say poetry and is that nothing and am I saying it
> I am and I have poetry to say and is that nothing saying it
> I am nothing and I have poetry to say and that is saying it
> . . .
>
> ('Opening the Cage')

The poet's fine talent for the evocative and elusive image transcends all the many categories of verse he has written, from the playful found poems to the sonnets in *Sonnets for Scotland* that imagine the state of the nation from its geological beginnings to independence, apocalyptic destruction and a mythical future far beyond that. But he rarely speaks directly and personally. 'The New Divan' (1977) is a long poem sequence echoing the Persian poet Hafiz from the fourteenth century, famous for his collection (the 'divan') of romantically spiritual meditations on love and death. Some sections deal with Morgan's sexuality and his experience of comradeship and war in the Middle East, yet the 'I' of the sequence seems to shift between different people and different times and the sequence as a whole remains exotic and opaquely elusive, ending with the poet's commitment to the sensual moment only – beyond all the preferred illusions of an afterlife:

> The dead climb with us like the living to the edge.
> The clouds sail and the air's washed blue. For you
> and me, the life beyond that sages mention
> is this life on a crag above the breakers. Oh I can't speak
> of that eternal break of white, only of
> Memories crowding in from human kind . . .

His poem in memory of the music-hall juggler 'Cinquevalli' carries something of the poet's own identification with a man of skill and balance who made the impossible happen in the years before the Great War. And yet, perhaps like all artists, he belongs to a circle that never will be 'respectable' or fully accepted by society:

> Cinquevalli tosses up a plate of soup
> and twirls it on his forefinger; not a drop spills.
> He laughs, and well may he laugh
> who can do that. The astonished table
> breathe again, laugh too, think the world
> a spinning thing that spills, for a moment, no drop.

In a long and very productive creative life Edwin Morgan has indeed been entranced by the world as a 'spinning thing'. He is fully aware that many drops of human pain and humiliation have been spilled in its time, yet his indefatigable curiosity, like his best work, is all the more profound for never having attempted the grand manner or a proper bardic solemnity. In the last poem of the *Collected Poems* of 1990, the poet reflected on his seventieth year – looking forward to 'figures and voices' that 'might be surprising yet', and pushing forward into the future, as if 'parting a bead curtain in Port Said':

> . . . The beads clash faintly
> behind me as I go forward. No candle-light
> please, keep that for Europe. Switch the whole thing
> right on. When I go I want it bright,
> I want to catch whatever is there
> in full sight.
> ('Epilogue: Seven Decades')

If the first half of the twentieth century belonged to MacDiarmid and the cultural nationalism of the literary Renaissance movement, the second half belongs to Edwin Morgan, Alasdair Gray and political devolution.

The political scene: new verses of an old song

Political and economic perspectives were shifting during the 1960s and 1970s with hints, indeed, of the 'second life' that Morgan hoped for. Voters in the north were becoming disillusioned by the two main parties and their inability to deliver significant change. The Scottish National Party began to collect votes from a new sector of the population, and this message was delivered in no uncertain fashion in 1967 when Winnie Ewing won the by-election at Hamilton, near Glasgow. Ewing took 46% of the vote for the SNP in the safest Labour seat in Britain, a traditional stronghold of coalminers and steelworkers who had seen Harold Wilson's Labour government fail to do anything to arrest the decline of heavy industry throughout Scotland. The seat was regained for Labour two years later, but Hamilton, and 101 further by-election gains for the SNP (against 81 Labour losses) had made a memorable impact on how Westminster was coming to think about the Scottish question. Edward Heath, speaking for the Conservatives in opposition, began to mention the possibility of a Scottish Assembly and although little came of it then, the idea had entered the vocabulary of Westminster politics, if only as a way of resisting any more challenges from the north at a time when the economy was not doing well. When

Heath and the Conservatives came to power and tried to close down shipbuilding on the Clyde, nation-wide support for the men who defended their industry (at the Upper Clyde Shipbuilders' work-in) once again showed which way the wind was blowing. Ironically, the Scottish Office had moved north and been greatly expanded in response to the decline of manufacturing industry and it became apparent that a more devolved structure of government was already in place, if only the will could be found to empower it.

The 1970s and 1980s were marked by fears that Scotland was benefiting less than she should from the discovery of North-Sea oil, and the Scottish National Party campaigned boldly on the ticket of 'It's Scotland's Oil'. The traditional Labour response that a separate Scotland was not economically viable was beginning to look less convincing now, just as it was beginning to dawn on Labour politicians at Westminster how dependent they were on Scotland's delivery of a broadly socialist vote in every national election. Nor were the SNP slow to suggest that Scotland might have a place in a federation of European States when the debate on whether Britain should join the European Union was under way. The possibility of some form of devolution was now clearly on the table, as all the major parties at Westminster began to recognise that pleasing Scotland, or at least resisting a too radical change there, might be a good idea. However, there was still a certain amount of nervousness about how far this process should go, and when a devolution referendum was proposed for 1979, there were mixed messages, muddled advice and quibbles from all sides, along with a last-minute amendment (never seen before or since) that required 40% of the total eligible electorate to vote 'yes', rather than a simple majority of those who actually turned out at the polling booth. In effect this meant that not to vote was to vote 'no'. The much-heralded devolution referendum produced a 63.8% electoral turn-out and a 'yes' majority of almost 100,000. This was 7% short of the required *total* majority and the bill failed.

There followed a period of bitter retrenchment and recrimination on all sides. Yet the possibility of devolution would not go away, least of all in the ensuing years that saw the rise of the Thatcher government, the turmoil of the miners' strike and (with the launching of the hugely unpopular poll tax in Scotland in the late 1980s) an increasingly disaffected population north of the border. Many Scottish voters wanted either a Labour government for Britain or a leftish Scottish government – whichever came first – and a cross-party Campaign for a Scottish Assembly began to gather force. A 'Constitutional

Convention' of public figures drew up 'A Claim of Right for Scotland' to make the case to the public and their elected politicians and, in the light of all this, the devolution issue became a plank on Labour's platform for re-election, with the promise to grant a greater degree of autonomy to both Scotland and Wales. Accordingly, when the Blair government came to power in 1997, a referendum was held again and this time 74% of the voters called for the re-establishment of a Scottish parliament, with 64% in favour of its having tax-raising powers. A number of key areas such as defence and international relations were still to be reserved for Westminster, but the result was unequivocal. The Scotland Act was passed in the following year and a Welsh Assembly with lesser powers was also established, all under a 'New Labour' agenda to 'modernise' Britain.

So it was that in 1999 a Scottish parliament in Edinburgh was convened for the first time since its closure in 1707. The event made an enormous symbolic and emotional impact, doubly reinforced by the singing of Burns's 'A man's a man for a' that' at the ceremony. Nor was the cultural connection inappropriate, for although Scotland's sense of its own distinct identity had expressed itself in different ways since the eighteenth century, it had never diminished, least of all since the cultural renaissance of the 1920s, or indeed the remarkable revival of creative confidence among writers and artists since the 1970s. And some of these writers had taken a leading part in the debates of the day. Thus, for example, after the general election of 1992 (which saw a Tory government returned under John Major despite a clear Scottish majority against it), James Kelman wrote a bitter essay on the need for constitutional change. In the same year Alasdair Gray produced his quirky and trenchant booklet *Why Scots Should Rule Scotland* (with a new edition produced for 1997), in which he summarised his vision in a seemingly artless and drily prophetic style:

> I think . . . a new Scottish parliament will be squabblesome and disunited and full of people justifying themselves by denouncing others – the London parliament on a tiny scale. But it will offer hope for the future. The London parliament has stopped even pretending to do that. I believe an independent country run by a government not much richer than the People has more hope than one governed by a big rich neighbour.

Several of Gray's books also contain the epigraph: 'Work as if you live in the early days of a better nation.' That cautionary 'as if' should not be forgotten, but the creative output from authors, and the rise of vernacular Scots or urban demotic in these years, might be compared to the similar determination to find a Scottish voice (and the vernacular revival) that followed the loss of the Scottish Parliament in 1707.

Alasdair Gray (b. 1934)

There is no doubting the imaginative impact made by the publication of Alasdair Gray's first novel *Lanark: A Life in Four Books* in 1981. Here was a book with the postmodern mastery of Salman Rushdie's *Midnight's Children* (also published in 1981), which looked to European and American narrative modes while also engaging with twentieth-century Scotland at the deepest personal, cultural, political and global levels. It won a Scottish Arts Council award and the Scottish Book of the Year award. Anthony Burgess hailed Gray as 'the first major Scottish writer since Walter Scott' and indeed the book's scale was appropriate to the claim, for the work was over 560 pages long. It also used typography in an innovative way, and was illustrated throughout by the author's own hard-edged line drawings, rather in the manner of Eric Gill. *Lanark* was nearly thirty years in the making and had started out as a realistic *bildungsroman* with a strongly autobiographical element, about the wartime childhood and college days of a young art student. In the novel as it stands today, the character Duncan Thaw suffers from asthma, eczema and social ineptitude in equal measure. Duncan finds relief in the solitary pursuit of his art (and also masturbation), haunted at every turn by a vision of the world that is acutely sensitive to gross physical detail, from the mushy food on his plate to the horrifying moment when he sees the faces of those around him in a negative epiphany:

> The skin on the skulls crawled and twitched like a half-solid paste. All the heads in his angle of vision seemed irregular lumps, like potatoes but without a potato's repose: potatoes with crawling surfaces punctured by holes which opened and shut, holes blocked with coloured jelly or fringed with bone stumps, elastic holes through which air was sucked or squirted, holes secreting salt, wax, spittle and snot. He grasped a pencil in his trouser pocket, wishing it were a knife he could thrust through his cheek and use to carve his face down to the clean bone.

His is indeed an artist's vision, but deeply alienated at such moments, which are reminiscent of how Sartre describes the terrifyingly existential otherness of the world in his novel *La Nausée* (1938). Thaw's difficulties accumulate when he enters his twenties, and his story ends in a violent confusion of sexual attraction, self-disgust and mental breakdown that may or may not have resulted in the death of a girl, followed by his decision to drown himself.

But this life in four books is really two lives, for half the novel seems to be taking place in another realm altogether, following the progress of a character called Lanark, who finds himself thrust into the strangely sunless city of Unthank, as if suddenly born, or indeed deceased and transported by train, to some sort of underworld where the streets are perpetually overcast, bureaucracy rules, and the first thing to do is to check-in to social security. Here Lanark meets an attractive girl called Rima, only to discover that he is suffering from dragonhide, the growth of scaly excrescences over his body. Caught up in an increasingly nightmarish scenario he finds himself being cured at the Institute, which is something between a hospital and a vast university research centre that turns out to be powered by the imploding bodies of the very people it sets out to cure. Professor Ozenfant explains how people afraid to love or to give, grow dragonhide to trap their heat within themselves, until they explode like stars going nova, providing light and warmth for the professionals. Other forms of illness provide a spongy food that nourishes staff and patients alike. The motto for this institution seems to be 'Man is the pie that bakes and eats himself, and the recipe is separation', and Ozenfant points out the logical elegance of such a closed and scientific system, so much more economical than a Christian morality, that would bury the dead or condemn the fallen to rot wastefully in hell.

Slowly the reader comes to realise that 'Lanark' and 'Unthank' are dystopian versions of Thaw and Glasgow and that their two lives are reflections of each other. The reiteration is made doubly complex and engrossing because the two narratives are entwined together without explanation, and the chronological order of the stories, so to speak, is mixed up. If Lanark is a version of Thaw, he must be Thaw after his apparent suicide. Yet the novel begins with Thaw arriving in Unthank in what is signalled as 'Book Three'. This is followed by a 'Prologue' and then by 'Book One', which starts the story of Duncan Thaw, aged five, during the Second World War in Glasgow. Then there is an 'Interlude' followed by 'Book Two', which continues the story of Thaw until his suicide, before finally returning to the Lanark narrative in 'Book Four'. Our sense that the two stories are linked is strengthened by the strange echoes that appear in each thread: the obsession with food and eating, for example, or with swallowing, being swallowed and excreted; or the parallels between dragonhide and eczema. Different locations also echo each other, while specific spoken phrases are even carried across, as if overheard, from one narrative strand to the other.

Later in the novel it is proposed that 'the plots of the Thaw and Lanark sections are independent of each other and cemented by typographical contrivances rather than formal necessity'. But this is deliberately disingenuous, for it does seem as if Thaw has indeed been given a second chance as 'Lanark', in some Dantesque circle of hell where he will try to redeem himself and learn how to love. And in fact he manages this after a fashion, doggedly navigating a world of corrupt bureaucrats and strange international corporations, while trying to love and stay true to Rima and the son she bears him, despite his own accelerating age and innumerable setbacks. Part of this particular pilgrim's progress is also to learn more about Unthank and the social cannibalism of the Institute:

> it is like all machines, it profits those who own it, and nowadays many sections are owned by gentle, powerless people who don't know they are cannibals and wouldn't believe if you told them. It is also amazingly tolerant of anyone it considers human, and cures more people than you realize. Even the societies who denounce it would (most of them) collapse if it vanished, for it is an important source of knowledge and energy.

Two-thirds of the way through Book Four there is an 'Epilogue' in which Thaw meets his maker, who explains the whole novel to him, rather belatedly perhaps, on page 480. This cheerfully garrulous authorial figure (not so very different from the Wizard of Oz behind the scenes) goes on to describe the genesis of the novel, his hopes for its critical reception, its literary predecessors and archetypes and his need for Arts Council grants. (His name is 'Nastler', which was in fact Alasdair Gray's baby name for himself.) This section also includes an extensive 'Index of Plagiarisms' by which the author confesses to having lifted ideas from Anon to Zoroaster, including authors as diversely sympathetic as Kafka, Carroll, Borges, Walt Disney, James Joyce, Blake, George MacDonald, Kurt Vonnegut and Sartre.

If this seems like postmodern playfulness gone mad, then the novel is wholly redeemed by what has been emerging as an increasingly pointed political message. In fact, despite the dazzling technique, Gray's true philosophical position, in this and all his other books, is closer to the Enlightened scepticism of Edinburgh in the eighteenth century (matched by a Swiftean rage) than it is to any more radically postmodern ethos. What Nastler explains to Thaw is very simple and entirely serious, and by this time in the book it is clear enough to the reader as well:

> 'The Thaw narrative shows a man dying because he is bad at loving. It is enclosed by your narrative which shows civilization collapsing for the same reason.'

One of the key intertexts to *Lanark* is Hobbes's *Leviathan* from 1651, which proposes that man is the ultimate and wholly material measure of all life. Christian theology and morality are dismissed as mere 'insignificant sound'; war is our natural condition and laws are made to control man's rapacious nature, to protect us from ourselves. The best ruler is an absolute ruler presiding over his commonwealth (the great beast of the state), which is envisaged as a surplus of manpower, to be directed according to the needs of the state to sustain and protect itself. Gray provides his own version of Hobbes's title page as the frontispiece to Book Four, with a picture of the state as the 'leviathan' mentioned in the Book of Job as 'king of all the children of pride'. In *Lanark*, however, the state has given way to corporate capitalism and its true objective is no longer territory and conquest through manpower, but total control of wealth and time. (Nastler confirms that he sees Hobbes's metaphor as a monstrous one with the state as 'the sort of creature Frankenstein made . . . full of strength got from people forced to supply its belly, the market'.)

This new Leviathan is 'the Creature' – 'a conspiracy which owns and manipulates everything for profit', that working like a global extension of the Institute, in which international conglomerates like Volstat, Quantum-Cortexin or Algolagnics take the materialist adage that 'time is money' all too literally, for if time is money, money is also time, leisure and life – so they set out to plunder space by launching an orbital platform to steal energy from the sun itself, quite possibly altering the calendar and shortening all our lives. (The normal passage of time and the links between cause and effect have already been strangely distorted in the 'intercalendrical zone' of this realm.) Lanark meets the Council for the Creature, where its chairman Lord Monboddo explains the plan and summarises the acceleration of time and the triumph of the Northern hemisphere in a fabular version of our own world that dares us to disagree:

> 'by the twentieth century, wealth has engrossed the whole globe, which now revolves in a tightening net of thought and transport woven round it by trade and science. . . . Two world wars were fought in thirty years, wars the

more bitter because they are between different parts of the same system. It would wrong the slaughtered millions to say these wars did no good. Old machines, old ideas were replaced at unusual speed. Science, business and government quickly became richer than ever before. We must thank the dead for that.

Grays's allegory is many-sided and darkly comic, but his nightmare analysis of capitalist society becomes more and more disturbing when it is so blandly explained as literal cannibalism; or when the principle of the mortgage to buy a home is explained in terms of time rather than money, for 'the energy to pay for it would be deducted from your future'.

MONEY IS TIME. TIME IS LIFE. BUY MORE LIFE FOR YOUR FAMILY FROM THE QUANTUM INTERMINABLE. (THEY'LL LOVE YOU FOR IT.)

It is here that Gray's dread of eating and being eaten (the novel is haunted by an imagery of mouths and excretion), or Thaw's disgust at the food on his plate, comes to have a specifically political and economic force. Thaw's horror of materiality and the Darwinian struggles of nature, along with Lanark's well-meaning but bumbling ineptitude in the face of the Creature's materialism and all its doings, sum up Gray's vision of our plight in the modern world. This psychological/moral/political vision is central to all his later work, and in *Lanark* it is as if Mervyn Peake and Kafka have been recruited to serve a secular and socialist John Bunyan. Gray's very Scottish combination of pedantic weight and scholarly flippancy is fully alert to the modernist tradition of fantastic literature in Burroughs and Borges, but it can be traced equally convincingly to Stevenson and Hogg, or the high style and philosophical rage of *Sartor Resartus*, the Nietzschean outlook of John Davidson, the allegorical visions of *The City of Dreadful Night*, Oliphant's 'Land of Darkness', George MacDonald's *Lilith*, Lindsay's *A Voyage to Arcturus* or even Edwin Muir's poem 'The Labyrinth'.

Several aspects of Duncan Thaw's life clearly correspond to the experience of his creator, as Gray made clear in the brief personal memoir he wrote in 1988 for a series of 'Saltire Self-Portraits'. The young Gray suffered from asthma and was evacuated to the countryside during the war. Even as a child he was writing stories and drawing pictures to accompany them. His mother died in the same year that he went to study at Glasgow School of Art in its famous Rennie Mackintosh building, where he specialised in mural painting, started to write short stories and began work on an autobiographical novel to be called 'Thaw'. Over the next few years he continued to suffer from severe asthma attacks, but he trained and found employment as an art teacher while also writing and working on commissioned murals. One of these was a Creation scene at Greenhead Church (four years of work, now alas destroyed) that features in the 'Genesis' chapter of *Lanark*. In 1961 Gray met Inge Sørensen at the Edinburgh Festival, and shortly after they married he gave up teaching to work for a spell as a theatrical scene painter. The couple had a son and Gray struggled to make a living by writing, painting and part-time teaching, but had no success in finding a publisher for 'Book One' of *Lanark* – the first half of the Thaw narrative. A BBC television documentary showed his work at this time, and he made use of the connection by writing TV plays, finding success with *The Fall of Kelvin Walker* in 1968. Remounted as a stage play in 1972 and re-written as a novella in 1985, this 'fable of the sixties' gives a satirical account of the media industry, and the differences between north and south, by following the adventures of a young Scotsman-on-the-make in London. Over the next eight years Gray had over twenty plays produced, some on television, four for small theatre companies and others on radio, many under the direction of Stewart Conn. *McGrotty and Ludmilla* pursued similar themes to *Kelvin Walker*, but was set in the corridors of Westminster rather than the BBC. It appeared first as a radio play in 1975 and then as a book in 1990. In the meantime Gray continued to work on *Lanark*, attending an informal writers' group run by Philip Hobsbaum of the University of Glasgow, along – at different times – with Liz Lochhead, Tom Leonard, James Kelman, Aonghas MacNeacail and Agnes Owens. On the strength of his plays Gray also found employment as a writer-in-residence at Glasgow University from 1977 to 1979. After a disappointment with another publisher, Gray finally signed a contract for his novel with the Edinburgh company Canongate, who published the book to great acclaim in 1981, and followed it with a collection of stories containing some of Gray's best short fiction.

Unlikely Stories, Mostly (1983) won the Cheltenham prize for that year and Gray's penchant for Kafka-esque fables with echoes of Borges or Calvino is never clearer than it is in a tale such as 'Five Letters from an Eastern Empire', or his two stories about the 'Axletree', all of which invoke labyrinthine empires or projects that overwhelm the individual. At the same time the author's postmodern playfulness is given free reign, from the *erratum* slip in the first edition, which reports 'this slip has been inserted in error', to the typographical extravagance and totally mad pedanticism of 'Sir Thomas's Logopandocy' – a project that might well have been written by the illustrious Sir Thomas Urquhart himself. In complete contrast the calm narrative translucence of 'The Comedy of the White Dog' might have been written by a modern-day Barrie.

Gray's next novel was to be simpler than *Lanark*, though no less challenging and perhaps even more disturbing. *1982 Janine* (1984) mixes fantasy and reality just as before, except that this time both modes operate within the same realistic field. As Gray describes it, the whole novel takes place:

> inside the head of an aging, divorced, alcoholic, insomniac supervisor of security installations who is tippling in the bedroom of a small Scottish hotel. Though full of depressing memories and propaganda for the Conservative Party it is mainly a sado-masochistic fetishistic fantasy. Even the arrival of God in the later chapters fails to elevate the tone.

The prevailing metaphor for the politics of the novel, and the theatre within which much of its imagined action is played out, is to be found in the pornographic fantasies of Jock McLeish – whose name might indeed be translated as 'John, son of the leash', given his dreams of bondage, whipping and humiliation. In a single long night of the soul, McLeish confronts the truth of his own and his nation's past, for as Gray reminds us in another 'Epilogue' his book is concerned with 'the matter of Scotland refracted through alcoholic reverie' in the manner of MacDiarmid's *A Drunk Man Looks at the Thistle*. In this case the thistle's phallic implications (already present in MacDiarmid's poem, after all) entirely dominate the landscape as this particular drunk man manifests all the pathology of damaged masculinity and diminished self-esteem because of his personal and political circumstances. McLeish's world has become entirely alienated, as he himself has become objectified, working for the 'National' company team in a mirror-maze of faceless mutual exploitation, with fear and the need for security as the bottom line:

> I am the instrument of a firm which installs instruments to protect the instruments of firms which produce meat cloth machines and whisky, instruments to feed, dress, move and stupefy us. But the National instals most of its instruments around nuclear reactors – instruments powering the instruments which light, heat and entertain us – and banks – instruments to protect and increase the profits of the instrument owners – and military depots where the weapons are kept which protects the nation's instruments

and profits from the protective instruments of the Russian instrument-makers. Mirrors reflecting mirrors are the whole show? No. Instruments serving instruments are the whole show. . . .

Most of us become instruments to get something NOW, what? Safety and pleasure. The safety and pleasure of big houses, rounds of golf and safaris in Kenya drive shareholders to operate the bank and Stock Exchange. . . . Safety and pleasure drive me to drink and wank in a Peebles hotel but I am SICK of being an instrument joining instruments to instruments so that an imaginary Superb, handcuffed and nude, facedown and writing screams NO NO PLEASE PLEASE DON'T DO IT AGAIN as Charlie, gripping her lovely buttocks, drives his stiff etcetera again and again through her etcetera etcetera. In my coat pocket is a bottle of barbiturate pills to be swallowed with the emergency whisky if the bombs drop before I reach the shelter. Why not swallow them and return to pre-birth nothingness now?

Emotionally inhibited all his life, unsure of his paternity, and disen-franchised again after the failure of the 1997 Referendum, McLeish's answer to the installation that 'encloses and controls' him is to turn to his imagination, where he can stand outside the system, like a cruel little boy, 'manipulating it and peering in upon, Janine?' Yet this results in even more self-contempt and a vision of human congress that is exclusively based on solipsism, will and power:

Men who gossip spitefully about women are not the arrogant bastards they want to seem. . . . They talk nastily about sex because they resent being unable to enter this world, or feel much ecstasy. Or replace themselves, or respect themselves, without help from a woman. What sex does not hate the other for threatening its independence?

From such a standpoint McLeish's preference for Burns's song 'A man's a man for a' that' rings particularly hollow, signalling nothing so much as desperation and a deep contempt for his own and his nation's favourite myths:

The truth is that we are a nation of arselickers, though we disguise it with surfaces: a surface of generous openhanded manliness, a surface of dour practical integrity, a surface of futile maudlin defiance . . .

Here, translated to a middle-class Tory businessman in the Scotland of the 1980s, is all the damaged self-esteem and sexual insecurity of Dunky Logan in *From Scenes Like These*; here is Docherty's sense of futility and entrapment, now shown to be even more acute in the aftermath of the 1979 *referendum interruptum* and the arrival of a government led by Margaret Thatcher, who held that 'there is no such thing as society'. *1982 Janine* brings all these elements together: the social, the sexual, the public, the political – and the disturbingly private. Yet despite everything, McLeish does finally manage to come through. The undoubtedly pornographic fantasies of the first half of the book give way to a searching exploration of his own past. Jock comes to a degree of self-knowledge that takes him to the edge of suicide before he rises to a new day with some hope that he has exorcised the demons of his personal and national situation. No longer quite so trapped in the machine, there is the possibility of agency and even, perhaps, of love:

> history is what we all make, everywhere, each moment of our lives, whether we notice it or not. I will work among the people I know; I will not squander myself in fantasies. . . . I will find friends, allies, enemies if need be, and l(don't name it).

The dynamic tension between the sexual drive and our need for love is a theme that Gray keeps returning to at a personal as well as a political level. It appears in *Lanark*, when Duncan Thaw remembers Blake's poem 'The Clod and the Pebble' and puzzles over our capacity for both selfless and selfish sexual desire, and of course Jock McLeish's fantasies of bondage would seek to 'bind another to [his] delight' in the most literal way. This exploration appeared again in *Something Leather* (1990) when Gray tried to write – not without a sexual charge – about the experience of four different women all of whom have suffered abuse in one sense or another. The gender politics implicit in such texts have given rise to considerable critical debate, not least in the suspicion felt by some readers, and some feminist critics, that there is a disturbing complicity between the author and his fevered creatures. Gray himself has not sought to underplay the genuinely pornographic drive in parts of *Janine*, nor does he deny exploring this still further in *Something Leather*. On the other hand, he was honest enough to admit in that same book that he just did not know what women think when they are alone. In fact Gray's work in this vein can be seen as an unusually honest attempt to explore the masculine psyche (or at least the psyche of a Scotsman of a certain generation), with no attempt to shirk what he finds there. And the ambiguously ironic admission he makes in *Something Leather* ('While writing the first chapter of this book I enjoyed a prolonged, cold-blooded sexual thrill of a sort common among some writers and all lizards') indicates a provocative determination to explore this territory in both himself and his readers' responses to it. In this respect, Gray's complex engagement with the nature of Scottish masculinity – part critical analysis, part symptomatic exposure – has indeed been shared by George Douglas Brown, William McIlvanney and Gordon Williams as well as by younger writers such as Tom Leonard, James Kelman, Janice Galloway, Laura Hird and – most provocatively of all – Irving Welsh.

The 'woman question' was to be explored further in a wittier and less rawly exposed fashion in Gray's third major novel *Poor Things*, which won the Whitbread Award and the Guardian Award for Fiction when it appeared in 1992. This 'up-to-date nineteenth-century-novel' adopts a conceit that would have been familiar to Scott and Hogg, when Gray purports to be merely the editor of a unique autobiographical volume and various associated papers to do with Dr Archibald McCandless, a Scottish Public Health Officer in the nineteenth century. Gray plays the game to its limits with the fiction that this material was initially found by a (real) historian friend of his, followed by an editorial apparatus; a variety of typestyles for different original sources; letters and holograph MSS; apparently contemporary illustrations; 'etchings by William Strang'; many embedded references to real historical people and events in Glasgow at the time; a title page for 1909; and of course an appendix of 'historical notes' not all of which are untrue. In this 'complete tissue of facts' Gray sets out to tell us about a daring medical experiment in Glasgow in the1880s by which the brilliant surgeon Godwin Baxter transplants the brain of a baby into the drowned body of a mature woman to create 'Bella Baxter', subsequently to marry Archibald McCandless. The woman in question committed suicide, perhaps because she was pregnant, and it is the brain of her unborn baby that Baxter makes use of. The *Frankenstein* parallels are obvious, as Gray reminds us by transplanting Mary Shelley's father's surname into Baxter's Christian name – not just for its echoes of divinity. There is undoubtedly something of Dr Jekyll in Godwin Baxter's character, and of course Stevenson's tale also uses different narratives and 'documents' to tell itself. Nor is the setting entirely accidental, for Glasgow was indeed at the forefront of radical medical advancement in those years.

Thus it is that Bella Baxter is simultaneously her own mother and her own child, and Gray sets out to explore the limits of male intellectual arrogance, emotional possessiveness – and perhaps delusion – in all that follows. In his story (McCandless's 'document') we see Bella (or 'Bella Caledonia', as her creator refers to her) learn that her genetic husband/father was a corrupt imperialist called General Blessington, before going on to declare her own independence by becoming a distinguished doctor herself and a campaigner for female suffrage. However, the novel ends with Bella's own version of the story, which completely contradicts all that has gone before, including the political allegory to do with Scotland and Empire – her paternity and creation. Thus a concluding letter (also among the book's many 'papers') from an elderly 'Victoria McCandless' describes her violent father as the foreman of a Manchester foundry, remembers her brutal sexual initiation at the hands of her first husband, 'Thunderbolt' Blessington, and tells of her rescue by Godwin Baxter, whom she called 'God' ('the only man I have ever truly loved'), who gave her the 'Bella Baxter' identity to protect her until she makes a marriage of convenience with old McCandless. We learn from the editor's notes that this ruthlessly strong-minded and successful woman became a spokesperson for public health and socialist revolution, who later saw the Great War as an outbreak of collective 'suicidal obedience' on the part of men, brought about by 'bad mothering and fathering'. Victoria's version of events reveals her ineffectual second husband's narrative (and therefore much of Gray's novel) to be a self-serving fantasy of god-like masculine prowess and second-hand Gothic fiction to the effect that men create women. On the other hand, she has her own agenda, too. So the 'Poor Things' of the title can apply to the impoverished classes that Victoria supported during her working life; or to women as they are perceived under the mentorship of men; or, finally and most tellingly, to men and their sad delusions of authority and authorship.

Gray married his second wife Morag McAlpine in 1991, and produced further short stories in *Ten Tales Tall and True* (1993) and *The Ends of Our Tethers* (2003). He presented a Wellsian future fiction in *A History Maker* (1994), while *Mavis Belfrage* (1996) billed itself as 'A Romantic Novel' (along with another five tales) to offer a rather sour account of the relationships between men and women, teachers and pupils and the emotional damage generally delivered by a good sound Scottish education. Gray's delight in editorial apparatus and his own considerable scholarship inspired him to work for some sixteen years on his edition of *The Book of Prefaces* (2000), a remarkable collection of introductory material by 'Great Writers of Four Nations from the 7th to the 20th Century' with his own brilliant insights and graphic designs, along with glosses and commentaries by other writers – many of them his Scottish contemporaries. In 2001 Gray was appointed as Professor of a postgraduate creative-writing programme at Glasgow

University, a chair that was shared with Tom Leonard and James Kelman.

Full of the confidence of youth, Duncan Thaw dismissed Glasgow in a now famous passage in *Lanark* by explaining that 'if a city hasn't been used by an artist not even the inhabitants live there imaginatively'. This was about to change of course and books by Gray, Kelman and Leonard during the 1970s and 1980s put Glasgow very much on the imaginative map. However, they quite rightly resist any attempt to call them 'Glasgow writers' for Gray's explorations of power in all its manifestations, and Leonard's quarrels with the hegemony of the literary canon and the English language, go far beyond whether their work happens to be set in the West of Scotland or not. This is particularly true of James Kelman, whose writing has a consistently politicised engagement with questions of literary realism, language and class, and, in the last analysis, an existential focus that transcends its origins in region or nation.

James Kelman (b. 1946)

Kelman has explained his position as a writer in the clearest possible terms:

> The stories I wanted to write would derive from my own background, my own socio-cultural experience. I wanted to write as one of my own people, I wanted to write and remain a member of my own community.

This was a position already established by the poet Tom Leonard with regard to his own poetry and his determination to use West of Scotland urban speech (frequently dismissed by literary critics of the day as corrupt Scots and a despised patois) as the proper medium for what he wanted to say in free verse. In Kelman's case, as a writer of prose, it meant that he was unwilling to make any distinction between the working-class speech of his characters and the narrative voice of his own text, for he sees this not just as a kind of class distinction, but as an abuse of moral and intellectual power. In a talk to students at Glasgow School of Art in 1996, he put it this way:

> I was uncomfortable with 'working class' authors who allowed 'the voice' of 'higher authority' to control narrative, the place where the psychological drama occurred. How could I write from within my own place and time if

I was forced to adopt the 'received' language of the ruling class? Not to challenge the rules of narrative was to be coerced into assimilation; I would be forced to write in the voice of an imagined member of the ruling class. I saw the struggle as towards a self-contained world. This meant I had to work my way through language, find a way of making it my own.

The short stories in his first two books *An Old Pub Near the Angel* (1973) and *Not Not While the Giro* (1983) use both first- and third-person narration, but Kelman starts to break down the distinctions between internalised and externalised discourse, and the orthographical conventions by which they are signalled. (This was an elision already made, for similar reasons, by Lewis Grassic Gibbon in *A Scots Quair*.) Thus Kelman dispenses with inverted commas for reported speech in several of the stories; others use free indirect discourse so that the 'mind-style' of the character and the voice of the narrator slide into each other; and the long title-story 'Not not while the giro' is a free-associative internal monologue on the possibility of suicide (but not when the 'Giro', the unemployment cheque, is ready to be collected), with echoes of Beckett and Dostoevsky's *Notes from Underground*. In every case Kelman's focus is on the inner experience of ordinary people and the routines of their daily lives at work, in the pub, at home, or in lodgings – often alone. For Kelman there is little distinction between the conditions of every day and the horrors of existential being, and he feels that this is clearest of all in the lives of his working-class protagonists, many of them in menial tasks, or unemployed, marginalised and despised by those whose affluence and indifference shields them from a similarly stark philosophical exposure.

I think the most ordinary person's life is fairly dramatic; all you've got to do is follow some people around and look at their existence for 24 hours, and it will be horror. It will just be horror.

This is more than just philosophical, of course, for Kelman is strongly opposed to the economic injustices suffered by underpaid and under-valued workers at the hands of a system that exploits or dis-employs them to satisfy share-holders. Yet he feels that such people are disenfranchised again by a conception of 'literature' and a critical establishment before which they are all but invisible. He has expressed contempt for an 'Anglo American literary tradition' that has no sense of 'concrete reality, no economic detail' and reflects that 'the way that literature generally works in our society you never have to worry about these very routine horrors, the things that make up everyday reality for

such an enormous proportion of the population'. This also has structural implications for Kelman, for he goes on to note that 'you don't
need any beginning, middle and end at all. All you have to do is show
this one day in maybe this person's life and it'll be horror.' This is not
to say that there are not finely crafted stories, such as 'Old Francis'
from *Greyhound for Breakfast* (1987) and 'By the Burn' from *The Burn*
(1991), which achieve a poetic force as powerful as anything written by
Joyce, Beckett, or Franz Kafka – a favourite author whom Kelman
regards, incidentally, as 'the greatest realist in literary art of the 20th
century'. In fact the Scots writer's prose generates a uniquely recursive
poetic cadence of its own, not least in his use of so-called 'bad
language', which is much more expressive than it is usually given credit
for. His treatment of narrative time is equally original, in that he
manages to focus on and slow down the trivia of day-to-day existence
– making a cup of instant coffee, a recipe for mince and tatties, crossing the street, watching a film, worrying about the rent – until we
realise that this is where life is most truly to be found, without benefit
of drama, symbolism, epiphanies or denouement. This is why the
considered cadences and textures of his text are so important – they
should not be rushed in the reading – and it's also why his work can be
misunderstood or crudely parodied.

Kelman was in his mid-twenties when he joined Hobsbaum's informal creative writing group in Glasgow. He had left school at fifteen to
take up an apprenticeship in the printing industry, later working as a
bus driver and at the Barbican in London before marriage and a family
brought him back to Glasgow. His first two collections contain many
of the most vivid and occasionally hilarious accounts of working life in
modern fiction and his first novel was a stylistic and thematic *tour de
force*. In *The Busconductor Hines* (1984) Kelman's apparently episodic
and inconsequentially mundane narrative is enlivened at every turn by
the free indirect discourse of Rab Hines's anarchic and imaginative
inner life as he reconciles himself to the daily grind. It is the energy of
the constantly shifting registers in Kelman's prose that gives the book
its drama, especially when Hines's ironically frustrated tones are
matched by the text's own ironic relationship to its chosen genre of
literary realism:

> Although predisposed towards speculative musings the Busconductor Hines
> cannot be described as a dreamer. Yet certain items do not always register.
> The itchiness for example: the material of standard issue uniform breeks is
> thick and reminiscent of wool; it probably isn't wool a 100% but it seems as
> if this is all it can be, because of the itchiness – the coarseness of the cloth

somehow making you think of the fleecy coat of a wee sheep, the straggly bits left on the barbed wire fence you can picture as hell of an itchy if dangled against the skin. Now: towards the latter stages of his last spell on the broo a certain husband and father's marked aversion to nought led him into what can authentically be called a pragmatic assessment of life, the outcome of which was his renewed determination to become the Busdriver Hines.

The unforced tenderness of Hines's care for his wife and family, his handiness with humble domestic chores and his worries about the well-being of old people and children in the street make a striking contrast to, and their own comment on, the generic expectations that have grown up around west of Scotland realistic writing in which a damaged and insecure masculinity shelters behind the violence of a 'hard-man' culture.

Kelman's next novel adopted a much more rigorous narrative ethic. With almost no interiority whatsoever, *A Chancer* (1985) was stripped as bare as a *nouveau roman* in its determination not to offer anything other than the starkest documentary surface description of what happens, moment by moment, in the actions of an inveterate young gambler. In a grey world of betting shops and backrooms Tammas seems to have pared his life down to the next turn of chance without the sensuality that was available to Camus's Meursault in *L'Étranger*. Such extreme minimalism makes for a particularly demanding read. *A Disaffection* (1989), however, returns to a more conventional narrative style and a more conventional hero, perhaps, as twenty-nine-year-old schoolteacher Patrick Doyle confronts his infatuation with a married colleague and a crisis of faith in his work. Kelman's capacity to move from interior to exterior life, seamlessly, darkly and humorously conveyed in free indirect narrative, makes this one of his richest and finest novels. (It was shortlisted for the Booker Prize and won the James Tait Black Prize.) His account of Doyle's recursive, frustrated and questing intelligence, in a black comedy of despair, rage, longing and the desire for love, is one of the most sympathetic and also the most acutely critical explorations of Scottish masculinity in contemporary fiction. Robin Jenkins and George Friel occupied similar territory, not least in Friel's account of another teacher's breakdown in *Mr Alfred MA*, but Kelman's novel is more directly political in the challenge it makes to institutionalised education in the materialistic 1980s, and also more clearly existential in Doyle's crippling sense of the absolute groundlessness of all things. His alienation is doubly felt as a man from a working-class background who finds himself cast in what he sees as the middle-class role of a state-employed imparter of 'knowledge'. Drawn to his unemployed brother's family (the scenes between them are sharply and movingly observed) and thinking himself in love with Alison Houston, a married fellow teacher, Doyle seems incapable of making any clear decision or commitment, except that his increasingly self-destructive behaviour seems to be narrowing his choices at every turn. He hopes to explain the world to the children he teaches and make them angry about the inequalities of society, and he is endlessly articulate about his situation, and yet the unfathomable rage that drives and seethes within him also paralyses him. Frustrated and longing for some form of creative expression to stave off his overwhelming loneliness, he finds some expressive relief by blowing musical sounds through some old industrial pipes he has found and taken home. The image is at once pathetic and heroic. Yet Doyle feels defeated by history before he has begun:

> Look at my da then right, it's no just because he smokes and likes a drink he's ended up with three bloody heart attacks Christ Nicola he's been working in the crazy job for fucking donkeys' years and worrying himself sick about it. Bloody job! It's a joke too! It's a joke-job. Most working-class jobs are the same, they're jokes. Joke-jobs. Just a fucking joke! Patrick laughed briefly. He closed his eyes.
> 'Are you as bitter as ye sound?'

In the end he has come to feel the same about his own job and the novel stops (it cannot be called a conclusion) with a self-pitying drunken mid-week spree and his running away from policemen in the night streets: 'It was dark and it was wet but not cold; if it had not been so dark you would have seen the sky. Ah fuck off, fuck off.' Yet perhaps this is a kind of conclusion, after all, of the most despairing sort.

Kelman returned to the streets with *How Late It Was, How Late* (1994), which follows the adventures of Sammy Samuels, a drifter and ex-convict who ends a two-day drunken binge by getting into a brawl with the police – largely his own fault – that leaves him permanently blind. Sammy now has to live his life inch by tentative inch as he gropes his way through Glasgow and the equally labyrinthine offices of the welfare state in what was an already minimal existence now razed to the ground. The so-called 'bad language' of the book caused a foolish critical stir when the novel was awarded the Booker Prize, but this is to miss the heroic point about Kelman's protagonist – who is certainly no better than he should be – who has found himself in an existential comedy in which he does rather better than Patrick Doyle could manage:

These things were a rigmarole, ye just kept the nerve. Ye got by on the situation, your situation. It took time and effort; concentration, attending to
detail. That was one thing he liked about being blind: see at night man he
slept like a fucking trooper. All down to the effort that went into the day-
to-day stuff, the minute-to-minute points of order. The actual living! That
was what fucking knackered ye, the actual living! Sammy chuckled.

Kelman's radical politics are clearly evident in his active support for the
victims of asbestosis in the Clyde shipyards; in his play about the radical
martyrs of 1820, *Hardie and Baird* (1991); and in the more controversial essays collected in *Some Recent Attacks* (1992) and *And the
Judges Said* (2003). Yet the prevailing condition of his fictional protagonists rarely manages to advance beyond resentment and resistance –
intelligent resentment undoubtedly – but they remain existentially solitary in the end and rarely tied to any sort of practical collective action.
Sammy, however, is indefatigable.

Kelman's time as a visiting professor at the University of Texas in the
late 1990s produced the novel *You Have to Be Careful in the Land of the
Free* (2004), an entertaining and searching account of a Scottish immigrant – another misfit trying to make a commitment – in a land grown
increasingly paranoid in the aftermath of September 11th. But the most
radically conceived and creatively challenging of his recent work is to be
found in *Translated Accounts* (2001) a terrifying and difficult masterpiece directly derived from its author's long-held understanding of the
relationship between the state, language and power – except that the
language here is corrupted, badly and blandly translated, censored, and
so mis-transcribed in places as to be almost indecipherable. The novel
contains 54 'translated accounts' as given by a number of individuals in
what seems to be 'an occupied territory or land where a form of martial
law appears in operation'. One imagines that this might be somewhere
like Bosnia, but it is never specified, and the sad fact is that such atroci-
ties could be happening anywhere in the world. These various testaments describe meetings and partings, acts of courage and endurance as
well as cruelty and oppression, but it is not always clear whether it is the
victims or the oppressors who are speaking. The obfuscating jargon of
officialdom mixes with clumsy translation and already fragmented first-
person accounts until we are never quite sure what has been happening,
or why. Nor can we tell the most innocent from the most oppressive of
situations – except that we constantly fear the worst:

But I am your friend.
   You are not my friend.
   I could be your friend, if I could be.

You are the fool, doing such injustice to us. You do not understand,
cannot, will not learn. It is you.
Yes he was the fool and I could have killed him. Not then. I did not say
then. But what account is this? I can return over everything. Tell me? What
is the detail required? If I know I can speak of it, I state only the truth.
What else, what else is there?
Not now, not for myself, for us, speaking of we, all of we, or us.
The other girl also, I can speak of her.

The result is intellectually and emotionally exhausting. The text's crippled English is both grammatically and morally ugly, with neologisms
such as the frequent references to the deeds of 'securitys' and 'mili-
tarys'. And yet such language is entirely suited to the horrors it tries to
describe and its flat, obfuscated inadequacy is more dramatic than the
most vivid descriptions would be. Adorno said that to write poetry after
Auschwitz is barbaric –and yet Kelman has found a sort of poetry for
the brutal realities of a world of 'final solutions' and 'ethnic cleansing'.
This is the language of technical and moral exhaustion – a broken,
tired, repetitive, dulled and occasionally censored officalese – and yet it
is the perfect paradigm for what it describes, and under Kelman's care
it achieves its own terrible eloquence.

Later novelists of voice and place

Jeff Torrington (b. 1935) and Agnes Owens (b. 1926)

Plays of the 1970s such as *Willie Rough*, *The Bevellers* and *The Slab Boys*
had taken drama into the workplace and the language of the workplace
into the theatre, and the stories in *Not Not While the Giro* did the same
for fiction ten years later. Kelman's example inspired other writers in
their turn and this was certainly the case with Jeff Torrington, who came
to write as a mature man, via his friendship with Kelman and the
Hobsbaum group in Glasgow. His novels *Swing Hammer Swing!*
(1992) and *Devil's Carousel* (1996) have a surreal humour and a linguistic extravagance that is completely different from Kelman's style – closer
to Byrne, perhaps – but they indicate a new confidence in writing about
what you know, and getting it published. (Torrington's first novel,
which was about dispossession, housing relocation and unemployment
in Glasgow, was the outright winner of the Whitbread Prize in 1992.)
Agnes Owens also came to writing later in life, much encouraged by her
experiences at a writers' workshop, the support of Liz Lochhead and a
shared publication with Kelman and Gray in the collection *Lean Tales*

(1985). If her chosen field seems to be closer to the relentlessly grim realism of Patrick MacGill's novels from 1914, it is considerably spiced by her own darkly surreal vision of what life has, or has not, to offer. Her first two books, *Gentlemen of the West* (1984) and *Like Birds in the Wilderness* (1987), deal with the trials of a character called Mac in a world of unemployed, dispossessed and rootless men like himself. This is a vision of a society outside 'society', the world of Howson's heroic dossers, living in the moment between drinks in a world where nothing and nobody can be trusted. These accounts of fecklessness and entrapment are memorable, but as with Howson's dossers, the final effect may be closer to an exploitation of futility than it is to any more profound existential or political insight. On the other hand, it is Owens' deadpan humour that seeks to turn what may seem like an excess of sentimental realism into an almost ironically Gothic comment on the genre itself. *A Working Mother* (1994) and *For the Love of Willie* (1998) focus on the experience of women with their dysfunctional menfolk in an ultimately comically absurdist world of deprivation and exploitation where the protagonists (Betty and Peggy respectively) are finally revealed as anything but reliable narrators themselves.

Life on the margins and dispossession were to be the main themes of several equally talented but much younger writers who might be said to have followed Kelman's example, but without his (or Gray's) directly political focus or their affection for the values of an older working class. In particular, Gordon Legge and Duncan McLean have produced a body of work dealing with the ups and downs of daily life in the central belt and small towns of Scotland. Despite often rather bleak settings, their books are notable for their focus on the liberating energy and expressive force of urban demotic speech as a measure of their protagonists' own anarchic vitality. Learning from Kelman, and from his contemporary the poet Tom Leonard, these writers have produced what amounts to a new genre of literature that takes what the Dochertys and Dunky Logans saw as the shameful limitations of their own voices and places only to turn them into celebration. The result is a vivid account of what life is like for many young people – almost always young men – in the housing estates, pubs, dance halls, record shops and streets of non-metropolitan Scotland.

Gordon Legge (b. 1961)

This was precisely the setting for Gordon Legge in his entertainingly good-humoured first novel *The Shoe* (1989), whose informed obsession with popular music anticipates Nick Hornby's *High Fidelity* by six years. Legge's book describes three days in the life of Archie and his friends, arguing about football, boxing and recorded music – young men in their mid-twenties, student drop-outs, unemployed or in dead-end jobs, still living at home in a town like Grangemouth (Legge's home town) in the industrial central belt of Scotland in the 1980s. The short stories and brilliant vignettes of the collection *In Between Talking About the Football* (1991) explored the same world (the running title for three of the stories is 'Life in a Scottish Council Estate'), with young couples, single mothers, lonely pensioners, classroom clowns, little children run wild, and awkward young men with high hopes and low expectations. Another episodic novel appeared as *I Love Me (Who Do You Love?)* (1994), and a further collection of short stories in *Near Neighbours* (1998). Legge has a fine ear for demotic dialogue and the apparently episodic and fragmentary progress of his prose has more structural finesse than its relaxed style might suggest. Most notable of all, however, is his capacity for humour and a Chekhovian care for his characters that is similar to the writing of Alan Spence (whose short stories were first published in 1977). Legge's compassion sets him significantly apart from Irvine Welsh, whose work was to inhabit a much darker version of the same territory.

Duncan McLean (b. 1964)

In fact Irvine Welsh's early fiction, including passages that would reappear in *Trainspotting*, first appeared in a booklet publishing enterprise founded and edited by Duncan McLean. McLean's Clocktower Press did much to signal the arrival of an important new generation of young prose writers in the early 1990s, including Gordon Legge, James Meek, Janice Galloway, Alan Warner and McLean himself. (The Clocktower output was later anthologised in the aptly titled *Ahead of Its Time*, 1998.) McLean was born in Fraserburgh in the North-East and, like that of Alan Warner, his work speaks for those who live far from Glasgow and the central belt. Yet when he first read Kelman it came like a revelation: 'When *The Busconductor Hines* came out in 1984 it just blew my mind. It was the voice. For the first time I was reading a book about the world I lived in. I didn't know literature could do that.' McLean was not slow to take up the challenge, and his first collection of stories, *Bucket of Tongues* (1992), won the Somerset Maugham Award. Set in Aberdeen and Edinburgh, dealing with a drunken wedding reception ('Bed of Thistles'), or a night on the town ('Cold Kebab Breakfast'), or violent teenage football casuals ('The Druids Shite It, Fail to Show'), some of these have a darker twist to them than Gordon Legge's work, although they share his energy and wild humour. McLean's novel *Blackden* (1994) offers a sweeter account of young maturity in the coming of age of Patrick Hunter, a fatherless eighteen-year-old left to his own devices over a cold November weekend in a small country town (rather like Banchory to the west of Aberdeen). Quartering the rural landscape on his bicycle, Paddy is a kinder sort than his layabout friends. In the course of the novel he looks after his grandparents and tries to make it with a local girl (if she would only leave her brutal boyfriend) while chasing rumours of local witchcraft, and trying to figure out his place in the world and his own family history. Hilarious and touching by turns, *Blackden* offers a modern version of the rustic concerns of *A Window in Thrums*, and a warmer account of small-town life in the North-East than Lewis Grassic Gibbon's Kinraddie. In complete contrast, McLean's second novel, *Bunker Man* (1997), is a darkly disturbing sexual and psychological thriller – although it would be true to say that his work has always contained seeds of deeply physical unease, as in the *Bucket of Tongues* stories 'Hours of Darkness' and 'Tongue'. The protagonist of *Bunker Man* is Rob Catto, a small-town school janitor whose wife has a high-powered job in the North-East oil industry. Rob's growing feelings of masculine inadequacy and frustrated desire lead him to a psychotic break-down in which he projects all his sexual rage, fantasies and fears onto the 'bunker man', a mentally handicapped local down-and-out whom he persuades to rape his wife. By blurring the borders of reality and indeed the borders of Rob's own identity and sanity as he becomes obsessed with the bunker man and disintegrates into gruesome acts of sexual abuse, voyeurism and murder, the novel offers specific homage to the theme of the double in the *Justified Sinner*. It also dares to delve deep into the misogyny at the heart of male violence in the Scottish tradition, an uncomfortable theme that also features strongly in the work of Irvine Welsh. In a completely different vein, the highly entertaining travelogue of *Lone Star Swing* (1998) has no such horrors, as McLean describes his passion for Western swing music and the pilgrimage he made to Texas in 1995 in appreciation of the music of Bob Willis and his Texas Playboys, a long way from the author's present home in Orkney – although both places do appreciate good fiddle music.

Irvine Welsh (b. 1958)

Irvine Welsh achieved instant fame, or notoriety, when *Trainspotting* (1993) gave a memorably vivid account of the drug abuse in

Edinburgh. What had been a counter-cultural exploration of 'inner space' by Alexander Trocchi's intellectual loners in the 1960s, now reappeared as outright nihilism in the housing estates of Scotland's most romantically iconic city, now also known as the heroin capital of Europe. The book describes a series of episodes in the lives of University drop-out Mark Renton and his fellow addicts, often told from the first-person point of view of Renton, Spud, Begbie and others. Welsh's rhythmic facility in catching the outright obscenity of their speech meant that these first-person narrative voices in East-coast urban Scots were at least as shocking to many readers as the book's grim accounts of heroin dependency. Yet, as with Legge and McLean, there is also great linguistic energy here and a kind of exhilaration in its uncensored free expression. And even these ghettos of addiction have something to say about the state of Scotland and the body politic at large. Thus there are echoes of Alasdair Gray's own political disillusionment in the raw humour of Renton's reflection on Begbie, the archetypal hard man, and his habits of defensive violence:

> Ah hate cunts like that. Cunts like Begbie. Cunts that are intae baseball-
> batting every fucker that's different; pakis, poofs, n what huv ye. Fucking
> failures in a country ay failures. It's nae good blamin it on the English.
> They're just wankers. We are colonised by wankers. We can't even pick a
> decent, vibrant, healthy culture to be colonised by. No. We're ruled by effete
> arseholes. What does that make us? The lowest of the fuckin low, the scum
> of the earth. The most wretched servile, miserable, pathetic trash that was
> ever shat intae creation. Ah don't hate the English. They just git oan with
> the shite thuv goat. A hate the Scots.

The shocking self-hatred evident in such passages is in part a measure of the country after the failure of the 1979 referendum and the sourness felt by many Scots during the Thatcher years that followed. But there is a deeper and more personal trauma within these lines – a rage of insecurity and unfocused guilt that Robin Jenkins and Gordon Williams had identified in the 1960s, and a sense of cultural and personal unworthiness of almost sexual intensity. The internal politics of disgust and self-disgust were to be key elements in Welsh's writing from now on, extending Kelman's scepticism, without his sense of the saving sense of ordinary heroic endurance. Not that Renton does not understand his condition perfectly clearly:

> Tom refuses tae accept ma view that society cannae be changed tae make it
> significantly better, or that ah cannae change tae accommodate it. Such a
> state ay affairs induced depression on ma part, aw the anger gets turned in.

That's what depression is, they say. However depression also results in demotivation. A void grows within ye. Junk fills the void, and also helps us tae satisfy ma need tae destroy masel, the anger turned in bit again.

And yet Welsh, too, has a political focus that is socially challenging – all the more challenging for being in the mouths of drug addicts who will not sign up to the corporate 'creature', as envisioned by Gray, that enjoins them to 'choose life', mortgage payments, washing machines and cars:

> Choose sitting on a couch watching mind-numbing and spirit-crushing game shows, stuffing fuckin junk food intae yir mooth. Choose rotting away, pishing and shiting yersel in a home, a total fuckin embarrassment tae the selfish, fucked-up brats ye've produced. Choose life.

Renton's heroin philosophy even has a certain challenging existential honesty:

> Basically, we live a short, disappointing life; and then we die. We fill up our lives wi shite, things like careers and relationships tae delude oorsels that it isnae aw totally pointless. Smack's an honest drug, because it strips away these delusions. Wi smack, whin ye feel good, ye feel immortal. Whin ye feel bad, it intensifies the shite that's already thair. It's the only really honest drug. It doesnae alter yir consciousness. It jist gies ye a hit and a sense o well-being. Eftir that, ye see the misery ay the world as it is, and ye cannae anaesthetise yirsel against it.

Needless to say, this is a vision of a world totally without love, but Welsh challenges us to say it isn't true. There are moments of potential tenderness towards women in the book and even a feminist awareness, as when Renton feels an affinity with everyone around him at a rave, affirmed by the taking of ecstasy; or when he shows an understanding of homosexual attraction that reveals the homophobic hard-man Begbie for the insecure dinosaur that he is. But in the end there is no sense of how love and respect might be sustained on a personal level in a milieu where sex exists as either a grimly abusive mechanical act or just another brief kick. The group remains deeply disaffected and tied to chemical self-abuse and Renton will come to betray his friends for money. What happens to them all in later life is taken up in more comic terms in the novel *Porno* (2002), which allows us to laugh at their plans to make money with a pornographic film, yet makes us care about the eventual disintegration of Spud, perhaps the most harmless of the group, and the only one who has completely succumbed to addiction.

Welsh was right to point out to his critics that his writing could never be accused of recommending hard drugs to susceptible readers, so horribly graphic is his description of dependency and physical deterioration. Yet this is to miss the element of gross comedy that also exists in all his work, with its outrageously Rabelaisian delight in physical repulsion and grotesque fantasy. This is especially evident in the short stories of *The Acid House* (1994). In 'The Granton Star Cause', for example, Boab Coyle insults God, whom he meets in a pub, and is turned into a housefly to confront the uselessness of his own life. He ends up being swatted by his mother, but not before he has watched her (as the veritable fly-on-the-wall) pleasure his father with a dildo. Sexual stereotypes are reversed in 'Where the Debris Meets the Sea' when Madonna, Kylie Minogue and Victoria Principal lust over pin-up photographs of 'Deek Prentice fi Gilmerton' or 'Tam Mackenzie of the Young Leith Team', in magazines called *Scheme-Scene* and *Bevy Merchants*: 'Victoria was enthusiastic. Total fucking ride. Ah bet eh's hung like a hoarse.'

Whether this reversal undermines the gross sexism of male objectification or actually validates it may be another question, and there remains a crucial ambiguity about women at the heart of Welsh's work. On the one hand he can be seen to be laying bare the roots of Scottish misogyny in its fears of sexual inadequacy or its violently repressed homoerotic drives. On the other hand, misogyny is so endemic in almost every one of Welsh's male characters, and the women in his books are so regularly and graphically disrespected, abused or raped, that the texts themselves may almost come to seem part of the problem. In particular, the female anatomy is so often described in such repulsive terms – admittedly by damaged men – that the reader is left wondering if this bracingly Swiftian disgust is about human sexuality in general, or just about women in particular.

Welsh's engagement with such questions is most directly and ambitiously presented in *Marabou Stork Nightmares* (1995), but this time with even more ambiguity. Roy Strang has left his dysfunctional family behind him in the housing schemes of Edinburgh (he graduated via a token stabbing at school and the cruel death by fireworks of his father's dog). He is now a well-paid computer expert, and a smartly dressed football casual about town. Violence is power for Strang, with a rush better than drugs and an almost sexual thrill: 'This cunt I was hitting was hitting me back but it was like I couldn't feel a thing and I knew that he could because his eyes were filling up with fear and it was the best feeling on earth.' But the book opens with him lying in a coma after an attempt at suicide, slowly rising to the surface of consciousness and some sort of realisation (through scattered typography) of what it is he has become. Sharing a motif from Iain Banks's novel *The Bridge*, published nine years earlier, Welsh has Strang's narrative switch between passages of gradual autobiographical recall and a coma-induced fantasy about hunting down the Marabou Stork, a particularly evil-looking and destructive African bird.

Strang and his family emigrated to South Africa when Roy was young and although they didn't stay, his fond memories of the place are clearly at work in his fantasy. These passages are written in a style that evokes the imperialist fiction of Rider Haggard and the John Buchan of *Prester John*. Welsh uses a parodically public school prose style, along with numerous homoerotic hints, but Strang's demotic tends to break through this discourse of 'dear chaps' and 'stout-hearted natives' when his concentration lapses. The South African connection also allows Welsh to reflect to some purpose on Scotland's engagement with the Imperial project. As Strang's right-wing father observes proudly: 'The Scots built the empire n these daft English cunts could-nae run it withoot us'; and Roy has his own observations to make:

> Edinburgh to me represented serfdom. I realized that it was exactly the same situation as Johannesburg; the only difference was that the Kaffirs were white and called schemies or draftpaks. Back in Edinburgh, we would be kaffirs; condemned to live out our lives in townships like Muirhouse or So-Wester-Hailes-To or Niddrie, self-contained camps with fuck all in them, miles fae the toon. Brought in tae dae the crap jobs that nae other cunt wanted tae dae, then hassled by the polis if we hung around at night in groups. Edinburgh had the same politics as Johannesburg: it had the same politics as any city.

The reader is challenged to deny that this is indeed the case.

From his nightmares we learn that the hunt for the stork is Roy's attempt to kill the worst in himself: 'If I kill the Stork I'll kill the badness in me. Then I'll be ready to come out of here, to wake up, to take my place in society and all that shite.' Strang's confrontation with the stork requires him to remember a terrible gang rape that he and his friends carried out, the guilt about which eventually led to his suicide attempt. We learn, too, that Strang was sexually abused by an uncle in South Africa, and that this is the reason for his sexual ambivalence, his defensive violence, and the homosexual fantasies that have been invading the stork-hunting dream. The novel clearly intends that this information should explain all, and that Strang's final acceptance of culpability is a step towards redemption. But the extent of Strang's psychopathology seems out of all proportion to the harm he has endured, and – more worryingly – the text itself has been delivering

Strang's violence with a disturbing relish throughout. The gang rape scene is prolonged, detailed and genuinely loathsome. The book's closing pages have the damaged girl turn up at Strang's bedside to cut off his penis and stuff it in his mouth. At this point the text makes play with the then current 'Zero Tolerance' campaign against the domestic abuse of women with its posters using a 'Z' logo and saying 'there is no excuse'. Despite his mutilation, Strang forgives his assailant, thanking God that 'she's got it back. What we took. I'm trying to smile.' But it has to be said that this is an extremely confusing or confused conclusion, for what the text actually shows us is that Strang's victim has herself become a Marabou Stork, and far from having regained herself she has become another Strang. The fact that she has rather more reason for her psychotic behaviour than Strang ever had in his own abused youth is not enough to excuse her actions, nor the transparent sensationalism of Welsh's description.

The very title of Welsh's next novel, *Filth* (1998), is an ironic comment on his reputation as a 'shocking' writer, and many passages in it demonstrate his characteristic brilliance in evoking a black comedy of abjection and disgust entirely worthy of Swift, delivered with the verbal exuberance of Urquhart's translation of *Gargantua and Pantagruel*. In adopting the persona of Bruce Robertson, a grossly abusive and corrupt police Detective Sergeant (hence the title), Welsh's first-person narrative scores many broad hits on government policy, police procedure, religious bigotry, racism, the masons and many other such targets in a *walpurgisnacht* of disgusting details and misanthropic grotesquerie. (Robertson's conscience appears to him, for example, as the voice of a tapeworm infesting his bowels.) As with *Marabou Stork Nightmares*, however, Welsh is less convincing when he attempts a psychological explanation for his antihero's degradation by calling up traumas in his past. Welsh's comic monsters neither need nor suit such extenuation, and in philosophical and political terms *Trainspotting* remains his most insightful work. The novel *Glue* (2001) returns to the schemes to produce a more sympathetic account of four friends and their very different fates as they grow up. Welsh has lost none of his scabrous humour, and his vision is as bleak as ever, but the historical scope of this novel – from the 1970s to the new millennium – and the importance its characters place on loyalty, aim to give it a more mature substance.

The huge popular success of Welsh's work has led some critics to wonder of this *fin-de-siècle* public taste for urban Scotland-the-gross, or for what Christopher Harvie has called the 'Satanic kailyard', may not be another – inverse – version of the rustic sentimentality that marked the end of the nineteenth century. It would be naive to suppose that Welsh's popularity is completely unconnected to the notorious shock-factor of his prose, but equally there is no doubt that in writing such as this many readers (especially younger readers) outwith the middle classes, the usual literary circles and the metropolitan centres, find issues that engage them and seem to speak on their behalf.

Kevin Williamson's Rebel Inc. magazine played a part in this development, too (following from Duncan McLean) with five issues between 1992 and 1996 taking an anti-establishment stance ('Peace, love and, fuck the mainstream'), a counter-cultural outlook, and a format based on punk or football fanzines. The Rebel Inc. magazine sponsored readings in clubs for a while but stopped when the *Trainspotting* phenomenon seemed itself to go mainstream. Williamson went into book publishing, linking up with Canongate in Edinburgh to produce the Rebel Inc. anthology *Children of Albion Rovers* (1996), followed by new fiction, non-fiction and underground 'classics' from American authors John Fante, Charles Bukowski and Richard Brautigan among others. Williamson went on to campaign for Amsterdam-style coffee-shops in Edinburgh, without much success, but the significance of Rebel Inc. was that it gave an unapologetically hip dimension to counter-cultural literature at a key time in Scottish publishing in the same – if more populist – spirit as had once been embraced by Alex Trocchi and Jim Haynes in the 1960s. Thus one of the most significant effects of the commercial and critical success of Kelman, Welsh, McLean, Legge, Warner and others, has been to generate a wider acceptance of youth culture and the demotic narrative voice by readers and publishers alike, and since then, a number of gifted younger authors have gone on to find publication and still further success in this vein. Nor is it an accident that so many of these writers should continue to engage with alternative cultures or cultural production, or come from small towns in the central belt.

Des Dillon (b. 1960), Alan Bissett (b. 1975), Suhayl Saadi (b. 1961), Anne Donovan and Laura Hird (b. 1966)

Des Dillon comes from Coatbridge and has written over seven novels including *Me and Ma Gal* (1995), *Duck* (1998) and *Itchycooblue* (1999). Dillon's work is characterised by the hugely positive energy of his demotic narrative voice, linked to typographical experiment. The same frenetically and cheerfully liberating force can be found in *Boy*

Racers (2001), the debut novel of Alan Bissett about growing up in the teenage car culture of Falkirk, and the uncheckable, narrative flow of *The Incredible Adam Spark* (2005) from a protagonist aged eighteen, 'going on eight and a half'. The heteroglot *Psychoraag* (2004) of Glasgow writer Suhayl Saadi is a novelistic *tour de force* mixing street Scots, Standard English and Urdu (the book has a large glossary) with an encyclopaedic knowledge of pop music from three continents. The comedy of domestic crisis in *Buddha Da* (2003) by Anne Donovan uses three different narrative voices, all in vernacular Glaswegian, to tell what happens when an archetypal West of Scotland male turns Buddhist to the delight and dismay of his wife and twelve-year-old daughter. Donovan's previous collection of short stories *Hieroglyphics* (2001) specifically focused on female experience with stories involving women from girlhood to old age. The short stories in *Nail and Other Stories* (1997) by Laura Hird, offer dark and humorous insights on urban misery and the comedy of the sexes, while her first novel *Born Free* (1999) gives a bleakly funny account of family life in Edinburgh.

There are passages in Laura Hird's work that are not unlike the spirit of Irvine Welsh, but many of these writers – and not just the women – would also acknowledge a significant debt to the work of Janice Galloway, whose engagement with voice and place has had as much to do with psychological issues of identity and with gender politics as it has with any particular concern about Scottishness *per se*.

Janice Galloway (b. 1956)

Some of Galloway's early short stories – later collected in *Blood* (1991) – give a grim picture of modern Scottish life, all the grimmer for being seen through female eyes. Galloway uses present-tense narration and a telegraphic descriptive style in many of these stories, as well as various typographical devices such as fragmented one- or two-sentence paragraphs, recurring capitals, and snatches of scene description and dialogue set out as if for a film-script. If this is realism, however, it is recounted with a greatly heightened intensity as Galloway's camera-like eye for detail gives even the most mundane scene a hallucinatory and almost metaphysical presence that is more than just a matter of what is being reported. Galloway's prose is constantly aware of the pressure of the physical world around us – overheard conversations, rain on the street, figures at a bus stop, stained wallpaper, water draining in a sink, blood on piano keys – as if the author had thinner skin than most of us, or senses sharpened by fever or fear. There is a running series of stories, or snatched vignettes, under the common title 'Scenes from the Life', for example, which describe a world full of petty damage as when a father hurts his baby son to teach him how to be a man, or the dignified desperation of a 'senior citizen' who waits until her community visitor has left before taking her own life. This is Sartre's nausea recruited to political, social or cultural ends as it describes a world of opaque threat, heightened at every turn by intimations of sexism and incipient violence against women, whether this is a Gothic–ghastly hint of marital murder ('Meat'), or simply the demented misogyny of a brain-damaged drinker shouting in the streets ('Fearless'). At every turn Galloway's hyper-acute sense of physicality gives the stories their own kind of indirect gender politics, as in the complex and unforgettable title-story of a menstrual school-girl having to suffer a bloody tooth extraction under the blithely offensive bonhomie of a male dentist. The short stories in a later collection *Where You Find It* (1996) deal with similar territory, and some of them are just as grim, with accounts of a young boy looking after himself and his baby brother in a flat with their dead father in the next room ('babysitting'); or child abuse ('someone had to'); or teenage abortion ('a proper respect'). If the title hints at the possibility of love, these are mostly moments of unrequited longing ('waiting for Marilyn'), or regretful compromise ('peeping tom'), or a comic glimpse of middle-class hell in 'proposal', or the bitter-sweet humour of a woman's-eye view of male sexuality, stimulated by the rituals of February 14th in 'valentine'. The story 'sonata form' is closest to finding love, perhaps, as it describes the subtle balancing act of the relationship between a talented musician and his pregnant wife, who knows so much more about the daily realities of the creative life than the admiring women flocking around her husband. (This is a theme that Galloway was to return to in much more developed form in the novel *Clara*.)

The existential intensity of Galloway's narrative style and her interest in formal experiment reach their fullest and finest expression in her remarkable first novel *The Trick is to Keep Breathing* (1989), which was shortlisted for the Whitbread award and announced as the MIND/Allen Lane Book of the Year. *The Trick* deals with the progressive breakdown and slow recovery of Joy Stone, a schoolteacher, who lost her married lover in an accidental drowning at a swimming pool while on holiday in Spain, only to find that her grief must be disallowed in favour of his widow. As readers however, we only slowly come to piece together this trauma from the recent past, as it comes to us as a sequence of fragmented italicised flashbacks that interrupt the text at intervals. In this respect the book operates rather as *1982 Janine* does, when McLeish recovers his own past, or as Bank's *The Bridge* from 1986, or indeed Margaret Atwood's brilliant novel *Surfacing* (1972). In fact the whole text is fragmented, but also immediate in its impact because it uses a running present-tense narration interspersed with Joy's memories (including her mother's attempts at suicide and eventual death) as she struggles to recover a life so currently beset by her own sense of unworthiness, grief, guilt, and the unsustainable contradictions of the society around her. Her odyssey can be almost unbearably intense – philosophically intense – as her depression and eating disorders bring her into contact with the existential horror of a physical world in which her own body, like everything around her, is reduced to brute matter and then to ultimate nothingness, as when she goes for a pregnancy scan:

> I looked. I was still there. A black hole among the green stars. Empty space. I had nothing inside me. The doctor smiled directly at me for the first time.
> Nothing for either of us to worry about then. Nothing at all.
> Tom held my arm and said nothing on the way back upstairs.

Galloway liberates the scrupulous detail of Kelman's realistic descriptive style to make a point about how the identity of women is generated by male perceptions and preferences, so that she is in a sense doubly estranged from her own body. Note the terrible animal objectification in her use of the word 'foreleg':

> I sit and soap each leg in turn, then lift the razor, checking the edge is keen. It gives a better finish slicing upward, against the hair: it severs more closely. I have to be careful it doesn't catch or draw blood. That would be unsightly. The water runs down each foreleg while I shave, carrying the shed animal hair away down the black hole under the taps. Fleeced, I turn off the taps and step out to rub my skin hard with the flat loops of the towel till it hurts. This makes me warmer.

She is 'fleeced', indeed. At the same time Joy retains a saving sense of the absurdity of it all, and the text has fun with the vapid materialism of women's magazines and the aridity of official discourse. Joy can make us laugh at her compulsion to make lists, at her inept sex life, at the hypocrisies of her fellow teachers and the pomposity of the social visitors and doctors who seek to help her, even as we recognise that under the banal condescension and unconscious sexism of such encounters, she is trapped and suffering.

Please god make boulders crash through the roof. In three or four days when the Health Visitor comes she will find only smashed remains, marrow-bone jelly oozing between the shards like bitumen. *Well*, she'll say, *We're not doing so well today, are we?* It's too cold. The hairs on my legs are stiff. I shiver and wish the phone would ring.
Needing people yet being afraid of them is wearing me out.

The novel has many telling points to make about what it is like to be a woman in a largely patriarchal society, and what it is like to be brought up in Scotland to be a 'good' girl:

> I can't think how I fell into this unProtestant habit. I used to be so conscientious. I used to be so *good* all the time.

> [where **good = productive/hardworking/wouldn't say boo**]

> I was a good student: straight passes down the line. . . . People made jokes, I was so eager to please. That's how good I used to be.

> [where **good = value for money**]

> I was very good at my mother's funeral though largely by default.

> [where **good = not putting anyone out by feeling too much, blank, unobtrusive**]

But Galloway never makes easy political points about the difficult paths that both men and women have to walk, and she resists simplistic claims to female victimhood. In the end, a significant part of what her novel has to say is to suggest what all our lives would be like if we had a 'layer of missing skin' like its protagonist, and male and female readers alike are challenged to recognise that 'You Can't Make Other People Love You Into Existence.' Gradually, however, Joy Stone begins to find a way to endure, to return from where she has been, in order to re-enter everyday life as if entering water to swim – 'I read somewhere the trick is to keep breathing, make out it's not unnatural at all. They say it comes with practice.'

One of the things that sustains Joy throughout the novel is her sense of connection to her friend Marianne, currently on the other side of the Atlantic; and friendship was to be the theme of Galloway's second novel. In *Foreign Parts* (1994) Cassie and Rona decide to take a holiday together in Normandy, where Rona's grandfather fought in the trenches of Arras in the First World War. They are an odd couple, for Rona is the organised one with the thermos flask, the lists and the guidebooks, while Cassie is impatient, intelligent, cynical and mildly depressive. They are both single women in their mid-thirties and while Rona is resigned to living on her own, Cassie has a history of unsatisfactory affairs and bad holidays with men, which come back to haunt her during this one. Galloway's narrative style is once again telegraphic, episodic, and typographically innovative, but this is a sweet comedy of wrong turnings and poor French, not without its sharper moments, as the two women come to terms with each other and where they find themselves – in France, in their lives – before they turn for home. In the face of the guidebook, with its peremptory commands ('DON'T MISS AZAY-LE-RIDEAU'); in the face of the size and strangeness of France; and in the face of national pride and the many dead boys in those huge war cemeteries, the book affirms the modesty of simple friendship. Learning to live in the minute (the book ends with them skiffing stones into the sea), Rona and Cassie realise an unsentimental and loving care for each other, incipiently sexual, that will sustain them: 'Rona and me. We stand in separate places looking out over water that is just water. Rona takes fresh aim, laughing. Defying gravity.'

Galloway's stylistic innovation takes a different form in her longest and most ambitious novel *Clara* (2002), which is the story of Clara Schumann, whose fate has been to stand in the shadow of the 'genius' of her husband the composer Robert Schumann, although she was the more famous of the two in their day. The novel is based on meticulous biographical research, and the facts of Clara's life have much to say about the rigidities of life and culture in nineteenth-century Germany and Europe. A celebrated concert pianist and composer in her own right, Clara had to deal with a domineering father who forced her to practise from the age of five. When she married Schumann, against her father's wishes, she bore him seven children and had to deal with his recurring mental instability while still trying to sustain her own career. The patriarchal expectations of the age are all too evident, and yet this is not Galloway's main topic. Instead she is interested in exploring the nature of creativity as it affects the couple, united in their passion for music, but very different in their capacities to direct or control that force. Looking back to her short story 'sonata form', Galloway takes a wholly unsentimental view of 'inspiration' while also showing the creative power and importance of love, and also of sheer endurance in an activity that is frequently difficult, fragmented, long-drawn-out and painful. Like Joy Stone, Clara is a mistress of 'lasting' and Galloway understands how beauty can be made from fragments and odd jottings, and how:

> sheer effort of will could construct a wholeness where none existed. Proof that music and those who made it could confront chaos, and find in it what was tender and fantastical and clear and true.

The special 'wholeness' of *Clara* is its narrative style, which is a sustained *tour de force* of free indirect narrative in a continuing present tense from within Clara's sensibility. Such a device (without using the first-person voice) gives a psychological immediacy and a chronological fluidity to the narrative, as we enter Clara's mind as it negotiates present action and past memories. More striking still, however, especially in the case of a 'historical' novel, it is an approach that thrusts us directly into Clara's world without recourse to authorial commentary or scene-setting explanation.

Iain Banks (b. 1958)

Iain Banks's first novel was distinguished by its symbolic complexity and an engagement with the instability of identity that would not have been out of place in *Lanark*. It also had such a gruesomely black sense of humour that there was something of a critical scandal when *The Wasp Factory* first appeared in 1984. Hailed by reviewers as either 'the literary debut of the year' or 'the lurid literary equivalent of a video nasty', this is the story of Frank Cauldhame, a teenage boy given to blowing up animals and torturing wasps in an elaborate mechanical maze-trap of his own invention (the 'wasp factory') that he uses as a prognostication device by which, along with many other obsessive and grisly rituals, he seeks to understand and above all to control his world. Frank would seem to be a particularly nasty piece of work, living with an eccentric father in a remote house on an island somewhere by Nigg Bay on the far north-east coast of Scotland. His mother left years ago and his father is an ex-hippy whose notion of education (in a parody of masculine rationality) is to make Frank memorise the exact measurements of everything around him, and to make his older brother Eric wear women's clothes. Told by Frank himself, the novel begins when he receives the news that his brother, a pyromaniac given to burning dogs and sheep, has just escaped from an asylum. Equipped with his combat knife and catapult, Frank thinks of himself as cut off from the mainland of life. He hates women and the sea and likes to make pipe bombs and kill rabbits with his flame-thrower. He marks out his territory with the severed heads of dead animals (the 'sacrifice poles') and in the course of explaining all this he lets slip that he murdered his young brother Paul and two female cousins in the most bizarre circumstances – but 'I haven't killed anybody for years, and don't intend to ever again. It was just a stage I was going through.' Frank may have a reason for this pathology, not to mention his misogyny, in that he regards himself as only half a man ever since an attack by his father's dog castrated him when he was young.

Reviewers who took offence at the tale completely missed the gloriously deadpan humour of Banks's style and its affinities with the black humour of Martin Amis, or the grotesquerie of Günter Grass's *The Tin Drum* (1959). As the book progresses we realise that Frank's boyish kingdom of violence may do no more than reflect the real world around us, and his naive commentary on it comes to seem more and more pointed. In this part of Scotland Jaguar jets practise bombing runs – and occasionally crash – on their test range down the coast, while Frank plays at blowing up plastic models and wonders if he is responsible for their fate. Frank's obsession with his 'war bag' and his 'defence budget', like the marking and protection of his own territory and his need to feel that he can control events, makes its own political comment on adult concerns with national security. He hopes to be the very model of a 'real man' and sees himself as the body politic itself: 'Often I've thought of myself as a state; a country or, at the very least, as a city', while the cruelty of the wasp factory is no less than a microcosm of life at large and the random horrors of fate.

As readers will know, *The Wasp Factory* is finally a black comedy about identity and gender stereotypes, for the book ends by revealing that Frank is in fact a girl, who has suffered a cruel deception played by his/her father. Banks has been playing with our preconceptions about masculine violence and the debates on nature versus nurture only to overturn them at the last minute. Yet on revisiting the text we find that it was always already dense with phallic symbols and clues about sexual ambiguity. This is much more, however, than a joke about sexual politics, for the final achievement of the novel is to make its own memorably ironic comment on those by now familiar Scottish literary obsessions with double identity, damaged masculinity and the difficult relationships between fathers and sons.

Banks's capacity to challenge conventions also featured in his next two books, both of which have complex multiple narrative strands mixing realism with what could be called science fiction or fantasy. The novel *Walking on Glass* (1985) has three narrative strands that may or may not connect up with each other at the end, and these strands alternate between textual realism, the paranoid fantasies of another realistic character, and a fantasy/science-fiction story set in a castle worthy of Kafka or Mervyn Peake. Something of a metafictional game, it is an ingenious and challenging read whose conclusion, as we see how the different narratives are contained within each other like Russian dolls, sends us back to the novel's first page and its opening lines. *The Bridge* (1986), which remains Banks's personal favourite, makes even more use of embedded narratives. The beginning, under the title 'Coma', offers a fragmented account of someone in pain in a hospital bed, and snatches of this voice are used to introduce each of the main three sections of the book. It becomes slowly apparent that everything that follows is the coma dream of this nameless character, who has crashed his Jaguar car and nearly killed himself within sight of the Forth bridges. (Banks's childhood home at North Queensferry, like his present address, both overlook the Forth at this point.) Later sections will tell us something about the protagonist's life as an upwardly mobile, hard-driving, hard-drinking and ultimately unhappy young technocrat working in Edinburgh. (His name is never mentioned, but via indirect clues we can deduce that it must be Alexander Lennox.)

But the greater part of the novel is the story of someone called Orr, who has lost his memory and is under treatment from a Dr Joyce, in order to discover who he is. Orr's story is told in the first person and the various vivid dreams he describes to Joyce are yet another embedded part of the narrative. Then there is a sword and sorcery fantasy of sex and violence, which also seems to be haunting Orr, as told in the first person by 'the barbarian' in a hilariously broad Glaswegian demotic that makes its own ironic comment on the hard-man genre. These dreams and interventions are almost as real and scarcely less strange than Orr's exploration of the vast bridge-like structure where he finds himself, inexplicably stranded and compelled to recover his own history. Modelled on the Forth Railway Bridge this is a retro-science-fictional world of trams, trains, planes and barrage balloons, mechanically and imaginatively baffling in its Kafka-esque maze of cabins, tunnels, lift shafts, platforms and linking-spans. Everywhere there are hints of messages, codes and communications, if only they could be deciphered. Banks's method is to weave these various narrative strands together so that fragments from each break through into the others in a densely symbolic web of distorted echoes and connections that gradually thin out towards a clearer and clearer commentary on the protagonist's life, on parodic versions of Scots identity (seen as either Glaswegian barbarians or engineers) and on the values of Thatcher's Britain.

Banks admitted a debt to the parallel narratives in *Lanark*, and the structural ingenuity of *The Bridge* can certainly match Gray's novel, although its political focus is more diffuse. Such doubled and doubling structures, along with parallel narratives that bleed into each other, amount to a structural subgenre in Scottish fiction – looking back, of course, to the *Justified Sinner* and *Jekyll and Hyde* – and they have proved particularly popular among contemporary writers as a way of exploring questions of identity, culpability and trauma in the past. Banks will use it again, more than once, and indeed it is the controlling pattern behind Mackay Brown's *Magnus*, Herdman's *Pagan's Pilgrimage* (among others), *Lanark*, *1982 Janine*, *Poor Things*, *The Trick is to Keep Breathing* and *Marabou Stork Nightmares*, as well as more recent works such as McLean's *Bunker Man* and James Robertson's *The Fanatic*.

Banks had started out wanting to be a science-fiction writer (some of his early attempts were revised and published after the success of *The Wasp Factory*); and certainly *Walking on Glass*, *The Bridge*, and later novels such as *Canal Dreams* and *A Song of Stone* all make use of elements that would be familiar to readers of the genre, if such labels have meaning any more in a literary field that includes 'serious' but markedly imaginative literature from Kafka, Orwell, Huxley, Mitchison, Borges, Vonnegut, Rushdie, Gray and Atwood. Nevertheless, in 1987 Banks committed himself to full-scale science fiction with *Consider Phlebas*, his first novel as 'Iain M. Banks' (an 'attempt on the Most Penetrable Pseudonym world record') and since then he has been at least as successful as a science-fiction author, particularly with his novels of 'the Culture', a liberal, anarchic, technological utopia in the far future, in a series deliberately designed as a counterpole to the many right-wing space operas that used to dominate the genre. The brilliantly realised surfaces of these other worlds generate an extraordinary energy which is itself a positive note in a universe of infinite possibility where people can change sex almost as a recreational activity, where artificial intelligences have become god-like entities in a godless universe, where talking weapons, undercover agents and high-tech feudalism add to the general fun and mayhem. In such fields Banks's enthusiasm for elaborate plotting is given full rein. His delight in parallel narratives and linguistic experiment reached new heights in *Feersum Enjinn* (1994), not a 'Culture' novel, but notable for its complex structure which includes a character called 'Bascule', who tells his own story in hybrid spelling that is reminiscent of Russell Hoban's 1980 novel *Ridley Walker* and prophetic of the vogue for texting that was to come ('Woak up. Got dresd. Had brekfast. Spoke wif Ergates thi ant who sed itz juss been wurk wurk wurk 4 u lately master Bascule, Y don't u 1/2 a holiday?').

Banks's own capacity for creative work has made him an extremely successful professional writer with 21 books of fiction to his name in 20 years. *The Crow Road* (1992) follows a pattern common to many of them in which a protagonist (often a young man) has his eyes opened about the world around him. There are several actual 'crow roads' in Scotland, but the phrase is also a metaphor for the road to death, and in this book young Prentice McHoan – one of Banks's most cheerfully engaging, if rather stubborn characters – has to come to terms with three generations of family history, death, secrets, class differences and his own and others' fallibility. When his grandmother's funeral brings him back to the McHoans' baronial pile in a remote part of Scotland, Prentice has to confront the past, including his infatuation with a girl called Verity (*sic*), brotherly rivalry, the split between his atheist father and himself, his father's subsequent death by lightning (with their differences unresolved) and the mysterious disappearance, perhaps the murder, of his uncle Rory. The novel links 1990s student life in Glasgow with the 1960s experiences of an older generation in a series of flashbacks, competing narratives and tantalising clues as Prentice gradually comes to a more mature assessment of the political and religious differences that estranged him from his father, and the forces that make people what they are. One of Banks's most endearing and affirmative novels, *The Crow Road's* thematic combination of a coming-of-age story, a lightly Gothic family saga and the solving of deaths and disappearances, all led to a successful TV serialisation in 1996.

Banks's next novel, *Complicity* (1993), was a much darker political satire on the values of Thatcherite Britain, as well as something of a crime thriller. Cameron Colley is a bright and cynical left-wing journalist who works for a daily paper in Edinburgh. A fan of Hunter S. Thompson, when he's not driving fast, drinking, taking recreational drugs or indulging in sado-masochistic sexual play, he spends his time playing a computer game about world domination. Tipped-off by anonymous phone-calls, Colley is hot on the trail of a corruption scandal, while the police are investigating a series of gruesome murders in which senior Conservative figures are killed in a number of hideous ways that are bizarrely appropriate to their own policies or actions. Colley's narrative is told in the first person, but the text is interleaved with horrifically graphic passages of direct second-person-singular description in which these murders are enacted in ways that inevitably engage the reader:

> You crouch down in front of him and make a deep downward incision into the left thigh, opening the artery to the air. The scream comes down his nose as he shakes the chicken-wire frame. The bright blood pumps out and up, spattering onto your gloved hand and jetting upwards in a pink

spray that soaks his underpants and rises as high as his face, freckling it with red.

The present tense and the technical precision of such passages, like the explicit descriptions of Colley's own sexual encounters, make a calculatedly direct assault on the reader's sensibilities. Thus the 'complicity' of the title goes beyond the specifics of political corruption, or a government whose leader does not believe in society, to embrace the values of a whole decade given over to material prosperity, selfish individualism and popular entertainment saturated with images of sex and violence. Of course the voyeuristic charge in Banks's own text makes the reader complicit as well, and the plot makes it clear that he has no intention of letting himself off the hook either, for indeed we are almost convinced – like the police – that the left-wing protagonist Colley is himself the killer. Once again double narratives, confusions of identity and a tissue of connections and parallel links are at the heart of Banks's vision, memorably charged this time by a sense of not quite controlled rage. The same political indignation marks *Dead Air* (2002) in the character of the 'devoutly contrarian' Ken Nott (his name is surely another of Banks's puns), a left-wing Scottish shock jock in a London radio station in the months after the destruction of the Twin Towers in New York, but the novel's political focus is much more diffuse. Like Colley, Ken is a smart and ambiguously driven character and as with Colley, Banks allows him a degree of redemption in the end, via an ultimately slight plot involving his affair with a gangster's wife.

Despite the amoral, violent and media-driven realm of *Complicity* and *Dead Air*, or the darker visions of the modern world in *Canal Dreams* (1989), or the allegorical wastelands of armed gangs and refugees in *A Song of Stone* (1997), the imaginative energy of Banks's writing amounts to a kind of celebration. His affection for cheerfully compromised and slightly naive protagonists, his complex plots, intertextual references and competing or parallel narratives, or his use of fantasy, dream, technology and far-future scenarios, are all ways of engaging with how we live in the inner and outer event-storms of hectic postmodernity – on our own, unsure of what we are, and without gods or devils.

Other ways of looking at it

The realistic prose fiction of urban experience, social despair or existential courage in the work of Williams, Friel and McIlvanney had its counterpart in much of the drama to be found in the theatres of Scotland during the 1970s. The technical innovation and the social awareness of Gray and Kelman were carried in new – and very different – directions by Welsh, Galloway and Banks, who were in turn to have a significant influence on many of the young prose writers to come. But there are other fine writers of Kelman's generation whose work is more conventionally realistic closer perhaps, to the poetic compassion of Elspeth Davie than to Kelman's technical rigour and radical anger. It will be useful to discuss some of these authors at this point, although full justice cannot be done to all of them or to their work.

Alan Spence (b. 1947)

The writing of Alan Spence is a case in point for he can be seen to antic- ipate and then to bridge many of the categories outlined above. His first collection of linked short stories, *Its Colours They Are Fine* (1977), took a familiar topic in its account of Glasgow and its street culture of wild children, old people, hippie students, sectarian difference and endemic unemployment. Yet the spirit of Spence's writing is completely different from Friel and Williams, being much more compassionate, with an almost tender regard for the rituals of the place and the fate of his characters, whether it's a working-class wedding ('The Rain Dance'), an Orange march ('Its Colours They Are Fine'), or the old man who spends his days in the glasshouse of the Botanic Gardens for the warmth ('The Palace'). Spence's vision is redemptive and his grasp of Glasgow demotic speech and his sense of period and place are fault- less. All these came together in an ambitious first novel *The Magic Flute* (1990), which traces the lives of four Glasgow boys from the 1960s to the 1980s. They take very different routes: Tam embraces the hippie life; Eddie is a street gangster who ends up serving with the British Army in Ulster; George, on the other hand, settles for a stifled life of business respectability and Masonic handshakes, while Brian tries to make his contribution as a schoolteacher in a deprived area of Edinburgh. The book's title invokes the flutes of the Protestant march- ing bands that were such a feature in all their boyhoods, but it also signals a different kind of magic by conjuring up the transfigurative spirit of Mozart's opera, and indeed of all music. In fact the novel is dense with references to popular music, tracking its own history and that of its characters from the exuberance of the early Beatles to Lou Reed and the Velvet Underground. Spence uses a subtle symbolism to suggest that all such histories and journeys are essentially spiritual, and indeed this intimation is at the heart of all his writing. (He and his wife run the Sri Chinmoy Meditation Centre in Edinburgh.)

The stories in *The Stone Garden* (1995) show the same capacity for insight and sudden illumination regardless of the place, time or difficult circumstances of the characters concerned, and the collection was awarded the McVitie's prize for Scottish Writer of the Year. Spence's second novel, *Way To Go* (1998) continues his concern with first and last things, in a lively account of a Scottish son – brought up under the repressed and repressive care of his undertaker father – who leaves home as soon as he can to expand his mind and take the hippie trail. When his dour father dies, Neil returns with his Indian wife to run the family funeral home and make some startling changes to a business that he refuses to see in solely economic terms. His vision of new ways to go includes audio-visual tapes, rock music, death jokes, extravagantly sculptured coffins, an aerial burial at sea and, when cancer finally overcomes him, his own ashes dispersed by pyrotechnic skyrockets. The book does not underestimate the fear and pain of bereavement, and different philosophical and cultural responses to mortality are scattered throughout the text, but in the end it celebrates the possibility that we can reach eternity in our own lives, if only we can really see what each living moment brings. The novel ends with one of Spence's own *haiku*-like poems to sum up something of this view of our life on earth: 'after the fireworks / cold and still / the moon'.

Spence has published several collections of poetry, all significantly influenced by eastern ways of responding to the world, and his interest in *haiku*. These include *Plop!* (1970); *Glasgow Zen* (1981) and *Seasons of the Heart* (2000). Spence is an exemplary figure in that the move from the grim urban realism – however tenderly realised – of *Its Colours They Are Fine*, to the wider and freer stage of his later work, with its philosophical and symbolic focus and frequent references to popular culture and rock music, marks a significant shift in how a younger generation of Scottish writers in the 1990s would come to see their field.

Andrew Greig (b. 1951)

Like Alan Spence, Andrew Greig, began his literary career by writing poetry but in later years has come to be better known and even more critically successful as a novelist. Brian McCabe has traced the same path, as have Ron Butlin and John Burnside. (Quite apart from the versatility of the authors concerned this is also a measure of the commercial realities of the marketplace for those who seek to make a full-time living by their craft.) Greig's first full collection, *Men on Ice* (1977), was a metaphorical, even a metaphysical allegory about mountaineering in which 'Grimpeur', 'Axe-man' and 'Poet' reflect on the nature of wonderment, fear and aspiration in all walks of life, in a poem sequence dense with cultural and counter-cultural references – from Chuck Berry to Nietzsche, from Greek myth to Bob Dylan. He returned to the mountaineering theme and the same characters (under different names) in the ambitious poem sequence *Western Swing* (1994), which admits a debt to Ed Dorn's *Gunslinger* in its loose and associative progress, while being even more densely scattered with echoes and references in a wildly eclectic literary 'sampling'. Greig's intention in this book was no less than to bring the Black Mountain poets to Glencoe in a conscious attempt to modernise the familiar signifiers of Scotland, placing them somewhere between Kathmandu and the Rest and Be Thankful, if not the kingdom of Fife and the kingdom of heaven. The collection *Surviving Passages* appeared in 1982, and *A Flame in Your Heart* (1986) was a poem sequence about the romance between a pilot and his love during the Battle of Britain, co-written with the poet's then partner, the poet Kathleen Jamie. Greig later revised and retold the story as a novel called *That Summer* in 2000. The poet's most successful personal lyrics are contained in *The Order of the Day* (1990), which includes a telling section, 'In Love and Politics'. These poems, like many of the book's other verses on travel, work and mountain climbing – and indeed Greig's writing in general – are notable for his belief in the possibility of a redemptive and romantic masculinity.

Mountaineering had become part of Greig's life by this time, for a friendship with the climber Mal Duff – based on the poems in *Men on Ice* – had led the climber to introduce the poet to the real thing. Greig recounted his adventures with Duff as 'the story of an armchair climber' in his remarkable book *Summit Fever* (1984), which describes their expedition to climb the Mustagh Tower in the Karakorum Mountains in Pakistan. *Kingdoms of Experience*, about an Everest expedition, followed in 1986 and Greig's career as a mountaineer and a successful writer of prose was well under way. His first novel *Electric Brae* was subtitled 'a modern romance' and indeed there is a romantic element in all Greig's prose fiction, not least in his entertainingly contemporary version of an adventure classic about poaching in *The Return of John McNab* (1996), which was hailed by Duncan McLean as reading like a cross between the original John Buchan and Iain

Banks. *Electric Brae* (1992) revealed a fine eye for the emotional complexities between its characters, in the relationship between Kim, a passionate and withdrawn young visual artist, and her climber boyfriend Jimmy who works on the North Sea oil rigs. Determined to counter the literary vogue for urban settings and brutal masculinity, Greig sets his story in the more remote parts of Scotland (Orkney, Shetland and the Borders) and has Jimmy tell the story in a sustained act of sensitive and nostalgic recall. Jimmy's account is prompted by playing a version of 'Kim's game', in which a collection of trivial objects and mementos act as the trigger for reminiscence and the gradual unfolding of the story. (Greig returned to this engaging narrative device for his novel *In Another Light* in 2004, and in fact when he writes prose his poet's imagination is frequently responsive to objects in this way, as with Proust's madeleine.) *Electric Brae* (the title invokes both a famous natural feature of a deceptive gradient in Ayrshire, and a paradoxical modernity) offers an account of Scotland in the 1980s, from North Sea oil to the referendum debate, but most of all it engages with questions of inheritance, mental stability, and creativity and the terrible demands it can make on an artist and those close to her. It is significant, however, that the book is allowed to end on a wholly affirmative note.

Greig's third novel, *When They Lay Bare* (1990), continues his interest in portraying strong women characters and his determination to write about rural Scotland in a fresh way. In this last respect at least, Greig's eye for landscape and weather and his delight in their interplay is easily a match for John Buchan. *When They Lay Bare* invokes a mystery about violent deaths that happened twenty years ago at a decaying country estate in the Borders. The story is told from several points of view and is given a sinister intimacy by its habit of slipping in and out of different first-person narrations to do so. Its events are triggered by the arrival of a mysterious woman seeking the truth about the past. She is obsessed with a set of antique plates, the Corbie plates, whose patterns seem strangely apposite to her quest. These plates, like the novel itself, draw on the Scots ballad 'The Twa Corbies', which tells of adultery, betrayal and death. The book is full of Border lore, with historic names (Allan, Elliott, Lauder), and Greig uses this, and especially the Border ballads with their affinity for the supernatural, as a controlling metaphor. Thus the book offers us a vision of the world as a liminal place, a 'debatable land', indeed, with a thin boundary between the living and the dead, or what's past, passing or to come. The strangeness of this world is matched by a strong sense of the power of sexual attraction and the psychological vertigo of erotic surrender when all individuality is extinguished in the heat of the moment – a kind of supernatural enchantment indeed. As Greig's most poetic novel this is a complex, wholly contemporary and brilliant homage to an older literary tradition.

Carl MacDougall (b. 1941)

Carl MacDougall shares fictional territory with Alan Spence and although he rarely uses Glasgow demotic speech, his work in English has an oral zest and an often surreal humour to it. His first publication made the most of this talent with a collection of Scottish folk tales for children in *A Cuckoo's Nest* (1974). He adapted the same mode with the 'tales' in *A Scent of Water* (1975), some of which were derived from traditional sources and urban myths, while others used the old structures of oral delivery to make something new. (The book was profusely illustrated by Alasdair Gray.) MacDougall's story-telling skills feature again in the collection *Elvis Is Dead* (1986) in a series of accounts and vignettes – often in direct first-person address and not without a certain savage humour – of lonely lives, fading dreams and final emptiness. The novel *Stone Over Water* (1989) presents itself in three parts to reflect on identity, duplicity and unreliable texts as it gives different insights into the life of Angus McPhail via his own narrative, the book he is writing and his dairies, none of which can quite be trusted. Angus was adopted into a highly eccentric family at the age of twelve, so his own past is doubly obscured. MacDougall uses this and numerous reflections on the truth of fiction and the fiction of truth (including a lecture from the old father on the identity myths of Scotland) to offer his own variation on the unreliability of texts, looking back to Hogg and Stevenson and forward to Gray's *Poor Things*. A hard-won stability and a sense of tradition and place are ultimately redemptive for the protagonist of *The Lights Below* (1993), even in the grim and exhausted cityscape of Glasgow, or in a Scotland given over to tourist clichés. MacDougall was to follow these insights in his cultural essay *Painting the Forth Bridge: A Search for Scottish Identity* (2001), and he took up the challenge again in presenting the 2004 TV series *Writing Scotland*.

John Herdman (b. 1941)

The fiction of John Herdman is still more haunted by the myths and puzzles of Scottishness – he has written a scholarly study of the double in nineteenth-century literature – and the ghost of Hogg's *Justified Sinner* is never far from his work, which operates in a vein that could be described as the psychological Gothic, with a surreal and strongly satirical strain. Herdman's short fiction, novellas and novels involve often grotesque characters who show a Dostoyevskian capacity for ever more desperate or shameless behaviour, recounted in a highly formal and deadpan narrative voice that is very characteristic of the author's black humour. *Pagan's Pilgrimage* (1978) begins: 'My imagination has been haunted by the wrinkled-nosed laundry-man for as long as I can remember,' before going on to tell of its hero's Wringhim-like determination to assassinate the local aristocrat, Viscount Gadarene, the Laird of Teuchtershards. Herdman's style has a constantly ironical awareness of its literary predecessors, as if marrying the light fictional satire of Compton Mackenzie to the terrors of 'Thrawn Janet' and playing darkly Kafka-esque variations on the outcome. The early grotesquerie and broad humour of tales such as *Clapperton* and *Memoirs of My Aunt Minnie* (1974) can be found in the collection *Four Tales* (2000), while *Imelda* (1993), *Ghost Writing* (1996) and *The Sinister Cabaret* (2001) show a continuing awareness of the Russian and German Expressionist tradition in a uniquely distinctive Scottish voice. Other authors, such as John Burnside, A. L. Kennedy, Frank Kuppner, Ron Butlin and Laura Hird, can also be seen to work within a modern Gothic genre. Indeed, a trend in 'contemporary Scottish Gothic' was identified by David Punter in 1999 and a collection of such work, *Damage Land: New Scottish Gothic Fiction* was edited by Alan Bissett in 2001.

Ronald Frame (b. 1953)

Ronald Frame could not be more different from these writers and his work is at the opposite end of the literary and social spectrum from the worlds of Kelman, Spence or MacDougall, focusing, as it does, on upper middle-class life in London, the south of England, France, or the wealthy suburbs of Glasgow in the 1950s. He is a prose stylist alert to the nuances of appearance, behaviour and dress – especially the minute details of fashion and class – in smart milieus where much is left understated or entirely unsaid. This is not to say that he does not have a unique capacity to evoke subtly disturbing undercurrents, and his fiction often engages with matters of betrayal that either generate a light comedy of manners or lead to the most painful of realisations, according to the book in question. Frame's recurring fascination with the 1950s is curious for a man who was only a baby at the time but it marks his determination to research and adopt the manners of the period as a matter of conscious literary style, re-creating this fiction-alised habitat as a paradigm of his own moral vision. Thus Frame's 1950s have a special air of either comedy or corruption – or both – where ambiguous histories, charming façades, elegant deceptions and genteel sexual betrayals are to be found behind the bay windows, gravel drives and high hedges of bourgeois villas. Yet things do come to the surface in Frame's work as his characters learn about their pasts, or belatedly realise what their own future holds, in what sometimes seems like a stylistic collaboration between Daphne du Maurier and Ibsen, with added fashion notes. The novel *Underwood and After* (1991), for example, tells of a young man hired as a driver to a grand house, grad-ually realising that his benefactor Mr Chetwynd is not as he seems. The novel uses the intricately patterned oriental carpets in the house as a metaphor for the web that traps Ralph in the devious interplay of the plot. Douglas Dunn has argued that Frame's 'impersonation' of such 'classic English "respectability"' is an almost conscious decision in favour of pleasure, grace and elegance, as opposed to the 'vernacular impulse' in so much contemporary Scottish writing. It is certainly the case that Frame has little sympathy with proletarian realism, but we should not underestimate the author's ironic awareness of the very genre he is exploiting, and the often sinister nuances of his work. (Some critics have likened him to Hitchcock in this respect.)

Frame has written many radio plays over the years, a genre that often operates on what is left unsaid, and in fact his novel *The Lantern Bearers* (2001) started as a radio play in 1997. Awarded the title of Scotsman/Saltire Book of the Year, this novel tells the story of an adolescent boy with a good singing voice who is taken up by Euan Bone, a Scottish composer in the early 1960s, to help him write a part for solo treble voice, based on R. L. Stevenson's short story 'The Lantern Bearers'. Young Neil is seduced by the lavish lifestyle and sophisticated tastes of his new companions, and indeed he is beginning to discover something about his own sexuality. But when his voice breaks he is cast off and, obsessed by the project, he starts to take his own revenge for what he sees as a betrayal. This narrative of hints and nuances, of unclear motives and unspoken commitments is compounded in its complexity by being told by Neil himself, now grown up and commissioned to write a biography of Bone. But Neil is terminally ill, and this densely atmospheric novel is a belated act of reparation in which a narrator – who must be recognised as unreliable – attempts a re-membering of the past, and a recognition of the price that all those who give themselves to art must pay. Stevenson's original short story is a subtle masterpiece about the roots of creation in a story about secrets and the complicity of imagination between boys on the edge of sexual and social maturity, and Frame does it more than justice in what may well be his best novel to date.

Brian McCabe (b. 1951)

Brian McCabe is a poet who is equally skilled as a writer of short stories. The title-story in his first collection, *The Lipstick Circus* (1985), is a memorably sensitive account of gender identity and a teenage boy's growing self-awareness. His second collection, *In a Dark Room with a Stranger* (1993), shows the same sensitivity to people and small moments of isolating and defining experience in their lives. McCabe's skill is to convey these shifts in an understated, elliptical and often heart-breaking manner and in this respect he is a master of the classic short-story format. He published a novel, *The Other McCoy*, in 1991 and has continued the theme of male experience and identity in many of the stories, some satirical and some downright bizarre, in the collection *A Date with my Wife* (2001). McCabe's poetry is observant, witty and alert. *Spring's Witch* (1984) showed a technical mastery of the sonnet form and the relaxed but incisive colloquial voice that is typical of all his work. *One Atom to Another* (1987) and *Body Parts* (1999) are equally strong, with the latter collection addressing simple objects in poems that are often touching, while also giving people, animals and finally parts of the body their own voices in a series of poems that are perceptive, funny and thought-provoking by turns.

Dilys Rose (b. 1954)

Dilys Rose is also a poet with three collections of short fiction: *Our Lady of the Pickpockets* (1989), *Red Tides* (1993) and *War Dolls* (1998). Her themes are consciously and sometimes ironically engaged with female protagonists and the compromises and complications of their experience. Whether they are girls travelling abroad or women working (or trying to write) at home, they seem to be on the edge of things or the brink of change, looking for location and connection. Rose has travelled widely herself and foreign locations feature in many of her stories. She has a poet's eye for metaphor, as in the 'red tides' of love, jealousy, anger or pollution on a beach, or in the imagery of blood as both inheritance and infection in her novel *Pest Maiden* (1999), which also plays on the comically painful treacheries of the creative life, as when the hero has to endure his lover's seducer publishing details of that very seduction in his bad prose.

Bernard MacLaverty (b. 1942)

Bernard MacLaverty was born and brought up in Belfast, working there as a medical lab technician before coming to live in Scotland in 1975. Many of his books deal with this Irish background and upbringing, most notably *Lamb* (1980) and *Cal* (1983), both of which were successfully filmed. MacLaverty's short stories often come from the same place, and the title-story of his third collection, *Walking the Dog* (1994), is an unforgettably brilliant account of what it is like to live with both sides of sectarian terror. *Grace Notes* (1997), his finest novel, tells of Catherine McKenna a woman composer living on Islay, with work commissioned in Glasgow, who has to return to Northern Ireland to bury her father and confront her own ghosts. Short-listed for the Booker and awarded the Scotsman/Saltire Prize as Book of the Year, *Grace Notes* is suffused with MacLaverty's own love of classical music (he hosted a music programme for BBC Radio Scotland) and it gives as fine an account of the joys and costs of creativity as Janice Galloway's *Clara*. It ends on a wholly uplifting note, but it also recognises that issues of national or sexual identity, responsibility, creation and grace have to be negotiated, made, remade and welcomed minute by minute, case by case, in an imperfect world.

Allan Massie (b. 1938)

Allan Massie was born in Singapore and worked as a schoolteacher in Scotland for ten years before turning to writing full time as an author, journalist and television critic. His first novel *Change and Decay in All Around I See* (1978) was a satire on middle-class life in London. Since then he has published over seventeen novels, including a fictionalised life of Scott, *The Ragged Lion* (1994), and an expanding series of successful novels about the Roman Emperors that includes *Augustus* (1986), *Caesar* (1993) and *Caligula* (2003). Massie was interested in history, which he studied at Cambridge, and his finest novels have been explorations of modern history and the complex issues of our time to do with conscience, morality, action and accountability. These include *The Death of Men* (1981), about terrorism in Italy in the late 1970s, and what he sees as a 'loose trilogy', three of his finest books, dealing with the events and aftermath of the Second World War: *A Question of Loyalties* (1989), *The Sins of the Father* (1991) and *Shadows of Empire* (1997).

William Boyd (b. 1952) and Shena Mackay (b. 1944)

The novels of William Boyd are equally various as one might expect from an author born in Africa and mostly resident in London, and indeed his award-winning work has often concerned itself with life in Africa, the Americas and London. His first novel, *A Good Man In Africa* (1981), has its own lightly satirical take on the imperial experience. *The New Confessions* (1987) is nothing less than a picaresque history of the whole first half of the twentieth century by way of the autobiography of a garrulous Scot on the make, from his first days in Edinburgh to his career as a film producer in Hollywood. *Brazzaville Beach* (1990) is a brilliantly thoughtful exploration of scientific enquiry and the challenges of new knowledge, set against personal drama and guerrilla war in Africa. *Stars and Bars* (2001) is a Waugh-like comedy about an Englishman in America's deep South, while *Armadillo* (1998) is a thriller about class, materialism, and the ruthlessness of the insurance adjustment business in London. Shena Mackay is an equally successful author with a similar reach. Like Boyd she has written many fine short stories, though her focus is more usually on women's experience of middle-class life in the home counties and her characteristically perceptive eye for sadness, eccentricity and the blackly comic operates somewhere between the territories of Muriel Spark and Elspeth Davie. *The Orchard on Fire* (1995) reveals village life in Kent in the 1950s through the eyes of a young girl, in a bittersweet and poignant comedy of experience and Edenic expulsion into adult life. Mackay's enjoyment of eccentric characters appears again in *The Artist's Widow* (1998), about supposedly 'artistic' people ('the good, the bad and the untalented') in London. Her most ambitious novel and the most relevant to the present context is *Dunedin* (1992), which links the history of a Scots Presbyterian minister's arrival in nineteenth-century New Zealand (with much to say about colonial exploitation) to the sad lives of his middle aged great-grandchildren in contemporary London. Here again Mackay invokes a sense of Edenic promise only for it to be followed by expulsion and loneliness.

Candia McWilliam (b. 1955)

Like Mackay, Candia McWilliam was born in Edinburgh and lives in England. Her first novel, *A Case of Knives* (1988), was notable for matching its macabre imagination to a highly stylised prose, as also did its successor *A Little Stranger* (1989). McWilliam has declared herself an admirer of Stevenson and her work shows a clear interest in questions of identity and place. Several stories set in Edinburgh appear in her collection *Wait Till I Tell You* (1997), whose contents are divided into 'North' and 'South', with a linking story about a train journey between the two. Stevenson's spirit is most present, perhaps, in the novel *Debatable Land* (1994), which has six characters aboard a yacht sailing from Tahiti to New Zealand. The book's title refers to several debatable lands: the French-colonial islands and hybrid cultures they encounter along the way; the past history of the characters themselves, three of whom are Scots; and indeed Scotland itself. McWilliam has a meticulous, insightful and slightly sardonic insight into human motivation, yet the book is haunted by memories of Edinburgh and a sense of how fragile our identities are and how dependent on a sense of place, without which we may well be like unshelled eggs. With their world shrunk to the hull of a yacht in the vastness of the Pacific, the final debatable land for these characters comes down to what lies within the shell of each vulnerable self.

New voices, new directions

By the end of the century the creation, reception and publication of Scottish fiction had been greatly boosted by the critical success of Kelman, Gray and Galloway with their willingness to break the conventions of textual layout and narrative structure. Fresh audiences had been opened up by the gross carnival energy of Welsh, whose books spoke to a new generation of readers and could be found on sale alongside CDs, videos and computer games; and the imaginative generosity and ultimately affirmative spirit of Iain Banks had been equally successful in mainstream and science-fiction genres. Scottish writers were finding new topics and new voices. English, European and American modes were just as familiar as the old themes, after all, and younger writers had the confidence to follow them, or not, just as they pleased. They also had the confidence to look for a different view of Scotland and the world, moving beyond the brutal pessimism and the male despair of Dunky Logan and his friends.

A. L. Kennedy (b. 1965)

Alison Kennedy shares Galloway's capacity for narrative innovation, as do Frank Kuppner, Alan Warner, Ali Smith, Jackie Kay and Andrew Crumey – all of whom have been prepared to take Scottish fiction into new territory in both subject matter and delivery. Some of the short stories in the Saltire Prize-winning *Night Geometry and the Garscadden Trains* (1990) by A. L. Kennedy seemed to be starting from the grim realism of what had gone before, with stories of urban decay, loneliness, misconnection and sexual betrayal. Kennedy herself acknowledged that writers such as Byrne, Leonard and Kelman 'made my generation of writers possible'; but by this she meant that they had given Scottish writers licence to be themselves, and she has since resisted any attempt to class her by her subject matter or her gender. Kennedy's work reveals a witty and sharply analytical intelligence and her preferred use of first-person discourse only gradually reveals what is going on in some of these stories, leading to doubts about the narrators' reliability, or indeed their sanity. Seen from these inner perspectives, or from her skilful use of free indirect discourse, Kennedy's world is shifting and provisional in its boundaries, sometimes surreal, always memorably crafted with a very writerly awareness of the nature of her medium. In the title-story, a wife recounts her husband's infidelity and the break-up of her marriage (it is the unreliability of the trains that brings her home unexpectedly) and reflects on the anonymity of her own life and that of so many others 'who live their lives in the best way they can with generally good intentions and still leave nothing behind'. The wife tells her story in a quirky and low-key tone, but ends with a memorable observation about mass culture and a plea for dignity drawn from the Hillsborough football stadium disaster in 1989:

> There is only one thing I want more than proof I existed and that's some proof, while I'm here, that I exist. Not being an Olympic skier, or a chat show host, I won't get my wish. There are too many people alive today for us to notice every single one.
> But the silent majority and I do have one memorial at least. The Disaster. We have small lives, easily lost in foreign droughts, or famines; the occasional incendiary incident, or a wall of pale faces, crushed against grillwork, on Saturday afternoon in Spring. This is not enough.

The cool precision of such writing, with its elegance and its awareness of pain, is characteristic of Kennedy. In an interview in 1999, she explained her feeling for those who leave nothing behind: 'So many people, if you actually get to know them at any level, are enormous inside and their life doesn't actually permit them to express what they want to.' Her narratives convey this inner scale by following the flow of her characters' thoughts from past to present and back again so that the reader has to work quite hard to reconstruct their stories in an inner landscape of immediate sensation, memory and old hurts. She is equally interested in the writer's task, giving early notice of this in the story 'The role of notable silences in Scottish history', which is told by a professional researcher. Kennedy uses this device to comment on authorship ('Now while I'm working I try not to think about the truth, but concentrate my full attention on the words instead'), as well as on literary genre, the manufacture of tradition, violence in Scottish culture and most of all perhaps on how she sees the world and her own books:

> This city makes you think like that. The roads come together, cross and go on and little strands of history follow them. In some places, many lines will cross: what has been, what is and what will be and you can walk from one coincidence to another, not step on a crack. It's like strolling across a book, something big and Victorian with plenty of plots. It makes you wonder who's reading you.

Kennedy's first novel, *Looking for the Possible Dance* (1993), is notable (and exceptional in modern Scottish fiction) for its sweet evocation of fatherhood and a daughter's care for the man who brought her up on his own. Yet she must also learn to let go in order to make a fuller commitment with her lover Colin. The novel understands what it is to be alone even as we love others, but then again Margaret also realises the need to make contact with people, in that 'possible dance', without the ties of family and romance. She has a memorably positive encounter with a spastic boy on a train journey. On the other hand the envy of a colleague and the sexism of her boss have cost her the job she enjoyed. The narrative asks a lot of the reader as it moves backwards and forwards through time, seemingly in step with Margaret's memories, on her train journey to London. Kennedy is not above offering a few withering insights on Scottishness: 'As the Israelites in slavery had their psalms, so we have the ceilidh'; and under the rubric of 'THE SCOT-TISH METHOD (FOR THE PERFECTION OF CHILDREN)' we learn, among other things, that: '1. Guilt is good' and '2. The history, language and culture of Scotland do not exist. If they did, they would be of no importance and might as well not.' This suggests a social as well as a personal cause for Margaret's sense of personal un-rootedness – something that many of Kennedy's characters feel. Yet in the end the novel's spirit is affirmative, despite what happens to her lover – Colin falls out with a local gangster and pays a terrible price: he is nailed to a wooden floor in a punishment borrowed from the actual exploits of Glasgow hard man Jimmy Boyle. This scene is reminiscent of the encounter with evil that closes Friel's *Mr Alfred MA* – 'This is our own small Terror, Colin', the psychopath explains, as he wields the hammer to the strains of Mozart. But this is not how the novel ends and the implications of such ultra-violence are mediated and countered by Margaret's capacity for maternal care and her decision to return to her wounded lover.

Kennedy explores the darker side of 'guilt is good' in some of the stories in *Now That You're Back* (1994), but the account she gives of child abuse in 'Perfect Possession' takes such utterly chilling pleasure in imitating the calmly authoritarian tones of psychotic parents that the final effect is very far from either sentimental realism or the more empathetic sensibility of Janice Galloway in the *Blood* stories. Kennedy's capacity for a darkly surreal vision and her incisive wit enlighten many of the stories in this and other collections, contributing a modern Gothic flavour to their accounts of trauma and obsession. Some of the other epigrams under 'The Scottish Method' would surpass Alasdair Gray and give a not inaccurate sense of Kennedy's characteristically sardonic voice – not without its own echoes of pain:

6. Pain and fear will teach us to hurt and petrify ourselves, thus circumventing further public expense.
7. Joy is fleeting, sinful and the forerunner of despair.
8. Life is a series of interwoven ceremonies, etiquettes and forms which we will never understand. We may never trust ourselves to others.

The stories in *Original Bliss* (1997) reflect specifically on sexuality and sexual obsession, once again with an underlying sense of emptiness, the loneliness of the human condition, occasional comedy and the terrible sadness of desire. Perhaps Kennedy's strangest and most fascinating imaginative fiction is to be found in the novel *So I Am Glad* (1995), whose first-person protagonist is Jennifer Wilson, a professional 'voice-over' and a disembodied presence on night-time radio who slowly falls in love with a mysterious stranger who appears unannounced, like a fallen angel lightly glowing, in her flat one night. Kennedy is more than happy to echo the strategies of Hogg, Stevenson and Gray in what is virtually a Scottish tradition of leaving the reader unsure as to whether this is a supernatural visitation or evidence of psychological derangement. Certainly other people see someone like Savinien who answers to the name 'Martin', but do they see what

Jennifer is seeing? Or is it the visitor who is mad? Nevertheless, the author does gradually persuade us of the 'reality' of it all, even when Savinien is revealed to be the French poet, soldier and thinker Cyrano de Bergerac, somehow back from the dead for a spell, before he has to return. Kennedy imbues the whole narrative with the spell of Jennifer's own estrangement – she was orphaned when her abusive parents died in a car crash and her sado-masochistic affair with a previous lover has been only another reflection of her emotional numbness, in a world where shop doorways shelter sleeping street-people at night, and torture has become an instrument of the state. Jennifer is as isolated as an astronaut, in the recording booth where she makes her living as an always-neutral soundtrack voice, and yet she comes to care for her supernatural visitor, who is as strange as Muriel Spark's Seraph in Zambesi and, like him, just as out of place. It is through this care that she manages to make a commitment to the world again, glad for the experience – whatever it has been – even if it ended in loss. Neither fantasy fiction, 'magic realism' nor allegory, *So I Am Glad* is an opaquely poetic fable in prose, deeply coloured, as so much of Kennedy's work is, by her interest in the peculiar nature of literary space. Her third novel, *Everything You Need* (1999), links this fascination to the nature of artistic ambition and returns to the theme of fathers and daughters in the story of Nathan Staples a burned-out and self-destructive thriller writer who arranges a scholarship to a writers' colony for the daughter he hasn't seen in fifteen years, and attempts to mentor her without revealing his identity. The novel contains a number of short stories as exemplars of the craft, each dealing in different ways with the denial or loss of love, while Kennedy also gives a scathing account of the London literary world and the pressures faced by authors and publishers alike. The essence of her work, however, is to be found in her unflinching and sometimes blackly comic vision of the loneliness of the individual subject, lost in desire and yet open to the possibility – as between fathers and daughters – of a sweeter human contact.

Alan Warner (b. 1964)

The world of *Morvern Callar* (1995) by Alan Warner is rather different. The 21-year-old protagonist wakes up one morning just before Christmas to find that her boyfriend – a writer in his thirties – has cut his own throat. Morvern cries for a bit and then has a long hot bath, chooses her clothes and sets off as usual to the local supermarket where she stacks shelves. Later she will dismember and dispose of his decaying body, claim his inheritance, along with his novel and literary success, for her own, and travel to Spain to give herself over to rave culture. The cool detachment of Warner's first novel made an immediate critical impact, not least because it was also a first-person female narrative written by a young man apparently alert to every nuance of feminine dress, make-up and intimate hygiene. Morvern seems to be a child of the ecstasy generation – she never leaves the house without a Walkman and her favourite compilation cassettes – but to typecast Warner as a spokesperson who celebrates youthful counter-culture, even though his books rather invite this simplification, is to miss the real focus of his work.

Callar lives in 'the Port', a seaside town that is never named but which has a clear resemblance to Warner's native Oban. This town and the north-western Highlands will be the setting for all his novels, and he joins Legge and McLean as a writer who celebrates the life of young people outside the large cities. Morvern and her friend Lanna, like many of their friends (and their parents and grandparents before them), have menial jobs and little prospect of doing better in a small town where everyone is already known to each other in a familiar round of pubs, disco clubs and heavy drinking. Neither disaffected nor politically inclined, Morvern seems to live only in the moment – an effect greatly enhanced by the first-person narrative and the scrupulously detailed account Warner gives of her every movement, from painting her toenails to her sensual enjoyment of the air and water on a rough hillside where she goes camping (and also to bury the severed parts of her boyfriend's body). She is a female protagonist quite unlike Chris Guthrie, who felt connected to an ancient timelessness in the hills, and yet her response to the physical moment is just as strong:

> You could hear the waterfalls down in the gulley. They would be spraying onto ferns there and drops of water would be hanging from their tips. I looked out at the landscape moving without any haste to no bidding at all. I yawned a big yawn. Two arms and a leg were buried on the cliff above the sycamore tree and higher up the torso and leg would be helping flower the sheets of bluebells below the dripping rocks. All across the land bits of Him were buried.

The final effect is bizarre but curiously undisturbing, for this is not *The Wasp Factory* and Morvern retains an oddly unfocused sweetness that defuses what might otherwise come across as a psychopathic dissociation. In fact Callar's refusal to follow the usual rituals associated with death after the absurdist and never-explained suicide of her partner could be seen as heroic. Indeed the spirit of *Morvern Callar* is closer to the unforced existential detachment of Camus's *L'Étranger* in sunny Algiers, than to Banks's Gothic glee or Irvine Welsh's violent nihilism. The sensual immediacy of Warner's prose creates and enfolds Morvern Callar's sensibility, especially in the last memorable scene when she returns from Spain after a few years and finds herself walking back to the Port as snow falls all around her, pregnant and full of unearned and unmediated hope, almost a kind of grace.

The cover of Warner's next novel, *These Demented Lands* (1997), described itself as 'a sequel to Morvern's odyssey' but it belongs to a different genre altogether. A pregnant and unnamed female narrator (who is revealed as Callar on the last page) crosses to a small island somewhere off the west coast to take part in DJ Cormorant's Millennium rave at New Year in a hotel by an aerodrome. The text includes road signs, faxes and documents and the narrative is shared by a male character known as Aircrash Investigator, who describes his encounters with (Morvern) from his own point of view. This is a surreal place of unlikely signs and place names – the Phosphorous Beds (ammunition dumped during the war); Outer Rim; Far Places – and is inhabited by people answering to names such as Brotherhood, Chef Macbeth, Knifegrinder and the Devil's Advocate. In fact these 'demented lands' come to seem increasingly spectral, haunted by Christian images of birth and crucifixion (Morvern gives birth to a girl at the end), and allegorically suggestive without being finally decipherable. One possible reading would be to see the whole setting as Warner's version (after Callar drowns) of the netherworld of *Lanark*, but in the end it lacks Gray's controlling political vision. Much more successful was *The Man Who Walks* (2002), a picaresque novel in which a nephew pursues a weird uncle who has absconded with the local pub's World Cup cash fund. Warner delivers a deeply defamiliarised vision of life in the modern Highlands, as a place where cannabis smokers, wanderers, hippie snowboarders, gangsters and film makers all rub shoulders in a hilariously alternative mountainscape of housing estates, motels and theme bars, guaranteed to undermine the old myths of history, identity and sexual repression. Warner's prose style is memorable in this novel, as in all his books: not just because he uses Scots dialect words, but because he seeks a musical cadence of his own by dislocating conventional English syntax in a way that seems entirely colloquial, yet which is unique to him: 'Varieties of routes presented themselves to the Nephew for reaching his Uncle's place over other side of the railway as varieties will insist on doing'; or more poetically: 'The Nephew came into woke-ness of vibrated daylight.'

Warner's interest in writing from a female point of view appeared again in *The Sopranos* (1998), which follows the experiences of five Catholic schoolgirls on a bus excursion to Edinburgh to sing in a choir competition. Once again the narrow life of the Port is invoked along with the girls' different backgrounds, as they thrill to the possibility of getting way from school, meeting boys, drinking alcopops, shopping and shoplifting in the big city. Warner catches the intense life of adolescent friendships, betrayals and burgeoning sexuality with remarkable skill. As with *Morvern Caller*, however, there is a voyeuristic element in such writing as these girls come under his male gaze, which is more fascinated by the erotic potential to be found in the minutiae of sexual difference than a female author would consider relevant. Having said that, Warner's grasp of the anxious innocence that underlies rowdy teenage crudity is genuinely compassionate, and although several difficult personal issues are raised and resolved during their trip, the book's final celebration of youthful energy cannot help but have a tenderly defiant and elegiac note for the girls back in the Port again, hanging out in the local dive, 'already in full summer flush in this time of their lives'.

Ali Smith (b. 1962)

The short stories of Ali Smith have a very powerful feeling for that 'summer flush' and the fleeting and fragmentary nature of how our lives are put together. She is especially sensitive to the glow of desire and the unexpected 'moments and material of which love gets made', which are the themes of her first collection *Free Love and other stories* (1995). The short-story format particularly suits Smith's eye for the way small details can be used to suggest a larger picture, while remaining open-ended and contingent. The story 'Virtual' in *Other Stories and other stories* (1999), for example, makes a mysterious but heartbreakingly apposite connection between an anorexic girl in hospital, and the Tamagotchi 'virtual pet' her family bring her because she is missing her cat. Every element of the tale, in Smith's spare and lucidly balanced prose, works to great effect without ever even hinting at symbolic 'importance', and indeed the controlling theme of her third collection, *The Whole Story and other stories* (2003), is that the whole story can never be known. Smith's first novel *Hotel World* (2001) has the same feeling for the subtle connections between the disconnected and the disaffected as it traces a day in the inner life of five very different women associated with a city-centre hotel. Each internalised narrative is characterised by a different voice and different grammatical and textual structures, from damaged Else begging for spare change in the street outside; to Lise trammelled by the organisational discourse of 'Management' in Reception; or Penny, the weary 'style' journalist inventing copy for the Globe Hotels, which pride themselves on being the same wherever you go. Then there is Sara, the student worker whose prank went tragically wrong when she fell to her death down a service lift-shaft a year ago, and Sara's sister who haunts the street opposite the hotel because she cannot come to terms with this accident. Sara has a narrative, too, for she is a ghost caught between this world and the next, seeking closure, like her sister, and permission to go. Under the eye of her particular eternity, the fragility and mortality of the other protagonists and the tenuous links between them become doubly moving. Sara begins to forget words, or to muddle them up ('remember / you / must / live . . . remainder / you / mist / leaf') as her own spirit starts to fade away, and this memorably poetic short novel ends with a vision of the world as a place entirely and life-affirmingly populated by the ghostly connections between us all.

Andrew Crumey (b. 1961)

The fiction of Andrew Crumey is much more self-consciously postmodern in its practice, and the author acknowledges the influence of Borges and Calvino in his work. His first novel set the mould with *Music in a Foreign Language* (1994), which imagines what life would be like if Britain was a communist state. Yet this scenario is not really central to the novel, which pursues instead a complex plot, with stories within stories, in an account of how two friends, a historian and a physicist, fare in such chaotic times when their interests in science, music and writing may, or may not, be enough to see them through. *Pfitz* (1995) borrows a theme from Italo Calvino in its account of an eighteenth-century prince who invents an ideal but entirely fictional city, only to have the boundaries between the real and the fictional endlessly blurred, as the cartographers and biographers of the city and its 'inhabitants' jostle for advantage both within and without the world they create. Crumey graduated from St Andrews with a degree in Mathematics and Theoretical Physics and in places his books can read like a witty but rather demanding introduction to poststructuralist critical theory, as if rewritten by an author from the Age of Reason.

D'Alembert's Principle (1996), *Mr Mee* (2000) and *Mobius Dick* (2004) are equally informed by their author's fascination with metafictional textuality and the unstable worlds of memory, reason, writing, indeterminacy and quantum physics in their tales of eighteenth-century intrigue, forbidden encyclopaedias and parallel universes.

Margaret Elphinstone (b. 1948) and Sian Hayton (b. 1933)

Further evidence of how modern Scottish fiction has moved away from the largely realistic and urban models that characterised the 1960s and 1970s can be seen in the development of serious historical fiction in the work of Margaret Elphinstone and James Robertson and in the use of myth and fantasy in that of Sian Hayton and Christopher Whyte. The early short stories of Margaret Elphinstone mixed realism and magic realism with a feminist sensibility in *An Apple from a Tree* (1991). Her novel *The Sea Road* (2000) tells of the voyages of the seafarer Gudrun and the Viking discovery of North America. This book has been widely translated and Elphinstone's capacity to re-imagine the densely mythopoeic otherness of ancient times is reminiscent of Naomi Mitchison. *Hy Brasil* (2002) is a modern adventure about a would-be travel writer visiting a remote (imaginary) island to the west of Ireland. One critic described it as a combination of *The Shipping News* and *Whisky Galore*, but it also has much to say about the tricky differences between writing fact and writing fiction. *Voyageurs* (2004) is a fully historical novel set against the 1812 war between Canada and the United States. The author has a remarkable feel for the nature of wilderness supported by an extensive research into period details and a sense, once again, of the utter otherness of the past. Sian Hayton, on the other hand, has chosen a more consciously mythic engagement with the past, most especially in her trilogy *Cells of Knowledge* (1989), *Hidden Daughters* (1992) and *The Last Flight* (1993), about the daughters of a Celtic god who enter the male world of monks and warriors in tenth-century Scotland. These interrelated texts – as complex as a Celtic knot – invoke a mythopoeic sisterhood whose wisdom and magical powers are scarcely compatible with ancient patriarchy and the authority of the Church. Looking back to the genre of Gunn's *Sun Circle*, or more properly to Mitchison's *The Corn King and the Spring Queen*, Hayton has taken still further steps to reject the melancholy fatedness of nineteenth-century Celticism in order to re-create the Celtic woman and her alternative values as a significantly empowered subject.

Christopher Whyte (b. 1952)

Christopher Whyte invoked a magical past via a retired schoolteacher-editor worthy of Sir Walter himself, who has discovered an old manuscript that will tell the story of *The Warlock of Strathearn* (1997). Whyte's fable goes beyond the supernatural, however, to examine questions about our relationship with the natural world – the warlock narrator discovers he has the ability to talk to animals and heal – as well as our culpability in the use of such powers. With his capacity to enter other realms of being and the ability to change shape and even his sex, the young warlock is a living challenge to rigid Presbyterianism and orthodoxy in general, then and now, but especially in seventeenth-century Scotland, which was so obsessed with witchcraft. Whyte re-imagines these magical powers as an experience of welcome seduction, liberation and gender-unspecific sexual exchange. In his first novel, *Euphemia MacFarrigle and the Laughing Virgin* (1995), Whyte had used the fantastic to similar ends, in a contemporary setting this time, by imagining a demon who generates a windy blast of Rabelaisian farting in Roman Catholic Glasgow, rather in the style of Edwin Morgan's demon, or Bulgakov's *The Master and Margarita*. In this respect Whyte's conflation of the sexually and magically other to challenge convention is similar to that of Ellen Galford's entertaining *Queendom Come* (1990), which imagines a lesbian priestess from ancient times recalled to Arthur's Seat to upset the male complacencies of Thatcher's Edinburgh.

James Robertson (b. 1958)

Two collections of short stories (*Close*, 1991 and *The Ragged Man's Complaint*, 1993) marked the fictional debut of James Robertson, who also has two collections of poetry to his name. His first novel *The Fanatic* (2000) was notable for the extent of its historical research into the dark days of the 1670s and the sufferings of James Mitchel, a 'justi-fied' covenanting martyr to the cause. The pains of the period, its convictions and its cruel obsessions are vividly realised and based on scrupulous research. Yet the book has a contemporary setting as well, in which an unhomely drop-out called Andrew Carlin finds himself signed up as a 'ghost' for a ghost tour in the Edinburgh of the 1990s. Carlin must play the part of (an actual) Major Weir, a notorious reli-gious extremist who was burnt at the stake in 1670 on a charge of incest and reputed witchcraft. Carlin starts to research Weir more thor-oughly, and (by means that would do justice to James Hogg)

Robertson leaves the reader uncertain as to whether Carlin is in some uncanny way possessed by Weir, determined that his story should be told. In the meantime the novel has a very strong sense of what religious conviction means, even in the mouth of a 'fanatic', compared with the triviality and vanity of the modern world with its own shallow iniquities and its theme-park approach to the past. Robertson uses the two strands of his tale to explore how the past inhabits the present and yet how irrecoverable it may still be in the end. The same theme in a more limited and wholly historical setting features in the masterful *Joseph Knight* (2003), in which a now wealthy ex-slave-owner from Jamaica (who fled to the Caribbean as a frightened boy after the defeat of the Highland 'rebellion' at Culloden) returns to his homeland with Knight as his black slave, only to have him win a law case against his master and gain his freedom. Now in later years, old Wedderburn, the master, wishes to know what happened to Knight and sets a private detective on his trail. Based on an actual law case of those days, Robertson's novel offers a succession of piercing and ironic insights into the imperial project, the Scottish condition after the Jacobite rising, the fragile and paradoxical nature of independence and the darker paradoxes of 'enlightenment' and 'freedom'. The presence, or rather the absence, of Joseph Knight haunts the whole book, for we almost never get to meet him and (like the detective who seeks him) we can only slowly piece together his story in fragmented narratives and differing reports. Knight is a man who never knew his birth name, having been abducted from Africa as a small boy and 'named' by others ever since. In this way – in a perfect paradigm of the marginalised and 'invisible' slave – he is a hole at the centre of the very novel that bears his name, but paradoxically he is also its heart, raising much larger questions about the nature of all identity. At the very end of the book we find that he has made a tolerable life for himself (if much harder than being a rich merchant's manservant) by working in darkness with the coal-miners of Fife – a class of native and supposedly freeborn Scots who are little more than slaves themselves.

Poetry in English and Scots

In the last thirty years of the century it became possible for authors, including many poets, to make a living from their writing: as reviewers, as writers-in-residence for local authorities, or as tutors or lecturers in Creative Writing for universities, schools and colleges. The availability of grants and awards from the Scottish Arts Council, or from the lottery funded 'Creative Scotland' initiative, also helped – although it has to be said that the sums in question are still sadly inadequate compared with what is made available for the performing arts. Poetry, nevertheless, continues somehow to happen.

In the same thirty years, the contradictory (antisyzygetical) qualities of 'Scottishness' that MacDiarmid set out to celebrate with such single-minded zeal have evolved into a broader and more relaxed field of utterance, more various and polyphonic, more alert to differences of gender and place, less prescriptive, and more open to irony and playfulness – modes almost entirely unknown to the old man. It is equally notable that many contemporary poets can move between Scots, Gaelic or English without feeling that they have to explain, theorise or apologise. And indeed the same is true of their ability to embrace different genres as well, for Dunn, Greig, Butlin, Kuppner, Burnside, White and MacNeil, for example, have all published fine prose fiction as well as poetry.

Douglas Dunn (b. 1942)

With over thirteen poetry collections to his name and numerous literary awards, Douglas Dunn has also written screenplays, critical essays (*Essays*, 2003) and two collections of short stories, as well as translating Racine (*Andromache*, 1990) and editing and introducing several anthologies. As a professor at the University of St Andrews, he has become a significant creative and critical presence with a firm commitment to the craft of poetry and to what might be called the balance between rationality and empathy that characterised the Scottish Enlightenment. Over the course of his creative career Dunn has come to make an increasingly strong identification with Scotland and indeed this has produced some of his best poems. Nevertheless, while recognising the creative achievement of MacDiarmid's early work, Dunn has little sympathy for his political and cultural extremism, and even less for the universalising ambition and the encyclopaedic modernism of his later poetry. Dunn has been equally unconvinced by the forces that claim Scottish writing as a special case with a single agenda – as if Scottish writers should not read and be influenced by their American, European or even their English contemporaries. Much of what he has to say on this issue is contained in the thoughtful introduction to his 1992 anthology of *Twentieth-Century Scottish Poetry*, and yet at the same time he still celebrates the fact that contemporary Scottish writers have sustained what he calls 'the liberty of three languages', and prevailed against the absolute cultural hegemony of 'standard English' and the erasure of class, regional and even national differences. Even so, Dunn remains suspicious of literary nationalism and cultural agendas, and he has welcomed the freedom of Scottish writers in the latter half of the century simply 'to write what they write'. In this respect he associates his own poetry with the values of formal craft, conceptual clarity and a humanist concern for common decency in a literary world too often given over to the pursuit of what he sees as obscurity, sensation and pretension.

Dunn was born to a working-class family in Inchinnan, near Renfrew on the Clyde, and began his career as a library assistant. He was a married man in his mid-twenties when he went to the University of Hull to study for a BA in English. On graduation in 1969 he stayed on to work as a librarian there and made the acquaintance of Philip Larkin. Perhaps he had the values of the English 'Movement' writers in mind, when he chose a particularly narrow palette for the poems in his first collection *Terry Street* (1969), but they show a certain Scottish austerity too, and a sense of not quite belonging. These poems set out to explore a world in which 'everything was there to be seen', with the poet determined not to invent 'when reality is good enough and lying to hand for the making of images'. In fact he often imagines himself as if he were simply standing at a window, looking out on this run-down street in Hull. He is sympathetic to the working-class lives and the deprivation he sees around him, but at the same time he is undeniably alert to all the subtle signifiers of class and values that he does not, or may no longer share.

> Young women come to visit their married friend.
> Waiting for their hair to set beneath thin scarves,
> They walk about in last year's fashions.
> Stockingless in coats and old shoes.
> They look strong, white-legged creatures
> With nothing to do but talk of what it is to love.

The 'Men of Terry Street' are no easier, for even 'at their Sunday leisure, they are too tired / And bored to look long at comfortably. / It hurts to see their faces, too sad or too jovial.' The prevailing spirit is one of frozen decay with glimpses of beauty and a sense of deep personal loneliness: 'What great thing have I lost, that faces in a crowd / Should make me look at them for one I know' ('The Worst of All Loves'). Yet there are flashes of rage, too, as in his bitterly ironic 'A

Poem in Praise of the British': 'how sweet is the weakness after Empire / In the garden of a flat, safe country shire, / Watching the beauty of the random, spare, superfluous'. Dunn's next collection (*The Happier Life*, 1972) was in somewhat similar vein ('They will not leave me, the lives of other people') but in *Love or Nothing* (1974) he began to speak more personally in poems that recall a wartime childhood in Renfrewshire, dense with references to the practical world and memories of class snobbery ('White Fields'; 'The Competition'; 'Boys with Coats'). Looking to his own background Dunn is proud to associate himself with labour (rather as Seamus Heaney did in thinking of his own roots) as he asks for 'A poetry of nuts and bolts, born, bred, / Embattled by the Clyde, tight and impure' ('Clydesiders'). His engagement with Scotland is clearer now, for he is 'No victim of my place, but mad for it' – although we should note that this is ambiguously expressed – for 'place' and 'mad' can also refer to class and anger.

With the appearance of *Barbarians* (1979) and *St Kilda's Parliament* (1981), Dunn came to his most fruitful themes and full maturity as a poet with great formal skill in rhyme and metre, as well as in the freer use of broken rhythm in a colloquial voice that is still finely musical. In 'Portrait Photograph, 1915', for example, he imagines a soldier remembering the one moment when he felt like an individual, before disappearing into the trenches to fight for a system under which he had always been, and always would be, faceless and nameless:

We too have our place, who were not photographed
So much and then only in multitudes
Rising from holes in the ground to fall into smoke
Or is it newsreel beyond newsreel
But I do not know and I have lost my name
And my face and as for dignity
I never had it in any case, except once,
I think, in the High Street, before we left
For troopships and the farewell pipers,
When it was my turn in the queue
In Anderson's Photographic Arcade and Salon.

Such insights were central to the opening 'pastoral' poems in the *Barbarians* collection, in which he speaks with a new political directness on behalf of the voiceless and the exploited, returning again to the theme of empire:

You work, we rule, they said. We worked; they ruled.

They fooled the tenements. All men were fooled.
It still persists. It will be so, always.
Listen. An out of work apprentice plays
God Save the Queen on an Edwardian flute.
He is, but does not know it, destitute.

                                        ('Empires')

This is not so far from the spirit of dramas such as *Willie Rough* (1972)
and *The Bevellers* (1973), or from McIlvanney's vision in *Docherty*
(1975) or the more compassionate insights in Alan Spence's *Its Colours
They Are Fine* (1977), or Alison Kennedy's care for the ordinary folk
who 'leave nothing behind'.

As an English poet from a working-class background, Tony Harrison
was making very similar points in his collections *The School of Eloquence
and Other Poems* (1978) and its sequel *Continuous* (1981), in which he
feels alienated from his parents by virtue of his education. From north
of the Border, Dunn can lay claim to a tradition of radical self education and actual rebellion in the Scotland of the 1820s ('The Student');
and as a boy who never went to public school he can excoriate the
niceties of Oxbridge culture in 'The Come-on', in which the wordplay
on 'sherry' and 'port(entous)' is typical of his scathing wit:

Brothers, they say that we have no culture.
We are of the wrong world.
. . .

Unless we enter through a narrow gate
In a wall they have built
To join them in the 'disinterested tradition'
Of tea, of couplets dipped
In sherry and the decanted, portentous remark.
Therefore, we'll deafen them
With the dull staccato of our typewriters.

Dunn uses the motif of gardens and gardeners in a country house in
several of these poems to express his admiration for beauty, and his
disquiet at how the toil of others is owned and enjoyed only by a
leisured few. In an imagined revolution set in '*England Loamshire
1789*' he has the gardeners speak: 'We did not burn your gardens and
undo / What likes of us did for the likes of you; / We did not raze this
garden that we made, / Although we hanged you somewhere in its
shade' ('Gardeners'). Dunn's play on the word 'likes' – suggesting also
a shared enjoyment of the garden – is notable for the way it qualifies
the poem's revolutionary zeal without defusing it.

St Kilda's Parliament was dedicated to Dunn's father (who had died the previous year) and several of the poems in it develop the historical sensibility already evident in *Barbarians* to offer a mature re-examination of the poet's relationship with his home country. Thus 'John Wilson in Greenock, 1786' offers a little parable on the state of the arts in Scotland by recalling that author (of a long poem about the Clyde) who had to promise to give up his interest in 'the profane and unprofitable art' of poetry in order to secure a job as a schoolmaster. Dunn reflects further on questions of literature, class and privilege in a specifically Scottish context with a scathing account of one of Walter Scott's youthful scrapes with a street boy in 'Green Breeks'; while 'Tannahill', to the poet Robert Tannahill, uses the Habbie Simson stanza (much favoured by the man himself) to ponder again on the vagaries of literary fame and reputation. The paradoxes of labour and the contradictions of Irish and Scottish experience within the British Empire are visited with great subtlety via the poet's own childhood experiences as a holiday-time potato picker, in 'Washing the Coins'. Another poem recalls the lame daughter of a woman who was burned as a witch, and the title-poem imagines a photographer revisiting a famous photograph of the elders on the remote outer Hebridean island of St Kilda in 1789. Here is a community – evacuated in the 1930s – whose language, values and communal life are all but incomprehensible to the modern viewer. Dunn's poem becomes a profound meditation on the mysteries of history and identity and yet the utter strangeness and irrecoverability of the past – for photographer and poet alike. Nevertheless, this collection marks Dunn's determination to figure out what Scotland's history means to him and the values he holds dear, and to take a place within that culture. The long discursive lines of the poem 'Remembering Lunch' reflect on where the poet might be going now, as an inescapably literary man in his forties, moving in smart metropolitan circles that he no longer enjoys. Dunn strikes a fogeyish pose with an air of self parody, seeing himself as a schoolmaster in tweeds 'circa 1930' who prefers to walk on the shore – 'In a pretence of being a John Buchan of the underdog, / with my waistcoated breast puffed against the wind'. (This is a persona he will adopt again and gradually grow into.) Other poems in the collection deal with love and travelling and have a relaxed and solemnly cheerful air: 'Ode to a Paperclip'; 'Ratatouille'.

The rather studiously symbolic poems of *Europa's Lover* (1982) set out to examine the tides of privilege, prejudice and imperial ambition that are European history: 'Lucid difficulties murmur / Contemplative stories of the West, / Martyrdoms, Reformations, Schisms'; but the event that was dominating Dunn's life at this time was his first wife's suffering and eventual death, in 1981, from cancer. The poems he wrote in an attempt to come to terms with Lesley's courage and his own loss were published five years later as *Elegies* (1985). It is a moving experience to read these verses as they chart the couple's history together, their mutual enjoyment of France, the unfolding of the disease, and the poet's own shaky progress in living with his grief. He complains wryly about running out of vases to hold the many flowers that are brought by friends; and there are moments when the necessary dull routines have their own symbolism, as at the Registrar's office:

> Death, too, must have looked in on our wedding.
> The building stinks of municipal function.
> 'Go through with it. You have to. It's the law.'
> So I say to a clerk, 'I have come about a death.'
> 'In there,' she says. 'You came in by the wrong door.'
> ('Arrangements')

And in the end, in 'Home Again', there is only an empty house:

> My open suitcase mocks me from the floor.
> The room is an aghast mouth. Its kiss is cold.
> I think of a piano with its lid locked
> And a carved, ivory silence in it.

Apart from their emotive power, lines like the 'aghast mouth' of the room and that 'carved ivory silence' remind us of Dunn's capacity to generate surprisingly surreal images from the quotidian objects around him. *Elegies* was widely praised and announced as Whitbread Book of the Year.

The short stories in *Secret Villages* (1985) spoke for Dunn's interest in observing people, as in *Terry Street*, with a sharp eye for the sometimes bizarre nuances of small town conventionality and behaviour. His second collection of short fiction, *Boyfriends and Girlfriends* (1995), was equally conventional in structure, taking the same delight in slyly observed Scottish middle-class and lower middle-class life. By this time Dunn had returned to Scotland and was living in Fife, with a sustaining preference for its rural landscapes along the Tay estuary and the small communities of that 'kingdom'. His next collection, *Northlight* (1988), confirms the commitment he had made to Scotland and the places where 'My accent feels at home'.

When prompted to reflect on his own roots in 1979, Dunn had this to say: 'Over the years my writing has tried to keep a promise with a

Scottish, rural working class background. It is a promise I don't remember making. What the precise nature of the promise is, I also don't know.' Nevertheless, the poems in *St Kilda's Parliament* and then those in *Northlight* were a more than sufficient clarification. *Northlight* made further explorations of Scotland's historical past including the fascination of the Picts ('Going to Aberlemno'), whose carved stones are to be found throughout the North-East, and whose history and language (in ogam inscriptions on the stones) remain completely unknown. Yet for the poet, as with 'St Kilda's Parliament', this unknowability is the point, as he imagines a 'previous Country' within the shell of modern Scotland in a perspective that calls all stable claims to identity into doubt. The question of perspective appears again in the long discursive poem 'Here and There' in which he imagines a debate with an English friend who fears that Dunn has consigned himself to a provincial backwater. The poet's answer is that from the so-called margins he can see 'civilisation' more clearly for what it is:

> You're wrong again, old friend. Your Englishness
> Misleads you into Albionic pride,
> Westminstered mockery and prejudice –
> *You're* the provincial an undignified
> Anachronism. The Pax Britannica's
> Dismissed, a second-rate Byzantium,
> Self-plundered inner empire's Age of Brass.

As if to make his point, a number of other poems in this collection look beyond Scotland to Italy, Africa and Australia, recognising, as he does in 'The War in the Congo', that the world is our parish now, haunted by echoes from other villages, and messages undelivered or undeliverable, while our leaders, like little boys, collect countries like stamps in foreign conquest or 'pacification'. From the vantage point of post-imperial Scotland, and in the light of the troubles in Northern Ireland, Dunn reflects on the role played by its humble servants ('Adventure's Oafs') the soldiers of the Crown. The danger of national pride when it seeks to exercise its muscles on the world stage was precisely the theme of his book-length poem *The Donkey's Ears* (2000), which retells the story of the Russo-Japanese War, when a Russian fleet sailed half way round the world to settle a territorial dispute with Japan only to have its ironclads ignominiously and decisively defeated at the battle of Tsushima in 1905. Dunn's interest in long poems, and his ability to produce thoughtfully discursive verses replete with researched detail and human interest, led him to imagine these events in the words of a Russian engineer writing home to his wife.

An increasing number of other poems in his later collections have taken up this extended and reflective approach, although it can slip into a rather professorial mode at times, as if we were overhearing the poet debating quietly with himself in his study. Dunn is committed to this voice, however, as a conscious contribution to the Scottish literary scene, as if to invoke Enlightenment rationality and a Horatian manner as his counter to the emotional and ethical violence of modernism and the cultural challenges of Leonard, Kelman and Welsh. In fact Dunn's poetic career can be seen – to his credit – as an exploration of his own understanding of what it is to be Scots in a creative dialogue (from a respectful but wholly different position) with the radically politicised cultural agenda that characterised MacDiarmid's early vision.

Stewart Conn (b. 1936)

Poets who have pursued a similarly humane muse include Stewart Conn, equally well known as a dramatist and BBC producer. Conn has written more than twenty plays, mostly for theatres in Edinburgh, and his productions for the Lyceum include *The Burning* (1971), which dealt with Scotland's witch trials, and *Play Donkey* (1977) about a Scottish mercenary on trial in Angola. As a poet Conn's characteristically gentle response to the world was established in his first collection *Stoats in the Sunlight* (1968), containing memorable reflections on his family and childhood on Ayrshire farms. The sequence 'Todd' remembers an uncle's skill with horses in what is in effect an elegy, not just for a way of life, but also for an earthy and unpretentious integrity of individual being. Many of Conn's poems look to the past in this way, or to landscape, seeking for a way to ground ourselves as a measure of how to live decently – always with a sense of passing time ('Family Visit'; 'To My Father'; 'Reiteration'; 'North Uist'). As alert to art as to landscape, Conn used the title-poem of *The Luncheon of the Boating Party* (1992) to enter the world of Renoir's famous painting as if it, too, were a recoverable memory or a visitable world. At the end of the sequence he has Renoir speak for him on behalf of an art of simple decency and sensuous enjoyment that will outlast its makers and its critics, reminding us 'that the eye ultimately sees / not through itself, but by some other thing'.

Tessa Ransford (b. 1938), Valerie Gillies (b. 1948) and Tom Pow (b. 1950)

Tessa Ransford was born in India and came to Scotland at the age of ten where she has lived ever since, apart from eight years in Pakistan in the 1960s where she worked as the wife of a missionary. As the founder of the Scottish Poetry Library she has made a significant contribution to the arts. Her poetry is consistently and consciously spiritual, ecological and ecumenical in its outlook with a strong sense of care for the dispossessed or the underprivileged. Valerie Gillies shows a similar concern about how we interact with the world, especially in the realm of nature, as in the sequence 'Rabbit Voices' in *Bed of Stone* (1989), and in this and subsequent collections (*The Chanter's Tune*, 1990) she shares something of Gaelic culture's sense of the interfusion of landscape, history and myth – from a broken Roman sculpture at Tweedsmuir ('The Hawkshaw Head') to the echoes of Gaelic women poets in the mouth of a singing girl ('Lullaby on a Country Bus'). The poetry of Tom Pow has shown a similarly open and direct engagement with places, people, landscape, travel and events, from his first volume *Rough Seas* (1987) to *Landscapes and Legacies* (2003). This last title is appropriate, for it catches Pow's alertness to the world around him and to the stories behind it, as he reports back, so to speak, in the subtle precision of his disciplined and tactful verse. Thus it was that many of the poems in *The Moth Trap* (1990) dealt with the hills and history of Scotland, from dry stane dykes, standing stones and modern sculpture in the sequence 'One Afternoon in Early Summer', to the myths, tales, deaths and martyrdoms of Dumfries and Galloway where the poet lives and works as Head of Creative and Cultural Studies at the Crichton campus of the University of Glasgow. Other collections go further afield and *Red Letter Day* (1996) contains poems from visits to Brazil and Peru, and the experience of Arctic Canada that produced the sequence of prose and verse 'The Hunt'. Pow's poems from Peru were gleaned from a visit there in 1989 that was recounted in prose as *In the Palace of Serpents* (1992), to give an engaging and utterly honest account of the delights and horrors awaiting the naïve traveller in a country that was descending into anarchy and terrorism.

Ron Butlin (b. 1949)

Ron Butlin was born in Edinburgh and brought up in the Borders. He left home at 16 and has made his living as an author, a journalist, a radio playwright and a writer-in-residence ever since. His first substantial collection, *Creatures Tamed by Cruelty* (1979), contained poems in both English and Scots (notably an elegy to Jimi Hendrix and a satirical commentary on *Paradise Lost*) as well as translations from French, Spanish and Chinese originals. Many of the English poems in the book have a delicate lyricism and a symbolist sensibility, as in the series 'Woman and Music', 'Woman and Stone' (another verse is called 'Anima'), or the numbered sequence of 'Fiction' poems: 'My mother and father are burning: / they rise from the fire having brought me flowers' ('Fiction No. 3'). Other poems are closer to the world of events and personal memories while still retaining a visionary element, and these show how his best work was to develop ('My Grandfather Dreams Twice of Flanders'; 'Different Moments in Piccadilly and Savignac'). *The Exquisite Instrument* (1982) sustains the poet's sense of magical suspension in a set of free translations from the Chinese, while *Ragtime in Unfamiliar Bars* (1985) continues his ability to make strange music from moments remembered when travelling abroad, or standing in the street, or talking to an absent lover on the phone ('The Night Sky, the River and the Scent of Sycamore'). There is a cheerfully surreal imagination at work in 'Preparations for a Sea Voyage' and in the title-poem, which also shows an informed fascination with music that would reach full expression in the short stories of *Vivaldi and the Number 3* (2004). The title-poem in *Histories of Desire* (1995) remembers a childhood moment splashing in a burn ('that was when the earth and sky first slipped / between my fingers') to reflect that 'all histories are histories of desire'. In fact Butlin's childhood circumstances were far from easy and his poems continue to be haunted – very indirectly – by early trauma and the death of his parents, as in 'Ryecroft', a sequence in memory of his mother's dying. ('The walls were as mist when mist disappears, / the door falling rain that no longer falls; / the corridor ran the length of the world / and she wasn't there.') The collection also contains witty and cheerful pieces, but Butlin remains essentially a poet of lyrically beautiful disturbance in a tender engagement with the world.

The same sense of disturbance, but far less affirmative and much more sinister, characterises his prose fiction. All but four of the fine short stories in *The Tilting Room* (1983) are first-person accounts and many of the narrators seem obsessive or unbalanced in oppressive circumstances. The title-story is reminiscent of how Kafka's fiction delivers detail without context, until we begin to suspect that the story itself is a 'tilting room' that has trapped us. Butlin mastered this dislocated, dislocating voice to extraordinary effect in *The Sound of My Voice*

(1997), a forensic triumph of the imagination to set beside Alasdair Gray's *1982 Janine*. In this short novel he has his protagonist use second-person locution and the present tense throughout ('You are thirty-four years old and already two-thirds destroyed') so that the reader is implicated to an almost unbearable degree in the story of Morris Magellan, a successful businessman in Thatcher's Scotland and a desperate alcoholic struggling against his need to destroy himself. Butlin's second novel *Night Visits* (1997) is even more powerful, and equally sinister in its exploration of family loss, past pain, repression, and obsession. It tells of 10-year-old Malcolm, whose father has just died, who goes to stay with his aunt Fiona who runs a nursing home for the elderly in the old family house in Edinburgh. The story is recounted from both Malcolm's and his aunt's point of view, with the boy's narrative made so much more immediate by the author's use, once again, of 'you' in a running present tense. In Fiona's Bible-ruled life, with her mysterious night visits to the bedside of a comatose old lady – and then to Malcolm – Butlin offers a vision of Scottish Presbyterian bourgeois hell, lightened only by his deeply sympathetic understanding of his characters' fear and grief and their need for peace and closure from old abuses in the past. The novel's poetic symbolism of reflections and windows and its use of motifs such as a tiny toy yacht, a compass and a piper in a snowglobe, give the story a capacity for wider significance and a more compassionate coherence than its Gothic aspects, or its links to the God-haunted Scottish tradition of Stevenson and Hogg, might at first suggest.

Liz Lochhead (b. 1948)

Liz Lochhead trained as an artist at Glasgow School of Art. Graduating in 1970 she made a brief visit to the United States before returning to Scotland where she worked as an art teacher at various schools until a Scottish–Canadian writers' exchange scheme took her to Toronto in 1978, after which she spent a year in New York. Back in Scotland again in 1980 she had a spell as writer-in-residence at Duncan of Jordanstone College of Art in Dundee and has worked in Scotland as a full-time poet and dramatist ever since. She began her commitment to verse while still an art student in Glasgow as a member of a small workshop organised by Stephen Mulrine, a poet and translator in the Liberal Arts department. On leaving college Lochhead attended some sessions with Philip Hobsbaum's writers' group, where she met James Kelman and Alasdair Gray – an older Arts School graduate who was to prove especially supportive. Lochhead was soon to join these writers, along with Tom Leonard, in the upsurge of new writing in the West of Scotland that had been heralded by Edwin Morgan. Most of the poems in *Memo for Spring* were written in the poet's student years and the collection received a Scottish Arts Council Book Award when it appeared in 1972. Lochhead's future course was clear, even in this first book, especially in her capacity to imagine dialogue and to marry relaxed and colloquial language to a strong and markedly original sense of rhythm in both formal and free-verse structures. She also uses frequent shifts of register – signalled by capitalising the initial letters in a phrase, or by using apostrophes or parentheses – to indicate a calculated ingenuousness, or an ironic aside, or the knowing use of cliché. Her work is characterised by such signifiers of what are, in effect, oral dynamics, which are especially evident when she reads her own poetry aloud. The opening of 'Box Room', making skilful use of couplets and half-rhymes, catches the wonderfully chilly welcome from a boyfriend's mother when the speaker has come to spend a weekend:

First the welcoming. Smiles all round. A space
For handshakes. Then she put me in my place –
(Oh, with concern for my comfort). 'This room
Was always his – when he comes home
It's here for him. Unless of course,' she said,
'He brings a Friend,' she smiled 'I hope the bed
Is soft enough?' . . .

One of Lochhead's first poems, 'Object', links her visual training with what was to become a central theme in her poetry. Sitting for a portrait under the eye of another artist she is all too aware that he can only pick a single point of view while 'I, love, / am capable of being looked at / from many different angles.' The tone is playful but wholly serious in its understanding of the tensions between artist and subject, ('I do not relish it, being / stated so – my edges defined / elsewhere than I'd imagined them / with a crispness I do not possess'); not least when the subject – or rather the 'object' – is a woman under the male gaze: 'I am limited. In whose likeness / do you reassemble me? / It's a fixed attitude you / force me into.' The title of the poem can now be seen to be a verb as well as a noun, and the verses end with a wry recognition (worthy of Christina Rossetti's 'In an Artist's Studio') of what art does, and also of what love does: 'But you, love, / set me down in black and white exactly. / I am at once / reduced and made more of.' Lochhead will return to the theme in this and later collections. How art can never quite capture the world is also the topic of 'Notes on the Inadequacy of a Sketch', while 'Fragmentary' looks at a cityscape of lit windows in the early evening to see 'so many / simultaneous / home movies, situation comedies, kitchen sink dramas / I can't make sense of them'. Her own situation appears in several poems dealing with the awkwardness between lovers not quite in touch with each other – separated perhaps by a more than geographical distance ('How Have I Been'; 'Morning After'; 'Getting Back'); while 'The Choosing' wonders whether we ever really choose our own lives. The poet is prompted to ask this question when she meets a fellow prize-winner from her old school, whose father did not believe in higher education for girls. Seeing Mary again ten years later, on a bus with her husband, pregnant and happy, Lochhead thinks 'of those prizes that were ours for the taking / and wonder when the choices got made / that we don't remember making'.

Memo for Spring has many such stories, from witnessing the end of a neighbour's marriage at a warrant sale ('After a Warrant Sale'), to the fading mementos of distant times and lost connections in 'Grandfather's Room'. Gradually in these poems it is the women's stories that come to the surface, especially in the contrasts between old women – often alone – and young girls with their illusions of romance culled from a world of perfume adverts and women's magazines with their advice on how to 'tangle him in your curls / and snare him with your fishnet / stockings' ('Cloakroom'). Lochhead's verses frequently show a cheerful delight in puns, but not without a sharper point. There are at least two such shifts in the closing lines of 'Cloakroom' which comment on the 'close-mouth kisses / which always / leave a lot to be desired'. Leaving a lot to be desired was the condition of teenage necking, at least in the early 1960s, but the poem makes it clear that this will also be a pattern for life; and while the word 'close' refers to the passageways at the entrance of tenement buildings, it can also be an adjective, as opposed to more desirable open-mouth kisses. The poet does not exempt herself from these sweet and tawdry enthusiasms, and in fact many of the poems in this and subsequent collections will offer ironic celebrations of what it was to be a 'desirable' woman in the years before feminism, with a more than sobering hint of the cost of such efforts, as when the poem 'Wedding March' ends with a promise that has more than a hint of desperation:

> I'll watch our tangled undies bleaching clean
> In the humdrum of the laundromat machine.
> I'll take my pet dog vacuum on its daily walk through rooms.

And knowing there is no clean sweep,
keep busy still with brooms.

The 'humdrum' of the spin drier is particularly well chosen, while walking a vacuum cleaner like a pet dog is at once an entertaining – if rather sad – conceit, with a darker suggestion that this woman's married life does indeed revolve around a quotidian vacuum. Lochhead took her exploration of the female condition much further in *The Grimm Sisters* (1981). Via its reference to the Märchen of the Brothers Grimm, this collection makes a subtle exploration of the points at which the sometimes frightening psychological complexities of sexuality and identity meet and collide with the shallow stereotypes of gender difference. Thus the poem 'The Grim Sisters' remembers those older girls who initiated teenagers into the mysteries of womanhood ('Wasp waist and cone breast') in the early 1960s. Lochhead enjoys nostalgic references to Radio Luxembourg (once the only source of broadcast pop music in Britain) and the period detail of beauty hints, 'Those days womanhood was quite a sticky thing.' But she also gives these 'sisters' a comically sinister and witch-like cast by referring to their 'mantrap' handbags containing 'hedgehog hairbrushes / cottonwool mice and barbed combs to tease', while their spiked heels collect 'dead leaves'. In effect the *Grimm Sisters* poems set out to re-examine, if not to deconstruct, familiar myths, legends and fairy stories from a female point of view. (Carol Ann Duffy was to take a similar line in her 1999 collection *The World's Wife.*) Thus the stories of Snow White, the furies, 'Rapunzelstiltskin', Beauty and the Beast, the ballad of Tam Lin, Ariadne and the clichés of 'bawd' and 'harridan' are revisited in an exploration of the many roles expected of women in such tales, only to be comically subverted, inverted or made fully strange again by Lochhead's poetry. The traditional constructions of femininity are seen as further examples of 'the choices we don't remember making', although the poems also recognise a certain complicity in our romantic attachment to them, not least by way of the continuing hope that a loving partner will make us better. (This is reminiscent of a finely ironic line in the early poem 'After a Warrant Sale' – 'But I am very young, / expecting not too much of love – / just that it should completely solve me.') In a volume of interviews with Scottish and Irish female writers (*Sleeping with Monsters*, 1990) Lochhead acknowledged that 'I'm interested in exploring issues without apportioning blame. I'm interested in female masochism, for instance. I suppose it's a feminist issue, but it's also a human issue.' In this respect she sees women and men both entangled by the inherited rituals of courtship and the commercial pressures to be 'attractive'. Lochhead does not simplify the outcome in what she sees as a shifting mutual balance between hopes, false hopes, exploitation and surrender.

A divided female self and all the ambivalences of sexual desire and resentment are invoked in 'The Other Woman' who 'lies / the other side of my very own mirror'; while the difficult relationship between mothers and daughters is the subject of 'Everybody's Mother', whose syntactically tangled last line enacts exactly the confused, stifled and stifling emotions at stake:

> [so] what if your mother did
> float around above you
> big as a barrage balloon
> blocking out the light?

> Nobody's mother can't not never do nothing right.

The erotic idealisation of the 'Song of Solomon' is revisited in the poem of that name, which recognises that the fragrant oils and myrrh of the original have been replaced in modern times by herbal shampoos and deodorants, not quite enough perhaps to mask 'the whiff of / sourmilk from her navel / the curds of cheese between the toes', until 'she banged shut her eyes / and hoped he would not smell her fear'. The fear invoked in this last line refers to so much more than the small embarrassments of personal hygiene. Lochhead has understood that the subtexts to many fairy stories are much darker than we allow and she uses them to invoke the complexities of living with another person and to make our domestic life doubly estranged – as with the man at work and his wife at home in the kitchen: 'In your innocent ticking fridge / I might find the forbidden egg / crowned with blood' ('Blueshirt'). Or there are the closing lines of 'Beauty & the' that promise soon 'Yes, sweet Beauty, you'll / match him / horror for horror'; or the mother who wakes up to her marriage feeling like a stage conjurer's stooge: 'I volunteered. It was / all my own idea to come up here. / I smile & smile & smile to show my rage' ('Stooge Song').

These themes, with echoes of knightly romance tales, spells and legends, were continued in several of the poems in the volume *Dreaming Frankenstein* (1984), which also reprinted work from *Memo for Spring* and *Islands* (1978). Lochhead's interest in the psychological – even psychoanalytical – undercurrents of Märchen and Gothic fiction had led her to write a play based on *Frankenstein* using Mary Shelley's initial 'conception' of the monstrous as an additional factor in a novel that was already a critique of patriarchal arrogance and science's usurpation of nature and the womb. *Blood and Ice* (1982) was not very successful on its first performance as a play (it has since been revised) but it contains passages of very striking poetic force. In the poem 'Dreaming Frankenstein', Lochhead's continuing fascination with the theme touches on theoretically challenging questions to do with who owns language, which Lacan, Cixous and Kristeva would claim to be a wholly patriarchal ('phallogocentric') sign system. If this is the case, then the female poet's muse may well be a male monster in what has always been the terror and the mystery of inspiration:

> She said she
> woke up with him in
> her head, in her bed.
> Her mother-tongue clung to her mouth's roof
> in terror, dumbing her, and he came with a name
> that was none of her making.

The poem 'Mirror's Song' offers a nightmare version of double identity in overtly feminist terms as a woman struggles to escape her own reflection in society's expectations, to smash her 'looking-glass glass / coffin' and emerge as 'a woman giving birth to herself'. The utter otherness of sexual attraction and release is explored in 'What the Pool Said, On Midsummer's Day', in which a pool by a stream, having seduced the woman on a hot day, now calls on the man to risk immersion, surrender, extinction as well: 'The woman was easy. / Like to like, I called her, she came.' The poem's sexual innuendos are clear – 'I watch. You clench, / clench and come into me' – but even so, this is an alien place fully owned by neither partner, although more difficult, perhaps, for men to trust. (Similar themes were to be revisited in Lochhead's next two plays.) Other poems are less intense, enjoying bittersweet memories of schooldays in Scotland, or dealing warmly with friends, relationships and the experience of places – including a visit to Canada and the United States ('In Alberta'; 'Fourth of July Fireworks'). Lochhead's most recent collection, *The Colour of Black & White* (2003), continues in this more personal and reflective vein, looking back to the 1960s, or to her parents' time in the war or post-war years, as well as dedicating poems to friends and fellow artists, including Carol Ann Duffy, Jackie Kay and Edwin Morgan.

The lively poetry-reading circuit of the later 1970s gave Liz Lochhead much experience of public reading and she is a consummate performer of her own work. She developed these skills in *Sugar and Spite* – a performance event she shared with Marcella Evaristi at the Traverse Theatre in 1978, and in subsequent years she has written and taken part in numerous humorous and satirical revues, such as *Tickly Mince* (1982); *The Pie of Damocles* (1983) and *Nippy Sweeties* (1985), shared with actors and other writers, including Alasdair Gray, James Kelman and Tom Leonard. Lochhead's ear for the telling banality and her skill with idiomatic speech produced highly entertaining dramatic exchanges, songs, raps and character monologues. Many of these were collected in the volume *True Confessions and New Clichés* (1985), including the memorable reminiscences of 'Verena', a fuller realisation of that woman taking her vacuum cleaner for a walk. Lochhead's ability to inhabit such *personae*, her fascination with the darker aspects of sexuality and identity and her pleasure in colloquially expressive language all come together in her work for the theatre, most especially in *Dracula* (1985), which is haunted by beautiful images, and the theatrical *tour de force* of *Mary Queen of Scots Got Her Head Chopped Off* (1987).

For Lochhead, the story of Scotland's most romantically doomed queen is only the starting point for a deeper examination of the national psyche and then, beyond that, an exploration of the Dionysian drives of sexuality and mortal desire. The poet's interest in sexual politics is doubly relevant to a time in history when England and Scotland were both so caught up in the political ramifications of female sovereignty (and the play has a lively grasp of the dynastic issues at stake), but this is not its final focus. Instead, and in order to reach the psychic heart of the matter, Lochhead conflates time and space so that John Knox can be the author of his famous *First Blast of the Trumpet* on the unfitness of women to rule, or a school bully in the playground, or (most tellingly of all) a bowler-hatted Protestant bigot in a modern-day Orange March. In the same spirit, the play conflates Elizabeth and Mary as sisters under the skin, making brilliant use of the economic realities of casting by having the same actor play both Mary's husband Darnley (groomed by the English Queen for this role) and Elizabeth's lover Leicester. The oddly incestuous echoes of this arrangement are reinforced when the actresses become, in a sense, each other's doubles, for Elizabeth plays Mary's servant 'Bessie' when the scenes are in Scotland, while Mary plays 'Marian' as Elizabeth's servant in the south. In a time of stress Marian comforts Elizabeth 'like a child'; and when Bothwell seduces Bessie, a sexual thrill runs through Mary like an electric shock. Elizabeth has been damaged by her father's treatment of her mother ('Don't want – I want – Don't want to be Daddy's little princess'), while an orgasmic moment between Mary and the brutally sexual Bothwell reaches a climax with the huge explosion that kills Darnley at Kirk o' Field. Issues of sexuality and violence and damaged masculinity are foregrounded at every turn. The actresses playing the two queens (or the servants of the two queens) also play children in a modern playground, as well as teenage urchins in Knox's Edinburgh who are rather over-heatedly chastised by the old man as whores of Babylon: 'Wi' yer lang hair lik' a flag in the wind an advertisement o' lust tae honest men an' they big roon een lik' a dumb animal. . . . Ah'll leave the rid mark o' ma haun on your white flesh afore Ah – . . .'

Scotland's record of patriarchal severity in the Reformation and the oppression of the witch trials is fair game for such comment, but in the last analysis the play goes behind the national condition to explore the universally deeper and darker drives of power and desire. Nevertheless, the whole drama is introduced and driven along by 'La Corbie', a ragged figure from the collective unconscious of the Scottish ballads, a circus-mistress of misrule speaking broad Scots and wielding a whip, under whose lash the actors, playing the great and the good, can only skip and gape like Dunbar's dance of the deadly sins. Indeed there is something of Dunbar's technical brilliance and cruel glamour to this extraordinary play, which adds a powerfully dark, even a psychoanalytical dimension to the vigour of the Scots language and the kind of historical subject that the earlier dramas of Robert McLellan (*Jamie the Saxt*) and Alexander Reid (*The Warld's Wonder*) had treated so differently.

Lochhead's engagement with the theatre and with the dramatic use of Scots had been early evident in her translation of Molière's *Tartuffe* (1986), which drew on a fully contemporary Scots idiom (as well as the national enjoyment of pantomime) to considerable popular success. Since then she has done more and more rewarding work in the theatre with a succession of scripts and plays for different theatre companies in Scotland and England (e.g. *Them Through the Wall*, with Agnes Owens, 1989; *Britannia Rules*, *Perfect Days*, both 1998), as well as sketches and translations, most notably her Scots version of Euripides' *Medea* for Theatre Babel in 2000 and Molière again for the Lyceum in 2002, this time set in the new Scottish Parliament as *Misery Guts* (*Le Misanthrope*).

The consistent power of Lochhead's work in both poetry and drama is to be found in her mastery of the rhythm, vigour and expressive energy of the speaking colloquial voice. Her commitment to her native idiom (whether in broad Scots or Scottish English) has been unforced and generous, and if she lacks the fiercer political agenda of James Kelman and Tom Leonard, it is not because she is unaware of the issues at stake. Her dual-language poem 'Kidspoem / Bairnsang' reflects on an education that taught her to write prize-winning essays in a language quite different from how she spoke:

> Oh saying it was one thing
> but when it came to writing it
> in black and white
> the way it had to be said
> was as if you were posh, grown-up, male, English and dead.

The poem describes a loving mother wrapping her child up warmly before going to school on a 'gey dreich' or 'really dismal' day. The socio-political point is well made by repeating the tale three times, in Scots, English and then Scots again. The affection of the description is plain in either language but the poem's impact comes when we realise that the second telling in Scots is what the school will teach her to 'learn to forget to say'.

Tom Leonard (b. 1944)

Tom Leonard made his name as a passionate opponent of the social discrimination that so often comes with local accents and speaking your mother tongue, and in this respect his poems anticipated the socio-political case James Kelman was soon to make for his narratives in prose. Leonard graduated from Glasgow University in the early 1970s and has made his living as a writer ever since. In 1993 he published *Places of the Mind*, a definitive study of the poet James Thomson. He is currently Professor of Creative Writing at his home University, a post originally shared with Kelman and Gray, both of whom he met while he was a student. Leonard's first collection *Six Glasgow Poems* (1969) created a stir by its fearless use of Glasgow urban speech in a phonetic spelling that catches the rhythms and nuances of actual utterance when read aloud, but which seems radically estranged on the page in its written form. One effect of this is to make the educated English speaker 'illiterate' again as he or she struggles to decode the printed word. By this means the poem becomes a spell against complacency and a retaliatory act against what Leonard sees as the educational establishment's intolerance of local (and working-class) expression and experience.

These six poems were a manifesto by example, the first of which, 'The Good Thief', was doubly determined to challenge convention by imagining what one of the two thieves crucified beside Christ might have said to the Lord: 'heh jimmy / yawright ih / stull wayiz urryi / ih' while wondering if he was a Catholic ('ma right insane yirra pape') and regretting a missed football match. The closing poem, 'Good Style', could not be more direct in its use of a voice and spelling that is so often regarded as 'bad' style, starting with an apparently sympathetic concession: 'hulluva hard tay read theez init', only to follow with 'if yi canny unnirston thim jiss clear aff then / gawn / get tay fuck ootma road'. The closing lines draw on a different meaning of 'style' to end with a direct threat: 'stick thi bootnyi good style / so ah wull'. In fact Leonard's poems often seem to be fully dramatic expressions – 'spoken' by hilariously rowdy girls in 'A Scream', or by savagely violent youths in 'No Light'. The disturbingly direct challenge of such aggression is a reminder that contempt begets contempt and another warning against cultural complacency, and this residue of rage in many of Leonard's poems gives the directness of their verbal address an almost physical impact. In a more tender mood the poem 'Fathers and Sons' is a recognition (in English) of the gulfs that education can open up within a family: 'I remember being ashamed of my father / when he whispered the words out loud / reading the newspaper.' Such shame can shame us all, and anger is never far away.

The poet's most explicit explorations on the theme of dispossession appeared in *Intimate Voices* (1984) with poems such as 'this is thi / six a clock / news', now widely anthologised and remembered for its preference for a BBC accent because:

        . . . if
    a toktaboot
    thi truth
    lik wanna yoo
    scruff yi
    widny thingk
    it wuz troo.

In the poem 'right inuff / ma language is disgraceful', the speaker reflects on the many people who have told him this, including language scholars who prefer a 'purer' form of Scots. The poem concludes with another blunt riposte: 'Ach well / all living language is sacred / fuck thi lohta thim.' Leonard has frequently declared his admiration for the patterns of breath, rather than metre, in the poetry of William Carlos

Williams, and his own commitment to 'living language' has to do with paying attention to how words actually sound in the mouths of the people around him. In this context he sees himself as a man committed to the local, and after that to the international, with little affection for nationalism and none for the early modern Renaissance's hopes for lowland Scots as a standard national tongue.

In fact Leonard sees institutionalised education as nothing less than an ideological apparatus in the service of the state – a view that has much in common with the critical theorist Louis Althusser, whose essay on 'Ideology and the State' was published in 1969. The poet's critique begins with the commodification of poetry in the classroom:

> I see 'English Literature' exams in schools and universities as central anti-creative rites in which Art is turned into property and students compelled to be witnessed in an act of acquisition.
>
> ('Poetry, Schools, Place' in *Reports from the Present*, 1995)

Then he looked at who decides what is and is not 'literature'. During his time as writer-in-residence at Paisley Public Library, Leonard edited a large collection of radical poetry, from the French Revolution to the Great War, most of which was local and almost none of which had ever appeared in any anthologies or Scottish literary histories. The introduction to *Radical Renfrew* (1990) makes clear his quarrel with the canon-makers and his resentment at the marginalisation of so many local and proletarian voices.

Janice Galloway has recalled her own sense of being made to feel that 'my language didn't make sense, was uneducated or stupid' and she suggested an affinity here with race prejudice so that somehow she 'signalled not through my skin but through my mouth that I was not capable of True Understanding of Culture. Something about my people, in a less blatant way, showed that we were "slave" class – fit to be grouse-beaters, crofters and soldiers.' In their prose fiction Archie Hind, Gordon Williams and William McIlvanney, from an earlier generation of writers, all made similar points, while Douglas Dunn, Liz Lochhead and Jackie Kay have all written poems about their own encounters with prejudice at school according to how they spoke. In their book *The Eclipse of Scottish Culture* (1989) Craig Beveridge and Ronald Turnbull cited the early postcolonial theories of Martinique-born French critic Franz Fanon to explain how this process of inferiorisation has been utilised on a larger scale to persuade native intellectuals to denigrate their own culture. If Fanon's observation is applied to questions of region and class, rather than national identity, then the socio-political grounding of Kelman's and Leonard's writing becomes clear. It is striking that such feelings of inferiorisation should be so prevalent in a culture that once prided itself on its democratic intellect, although of course a sensitivity about speaking Scots and using 'Scotticisms' can be traced back to the Union of the Parliaments and the universalising agenda of the Scottish Enlightenment. In modern times, in the industrial and post-industrial cities of central Scotland, the same sensitivity too often associates the use of Scots dialect or working-class speech with ignorance or poverty or with a long-standing prejudice against Irish immigrants. For some Scottish writers such experience has generated an especially intense engagement with language use and how it corresponds to the structures of power in society, even as they themselves negotiate the many different registers of vernacular speech and formal written English. As Leonard notes:

My work is made up of different voices: some high register English, some very low register, some written in phonetic dialect, some very formal, and some very informal. So I've *had* to have different voices in my work, because I have different voices in my life. I didn't have an abiding or what I would call a 'colonising narrative'. My cultural experience is made up of different voices: the voice I would have when I was (as I said) writing my English essays, or the voice that I would have when I was speaking in the house. These are two completely different voices. If, as an artist, I wanted to represent these voices, if I was to use my own culture, or if I was to try and make art of my cultural experience, I *had* to use different voices.

This plurality of literary voices is exactly what modern Scottish literature has brought to the British or indeed the international literary scene, from MacDiarmid, Gibbon and Garioch to Kelman, Lochhead, Leonard and many more. As a result many Scottish poets feel free to write in different languages as well as different registers of the same language. Thus it is that poets such as Crawford, Herbert, Kinloch and Jamie, all of whom write in English, can also write poems in Scots, or poems which contain Scots, without necessarily subscribing to the overtly nationalist agendas associated with the use of Lallans in the opening decades of the century.

Robert Crawford (b. 1959)

Robert Crawford is a professor and distinguished literary critic at the University of St Andrews. Born in Belshill in Lanarkshire, he went to Glasgow University and has written that it was his time as a research student in Oxford (working on the poetry of T. S. Eliot) that 'made me think hard about what and how much it meant to me to be Scottish. I wanted to write a poetry that relied on Scottish resources, without undue chauvinism and with a sense of humour.' This is exactly what he accomplished in his first collections *A Scottish Assembly* (1990) and *Talkies* (1992), which share something of Edwin Morgan's optimism, as well as the older poet's witty delight in technology and eclectic references. The poem 'Scotland', for example, celebrates the native land as a 'micro-nation', a 'Semiconductor country . . . crammed with intimate expanses', and it is interesting to note that here the small size of the nation is seen as a source of power and strength, when an earlier poet like Alan Jackson could only see 'Scotland the wee' as a tired measure of infantile sentimentality. Not that Crawford is uncritical, for 'The Land o' Cakes' satirises the exploitation of Scotland's resources as well as the country's willing commodification of the clichés of identity – both seen as a species of gluttony:

> Bens ran with venison. Green straths ripened with grouse.
> In the Highlands people didn't use knives and forks. They were cleared like
> a table
> To make way for shortbread.

Crawford's witty commitment to a Scotland beyond the essentialist stereotypes of national identity shines through these collections. His poetry is packed with a playful energy, often signalled by his liking for a certain linguistic density, idiosyncratic Scottish place names and puns. His is a constantly referential muse, engaged with past histories and personalities, new metaphors, unlikely (even surreal) flights of learned fancy and out-of-the-way facts, all recounted with an undisguised intellectual glee. Thus 'The Declaration of Arbroath', 'Insignia' and 'Hostilities' re-imagine Scottish history to produce alternative versions of the nation's prized myths:

> Accusing the D. C. Thomson group of continuing to hold the national mind intellectual hostage, the Scottish fleet has commenced its bombardment of Dundee.
>
> . . .
>
> At the Glasgow School of Art an outbreak of typhoid has been traced to tinned produce carrying cooking instructions in Scots and Gaelic.
>
> ('Hostilities')

In *Sharawaggi* (1990), Crawford took on the Scots language with similar irreverence. This was a dual collection in collaboration with a fellow Oxford graduate, the Dundee-born W. N. Herbert, in which the two poets construct a melange of urban Scots and dictionary invention to produce densely muscular and stilted lines that defy any musical rendition and make no claims to folk sources or lyric beauty. The project had started in 1985 with *Sterts and Stobies* (since included in the later volume) and their agenda was declared in Crawford's early poem 'Ghetto-Blastir', whose title alludes to both raucous modern music and the cultural 'ghetto' inhabited by professional Scotsmen:

Ghetto-makars, tae the knackirs'	Scots poets
Wi aw yir schemes, yir smug dour dreams	
O yir ain feet,	

. . .

. . . See us? We're foon	found

Wi whit's new, wi aw that's speerin oot	questioning
An cummin hame tae roost, set the feathers	
Flyin in yir kailyard.	

. . .

. . . we're grabbin

Whit's left o the leid tae mak anither sang	language

In the latter part of the book the poets interrogate the concept of translation (and translatability) by having poems in Scots where the foot of the page glossary is at least as long as the poem itself, or by offering a facing-page English version of an extremely dense Scots 'original' while making sure that neither account was by any means easy to read or understand. Thus the opening sentence of 'Fur thi Muse o Synthesis' is as follows:

Interkat intercommuner, intercommunin
At aw leid's interfaces, skeich
Tae interpone a hooch that intermells
An interverts auld jorrams tae reconduct
Aureat thru lingua franca, intercommoun
Thru joie-de-vivre-wurds, guttir thru dicitonar, it's yirsel's
Thi ane I T, thi richt wurdbank, fettle
Thru thi hert's printoot, wi'oot figmalirie tae spairge
Or jevel thi speerit.

Clearly this is not in any way colloquial Scots, and if an early complaint about MacDiarmid and his fellow makars in 'synthetic Scots' was that they had 'swallowed a dictionary', modern readers might be forgiven for suspecting that the dictionary has swallowed Crawford – except that this was precisely what the two poets were aiming for, in writing a poetry that set out to intensify, to the utmost possible degree, the already inevitable 'estrangement' of using the Scots language in a largely English-speaking world. Yet the formal English version is no happier:

> Intricate negotiator between factions at variance, having intercourse at all language's interfaces, apt to startlingly interpose a cry of joy that intermingles and appropriates to a new, unfamiliar use old slow, melancholy boatsongs to reconduct high diction through common speech, the language of conversation through exclamations of delight, gutter through dictionary, it's you who are the only Information Technology, the true word-bank, speech-energy through the heart's printout, without whim to spatter or joggle the spirit.

At one level this reads like a parody of MacDiarmid's diction in his later world-language poems, and certainly one gets a sense of a younger poet daring at last to twist the lion's tail in such writing. But at another level, the poem makes a serious claim for a muse of synthesis that will 'reconduct high diction through common speech' and bring the dictionary and the gutter closer to one another through 'speech energy' and a delight in what MacDiarmid called 'adventuring in dictionaries . . . / Among the débris of all past literature / And raw material of all the literature to be' ('The World of Words', *In Memoriam James Joyce*). Crawford and Herbert have robust fun with their method (the volume includes a traditional flyting between them) but the 'strangeness' of Scots and the estrangement of language itself are profound themes, and ones that will prove central to the more lyrical vision of the poet David Kinloch.

More recent collections *Masculinity* (1996); *Spirit Machines* (1999) and *The Tip of My Tongue* (2003), continue to entertain and engage readers with what Crawford has called – with justification – his 'evolving vision of a multilingual, pluralist Scotland'. *The Tip of My Tongue* contains love-poems as well as a further use of Scots words like 'flauchters' and 'shoogles' – those 'English-Scots-Gaelic hailstones' that identify us. 'Chaps' from *Masculinity* recognises the complicity between manliness and imperial aggression – and Scotland's role in that project:

With his Bible, his Burns, his brose and his baps
Colonel John Buchan is one of the chaps,
With his mother, his mowser, his mauser, his maps,
Winston S. Churchill is one of the chaps.

Crawford is expert at such high-energy games, but these volumes also contain more personal poems – if indirectly so – like the 'Spirit Machines' poem sequence in memory of his banker father; or an uncle's funeral in the wry melancholy of 'Old Tunnockians'; or 'Bereavement', which is a quiet and finely oblique meditation on death and loss. In the best of these poems Crawford's technologically heated imagination leads to a more profound metaphor in which the phrase 'spirit machines' (which might be taken to refer to the human condition, after all) is also applied to the invisible transactions of value that lie behind the exchange and accounting of money (his banker father again), or to the information technology by which we commit our words, memories and images to old tape recorders or the digital inscription of CD ROMs and hard drives. It is an unexpected but strikingly apposite metaphor for whatever it is that makes us something other than merely material bodies.

W. N. Herbert (b. 1961)

The dynamic Scots of *Sharawaggi* owed a lot to the poetic vision of W. N. Herbert, whose commitment to a Scots tongue of crammed lexical energy and surprising juxtapositions has been absolute. Born in Dundee, once regarded as the shabbiest of Scotland's larger cities and still burdened with its image as the home of jute, jam, journalism and McGonagall, Herbert has remained faithful to his family roots and to the history and achievements of his home town. Educated at Oxford – where he met Robert Crawford – Herbert currently lectures on creative writing and contemporary Scottish poetry at the University of Newcastle. He has given himself to writing in Scots more thoroughly and more daringly than any other contemporary poet. In the 'Author's Note' to his early collection *Dundee Doldrums* (1991) he realised that neither MacDiarmid's rural form of Scots, nor the Scots of the Makars, nor the modern Renaissance's hopes for a standard Lallans were really available to him, and yet 'the fact that I spoke an urban Scots as a child became immensely significant to me'. Inspired by the energy, confidence and verbal extroversion of Kerouac and Ginsberg, Herbert set out to find a voice of his own that might find space to operate 'somewhere in the gap between Garioch's urban poetry and that of, say, Tom

Leonard' but without what he saw as 'the aggression in Leonard's *personae*'. The final piece of the puzzle was his discovery of the Scots dictionary as a way of freeing the imagination and in a sense super-charging the basic urban demotic of his boyhood's 'playground voice'. The resulting 'Dundee Doldrums' visited the blighted streets and backlands and the raw concrete reconstructions of Dundee in the 1970s with a linguistic intensity that expressed rage at the city's history of cultural and economic decline and now brutal expansion:

> thi cheenge huz cum ower thum.
> Pubs o shite: glessy Amerikan waas replacing
> dreich American waas, auld stickirs;   miserable
> Hell spat intae nicht, hammirt phlegm,   drunken
> meditatin lack o money, joabs,
> no meditatin lack o luv, fear o daith;
> laithin ilk ithir an wir ain shabby thochts.   loathing each other
> An the thri estates: council, prehvut and thi ownirs' manshuns:
> aa the semm, aa waasht by thi cheenge.
> Tay huz owerfluddit,   (River Tay)
> bile o Noarth sea, choakt oan ships an ileymen   oilmen
>   ('6th Doldrum')

And yet the energy of the language – even the strength of disgust in such poems – almost becomes a kind of celebration of what the poet called, on the title page of the collection, 'an exorcism'. Unlike Tom Leonard (who does not use a Scots lexis at all), Herbert's phonetic spelling contains many words from the Scots dictionary, although the final effect is not entirely colloquial in a discourse that occasionally forces you to halt (as the poet himself admits) to decode a line. Some of Herbert's words are obscure compounds like 'hoolyhide' (membra-nous skin); some are pressed into new contexts and some are constructed compounds like 'snaaflinders' (a mixture of ash and snow), while others – still seemingly Scots – are neologisms like 'aasamied' (all the same); or darkly phonetic English like 'enchenned' (enchained) or simply very obscure English like 'apterous' (wingless). Such density had not been seen since MacDiarmid's early *tour de force* of magical incantatory Scots in 'Gairmscoile' – seeking 'Coorse words that shamble thro' oor minds like stots [bullocks], / syne turn on's muckle een wi' doonsin emerauds lit.'

The relationship between place, language and identity is one of the themes in the collection *Forked Tongue* (1994), which contained new poems in both Scots and English, and selections from earlier volumes. Herbert explained the title and his position as follows:

To be Scottish is to experience suppressed contrasts; it may be between your lifestyle and that of the affluent South, it may be between your speech patterns and the pervasive norm of standard English. Unlike Ireland, Scotland is not supposed to be 'different' or 'foreign'. It is the country which is not a country, possessing a language which is not really a language. To use English or Scots, then, seems to cover up some aspect of our experience, to 'lie'. The truth about Scotland, perhaps, can only be situated between the dominant and suppressed parts of language, in the region of the forked tongue.

'Other Tongues' (one of the English poems in the sequence 'The Cortina Sonata') considers the strangenesses of language and travel during a holiday on Corfu ('Other tongues try to shove their fierce / red meat of difference down your / throat'). In an imagined dialogue with a pebble (perhaps a symbol of Demosthenes and hard-won eloquence) the poet ends by realising that when he returns home he, too, has 'another tongue in my head / the like of which it's never heard'. The poem 'Pictish Whispers' invokes the strata of time and difference that lie across the borders between countries and across our own voices, as old vowels and echoes from a past way of speaking invade our present utterance, collecting 'like Pictish whispers, beneath / such incongruities as language can detect.' (And Pictish whispers, after all, like Chinese whispers might be open to misinterpretation or misappropriation.) Many of the poems in this collection reflect on the instabilities of travel and culture in Greece and Italy, along with memories of home, especially in 'The Beano Elegies', a recollection of the wonder of childhood comics (published by D. C. Thomson in Dundee) that becomes a moving elegy for dead family members and lost innocence. The poet recognises, as he did in 'Pictish Whispers', that 'the act of translation is always with us'. The sequence 'Ticka Ticka' mixes fond personal memories with angry recollections of exploitation in the radical history of Dundee as the poet recalls the closure of the Timex factory where his father worked for thirty years, as he himself did in his teenage summers. The sequence begins and ends with a beautiful 'Temporal ode' addressed to Time itself:

> Time you prove to me that trash
> can become precious, because it shows
> our brittle workings can endure, the dream
> of personality survive a little while.
> Time you turn the dog's head to a skull,
> you make my joke a penance to presumption,
> you do not mind looking ridiculous
> as long as one day you may eat me
> as you will.

Herbert uses the phrase 'Pictish whispers' again as the collective title for two sequences in his collection of wholly English poems *The Testament of the Reverend Thomas Dick* (1994). Here again the phrase refers to how echoes from the past inhabit the present, but this time applied to poems referring to figures from ancient culture and legend (among others, Ariadne, Noah, Judith and Holofernes) or from more recent historical times (J. S. Haldane, John Davidson, Hart Crane), yet all are also combined with contemporary references. The collection's title sequence remembers Thomas Dick, a nineteenth-century astronomer from Dundee who aimed to reconcile science and religion, but Herbert's capricious muse doesn't hesitate to include references to Rilke, Jean Tinguely, the planet Zog, Garbo and Buster Keaton. Indeed Keaton has a fine sequence of his own in 'A Dream of Buster Keaton', the lines of which brilliantly catch something of the spectral nature of Keaton's face and the disturbing comedy of those so-silent gags:

> The silence has left me. The silence is inside me.
> It has made a dark journey across the words
> to be within me. The silence is only the shadows.
> Now I have to make the moves that expel it.

Herbert rarely writes conventional lyrics but the quieter focus of such writing has produced some of his best poetry.

The well-named *Cabaret McGonagall* (1996) returns to the carnival with poems in Scots and English again, along with every kind of reference to popular culture, high art, ancient history, ballads and parodies. This imaginative hyper-drive includes 'Why the Elgin Marbles Must Be Returned to Elgin', 'Tarzan Visits Highland Region'; 'Ode to Scotty' (of *Star Trek* fame), and 'The Third Corbie' – who might well be Herbert's true mischievous muse. Here, as in so much of his work, Herbert is determined to revisit the stereotypes of Scotland in order to celebrate them in a cheerfully satirical but finally affirmative fashion:

> Surely those figures eating fried egg rolls
> behind the glass of Italian cafés
> are the philosophers of the Enlightenment.
> Surely that is Susan Ferrier gossiping
> outside the crappy dress shop
> with Margaret Oliphant. Surely
> Robert Burns is buying a haggis supper
> from that chipper in Annan,

William Dunbar is stotting from
The Cement-Mixer's Arms.
('The Postcards of Scotland')

The long title-poem of *The Laurelude* (1998) conflates Wordsworth's *Prelude* with the life of Stan Laurel, who was born near Ulverton, and although the concept seems characteristically surreal and even contrived, Herbert's blank verse produces moving passages, in strange echoes and reflections from the prior text – Pictish whispers indeed.

David Kinloch (b. 1959)

Herbert's enjoyment of all kinds of information and his fascination with abstruse Scots words is shared by David Kinloch, and indeed an article in 1991 by the poet and editor Richard Price (b. 1966) suggested that these two poets and Crawford, along perhaps with Alan Riach (b. 1957) and Peter McCarey (b. 1956), might be called 'Scottish informationists' because of the wide range of arcane references that invade and cross-pollinate their verses, and their enthusiasm for the new technologies of the 'information age'. Talking of MacDiarmid's later poetry in a recent interview with Price, David Kinloch admired the older poet's 'enthusiasm for information of the most diverse kinds', as well as his use of Scots and 'the way he miraculously re-ignites words long thought dead and forgotten'. In these respects it is tempting to see the spoor of MacDiarmid in the work of the young 'informationists' and in fact both Herbert, Riach and McCarey completed doctorates on his work. On the other hand they are equally familiar with modern American verse, especially the work of John Ashbery, Frank O'Hara and the more extreme strategies of the l=a=n=g=u=a=g=e poets; and equally telling links can be made between their work and Edwin Morgan's eclecticism or W. S. Graham's fascination with the abstractions of language. These poets are all very different, of course, but if there is a common denominator between them, it lies in their willingness to recognise verse as a literary or linguistic construction that can be made to go beyond the conventionally Romantic understanding of poetry as the utterance of a lyrically fluent and singular poetic identity. As a scholar of French language and literature, Kinloch is particularly fascinated by the *difference* of other tongues (not to say the Saussurean arbitrariness of language itself) and has come to be 'suspicious of any kind of expression that makes a claim to "naturalness"'. As with Herbert and Crawford, this explains his interest in Scots as a language that is simultaneously familiar and different, both within and without conventional society, as it operates somewhere in the gap between colloquial utterance in the street and the most abstruse dictionary researches. For Kinloch in particular this in-betweenness becomes a powerful metaphor for his own creative and sexual identity:

> I like that feeling of simultaneous nearness and distance partly because it echoes how I feel about the Scots language . . . and also on a much more general level because it speaks to what it feels like to live in 'straight' society as a gay man.

This was the theme of his first book *Dustie-fute* (1992), which contains a number of fine prose-poems in which the speaking 'I' finds itself in Paris, symbolised as a 'dustie-fute' or 'rintherout', meaning a pedlar, a wandering mountebank or a vagrant – looking back to old Scots words to catch something that is both familiar and alien:

> These words are as foreign as the city they have parachuted into, dead words slipping on the sill of a living metropolis. They are extremes that touch like dangerous wires and the only hope for them, for us, is the space they inhabit. . . . Old Scots word, big French city and in between abysmal me: ane merchand or creamer, quha hes no certain dwelling place, quhair the dust may be dicht fra hes feete or schone.

In a conscious act of homage to MacDiarmid's example – although in an entirely different mode – Kinloch's prose-poems meditate on the strangenesses of place, language and meaning via old Scots words from Jamieson's dictionary ('Dustie-fute'; 'John Jamieson's First Billy-Goat Primer'; 'Gurliewhurkie'). Dense and demanding, his poems yet manage a tender music of their own as they invoke both what he sees as the 'shared rootedness' of language and its impossibility. The poem 'Dustie-fute' finds him 'at a loss in the empty soul of his ancestors' beautiful language and in the soulless city of his compeers living the 21st century now'. He wonders if his poetic interest in texts and mean-ings is not 'medieval' and asks: 'Does the "auld alliance" of words and things stand a chance among the traffic and pimps in the Publicis Saint-Germain?' In his interview with Price, Kinloch remembered that 'that experience of foreignness touched or duplicated a much deeper sense of difference and enabled me to explore and express aspects of my sexu-ality which I had been unprepared or unable to articulate until that point'. Indeed, as the poems in the collection unfold he comes to speak more and more clearly about a friend dying of AIDS, using the remark-able public project of the AIDS Quilt as a recurring symbol of care, memory and creation in the face of extinction. He returned to this theme in the collection *Paris-Forfar* (1994) – which included the *Dustie-fute* poems – seeing both the living and the dying as 'tongue-tied. / Who travel further every year / Seeking their own small country' ('Needlepoint'). Kinloch's most recent collection *Un Tour d'Écosse* (2001) contains poems which speak more frankly of homosexual love – as Edwin Morgan's later poems have come to do – in an important development for Scottish literature when one recalls the many implicitly homophobic novels of macho self-destruction that characterised the 1960s and 1970s. On a subject that has also engaged the critic and author Christopher Whyte, Kinloch hopes that he has managed, as he said to Richard Price, 'to write about issues of sexual and gender identity in ways that link them to the problematisation of linguistic and national identities'.

Frank Kupper (b. 1951)

No less experimental in his way, but never likely to be an 'information-ist' in love with the buzz of the modern world, Frank Kuppner writes poetry that is haunted by the physicality of texts and by the textuality of things: by the stories that lie behind what we see around us, that may or may not ever be told. His first collection of poems signalled his interest in telling stories by the most oblique means, for *A Bad Day for the Sung Dynasty* (1984) offers 511 quatrains as if describing Chinese paintings, or as if translating Chinese texts – with lines missing or inde-cipherable words. The poems offer parodic echoes of Ezra Pound's *Cathay* verses, satirical comments on scholarly translation and hilarious moments of surreal humour; but other verses are genuinely moving, with a Zen stillness to them. Kuppner retained the quatrain format for the several long poem sequences in *The Intelligent Observation of Naked Women* (1987). These include meditations on the streets and tenement stairs of his native Glasgow, 'Passing Through Open Doorways', that prefigure how he would come to see the city in his later prose work. In 'An Old Guide Book to Prague' his typically distanced and scrupulously observant eye speculates on the human lives caught in the details of old photographs – which are another kind of textual trace to be translated – to produce verses that are essentially and characteristically elegiac in tone:

107

The sense of Sunday and a listless, fleeting crowd;
The familiarity of this distant scene haunting me;

Some of my German relatives must be here or hereabouts;
Oh, silver nitrate, silver nitrate, how much I have loved thee.

Kuppner's dream-like detachment and the formal scholarly diction of his verses, or his passages of Calvino-like prose-poetry, all make for a strangely lyrical and unique voice. The long poem 'Last Eternal Moments', from *Everything is Strange* (1994), has passages that share something of MacDiarmid's interest in a 'poetry of fact' and an outlook very similar to the cosmic perspective that characterised his early lyrics. But Kuppner's voice is entirely his own as he reflects on human life in a poem that switches from boring afternoons in the library, to momentary flashes of longing, to the mysteries of biochemistry and exploding stars:

A tentative golden light is caught by the window.
We hear a few details of an infinite story
Which has been spreading everywhere for billions of years.
We are given a few details to work upon;
And the strange thing is, we change it utterly.
We are smaller than one full-stop in any of these books
In this room which contains too many trivial books.
All our known universe is perhaps less than that chair.
Can I even begin to estimate how long I have had that chair?
The back is slightly broken, and I well remember
Already being bored with it five or six years ago.
How tensely she has gathered herself, a transient at its edge!
She moves her arms gently, to avoid alarming the cosmos.
And seeing the elegant watch lie so neatly on her wrist,
I find I am getting jealous even of Time itself.

(91)

Kuppner's prose has a similarly remote but engaged perspective on the world. He became fascinated by a famous murder in 1908, which had taken place near to where he lives in Glasgow. In a combination of investigation and autobiography he retraced the details of what has come to be known as the Oscar Slater Case in his book *A Very Quiet Street* (1989). He developed this method in *Something Very Like Murder* (1994), which uses the format of a daily journal to offer an extended meditation on his own life and his family's roots in Eastern Europe, linked to streets in Glasgow and also to another murder case – again near to where he lives – which had happened in 1929. *Something Very Like Murder* is a remarkable investigation into the nature of autobiography, social documentary and into causation itself as we begin to see the city streets like a palimpsest of collective memory, a web of ghostly connections and human endings all around us, as if faintly inscribed in the stone itself. Kuppner further developed the theme in his novel *Life on a Dead Planet* (1996), whose narrator orbits the streets of a city at dusk, wondering about the human lives around him, behind the doors and lit windows that will never quite let him in – the perennial fate, perhaps, of the scholar or the poet (Burns's 'chiel amang us takin' notes') as Kuppner understands it.

Donny O'Rourke (b. 1959)

The poems of Donny O'Rourke and Gerry Cambridge are more conventionally engaged with the world of people and, in Cambridge's case, animals too. The early ambition of Donny O'Rourke was to write song lyrics ('I wanted to be Leonard Cohen rather than Hugh MacDiarmid') and indeed he has produced a CD with Ceaolbeg singer and guitarist Dave Whyte (*Still Waiting to be Wise*, 1999). Growing up in the west of Scotland and going to school in Paisley, he recalls how empowered he felt by the writing of Alan Sharp, Gordon Williams and John Byrne among others: 'Poetry was not only permissible, it was possible' and he acknowledges a special admiration for Frank O'Hara. His own work has something of the relaxed and wryly conversational spirit of the American poet, much engaged with friends, family and places – especially the stir and buzz of city life ('It's So Beautiful Tonight You Wish', 'For James Schuyler', '(Another) Little Elegy'; 'Messages'). He also has poems that show a song-writer's feel for rhythm and clarity, and several songs are reproduced in *The Waistband and Other Poems* (1997). O'Rourke can write in Scots but mostly uses English, reflecting on his own family history in Scotland in the section 'A Letter from my Father' and in the long poem 'Marche Funèbre', which recounts the poet's return to Ireland for a family funeral. O'Rourke has co-published with Herbert and Kinloch and has worked as a writer-in-residence, a journalist and a television arts programme producer and presenter. He has edited an anthology of Scottish poets who have links with Ireland like himself (*Across the Water*, 2000), as well as two editions of *Dream State* (1994; 2002), a key anthology of work from this younger generation of Scottish poets.

Gerry Cambridge (b. 1959)

Gerry Cambridge was also born of Irish parents in Scotland. He trained as a journalist and photographer and came to specialise in natural history. The collection 'Nothing But Heather' (1999) derives from his time as Brownsbank Writing Fellow at MacDiarmid's cottage in Biggar, linking his own close-up photographs of animals and plants to poems about them. His special knowledge as a naturalist illuminates his work in this genre with an unusual precision that would have appealed to the later MacDiarmid. The sonnets and well-structured poems of Cambridge's first substantial collection *The Shell House* (1995) had been equally engaged with the landscapes, animals and people of rural Ayrshire where he has lived most of his life. In 1995 Cambridge founded the Scottish–American Poetry Magazine *The Dark Horse*, with a strong bias in favour of more formally structured verse. He still edits this prestigious journal and has written many critical and biographical essays on poets and poetry. *Madam Fi Fi's Farewell* (2003) contains some poems in free verse, a new direction for such a strong proponent of strict form, and indeed the collection as a whole shows a widening range, with addresses to friends and other writers, wryly observational poems about love, as well as verses boldly and unsentimentally rooted in the physical and cultural fabric of the countryside.

Jackie Kay (b. 1961)

The poetry of Jackie Kay is very much concerned with what we make of our lives in the here and now, and what it is to be a writer first, then a woman and then perhaps a Scottish writer. She belongs to the very remarkable generation of female poets to have appeared since Liz Lochhead's first books were published. In fact, as far as women writers are concerned, the real re-birth of Scottish poetry began in the 1980s and not the 1920s. (Not that any of them would have much truck with the term 'female poet' to begin with.) Even so, there is a deeply personal note to the poems of Jackie Kay's first collection *The Adoption Papers* (1991), which is a sequence of dramatic but reflective monologues, drawn from her own life, about the adoption of a black girl by a white working-class Scottish couple. The poems are constructed from the three different voices of the daughter, the adoptive mother and the birth mother in a starkly moving interplay (signalled by different typefaces) whose thoughtful engagement with the balance between constructed identity and genetic origin becomes much more than merely autobiographical. (The sequence was originally arranged for radio broadcast, where the interplay of voices and different points of view is especially effective.) Kay's continuing interest in identity is evident in much of her work, not least in the poem 'So you think I'm a mule?' which was prompted, as she explained, by the fact that many people cannot accept 'being Black and being Scottish without there being an inherent contradiction there'. So for Kay the question 'Where do you come from?' can never be entirely innocent nor, as a lesbian mother, is her sexual identity any less challenging to narrow minds. Out of such tensions, Kay produced *Other Lovers* (1993), which contains tough and joyful poems to explore the nature of love, equally alert to joy, pain and otherness – whether those states derive from physical ecstasy, separation or social exclusion. Poems such as 'Full Moon', 'A Country Walk', 'Mouth' and 'Inside' deal with the need that makes us savage and tender strangers to each other when we communicate so intimately, while 'Condemned Property' and 'No Way Out' expose the familiarity that breeds domestic violence in the family. The poem 'Gastarbeiter' looks at another kind of 'otherness', while 'Sign' reflects on the distances between one language and another, their mutual suspicions and the eloquence of the mute when they communicate by signing and not with sound. A cheerfully vulgar family sing-song generates an almost unbearable longing in 'Watching People Sing'; while a sequence of poems on the great blues singer Bessie Smith celebrates the transcendent power, but also the danger, rage and liberating joy, of her vocal art:

> Inside the house where I used to be myself,
> her voice claims the rooms. In the best room even,
> something has changed the shape of my silence.
> Why do I remember her voice and not my own mother's?
> Why do I remember the blues?
>
> ('The Red Graveyard')

Kay produced a collection of poems specifically about Bessie Smith in 1997. The travails of love and family, along with the power of jazz music and the strangeness of identity all reappeared in her first novel *Trumpet* (1998), which tells the remarkable story (based on the actual case of Billy Tipton) of a successful black trumpet player, Joss Moody, with a wife and adopted son, who is discovered on his death to have been a woman. The details of the story gradually come together in a series of narratives from Moody's wife, his son Colman and the tabloid journalist who only wants a juicy story, all interspersed with brief testaments from the doctor, the registrar, the funeral director, an old school friend and the drummer of the band. Moody's son is bitterly offended by the revelation, for the deception leads him to feel that his father 'has made us all unreal'. Yet Colman will slowly recover from his hurt and these unlikely and potentially sensational circumstances will come to seem less and less relevant – after all, what do we *ever* know of each other? And what does 'identity' mean anyway, when Joss 'unwraps himself with his trumpet' to tell real truths with his music every night?

> When he gets down and he doesn't always get down deep enough, he loses his sex, his race, his memory. He strips himself bare, takes everything off, till he's barely human. Then he brings himself back. . . .

The bandages that Joss uses to bind his breasts become a metaphor for all the other trappings that we use to cover our nakedness, and when they are stripped away, in the dark, all that matters in the end is whether there is love between us. This remarkable book was the novel that Kay had to write, as it touches on so many aspects of her own being (including her adoptive father's love of jazz), but it can also take its place as a wonderfully redemptive retelling of the Gothic Scottish interest in dual identity, balanced with the Enlightenment's understanding of how we are all 'made' to some extent – for better or for worse – by our relationships with the people around us. On the other hand, the short stories of *Why Don't You Stop Talking* (2002) look beneath the surface of society to explore the fantasies and fears that underlie so-called 'ordinary' lives, when people find themselves thrown on their own resources when they cannot meet the pressures of commitment, or when they come to recognise that they are finally and fundamentally alone.

Carol Ann Duffy (b. 1955)

Carol Ann Duffy has problematised identity in other ways. She was born in Glasgow of Irish extraction on her mother and her paternal grandfather's side, but her family moved to England in the early 1960s:

> It felt weird, distressing, to move. England was a foreign country. The accent! The condescension! And Stafford was the opposite of Glasgow. Glasgow was big, noisy, dark, glamorous, dramatic. Stafford was a wee toytown of a place, with little gardens, like green hankies, in front of all the houses. We kids were teased for about three years because of our Scottish accents. Eventually, we all developed English accents for outside and kept the Scottish ones for home – my father would shout at us if we talked with English accents! I still have a little Scots girl trapped in my head.

The poem 'Originally' recalls that journey south; yet the increasing distance between herself and her Scottish roots also leads her to recognise the ghostly and elusive nature of all origins:

Do I only think
I lost a river, culture, speech, sense of first space
and the right place? Now. *Where do you come from?*
strangers ask. *Originally?* And I hesitate.

This poem contains the insight that 'all childhood is an emigration' and many of the other verses in the fine collection *The Other Country* (1990) deal with that sense of loss, or of uncertainty when memory or reports from the past cannot be trusted ('We Remember Your Childhood Well'), or when we can never be sure of the thoughts or fantasies of others in that other country of the mind. Beyond any question of returning to Scotland, the poet's cry 'I want our own country' is about the impossibility of desire – which may well be the prevailing theme of all lyric poetry when all is said and done – and Duffy has certainly written powerful poems about both the fulfilment and the failure of love. It can be argued that her own lesbian sexuality (she was Jackie Kay's partner) might give her a particular sensitivity to the permeability of borders between supposedly separate countries, realms of being and experience ('River'). 'Two Small Poems of Desire' and 'Girlfriends' are openly sexual while 'Warming her Pearls', from the earlier collection *Selling Manhattan* (1987), gives a powerfully erotic charge to the thoughts of a personal maid as she imagines her lady's life in a world she herself can never – must never – know:

Full moon. Her carriage brings her home. I see
her every movement in my head . . . . Undressing,
taking off her jewels, her slim hand reaching
for the case, slipping naked into bed, the way

she always does . . . And I lie here awake,
knowing the pearls are cooling even now
in the room where my mistress sleeps. All night
I feel their absence and I burn.

'Disgrace', from *Mean Time* (1993), paints a terrifying picture of disconnection when love goes dead: 'We had not been home in our hearts for months. // And how our words changed. Dead flies in a web. / How they stiffened and blackened.' The poem 'Prayer' has an equally strong feeling for that moment when confidence is lost and the existential loneliness of the present opens like an abyss beneath our feet, echoing a line from the Catholic 'Hail Mary':

Pray for us now. Grade I piano scales
console the lodger looking out across

a Midlands town. Then dusk, and someone calls
a child's name as though they named their loss.

Darkness outside. Inside, the radio's prayer –
Rockall. Malin. Dogger. Finisterre

A significant number of Duffy's poems satirise the condition of
Thatcher's Britain with fiercely funny and cutting verses on the idle
racism of the young ('Comprehensive'); the excesses of the tabloid
press ('Poet for our Times'); poverty and financial greed ('Making
Money') or the debasement of plain speaking ('Weasel Words'). The
poem 'Foreign' identifies strongly with those whose own identities do
not quite 'fit' because of their race, who must daily confront 'a name
for yourself sprayed in red / against a brick wall. A hate name. Red like
blood.' In this respect Duffy frequently adopts a first-person persona
for her poems as dramatic monologues. She went on to have fun with
this form in *The World's Wife* (1999), allowing the female partners (the
'other half' of famous names in history or myth) to tell their side of the
story – seldom to the credit of their husbands. Thus we hear from Mrs
Faust, Mrs Freud (not envious of his private member after all) and Mrs
Midas, whose lines also make a subtle reference to the transformations
of art and the dangerous idealisation of women: 'I feared his honeyed
embrace, / the kiss that would turn my lips to a work of art. // And
who, when it comes to the crunch, can live / with a heart of gold?'
The Feminine Gospels (2002) developed the theme by proposing new
myths of female experience in funny, surreal but also in darker and less
programmatic terms. In this collection, as in her previous books,
Duffy's finest work comes from her engagement with the debatable
lands of identity and desire.

Magi Gibson (b. 1953) and Angela McSeveney (b. 1964)

Female stereotypes and the realities of women's lives feature once
more in the work of Magi Gibson and Angela McSeveney. The title
of Gibson's collection, *Wild Women of a Certain Age* (2002), almost
speaks for itself, mixing personal lyrics with poems that make a vigorous, broad and often comic reinterpretation of familiar myths,
legends and ballads – Tam Lin, Queen Maeve, the Sheila-na-gig,
Goldilocks – in a spirit not unlike Lochhead's *Grimm Sisters* or
Duffy's *The World's Wife*. Poems such as 'Weep Not for Me' and 'no
angel', however, have a serious and vividly political focus to their
anger. Her second collection *Graffiti in Red Lipstick* (2003) and a

poem sequence about a failing marriage, to be read aloud in collaboration with the cello of musician Sally Beamish, show a broadening and deepening of these themes. The verse of Angela McSeveney first appeared in *Other Tongues* (1990), a volume shared with Meg Bateman and David Kinloch, followed by her first full collection *Coming Out with It* (1992). As the name suggests, her poems are cool, minimal and strikingly honest accounts of common female experience ('Sunbathing'; 'My Breasts'; 'Crockery'; 'Smear Test'), which say all the more for their quietness and their sense of fragility, isolation and dignity. While seemingly very personal, the physical detail and the transparent frankness of these poems goes beyond the immediate moment to generate a quietly ironic but none the less almost metaphysical perspective of presence and evanescence via the most mundane events: 'back in the showers / we have only ourselves to tend, / shampoos, conditioners, footprints left in talc'. The collection *Imprint* (2002) continues McSeveney's rigorous determination not to say more than what is, and the closing lines of 'The Ventilator' could speak for much of her art, which so values 'an individual's persistence / in living without gall the life / they've found themselves in'.

Kate Clanchy (b. 1965)

Kate Clanchy takes a more cheerfully ironic and confident line in listing all the kinds of men she likes, whether they are 'the soft white collared ones / smelling of wash that someone else has done', or 'the athletes, big-limbed, / who stoop to hear' ('Men'). Born in Glasgow and educated in Edinburgh and Oxford (where she now lives), Clanchy has acknowledged an early debt to Carol Ann Duffy, and although the title of her first book *Slattern* (1995) suggests a challenge to the stereotypical decencies, her poems reflect on female experience in a gentler but no less sharply perceptive spirit. There is a frank and sensual enjoyment of the memories of love and lovemaking during domestic chores ('Afterwards'), and a sense of strangeness in the act ('Overnight' and 'One Night when We Paused Half-Way'). 'Double Take' hopes that a departed lover is missing her the way she is missing him, in a succession of assonances and internal rhymes brilliantly tapping out single words and phrases to capture loss:

. . . sleep badly, late, dream chases, shake,
send fingers out to pad the pillow, find
my hollow, start awake, roll over, hug a gap,

an ache, take a walk, damp dawn of course,
wrapped in a mac with the collar up, glimpse
a slice of face, tap a stranger's back, draw a blank:

as I have. . . .

The same technical skill informs the hauntingly sensual lines and the astonishingly delicate image that concludes 'Poem for a Man with No Sense of Smell' when she informs him that sometimes

In a breeze, the delicate hairs on the nape
of my neck, just where you might bend
your head, might hesitate and brush your lips,

hold a scent frail and precise as a fleet
of tiny origami ships, just setting out to sea.

Other poems invoke a powerful physicality in remembering an oil-damaged bird ('Gull') or a sick cat ('Towards the End'); or the poet uses vignettes from her work as a schoolteacher ('Timetable', 'Rain, Book, Classroom') to foreshadow with some compassion the futures that await us all, or the pasts from which we sprang ('Men From the Boys'). The poems in *Samarkand* (1999) are similarly attentive, compassionate and domestic, looking to married love, family history and friends in a world where the hay fields of Oxford are far more golden than anything to be found in Samarkand ('To Travel'). There are satirical barbs about the middle classes ('Lawyers', 'The Rich') and a fine closing sequence of poems 'The New Home Cabaret' in which the poet and her partner find themselves entangled in an archaeology of other peoples' pasts as they struggle with old carpet and blocked-up fireplaces. Yet this settled life is a rich treasure, too, as it invokes a recurringly aureate motif: 'all down our road, / the lights go on – the gold / of bulbs in potting sheds, ingots / of a hall, back bedroom, stair'.

John Burnside (b. 1955)

John Burnside published ten poetry books in seven years to deliver a remarkable body of work with an intensely singular and slowly evolving vision. The poems in his second volume, *Common Knowledge* (1991), set the scene for much of what was to follow:

The past keeps shifting around us
but each year the same milk-coloured spring returns:

whitebeams, the tug of meadows,
the first yellow sail in the bay.

In these lines from the sequence 'Home', Burnside establishes his territory, where 'home' is 'a series of lucid echoes / between a sky inscribed
with gulls and stars / and these strange or familiar houses / where love
is perfected'. The poet's engagement with space, memory and the
natural realm focuses on the small details of rooms, gardens and the
half-settled countryside with such intensity that the surrounding world
of people and affairs fades away to become no more than faint echoes,
or radio whispers from another room, while the moment stills to a
hyper-intensity of presence that is achingly indefinable, even slightly
and supernaturally disconcerting:

> Something is in the wood but nothing
> visible. Continuance; a filmy brackish
> misting of oak and moss,
> cold as shillings mined in the frost
> winking at break of day through dusted grass.
> (from 'Home')

Having been brought up in the Catholic faith, Burnside often draws
on a religious vocabulary to convey this sense of immanence, especially
in his earlier verses, but they are by no means conventionally religious or
'spiritual' poems. The poet invokes images of resurrection from 'the
notion of a Christ / we half-invent', which relates to the immanence of
a power 'not yet manifest', rather than to any sense of sure salvation. The
collection contains a set of prose-poems called 'Annunciations' that
explore this sense of ghostly immanence further, taking the conventional
gospel story into stranger realms – closer to the terrible metaphysical
immanence of Rilke's angels than to any assurance of God's love for man:

> I imagine travelling in a country where the existence of the soul is taken for
> granted. I imagine there is no difficulty in dealing with the soul on every
> level in every waking and sleeping moment of the day. To begin with, there
> is some resistance, but at last I succumb to the idea that the soul exists. Or
> rather, not the soul, but souls. I am even capable of believing all things have
> souls, not one each, but many, according to the time of day, or the light, or
> the season.
> (from 'Annunciations')

Burnside's typical 'season' for such insights, is at night alone in the
house, perhaps in the kitchen looking out at the moon over fields, or
early at dawn with frost on the grass, or in the suburbs:

In the late afternoon, the people indoors; catspaws of light on the honey-
dew leaves, sprinklers surging and hissing on deserted lawns. A mile away
the abandoned railway station is buried in grapevine and cherry laurel,
already half-surrendered to the woods, like a temple to some forgotten god.
(from 'Suburbs')

For Burnside the natural world – especially its marginal details –
becomes a vocabulary for the relationship between being and infinity.
The fine poem 'Domestic' has his characteristic intensity, like a
Vermeer interior that is deeply specific and yet also numinous with a
beautiful significance that can scarcely be traced:

Later afternoon in October:
light feathers the kitchen walls,
finds long-lost cousins
in saucepans and colanders.
. . .
We sit indoors, alone,
pressed to the silence
like wasps to a window pane.
. . .
At teatime, lamps go on
across the valley.
The marmalade cat stares in
from the window's gloaming
and, watched, we become what we seem
in the moth-coloured light,
like these figures we make in glass,
irredeemably bright.

Feast Days (1992) contains more prose-poetry and the author's
continuing sense of being haunted by a feeling of 'home' as something
that we seek, and may even inhabit, but can never truly possess. Born
in Dunfermline, Burnside spent the first eleven years of his life in
Cowdenbeath in West Fife until his family moved to the industrial
Midlands where his father worked in the steel town of Corby – a scene
that would provide the poet with the setting and the autobiographical
grounding for the protagonist's sense of exile in his fourth novel *Living
Nowhere* (2003). After training as a computer software engineer,
Burnside became a full-time writer in 1996, before returning to live in
Fife where he is now a Reader in Creative Writing at the University of
St Andrews. It is tempting to wonder if the spectral status of 'home' in
his poems is connected to this childhood move south (as it was for
Carol Ann Duffy) and he, too, remembers 'the feeling I had of being

uprooted from my community, and from the dialect and local land-scape of Fife'. But this alone seems scarcely enough to explain the intensity of Burnside's response to a natural world of smoke and frost, of lupins and moonlight – all quite specific, and yet finally uncatchable – as he makes them into a language for understanding the numinous nature of the ordinary. *The Myth of the Twin* (1994) introduced the concept of a ghostly double to this imaginative realm and spoke a little more clearly about his family past with tenderly opaque poems to his grandparents: 'They had moved to the centre of things, / rounded and smooth, and closed up on themselves / like mushrooms' ('My Grandparents in 1963'). Yet even when remembering past places ('The Pit Town in Winter'; 'The North') the poet must still recognise that 'mine is the other north', that 'figment of the wind / that always finds an echo in my hands' – the secret twin, perhaps, that he can neither see clearly nor forget, that must always lie beyond language and any actual place.

In the late 1990s Burnside began to write prose fiction and his first novel, *The Dumb House* (1997), made a considerable critical impact, not least because of its sensationally Gothic nature and an opening line that is worthy of Iain Banks's *The Wasp Factory*: 'No one could say it was my choice to kill the twins any more than it was my decision to bring them into the world.' Speaking in the first person, the novel's protagonist explains his obsessive interests in the nature of being, from his grisly animal dissections as a boy (equally grisly in his admiration for the interior structure of these 'wet machines'), to his mature decision to replicate an ancient experiment by which Akbar, the dyslexic Mughal emperor in sixteenth-century India, built a 'dumb house' for new-born children where they were to be raised entirely by mutes in order to determine if the gift of language was innate or learned. (Surely if they spoke at all in such circumstances, it would be in the tongue of Adam and Eve? Surely the capacity for language must be linked to the posses-sion of a soul?) Such questions have a long history (including the many tales of feral children) but in Akbar's experiment the children never spoke and the 'dumb house' was forever quiet: 'People would travel from all over the kingdom to visit the house. They would stand for hours outside its walled gardens, listening to the silence.' Nevertheless, Burnside's narrator sets out to do it again in the cellar of his own dwelling.

The novel is striking for the intelligent, mad and affect-free precision of the narrator's voice, beautifully rendered by Burnside; and striking again for the parallels between this grimly Gothic plot and the fact that

Burnside's own poetry is itself so strongly engaged with whatever it is we might want to call the soul – of things and people alike. His disturbed protagonist's account of language, for example, would be familiar to any writer:

> The trick and the beauty of language is that it seems to order the whole universe, misleading us into believing that we live in sight of a rational space, a possible harmony. But if words distance us from the present, so we never quite seize the reality of things, they make an absolute fiction of the past. Now, when I look back, I remember a different world: what must have seemed random and chaotic at the time appears perfectly logical as I tell it, invested with a clarity that even suggests a purpose, a meaning to life.
> . . .
> What disturbs me now is the possibility that language might fail: after the experiment ended so inconclusively, I cannot help imagining that the order which seems inherent in things is only a construct, that everything might fall into chaos, somewhere in the long white reaches of forgetting.

The poet's next novel appeared in 1999 as *The Mercy Boys*, an equally dark study, this time of damaged Scottish masculinity, in the plight of four heavy-drinking Dundee men long lost to hope but still haunted by dreams of escape, completion, or even love in their loveless and soon to be violently disrupted lives. The poet published short stories in the 2000 collection *Burning Elvis* ('Graceland didn't have to be in one place or another, it existed in people's minds, and everyone could have a Graceland, if they wanted'); and followed this with *The Locust Room* (2001), which ends on a more redemptive note, as Paul, a young photographer re-examines his life and his relationships with women in the summer of 1975, at a time when a violent rapist was (truly) at large in the town of Cambridge. The rapist's own thoughts intervene in short passages inserted through the novel to make an eerie counterpoint to the town's culture of 1970s laddish behaviour and – because of the crimes – vigilante panic and violence. Incidental to the main plot, but central to the novel's creative purposes, Paul's thoughts as a photographer echo Burnside's own work in verse, as Paul remembers a photographic exhibition and what it showed him:

> Images of frosted planks, rock pools, seaweed, a street in Alderney, they possessed, or were possessed of, that quality of estrangement that seemed to allow the things seen to move away from the viewer's gaze, to set each thing, each pebble and plank and scab of weed, in its own inviolable space, not a mere object, but as something respected, something loved and so left to be itself, beyond possession, beyond comprehension.

The poems in *A Normal Skin* (1997), *The Asylum Dance* (2000), which won the Whitbread Poetry Prize, and *The Light Trap* (2001) pursue the same themes, but become more autobiographically direct, with a more narrative approach, as in 'Snake', 'Restoring Instruments', 'Anstruther', 'Penitence' or the eight poems in the 'Epithalamium' sequence. In 'The Light Trap' the poet remembers catching moths on a torch-lit sheet, to invoke the mysteries of consciousness ('shapes we fail to name, / though they are bright and present'), and his task 'to draw in from the air what it conceals'; or he longs for the knowledge we had as children when 'we knew / that everything was finite and alive, / cradled in warmth against the ache of space' ('Being and Time'). *The Light Trap* also contains a beautiful sequence of six 'Birth Songs' written for his young son Lucas, along with poems engaging with people and places closer to the author's daily life ('History. St Andrews: West Sands; September 2001'; 'Heat Wave'). Burnside revisits Wallace Stevens's famous blackbird, with his own poetic blackbird, in several of these poems, confirming his commitment to the beauty and evanescence of the moment – simultaneously fragile and indestructible – as in the book's closing poem 'A Theory of Everything', which seeks:

> – a history of light
> and gravity   – no more –
>
> for this is how the world
> occurs: not piecemeal
>   but entire
>
> and instantaneous
>
> the way we happen:
>
> woman   blackbird   man

Don Paterson (b. 1963)

The poetry of Don Paterson is a good deal more worldly with its esoteric imagery drawn from bad football games, solo pool in an empty pub, jazz and folk music, disused railway lines and an ironic meta-literary awareness:

> In the poem you appear as a poet, a real one,
> with a book out, and two or three gigs in the diary
> though neither the taxman, your shrink nor the Gas Board
> is having it. Last week at the manse

for the cosy wee pep-talk arranged by your mother,
the minister, somewhere between the sweet sherry
and the meat-paste and cucumber sandwiches,
leant across, laid his fat paw on your shoulder
and whispered *For fuck's sake, get real son.*
('The Alexandrian Library Part II' from *God's Gift to Women.*)

Born and educated in Dundee, Paterson makes his living as a musician along with his work as a poet, journalist and editor. He spent the 1980s playing the acoustic guitar for various bands in Dundee and London before becoming a founding member of Lammas, with saxophonist Tim Garland, to deliver a sophisticated amalgam of Celtic folk music and jazz. The title-poem of Paterson's first collection, *Nil Nil* (1993) – the last poem in the book – is characteristic of his oblique, irreverent and powerful imagination. The poem begins with an epigraph from the *Pensées* of François Aussemain (a creature entirely of Paterson's own making, whose thoughts will bless several other poems) and goes on to meditate on entropy and fate by charting the processes of mortal decline via references to football, from an old team's glory days, to the Sunday League, and lower still to 'the unrefereed thirty-a-sides, / terri-fied fat boys with callipers minding / four jackets on infinite, notional fields', down to a boy kicking a pebble in the gutter without realising that it is the gallstone of a fallen wartime fighter pilot burned in his exploding plane over Fife. This bizarre chain of connections, simulta-neously serious and surreal, is typical of Paterson's capacity to amuse, challenge, disturb and be lyrical in equal measure:

> *In short, this where you get off, reader;*
> *I'll continue alone, on foot, in the failing light,*
> *following the trail as it steadily fades*
> *into road-repairs, birdsong, the weather, nirvana,*
> *the plot thinning down to a point so refined*
> *not even angels could dance on it. Goodbye.*

'Exeunt' pursues the same theme with a set of five poems that imagine a succession of individual deaths indirectly and phantasmagorically conveyed through the hobbies, settings, or lost memories of each one of the deceased. 'An Elliptical Stylus' recalls an insult to the poet's father, mocked in a hi-fi shop for his ancient record player, but the poem immediately subverts itself by recognising that this is indeed the subject for a poem and it even goes so far as to invent a counter-poem called 'Fidelities' as if written by the middle-class shop assistant in memory of *his* father:

The day my father died, he showed me how
he'd prime the deck for optimum performance:
it's that lesson I recall . . .

Paterson's lines produce a perfect imitation of just such a poem, only
to abandon it to return to his father's hurt, and a refusal to end his own
poem with any sort of moral or literary closure:

that man's laugh
stuck in my head, which is where this story sticks,
and any attempt to cauterize this fable
with something axiomatic on the nature
of articulacy and inheritance

The theme is already familiar in the work of Leonard and Kelman but
Paterson will not demean his father by making the point on his behalf,
choosing to end the poem with an angry challenge to the reader
instead:

But if you still insist on resonance –
I'd swing for him, and every other cunt
happy to let my father know his station,
which probably includes yourself. To be blunt.

This direct but deceptively subtle poem is elliptical in more ways
than one, not least in its last word, which returns us to that despised
record player with its 'needles, thick as carpet tacks'.

Many of the poems in *God's Gift to Women* (1997) – a title that can
be interpreted in more than one way – reflect on sexual experience,
from the rather startlingly epigrammatical conclusions of 'Buggery' or
'*from* Advice to Young Husbands' to the tenderly shocking wit of
'Imperial'. The memorable title-piece, a long and macabre love-poem,
traces the speaker's night-time journey into his own psyche and the
past abuses visited on his partner, in a dream-like exploration of our
separate and sometimes terrible histories of sexual initiation: touching
on male arrogance, family abuse, emotional damage ('God's gift',
indeed) and finally a surprising tenderness. Paterson mixes a postmodern wit with a ferociously erudite range of reference, a liking for arcane
words, and a capacity for direct rhymed address – an unusual combination. He delights in making the most unlikely imaginative connections
– as with the set of verses that link his own boyhood and emotional
history to the stations and timetables of the Dundee–Newtyle railway
(long since 'rationalised' and abandoned). The meditative contempla-

tion of a lost love, while drinking a collection of whisky miniatures, is a case in point, achieving a bittersweet and melancholy lyricism in 'A Private Bottling':

> So finally let me propose a toast:
> not to love, or life, or real feeling,
> but to their sentimental residue;
> to your sweet memory, but not to you.

The award-winning *Landing Light* (2003) contains sonnets, prose-poems, poems in Scots and a growing preference for metrical and rhymed verse forms. Infused with myth, dream and a typically exotic range of references, Paterson's longer poems return to the surreal but intriguingly postmodern monologues of 'The Alexandrian Library' (this time 'Part III'), or generate a bizarrely interrupted fairy story in the English and Scots quatrains of 'The Long Story'. There are moments, however, when the poet's mixture of postmodern awareness and Byronic narrative flow becomes, perhaps, just too exhaustingly clever, despite his reflexive caveats, as in 'A Talking Book', in which the book itself talks back to us, its readers:

> and a big hi! to those holders, old and new
> of the critic's one-day travel pass (I too
> have known that sudden quickening of the pulse
> when something looks a bit like something else . . .)
> ('A Talking Book')

Such is the stuff of poetry, of course, but the one certain thing about Paterson's muse is that the 'something else' will never be predictable.

Kathleen Jamie (b. 1962)

Kathleen Jamie came into her own with the Queen of Sheba, on the back of a carnival lorry in the Currie Gala, parading to the cheers of 'a thousand laughing girls' ready to ask 'Difficult Questions' of the masons, the elders, the police – of patriarchal Scotland in other words. Such was the title-poem of her second full collection, *The Queen of Sheba*, which signalled the arrival of a fully mature new voice. Recalling her childhood and schooldays in Currie, a village outside Edinburgh, Jamie remembered 'kicking very hard against the small options which seemed to be our lot, as though I'd glimpsed a huge world but felt it was being withheld from me'. She was soon to put this right. Jamie graduated with a degree in Philosophy from Edinburgh University in

1981, and an Eric Gregory Award for her poetry that year allowed her to travel. Her first volume *Black Spiders* (1982) has poems on Jerusalem, Istanbul and Scotland ('Cramond Island'), which are notable for their cautious and unjudgemental openness to experience, matched by an unwillingness to pander to the obvious connections, the exotic or the pastoral in any way. A co-authored book of verses with Andrew Greig, *A Flame in Your Heart* (1986), dramatises the evolving love affair of an RAF fighter pilot during the Battle of Britain. A climbing expedition with Greig took her to northern Pakistan and these travels led to the 'Karakoram Highway' poems in *The Way We Live* (1987), and her subsequent visits to Baltistan produced the prose volume *The Golden Peak* (1992), a more than 'travel' book about engaging with the culture and the people there and especially with the life of women. (The book was reissued in 2002 as *Among Muslims*.) In 1989 she set out to travel to Amdo and Tibet on the route of pilgrims, monks, traders and nomads, accompanied by the climber and photographer Sean Mayne Smith. This expedition produced *The Autonomous Region* (1993), a volume of photographs and poems about the beauty of the place and its people and their struggle to retain Tibetan culture in the face of Beijing's determination to see that ancient country as only one among many so-called 'autonomous regions' in China. (These were troubled times: the Tiananmen Square massacre happened that June and the two travellers were turned back by the Chinese at the borders of Tibet.) Jamie's poems relate to the folk she met, but she shared her journey with the writings of Fa-hsien, a wandering Buddhist monk of the fourth century, and the story of Princess Wen Cheng, the king of Tibet's Chinese bride who brought the art of writing to the mountains in the seventh century. In the preface to their book, Mayne Smith reminds us that there is still another 'autonomous region', which is the inner state of peace that Buddhism seeks to find, a state that recognises that the world's reality is ultimately only in the eye of the beholder. Thus it is that Jamie recognised Fa-hsien in the faces of the wandering monks she met on the road, and was haunted by Wen Cheng, that strong-willed traveller, along the way. So *The Autonomous Region* is an imaginative voyage (or a travelogue in time as much as space) as past and present merge in Jamie's poems, just as her mainly English verses are haunted by snatches of her own past: in her grandmother's sayings ('*Set a stout hert tae a stey brae*'), and every now and then by the Scots tongue:

Sits a lassie in red scarf,
wi her heid in her hauns, her heid

achin wi the weicht o so much saun
the weicht o the desert that waits every morn
an blackly dogs her back.

Jamie writes of beginning to see 'ghosts, lines of energy and wander-
ings' in her 'criss-crossed routes of travel', and it seems that one of
these ghosts was her own home, for the book ends with the lines: 'An
A'm waukenet, on a suddenty mindit: / A'm far fae hame, / I hae
crossed China.'

This new perspective was to be the key element in the poems of *The
Queen of Sheba* (1994), in which Jamie re-inhabits Scotland via the
streets, beaches and rubbish-tip playgrounds of her childhood, or the
high-rise flats and shopping malls of her adult life, to discover a
freedom to breathe as a woman, and a more magical anarchy in her
home country than previous generations might have expected to find.
In this respect her work shares a certain tough spirit of celebration with
those other writers who were born in the 1960s: Legge, Smith,
McLean, Warner, Kennedy, Herbert, Kay, Paterson, Clanchy, Dillon,
Bissett, Saadi et al., and (in Gaelic) Gorman and McNeil. The very first
poem in the collection makes its point as the phrase 'The Queen of
Sheba', which was for so long a Scottish put-down of any claims to
ambition or difference (as in: 'Who do you think you are? The Queen
of Sheba?'), returns personified as a triumphant affirmation of unfet-
tered sexuality, knowledge, difference and escape. She demands
nothing less than 'the keys / to the National Library' and '*All that she
desires, whatever she asks* / She will make the bottled dreams / of your
wee lasses / look like *sweeties.*'

The point about the promise of creative anarchy in this hugely good-
humoured poem is not that it comes from some other realm (despite
Sheba's oriental origins) but that her spirit can also be found in the
little girls and the old men all around us – so often unseen or kept to
the margins of polite society. In 'Mother-May-I' one of those wee lasses
wants to play by the dump 'where we're not allowed' or 'muck about
/ at the woods and burn / dead pleased / to see the white dye / of
our gym-rubbers seep downstream?' In the same spirit, and much the
same place, 'The Bairns of Suzie: a hex' are 'laughing like jackdaws' as
they make magic arrows out of scabs and the briars caught in their
body hair to hex all those with their 'laws and guns' who would 'shake
in the people's faces keys / to courtrooms and gates'. Such poems are
not without their hint of sexual danger and challenge. The protagonist
of 'Jocky in the wilderness', for example, is the personification of
damaged Scottish masculinity now incarnated as a mad old dosser who

hasn't yet learned to 'unclench' his fists and heart. Yet he, too, can achieve wildness and perhaps redemption, as he wanders through the parish and sleeps with the foxes, 'trails of sticky-willy on his poor coat'. The poet celebrates a homelier potential for anarchy in 'The Den of the Old Men' as she imagines them building a raft and sailing away on the Firth of Tay 'like captains', with their 'raincoats and bunnets, / wee dugs and sticks'. The old men with their dominoes and last year's calendar on the wall may be symbols of the dead hand of stifled Scotland (readers of the *Sunday Post*, no doubt, and complainers about the younger generation) but Jamie's challenge to them invokes change and new horizons, and her vision of their disreputable and shabby presence is an affectionate one.

These and many of the other poems in the collection show a finely nuanced grasp of the outlook, fittings and furnishings of lower middle-class Scotland in the 1960s – 'Royal Family Doulton' recalls the hardships of her grandmother's life, scrubbing floors in an old tenement with a shared lavatory, and the irony of her so precious Doulton porcelain ornaments with their bonnets and parasols 'Seized in coy pirouettes, little victims / of enchantment'. They may not be the only victims of 'enchantment' when such value systems can prevail so long in the face of reality. 'Mr and Mrs Scotland are dead', for example, is a veritable anthology of the bric-a-brac of genteel respectability – old postcards from Peebles, the 'John Bull Puncture Repair Kit' and the man of the house's 'last few joiners' tools / SCOTLAND, SCOTLAND stamped on their tired handles' – all now to be found 'On the civic amenity landfill site, / the coup, the dump beyond the cemetery' (where, no doubt, the wild bairns of Suzie play). The irony of Mr Scotland's inscribed tools lying next to the *John Bull* kit is a brilliantly delicate political touch, and one might think that such 'tired handles' should best be thrown away: except that the poet goes on to wonder when our turn will come – 'the sweeping up, the turning out'. 'Crystal Set' has the same mixture of irony and nostalgia, and yet at the heart of the poem is the sudden realisation – in the middle of a stereotypically cozy domestic scene from the late 1950s – that there is a larger world out there, just discernible on the primitive set's radio reception.

In poem after poem Jamie seems to be simultaneously evoking and bidding farewell to an older Scotland, with a curiously tender satirical eye. The same compassion can be found in 'School Reunion' and 'Hand Relief', which reflect on the death of early promise – yet without bitterness. 'Wee Baby' and 'Wee Wifey' on the other hand are invoked as if they were personal female demons: of fertility, perhaps, and compulsive tidiness or respectability. They may be kept at arm's length or even exorcised, but still the poet must admit a deeply and alarmingly intimate connection with them. Such poems join 'The Bairns of Suzie' and others in the collection with their references to the supernatural, whether hinting at witchcraft or echoing the old Scots ballads, and with such potential there is always hope for creative change or the hilariously liberating return of the Queen of Sheba to throw out Scotland's Presbyterian gloom, with its poverty of expectation and its 'thrawn streak' like 'a wally dug you never liked / but can't get shot of'.

Jamie finds the same capacity for magic in several fine poems of the cityscape. In 'Fountain' the coins at the bottom of a pool in the shopping mall bear witness to the possibility that ancient rites and strengths may not be entirely gone, alongside those stores with mythic and godly names: 'Athena, Argos, Olympus'. The poem 'Flashing Green Man' finds real enchantment in the early evening urban scene of shops and traffic lights and roundabouts, as a skein of geese catch the light beyond the multi-story flats, yet the poem's achievement is to make the flashing green man of a pedestrian crossing almost as meaningful a sign. 'Child with pillar box and bin bags' finds a similarly lyrical suspension in its account of a mother photographing her baby in a pushchair in the middle of the most unprepossessing street setting. Without denying the crowded and grubby scene, Jamie's poem still finds space for the possibility of love and beauty in a moment that has its own slightly daft but transfiguring power, even on the shadowed side of a busy road. All these elements come together in 'The Republic of Fife', which invokes the regional pride of the old 'kingdom' of Fife now revivified by revolution and re-imagined as a place with woods 'where my friend Isabel / once saw a fairy, blue as a gas flame', next to a motorway flyover with 'PAY NO POLL TAX' painted on it. This is a place where

. . . spires and doocots	dovecots
institutes and tinkies' benders,	hut-like tents of travelling people
old Scots kings and dancing fairies	
give strength to my house.	

And from the roof of that house – symbolic perhaps of a new Scotland – the poet imagines how it will be possible to see as far as Europe or Africa, and wave to the waving citizens of 'all those other countries'.

Jamie's ability to find other-worldly traces in the bustle of the everyday appears again in *Jizzen* (1999), especially in the beautiful lyrics of 'Ultrasound', a sequence dedicated to her baby son, whose ghostly presence and arrival the poems describe:

> Oh whistle and I'll come to ye
> my lad, my wee shilpit ghost   puny
> summonsed from tomorrow.

'Jizzen' is the old Scots name for childbed, and the poet slips into Scots again to write the tender lullaby 'Bairnsang'. Perhaps it is the prospect of family continuity that prompts her to consider her own and her child's inheritance, and so the challenge of what to make of Scotland's present place and past history appears in 'Forget It', as she remembers her childhood enthusiasm for a classroom study of the slums, when her mother would sooner leave such experience behind. Once again Jamie's poetry negotiates a complex passage between nostalgia and irony, recognising the need for sustaining myths, and yet also their capacity to enslave us. The ambiguous continuity of the past – even the imperial past – is evoked in 'The Soldier', in which an isolated war memorial, engraved with still familiar local names, overlooks the children's playpark and the old folk at their game of bowls. 'The Graduates' acknowledges that education plays a part in leaving the 'stories of the old country' behind and regrets that someday the poet's 'bright monoglot bairns' will find her graduation parchment, as if it were her 'visa' for an exile of the mind and heart, even though she has not actually left her own shores. The harshness of literal exile, in Canada this time, and 'the useless dead-weight / of your mother tongue' appears in 'Suitcases', 'Hackit' and 'Pioneers'; yet 'Rhododendrons' also recognises that such transplantations generate new beauty and are soon claimed as our own, to become as 'native as language or living memory'. The closing poems of the collection welcome the new Scottish parliament as a 'watershed' and turn to Celtic lore and ancient history for renewal ('The Well at the Broch of Gurness', 'St Bride's'). The final poem, 'Meadowsweet', recalls the tradition that some Gaelic women poets were buried face down, only to turn that seeming silencing into a vision of renaissance, as the seeds in the dead poet's hair flower, 'to dig herself out' with her mouth 'young, and full again / of dirt, and spit, and poetry'. A better image of Jamie's achievement, and its promise for the future of so many other young writers, could not be found. After 'Meadowsweet' it seems doubly appropriate to end this study with poems in Scotland's oldest language.

Poetry in Gaelic

In the introduction to his major twentieth-century anthology *An Tuil*, Ronald Black has noted how often Gaelic poetry – even in modern times – has engaged with traditional issues of religious belief, language and the homeland, even if poets such as Sorley MacLean, George Campbell Hay, Derick Thomson, Iain Crichton Smith and Donald MacAulay have added politics, symbolism, psychoanalysis, the anguish of doubt and contemporary urban experience to the mix. At the latter end of the twentieth century Gaelic literature has been notable for the increasing breadth of its outlook and an awareness of other literatures and cultures, and yet questions of language and homeland are still there to be faced, perhaps inevitably, when one considers the inescapably 'minority' status of Gaelic itself. Equally notable, however, is the number of non-native speakers who have learned the language and chosen to write poetry in it, either as a way of finding some finer personal or social expression, or as an act of resistance to cultural globalisation and the growing hegemony of English. William Neill, for example, learned Gaelic as a conscious act of cultural politics, although of course that can never be the only reason for choosing to write poetry. For Meg Bateman, on the other hand, access to Gaelic may have been a way of finding the right voice for the spiritual vision that characterises her work, although, here too, the complex interrelationship between language and utterance defies any simple explanation. Nevertheless, the creative success of non native-speaking Gaelic poets such as Neill and Bateman and Fearghas MacFhionnlaigh, Christopher Whyte, Rody Gorman, Peadar Morgan, and the late Alasdair Barden is a marked feature of the last third of the century.

Aonghas MacNeacail (b. 1942)

Born and educated in Skye and at the University of Glasgow, Aonghas MacNeacail has acknowledged an admiration for the poetry of William Carlos Williams and certainly his own verses utilise a modernist freedom in line spacing, layout and punctuation. However, his commitment to the landscape, history and culture of the Highlands, and to the role of the poet as one who celebrates the natural world and the passions of the heart, is wholly traditional. Long early poems such as *Sireadh Bradain Sicir / Seeking Wise Salmon* (1983) and *An Cathadh Mor / The Great Snowbattle* (1984) draw very strongly on the Gaelic tradition of nature description and poetry in praise of place, but go on to suggest a symbolic dimension as well. Thus *An Cathadh Mor* imagines a blizzard as if it were a battle in which the worlds of nature, memory and human scale vie with the inchoate blankness of a universe equally open to creation and extinction. The result – especially in the first edition of the poem with its innovative layout and beautiful illustrations by Simon Fraser – is a sustained and restrained lyric to potentiality, a remarkable meditation on whiteness and abstraction, with the two languages dancing together on equal terms, making something dynamically new of the 'facing page' gloss which is the usual fate of the English version. The title poem of the 1986 collection *An Seachnadh / The Avoiding* celebrates love in terms that are simultaneously spiritual and sensual, drawing on images from the natural world in a mode of high address that is self-consciously evocative of the bardic tradition, if now turned to a more modern or at least a post-Romantic purpose. This voice with its traditionally inspired and erotically charged imagery is characteristic of many of MacNeacail's poems in this vein:

> White your shoulders in my dream
> smooth your brow
> slender calf elegant as hind,
> snug sheltered harbour of your breast
> a shield for my floundering heart
> you sped through my senses
> in supple *cainntearachd*   eloquence (also oral music)
> a fiery shoal travelling
> (trs. A. MacNeacail)

Poems such as 'an dràda dà fleasgach' ('at this moment two heroes') invoke the modern world by reflecting on the astronauts who are walking on the moon, only to reinscribe the vision within the customary – perhaps ironic – account of a poet's expected status: 'and I am walking the shore / my eyes on the moon / my pockets empty'. When MacNeacail seeks a metaphor for inspiration, or for the beauty of the world, it comes to him as a traditional creature of beauty and delicacy in the poem 'an eilid bhàn ('the white hind'); or when he writes about Marilyn Monroe in his 1996 collection *Oideachadh Ceart /A Proper Schooling*, he opens the poem with a repeated epithet that could have come from any of the great eighteenth-century bards. (Sorley MacLean used a similar rhetorical device in the elegy for his brother Calum MacLean.)

> gold in your hair
> gold in the nails on your feet

gold in the sleepy lids of your living eyes
gold in your cheeks, in their rumour of a blush
red gold of your lips
gold in the raised shoulder that shelters your chin
gold in your breasts . . .

(trans. A. MacNeacail)

The same use of repetition energises the poem to his son 'beaul beag' ('little mouth'); while the title-poem of the collection, 'a proper schooling' (dedicated to two African poets), recalls the oral recounting of emigration and clearance in Skye with the opening lines 'when I was young / it wasn't history but memory'. MacNeacail is seldom free from such memory and even when he writes in English his eyes are never far from the past history and the present condition of the Highlands. The English sequence 'rock and water', for example, in the 1990 collection of that name, invokes a thin landscape of ageing communities and small prospects, in a poem sequence reminiscent of Mackay Brown's *Greenvoe*, or Iain Crichton Smith's Murdo stories without Smith's surrealist humour:

the young have left
a place propped up on the frail
bones of pensioners.
Crofts die under docken thistles nettles and
the absence of livestock.
. . .
elsewhere 'bed and breakfast' signs
invite the traveller to share
a traditional croft cuisine
bought from liptons mobile shop.

Fearghas MacFhionnlaigh (b. 1948)

The poetry of Fearghas MacFhionnlaigh has a more outward looking response to modernity in swiftly moving and associative lines that mix a strongly evangelical Christian Calvinist faith with a wide range of literary, scientific and cultural reference. MacFhionnlaigh trained at Duncan of Jordanstone College in Dundee and works as an art teacher. His was not a Gaelic-speaking upbringing, except for a great-grand-parent on his mother's side, but he and his family now live in Inverness and speak Gaelic, and he made the Gaelic form of his name official in the 1980s when he first started to publish poetry. His engagement with language and his faith come from the same roots, as he explained in a talk he gave in 2001:

It seems to me that Christians make a fundamental mistake when they understand the confusion of language at Babel as a curse. The 'Orwellian' totalitarian tyranny of the single language is surely the curse . . . there is a connection between language and control, between language and being controlled. In one of the essays in his book *Language and Silence*, George Steiner discusses the effects of Nazi manipulation of the German language. He suggests they ruined it for poetry. My burden is that God has delivered humanity from the thraldom of Babel by giving us many languages. The single language was the curse – the multiplicity of languages is the blessing.
. . .
One of those beams of light from Babel is called Scottish Gaelic. It is flickering and fading. It was in our stewardship but we have neglected it. If it goes out there will be one less route of escape for mankind. One less window through which to look for and find God.

With its neologisms, meditative asides and its breadth of reference, MacFhionnlaigh's work shows how the ethical and religious focus of much Gaelic verse in the nineteenth century can be sustained while still keeping fully in touch with scientific knowledge and the media-saturated world of contemporary experience. His is an exciting voice in contemporary Gaelic poetry and one that manages to speak – even in free verse – from within the tradition, without falling into too familiar tropes. His work has something of the ethical anxiety of George Campbell Hay and his delight in nature, and the questioning tone of Iain Crichton Smith; but he is equally aware of modern poets in other cultures, being influenced by MacDiarmid and Eliot and having translated poems by Pablo Neruda. MacFhionnlaigh has written a number of long poems, the first of which, *A' Mheanbhchuileag* (*The Midge*) was published in 1982 to reflect on questions of scale, power and compassion in the world, prompted by the sight of a midge – that tiny and infuriating biting insect – trapped in a spider's web. The opening lines give a good account of MacFhionnlaigh's characteristic tone and his marriage of metaphysics and politics:

It troubles me
that most of the world is under sea,
and half the day under darkness,
and the foliage of the two Poles under ice,
and Machu Picchu a ruin,
and the dodo extinct,
and gravity fighting against us,
and a third of our lives spent in sleep,
and two thirds of our brain out of use,
and the mask of the universe having slipped
so there is no correlation between beauty and truth,
and lies riddling our planet

like maggots in a cat's corpse,
and there is such a thing as that which is called death,
so that bones are more durable than brain
and plastic than love.

I'll tell you this –
I'm not Atlas;
I cannot bear the world.
I am only an atom on the surface of the globe,
struggling between fission and fusion.

It troubles me too
to see a country sink
like a sand-castle beneath the tide,
and a language thrown from us
like a faded paper flag,
and a weltanschauung forgotten
like an empty daydream,
and history disappear without a trace
like a child's footprint on the beach.
                                        (trans. F. MacFhionnlaigh)

The poem *Iolair, Brù-Dhearg, Giuthas* (*Eagle, Robin, Pine*) is a long meditation on his mother's early death from cancer, and again questions of scale, meaning and accountability haunt the poet:

Finding wisdom – that's not the problem. It's in wisdom
that we live and move and exist.
The problem is submitting to the wisdom we have found.

One leaf is big enough
to be a life-raft for the mind.
A tree rises like a boat before us.

A robin will do
as a beacon for the intellect.
An eagle will suffice as proof of infinity.
                                        (trans. R. Black)

Yet another poem sequence of nearly 2000 lines, *Bogha-Frois san Oidhche* (*Rainbow in the Night*), describes the anguish of a young son's long illness, mixing loose descriptive accounts of hospital visits with intense and prayerful lines from the Gaelic scriptures and quotations (translated into Gaelic) from Frank Baum's *The Wizard of Oz*. MacFhionnlaigh's eclecticism in this regard gives the spiritual dimension of his writing a new and truly fresh power.

Maoilos M. Caimbeul, Myles M. Campbell (b. 1944)

Born in Skye Maoilos M. Caimbeul served as a merchant seaman before returning to Scotland to take a degree at Edinburgh, since when he has worked as a Gaelic Development Officer in Inverness and a Gaelic teacher in Mull and the Gairloch. Given his profession it is not surprising that his poetry should be concerned with where his language and his homeland finds themselves in the modern world. 'An t-Eilean 'na Bhaile' ('The Island a Town') laments that the island of Mull has becomes a 'town of dispersed people / as the world grows to be a town, / the old values, tribe and kin, / withering in an industrial, technological world.' Yet in poems such as 'Do Chròcus air a Shlighe a Nèamh' ('To a Crocus on its Way to Heaven') he finds a continuing strength in natural beauty and the Gaelic praise tradition as he addresses the flower, if with an ambiguous twist towards the end:

For the sake of that beauty
that is between you and me,
dwelling in you or in me,
pouring through the fine mesh of our nature,
I will do as you desire,
I will tear you from your roots
and take you home to heaven
among the gods. You will be there
in a vase on the table
praising and being praised.
                          (trans. M. Caimbeul)

'Agus mar sin car a' Mhuiltein' ('And so a Somersault') is a long prose poem in the dream tradition of fantastic adventure, with echoes of the oral tradition in something between a surreal fairy story and a nightmarish trip.

Catriona NicGumaraid, Catrìona Montgomery (b. 1947), Mòrag NicGumaraid, Mòrag Montgomery (b. 1950) and Meg Bateman (b. 1959)

The sisters Catrìona and Mòrag NicGumaraid both reflect the homeland concerns of language, separation and the dilution of traditional communities, very much as they experienced these forces in their native Skye. They published a joint collection *A' Choille Chiar / The Gloomy Forest* in 1974. Catriona has published more than her younger sister (collected in *Rè na h-Oidhche / The Length of the Night*, 1994) and her early poems have something of the intensity of Sorley MacLean, whether dealing with love or religious anguish ('Sireadh' / 'Searching'). Her later work shows a lighter touch with the familiar issues of changing times and fading tradition, as in 'An Taigh Beag' ('The Wee House') but not without a sharper satirical edge, as in 'Rodhag, Anns a' Bhliadhna 2000 ('Roag, 2000 AD') which sees the once milky byres of her home township now filled with pottery and Beaujolais; or the wry comment on Highland gossip and godliness in 'Obhair-Ghrèis' ('Embroidery'). The verses of Morag Montgomery are a little more indirect and capable of a sly humour as in 'Muilemhàgag' ('Toad'), which describes the fate of a toad on a bench under the buttocks of a large lady. The love poems of Meg Bateman also share something of Sorley MacLean's intensity (without seeking his political range) as she interrogates the nature of love in her relationships with family, a lover, or her son, in verses that are at the same time strikingly honest, physically intimate, sensual and vulnerable. This is especially the case in her first complete collection *Aotromachd agus dàin eile / Lightness and other poems* (1997), which includes the poem series 'Do Fhear-Pòsda' ('To a Married Man'), or the poem 'Srainnsearan' ('Strangers'), which confronts the distance between a couple in the morning-after-the-night- before: 'A pale-yellow leaf / turning on its twig and dropping, / growing smaller, flatter, / like your face today . . .'. More recent poems, such as the fine 'Caraid an Dùn Eideann' ('A Friend in Edinburgh'), reflect on friends and family and the weight of the past as it manifests itself in changing landscapes, the fabric of buildings, the burdens of personal memory. Bateman took a degree in Celtic at the University of Aberdeen and a doctorate in medieval Gaelic religious poetry. She works as a lecturer at the Gaelic College in Skye.

Màiri NicGumaraid, Mary Montgomery (b. 1955) and Anna Frater (b. 1967)

Màiri NicGumaraid comes from Lewis and is no relation to the Montgomery sisters in Skye. Her relaxed verse makes use of short lines and single words, often echoing the same rhyme or assonance as she traces the course of her thoughts in response to the people and places around her, or to her own sometimes ironic, sometime angry relationship with a Gaelic culture under constant threat from diminishment on the one hand, or sentimental inflation on the other. Her poem 'Sean Bhalaist' ('Old Ballast') recognises the dangers of depending too long on a cultural identity so closely associated with defeat and exile

('I could come with a history / that was harvested whole / and sold as a prize to others'); yet 'Baile Ailein' ('Balallan') also recognises that her home village must always have a call on her. Anna Frater strikes a more regularly elegiac note (not unlike the work of fellow Lewis poet Derick Thomson) in verses that lament the island's many losses. Her collection *Fon t-Slige / Under the Shell* (1995) contains a moving poem to her grandmother whose father drowned as a returning soldier in the wreck of the SS *Iolaire*, within sight of home on New Year's Eve in 1919 ('Màiri Iain Mhurch' Chaluim'). In another poem ('Connadh' / 'Fuel') she is moved to anger when peats cut in the communal way are simply taken to town in a lorry and sold off.

Aonghas Pàdraig Caimbeul, Angus Peter Campbell (b. 1954)

Aonghas Pàdraig Caimbeul also writes of traditional community in the West, seeing it as a model for so many ways of life that are disappearing or under threat throughout the world. Born in South Uist, he has worked as a Gaelic reporter for news media and television, and has been writer – in-residence at Sabhal Mòr Ostaig, the Gaelic College in Skye. He has written novels in Gaelic specifically for teenage readers and his poems in Gaelic (he writes many in English too) were published in *One Road* (1994). 'Oidhe Chullaig' ('Hogmanay Night') celebrates the original joy of the old ceremonies and renews the act of blessing that is their essence, while 'Gearraidh na Mònadh á Smeircleit' ('Garrynamonie from Smerclate') lists all the houses in that township by way of the names of those who live there – or perhaps these are the names of the original inhabitants living on and forever attached to these stone walls only in local memory. 'Radar Beinn Sheaval' sees Ben Shieval and the modern world beyond its peaks – the 'free world' – given over to radar warning systems 'waiting for crumbs / On the mountainsides of our sloth and docility'. His poems in English are equally outspoken about the forces – and the moral 'sloth' too – that despoiled the Arctic and brought a different kind of 'clearance' to Native Americans ('Indians Dispossessed'). Reflecting on the ironies of his own time at the Sabhal Mòr (literally 'the big barn', now a place of Gaelic education) in 'Dan an t-Sabhail' ('The Song of the Barn'), he remembers bitterly how the animals inherited the Highlands, when so many people left:

> . . . who never saw a college
> alive with their songs and prayers
> in my memory, in my conscience, in my blood, in my head, in my poetry:

the Sabhal for the animals, and Canada for the people –
let's feed that into the computers and make a hì-ho-ro-hiù of it.

If there is pain here it may in part be due to a feeling of being trapped
in a tradition that will not let (cannot let) such memories die.

Rody Gorman (b. 1960)

Rody Gorman has also worked at the Sabhal Mòr. He has published
several collections in Scotland and Ireland, including his first volume
Fax and Other Poems (1996), followed then by *Cùis-Ghaoil* (1999),
Air a' Charbad fo Thalamh / On the Underground (2000) and
Taaaaaadhaaaaaaal! (2003). His poetry makes frequent reference to
contemporary culture while still alert to traditional associations, as in
the title-poem 'Fax', which likens the noise of the fax machine to 'a
corncrake in the meadow / or a pig grunting' while the 'printer beside
it is a waterfall / with white pages gushing out of it'. These things, the
poet concludes, 'will put their own form neatly / On today's world'.
Such lines are characteristic of his poetic position. Born in Dublin and
a native Irish speaker who has also learned Scottish Gaelic, Gorman has
lived on Skye for many years. He is committed to linguistic pluralism
by mixing lines in Gaelic and English in the same poem, or by allowing other poets to translate some of his own Gaelic work into English,
or (following George Campbell Hay's example) into Scots. He has
edited an anthology of Scottish and Irish Gaelic poetry and has translated European and American poets and Japanese *haiku* into Gaelic. In
fact his own work often has a *haiku*-like spareness to it that fits well
with the sardonic and tender freshness of his love-poems and his dry
and wry engagement with tradition. Both qualities are evident in the
poem 'Mise nam Ghaidheal' ('Me as a Gael'):

> I am a Gael
> Who has depended in his time
> On seaweed
> And on potato
> And on herring
> And every one of them has gone
> And now here's you packing your bags
> And going away in the morning.
> (trans. R. Gorman)

Gorman has written a Gaelic poem on the death of Charles
Bukowski, and his wide-ranging, humorous, experimental, spare and

eclectic muse promises well for contemporary poetry in Gaelic. In an interview in 2004 he recognised with regret that the old oral tradition was passing away in Scotland as in many other cultures around the world, but noted that 'there is a counter balance . . . with the literary tradition taking its place', and in this regard he recognised the importance of the many younger poets who have learned Gaelic and are writing poetry in it.

Crisdean Whyte, Christopher Whyte (b. 1952)

As a literary scholar and former academic in the Scottish Literature Department at the University of Glasgow, Christopher Whyte is a case in point, and his first writings in Gaelic included translations of the Spanish-language poet Constantino Cavafis. White has a wide interest in Italian, Spanish and Catalan culture and has translated verse from all these languages, while his own Gaelic poems have been translated into European languages in their turn. A verse sequence of Browningesque monologue such as 'Fontana Maggiore', from Whyte's first collection *Uirsgeal / Myth* (1991), demonstrates his determination to take poetry in Gaelic away from its familiar Highland settings and themes, as does his later sequence 'Bho Leabhar-Latha Maria Malibran' ('From the Diary of Maria Malibran'), which imagines a first-person monologue by this nineteenth-century opera singer, only to end with an authorial challenge to the reader and a reference to the myth of Cadmus and the founding of Thebes:

> . . . I am not a true Gael
> it would seem. But, gentle readers,
> I'll cast these words on hostile, barren,
> unsympathetic ground, and you can
> just believe me, even though they're not
>
> dragons' teeth, nor are they pebbles,
> in the long run they will start to grow.
> (trans. R. Black)

Kevin MacNeil (b. 1973)

Kevin MacNeil is outward looking in a different way. A native-speaker from Lewis, he shares Gorman's interest in *haiku* and, like his Scottish precursors Alan Spence and Neil Gunn, is strongly committed to Zen as a way of responding to – or rather living in – the world. The poems in his well-received first collection *Love and Zen in the Outer Hebrides*

(2001) include translations of Basho into Gaelic, but his own work has a specially surreal tenderness, half way between an ironic nod to the familiar clichés of Gaelic melancholy (reminiscent of Iain Crichton Smith's humour) and an invigorating sense of chilly space, poetic minimalism and Zen insight. The poem 'faclan, eich-mhara' ('words, seahorses') shows his image-making ability:

> i dreamt i was the seafloor and you were the weight of the ocean pressing
> down on me, your quiet words of love in my ears now and again,
> golden, elegant and strange, like seahorses, like grace-notes, tiny
> floating saxophones

MacNeil is a vigorous defender of Gaelic's right to a fair hearing in Scottish cultural circles, against those who would consign it to the dustbin of history: 'The contemporary Gael is well-educated, well-travelled, talented, open-minded – and sick fed-up of defending a language against bigoted remarks which, were they directed against Urdu or Cantonese, would surely constitute racism.' He has made his own contribution to a culturally plural Scotland by co-editing with Alec Finlay the anthology *Wish I Was Here* (2001), which contains the work of Scottish poets from the Gàidhealtachd, Shetland and Asia – each with their own insights into questions of community, language and identity and what it might mean to be a Scot, a Scottish poet, or indeed a poet at all, in the face of the globalising drives of commerce and the mass media, and the need to find space for what Fearghas MacFhionnlaigh saw as the 'blessing' of difference and multiplicity in our culture and all our languages.

Changing places and other tongues: envoi

It seems apposite to have ended this volume with a survey of contemporary poetry in Scotland, given that poetry played such a large part in the early years of the modern literary Renaissance as a signifier of cultural, socio-political and linguistic distinctiveness. In many of these younger poets, however, the agenda of difference and nationality has given way to a more complex engagement with a conception of identity that owes as much to psychology, gender and sexuality, or to a post-structuralist recognition that it is language that makes us (and the world around us), rather than vice versa. And part of that construction is the recognition, too, that we become who we are by way of culture, which is to say through the stories we tell about ourselves, whether these stories are predicated on conceptions of place, or the remembering (real or imagined) of what we take to be our personal or our collective histories. Such are the concerns of the poets discussed above, from Douglas Dunn's concern to sustain a tolerant and enlightened humanity in his sense of a northern identity without forgetting old differences, to the rage and pain of Tom Leonard's uncompromising quarrel with the social and political hegemony of English as a leading factor in class prejudice and cultural disenfranchisement. In complete contrast, the conceptually good-humoured extravagance of Robert Crawford and W. N. Herbert's engagement with Scots relishes that language's literary role as an 'other' to English, or as a 'forked' tongue that can overthrow, or at least call into question, all pretensions to authority and stability. Then again, the slippery nature of language and the part it plays in making us what we think we are – both sexually and socially – appears in the work of David Kinloch, Carol Ann Duffy and Jackie Kay. For other writers, however, the old ties remain and the beloved wounds of homeland, clearance and emigration can still be seen to feature, for example, in some contemporary Gaelic writing. On the other hand, poets such as Kathleen Jamie, Rody Gorman and Kevin MacNeil have discovered a creative, affectionate and not entirely unironic pleasure in cultural and linguistic marginality by playing with, or against, its now familiar tropes in a welcome and engaging release from old ghosts.

'Of the making of books there is no end', and the need to make some sort of coherent narrative (rather than just an encyclopaedic anthology of names) in this work has inevitably meant that there are good writers missing from or under-represented in my account. For such omissions I can only hope for the understanding of readers and authors (at least the living ones) alike. This is not the only possible version of the long narrative of the literature of Scotland, yet I hope it has left some space for readers to make their own connections, too, while remaining readable: for the story – and the fable too – is still unwinding in all three (and now more) of Scotland's languages. But let us 'mak up work heirof', as Gavin Douglas says, 'and clos our buke'.

Chronological table

Abbreviations: A = autobiography; B = biography; C = cinema;
D = drama; F = fiction; P = prose; V = verse; *d.* = dies; *r.* = reigned.

Date	Author	Event
1880–1	James Thomson, *City of Dreadful Night* (V) Oliphant, *A Beleaguered City* (F)	Dostoevsky, *The Brothers Karamazov* James, *Portrait of a Lady*
1882	Gaelic poetry of Mary Macpherson	The 'battle of Braes' on Skye Highland Land League
1883	Stevenson, *Treasure Island* (F)	Renan, *Souvenirs d'enfance et de jeunesse* Nietzsche, *Thus Spoke Zarathustra* Edison invents light bulb
1886	Stevenson, *Dr Jekyll and Mr Hyde* and *Kidnapped* (F)	Daimler Benz motor car Seurat, 'La Grande Jatte' English translation of *Das Kapital*
1887	Lang, *Myth, Ritual and Religion* (P)	Dunlop develops pneumatic tyre
1888	Barrie, *Auld Licht Idylls* (F)	Scottish Labour Party formed with Keir Hardie and Cunninghame Graham
1889	Stevenson, *The Master of Ballantrae* (F) Barrie, *A Window in Thrums* (F)	Yeats, *The Wanderings of Oisin* Carnegie endows libraries
1890	MacGonagall, *Poetic Gems* (V) Oliphant, *Kirsteen* (F) Frazer, *The Golden Bough* (P)	Forth Rail Bridge completed
1891	Conan Doyle, Sherlock Holmes stories (F)	
1892		Geddes founds the Outlook Tower in Edinburgh
1893	Davidson, *Fleet Street Eclogues* (V) Crockett, *The Stickit Minister* (F)	

Date	Author	Event
1894	Maclaren, *Beside the Bonnie Brier Bush* (F) Sharp, *Pharais* (F)	*The Yellow Book* Debussy, *L'Après-midi d'un faune*
1895	George MacDonald, *Lilith* (F) Sharp, *The Mountain Lovers* (F)	Trial of Oscar Wilde Yeats, *Poems* Marconi and wireless Lumière shows film of a train in Paris
1896	Stevenson, *Weir of Hermiston* (F) Barrie, *Margaret Ogilvie* (B) Munro, *The Lost Pibroch* (F)	
1898	Buchan, *John Burnet of Barns* (F)	
1899		Boer War (1899–1902) Wilde, 'Ballad of Reading Gaol' Zola, 'J'accuse'
1900	Charles Murray, *Hamewith* (V) Cunninghame Graham, *Thirteen Stories* (F)	Freud, *Interpretation of Dreams* Sibelius, *Finlandia* Chekhov, *Uncle Vania* Strindberg, *Dance of Death*
1901	George Douglas Brown, *The House with the Green Shutters* (F) Bell, *Wee McGregor* (F)	Edward VII (r. 1901–10) Kipling, *Kim*
1904	Barrie, *Peter Pan* (D) Geddes, *City Development* (P)	Rennie Mackintosh designs Willow Tea Rooms in Glasgow. Synge, *Riders to the Sea*
1905		Einstein, Theory of Relativity
1907		Picasso, 'Les Demoiselles d'Avignon' Bergson, *Creative Evolution* Kipling wins Nobel Prize
1908	Davidson, *Testament of John Davidson* (V)	
1910	Buchan, *Prester John* (F)	George V (r. 1910–36)
1911	Jacob, *Flemington* (F)	Marsh (ed.), *Georgian Poetry*
1913	Compton Mackenzie, *Sinister Street* (F)	Stravinsky, *Rite of Spring* Lawrence, *Sons and Lovers* Clydeside produces one-fifth of world shipping
1914	John MacDougall Hay, *Gillespie* (F)	First World War (1914–18) Yeats, *Responsibilities* Joyce, *Dubliners*

Date	Author	Event
1915	Buchan, *The Thirty-Nine Steps* (F) Jacob, *Songs of Angus* (V) Norman Douglas, *Old Calabria* (P)	Einstein, General Theory of Relativity Griffiths, *Birth of a Nation*
1916	Buchan, *Greenmantle* (F)	Easter Rising in Dublin
1917	Norman Douglas, *South Wind* (F)	Russian Revolution Jung, *The Unconscious*
1919	Smith, *Scottish Literature,* *Character and Influence* (P)	'40 Hour' strike in Glasgow. Troops called out: 'Red Clydeside'
1920	Grieve ('Hugh MacDiarmid') (ed.), *Northern Numbers* (1920–2) Lindsay, *A Voyage to Arcturus* (F) Barrie, *Mary Rose* (D) Carswell, *Open the Door* (F)	Prohibition in America (until 1933) Wells, *The Outline of History*
1921	Jacob, *Bonnie Joann* (V)	Lawrence, *Women in Love*
1922	Grieve (ed.), *Scottish Chapbook* Carswell, *The Camomile* (F) Angus, *The Lilt* (V)	Eliot, *The Waste Land* Joyce, *Ulysses* Mussolini marches on Rome and forms Fascist government Stalin becomes General-Secretary
1923	Grieve, *Annals of the Five* *Senses* (F) Mitchison, *The Conquered* (F)	John Maclean d. Shaw, *St Joan* Nobel Prize for Yeats
1924	Angus, *The Tinker's Road* (V)	MacDonald forms First Labour Government Forster, *A Passage to India*
1925	MacDiarmid, *Sangschaw* (V) Muir, *First Poems* (V) Gunn, *Grey Coast* (F)	Hitler, *Mein Kampf* Kafka, *The Trial* Woolf, *Mrs Dalloway* Fitzgerald, *The Great Gatsby* Baird transmits first moving televisual picture Shaw wins Nobel Prize
1926	MacDiarmid, *Penny Wheep* and *A Drunk Man Looks at the* *Thistle* (V) Gunn, *Grey Coast* (F)	General Strike Kafka, *The Castle* Hemingway, *The Sun Also Rises*
1928	Shepherd, *Quarry Wood* (F) Corrie, *In Time of Strife* (D)	National Party of Scotland formed Women get vote in Britain. Lawrence, *Lady Chatterley's Lover*
1929	Linklater, *White Maa's Saga* (F) Grant and Murison, *Scottish* *National Dictionary* (1929–76)	Trotsky expelled from Russia. Wall Street crash Labour government in Britain Hemingway, *A Farewell to Arms*

Date	Author	Event
1930	Bridie, *The Anatomist* (D) Carswell, *Life of Burns* (B) Shepherd, *The Weatherhouse* (F)	Gandhi starts civil disobedience in India
1931	MacDiarmid, *First Hymn to Lenin* (V) W. Muir, *Imagined Corners* (F) Linklater, *Juan in America* (F) Mitchison, *The Corn King and the Spring Queen* (F) Cronin, *Hatter's Castle* (F)	Scottish Party formed. MacDonald forms National Government to balance budget Riots in Glasgow and London; naval mutiny at Invergordon Scottish Colourists exhibit in Paris
1932	Gibbon, *Sunset Song* (F) MacDiarmid, *Scots Unbound* (V) Muir, *Poor Tom* (F) MacColla, *The Albannach* (F)	Hunger marches in Britain Faulkner, *Light in August*
1933	Gibbon, *Cloud Howe* (F) Shepherd, *A Pass in the Grampians* (F) Bridie, *A Sleeping Clergyman* (D) MacDiarmid, *Second Hymn to Lenin* (V) W. Muir, *Mrs Ritchie* (F) Soutar, *Seeds in the Wind* (V)	Reichstag fire; Hitler takes power: Jews persecuted in Germany Orwell, *Down and Out in Paris and London*
1934	Gibbon, *Grey Granite* (F) Linklater, *Magnus Merriman* (F) MacDiarmid, *Stony Limits* (V) Cruickshank, *Up the Noran Water* (V) McLellan, *Jeddart Justice* (D)	Scottish National Party formed Fitzgerald, *Tender is the Night*
1935	Blake, *The Shipbuilders* (F) MacArthur and Long, *No Mean City* (F) Soutar, *Poems in Scots* (V) Muir, *Scottish Journey* (P)	
1936	Muir, *Scott and Scotland* (P) Macpherson, *Wild Harbour* (F) Barke, *Major Operation* (D) Craigie, Aitken and Stevenson, *Dictionary of the Older Scottish Tongue*	Edward VIII abdicates George VI (r. 1936–52) Spanish Civil War (1936–9)
1937	Gunn, *Highland River* (F) Muir, *Journeys and Places* (V) Compton Mackenzie, *The Four Winds of Love* (F) (1937–45) McLellan, *Jamie the Saxt* (D)	Scottish Gaelic Text Society formed Aimé Césaire helps coin concept of *négritude* in anti-colonial movement of black liberation

Date	Author	Event
1939	Mitchison, *Blood of the Martyrs* (F) Barke, *The Land of the Leal* (F)	Second World War (1939–45) Steinbeck, *The Grapes of Wrath* Joyce, *Finnegans Wake*
1941	Gunn, *The Silver Darlings* (F) Buchan, *Sick Heart River* (F)	Battles of El Alamein and Stalingrad Pearl Harbor: America enters war
1942		Camus, *Le Mythe de Sisyphe* and *L'Etranger* (both 1942)
1943	Sorley MacLean, *Dain do Eimhir* (V) M. Lindsay (ed.), *Poetry Scotland* (V) (1943–9) MacDiarmid, *Lucky Poet* (A) MacCaig, *A Far Cry* (V) Bridie, *Mr Bolfry* (D)	
1944	Gunn, *The Green Isle of the Great Deep* (F) Bruce, *Sea Talk* (V)	D-Day Normandy landings Construction of atomic bomb Eliot, *Four Quartets*
1945		Bombing of Hiroshima and Nagasaki; end of Second World War
1946	Linklater, *Private Angelo* (F) Goodsir Smith, *The Deevil's Waltz* (V)	
1947	Stewart, *Men Should Weep* (D) Hendry, *Fernie Brae* (F) McCrone, *Wax Fruit* trilogy (F) Mitchison, *The Bull Calves* (F) Goodsir Smith, *Carotid Cornucopius* (F)	Independence of India; Partition and creation of Pakistan Sartre, *Huis Clos*
1948	Goodsir Smith, *Under the Eildon Tree* (V) Henderson, *Elegies for the Dead in Cyrenaica* (V) Gaitens, *Dance of the Apprentices* (F) Lindsay, *Hurlygush* (V)	Lindsay's *Satire of the Three Estates* performed at second Edinburgh International Festival Faulkner, *Intruder in the Dust* T. S. Eliot wins Nobel Prize
1949	Muir, *The Labyrinth* (V) Mackendrick, *Whisky Galore* (C) A. Scott, *The Latest in Elegies* (V)	Orwell, *1984* Faulkner wins Nobel Prize
1950	Reid, *The Lass wi' the Muckle Mou'* (D) Young, *Selected Poems* (V)	Korean War (1950–3) Pound, *Cantos* Stone of Scone stolen from Westminster by Scottish nationalists
1951	Derick Thomson, *An Dealbh Briste* (V) Gunn, *The Well at the World's End* (F)	School of Scottish Studies founded

Date	Author	Event
1953	Reid, *The Warld's Wonder* (D)	Coronation of Elizabeth II Stalin d. Beckett, *Waiting for Godot*
1954	Muir, *An Autobiography* (A) Soutar, *Diaries of a Dying Man* (A) Trocchi, *Young Adam* (F) McKendrick *The Maggie* (C)	Minelli films *Brigadoon* French in Vietnam: battle of Dienbienphu Hemingway wins Nobel Prize
1955	MacCaig, *Riding Lights* (V) MacDiarmid, *In Memoriam James Joyce* (V) Graham, *The Nightfishing* (V) Munro, *Para Handy Tales* (F) Jenkins, *The Cone Gatherers* (F)	Nabokov, *Lolita* Tolkien, *Lord of the Rings*
1956	Gunn, *Atom of Delight* (A) Kennaway, *Tunes of Glory* (F)	Suez crisis Russia invades Hungary
1957	Spark, *The Comforters* (F)	Macmillan leads Conservative government (1957–63)
1958	Kesson, *The White Bird Passes* (F) Hanley, *Dancing in the Streets* (F) Jenkins, *The Changeling* (F)	
1959	Brown, *Loaves and Fishes* (V) Goodsir Smith, *Figs and Thistles* (V) Spark, *Memento Mori* (F)	Pasternak, *Dr Zhivago* Grass, *The Tin Drum* Roth, *Goodbye Columbus* Vonnegut, *The Sirens of Titan* Bellow, *Henderson the Rain King* Buddy Holly dies
1960	Muir, *Collected Poems* (V) Finlay, *The Dancers Inherit the Party* (V) Spark, *Ballad of Peckham Rye* (F) Goodsir Smith, *The Wallace* (D)	Oil discovered in North Sea
1961	Crichton Smith, *Thistles and Roses* (V) Jenkins, *Dust on the Paw* (F) Kennaway, *Household Ghosts* (F) Trocchi, *Cain's Book* (F) Spark, *Prime of Miss Jean Brodie* (F)	Berlin Wall built Bay of Pigs débâcle Mass CND rally in Trafalgar Square Gagarin in space Green Berets in Vietnam Heller, *Catch 22*
1962	MacDiarmid, *Collected Poems* (V) Kesson, *Glitter of Mica* (F) Mitchison, *Memoirs of a Spacewoman* (F)	Cuban missile crisis Solzhenitsyn, *One Day in the Life of Ivan Denisovich*

Date	Author	Event
1963	Finlay, *Rapel* (V) T. Scott, *The Ship and other poems* (V) Spark, *Girls of Slender Means* (F)	Assassination of President Kennedy Home leads Tory government (1963–4) Baldwin, *The Fire Next Time*
1964	Friel, *The Boy Who Wanted Peace* (F)	Wilson leads new government for Labour (1964–70) McLuhan, *Understanding Media* Forth Road Bridge opened
1965	Crichton Smith, *Biobull is Sanasan Reice* (V); *The Law and the Grace* (V) Sharp, *A Green Tree in Gedde* (F)	200,000 American combat troops in Vietnam (1965–73)
1966	McIlvanney, *Remedy is None* (F) Garioch, *Selected Poems* (V) Hind, *The Dear Green Place* (F) White, *The Cold Wind of Dawn* (V) MacCaig, *Surroundings* (V)	Rise of SNP popular support Cultural Revolution in China Barth, *Giles Goat-Boy*
1967	Black, *With Decorum* (V)	Scottish Arts Council established Ewing wins strong Labour seat for SNP at Hamilton Homosexuality decriminalised in UK
1968	Morgan, *The Second Life* (V) Crichton Smith, *Consider the Lilies* (F) Williams, *From Scenes Like These* (F) McIlvanney, *A Gift from Nessus* (F) W. Muir, *Belonging* (A) Gray, *The Fall of Kelvin Walker* (D)	Oil rigs in North Sea Moves towards Devolution proposed Martin Luther King assassinated Tet offensive in Vietnam; My Lai massacre
1969	Friel, *Grace and Miss Partridge* (F) Brown, *A Time to Keep* (F) Dunn, *Terry Street* (V) Leonard, *Six Glasgow Poems* (V) Crichton Smith, *From Bourgeois Land* (V)	Fowles, *The French Lieutenant's Woman* Vonnegut, *Slaughterhouse 5* Armstrong stands on Moon
1970	Thompson, *An Rathad Cian* (V) Crichton Smith, *Selected Poems* (V)	Heath leads Conservative Government (1970–4) Students killed at Kent State, Ohio Greer, *The Female Eunuch*
1971	Davie, *Creating a Scene* (F) MacCaig, *Selected Poems* (V) Brown, *Fishermen with Ploughs* (V) Bruce, *Collected Poems* (V) Boyd, *The View from Daniel Pike* (C)	The Pentagon Papers published Work-in at Clyde shipyard

Date	Author	Event
1972	Friel, *Mr Alfred MA* (F) Brown, *Greenvoe* (F) Bryden, *Willie Rough* (D) Lochhead, *Memo for Spring* (V) Douglas, *My Childhood* (C) trilogy (1972–8)	Nixon visits China Bloody Sunday violence in Northern Ireland Watergate scandals in Washington
1973	McGrath, *The Cheviot, the Stag and the Black, Black Oil* (D) McMillan, *The Bevellers* (D) MacMillan, *The Sash* (D) Morgan, *From Glasgow to Saturn* (V) Brown, *Magnus* (F)	Ceasefire in Vietnam, US troops leave
1974	C. & M. Montgomery, *The Gloomy Forest* (V)	Labour in power again with Wilson (1974–6)
1975	McIlvanney, *Docherty* (F) MacDougall, *A Scent of Water* (F) Garioch, *Two Men and a Blanket* (A)	Wolfe, *The Right Stuff*
1976	Davie, *The High Tide Talker* (F) Campbell, *The Jesuit* (D)	Labour under Callaghan (1976–9)
1977	McIlvanney, *Laidlaw* (F) Spence, *Its Colours They Are Fine* (F) McLellan, *Linmill and Other Stories* (F) Graham, *Implements in Their Places* (V) Greig, *Men on Ice* (V) T. Scott, *The Tree* (V) T. McGrath, *The Hard Man* (D)	Devolution for Wales and Scotland, new Bills proposed Sex Pistols, 'God Save the Queen'
1978	Davie, *Climbers on a Stair* (F) Massie, *Change and Decay in All Around I See* (F) Campbell, *Somerville the Soldier* (D) Byrne, *The Slab Boys* (D) Herdman, *Pagan's Pilgrimage* (F)	Mass suicide in Johnstown
1979	Black, *Gravitations* (V) Lindsay, *Collected Poems* (V) Dunn, *Barbarians* (V) Jenkins, *Fergus Lamont* (F)	Devolution Bill fails on insufficient majority Labour lose election; Thatcher leads Tory government (1979–90) and repeals Scotland Act
1980	MacLaverty, *Lamb* (F)	John Lennon assassinated
1981	Gray, *Lanark* (F) Spark, *Loitering with Intent* (F)	Rushdie, *Midnight's Children* wins Booker Prize

Date	Author	Event
1981 cont	Boyd, *A Good Man in Africa* (F) Lochhead, *The Grimm Sisters* (V) Dunn, *St Kilda's Parliament* (V) Spence, *Glasgow Zen* (V)	
1982	Forsyth, *Gregory's Girl* (C) Thomson, *Collected Poems 1940–80* (V) Massie, *The Death of Men* (F) MacFhionnlaigh, 'The Midge' (V)	The Falklands War
1983	Gray, *Unlikely Stories Mostly* (F) Kelman, *Not Not While the Giro* (F) Kesson, *Another Time Another Place* (F) Forsyth, *Local Hero* (C) Jamie, *Black Spiders* (V)	Thatcher wins second general election, Labour majority in Scotland Golding wins Nobel Prize
1984	Gray, *1982 Janine* (F) Kelman, *Busconductor Hines* (F) Banks, *The Wasp Factory* (F) Frame, *Winter Journey* (F) Kuppner, *A Bad Day for the Sung Dynasty* (V) Leonard, *Intimate Voices* (V) Lochhead, *Dreaming Frankenstein* (V)	The miners' strike (1984–5) Bomb at Tory Conference in Brighton Macintosh produce first personal computer with graphic interface and mouse
1985	McIlvanney, *The Big Man* (F) Gray, *The Fall of Kelvin Walker* (F) McCabe, *The Lipstick Circus* (F) Dunn, *Elegies* (V) Greig, *Summit Fever* (P) Lochhead, *True Confessions and New Clichés* (V) Butlin, *Ragtime in Unfamiliar Bars* (V)	First British mobile phone call made
1986	Banks, *The Bridge* (F) MacDougall, *Elvis is Dead* (F) MacNeacail, *The Avoiding* (V)	Chernobyl disaster
1987	Lochhead, *Mary Queen of Scots Got Her Head Chopped Off* (D) Byrne, *Tutti Frutti* (D) Kuppner, *The Intelligent Observation of Naked Women* (V) Rankin, *Knots and Crosses* (F)	'The Vigorous Imagination' exhibition of new Scottish art Doyle, *The Commitments* Lockerbie aircraft bombing
1988	Jenkins, *Just Duffy* (F) MacCaig, *Voice Over* (V) McWilliam, *A Case of Knives* (F) Dunn, *Northlight* (V)	Rushdie, *The Satanic Verses*

Date	Author	Event
1989	White, *The Bird Path* (V)	Berlin Wall falls
	Kelman, *A Disaffection* (F)	Student protests in Tianamen Square
	Massie, *A Question of Loyalties* (F)	Fatwah declared on Rushdie
	Legge, *The Shoe* (F)	Exxon Valdez oil spill
	Byrne, *Your Cheatin' Heart* (D)	Vaclav Havel, President of
	MacDougall, *Stone Over Water* (F)	Czechoslovakia
	Rose, *Our Lady of the Pickpockets* (F)	
	Hayton, *Cells of Knowledge* (F)	
1990	Spence, *The Magic Flute* (F)	Conservative government under
	Galloway, *The Trick is to Keep Breathing* (F)	Major (1990–7)
	Gray, *Something Leather* (F)	Mandela freed and ANC in power
	Kennedy, *Night Geometry and the Garscadden Trains* (F)	Glasgow is 'Cultural Capital' of Europe
	Boyd, *Brazzaville Beach* (F)	World Wide Web
	Crawford & Herbert, *Sharawaggi* (V)	Reunification of Germany
	Crawford, *A Scottish Assembly* (V)	Roddy Doyle, *The Snapper*
	Greig, *The Order of the Day* (V)	
	Duffy, *The Other Country* (V)	
	Whyte, *Myth* (V)	
1991	Glover, *Bondagers* (D)	Operation Desert Storm, first Gulf War
	Black, *Collected Poems* (V)	
	Massie, *The Sins of the Father* (F)	Division and ethnic conflict in Yugoslavia
	Galloway, *Blood* (F)	DeLillo, *Mao II*
	Kelman, *The Burn* (F)	
	Frame, *Underwood and After* (F)	
	Smith, *Free Love and other stories* (F)	
	Kay, *The Adoption Papers* (V)	
	Herbert, *Dundee Doldrums* (V)	
	Burnside, *Common Knowledge* (V)	
1992	McLean, *Bucket of Tongues* (F)	Soviet Union dissolved
	Gray, *Poor Things* (F)	European Union declared
	Banks, *The Crow Road* (F)	
	Greig, *Electric Brae* (F)	
	Spark, *Curriculum Vitae* (A)	
	Burnside, *Feast Days* (V)	
	Kinloch, *Dustie-fute* (V)	
	McSeveney, *Coming out with It* (V)	
1993	Welsh, *Trainspotting* (F)	Bomb at World Trade Centre, NY
	Jenkins, *Willie Hogg* (F)	Proulx, *The Shipping News*
	Banks, *Complicity* (F)	Keneally, *Schindler's List*
	Herdman, *Imelda* (F)	
	Kennedy, *Looking for the Possible Dance* (F)	
	Kay, *Other Lovers* (V)	
	Paterson, *Nil Nil* (V)	

Date	Author	Event
1994	Kelman, *How Late It Was, How Late* (F)	Mandela President of South Africa
		Genocide in Rwanda
	Galloway, *Foreign Parts* (F)	Kelman wins Booker Prize
	Kuppner, *Something Very Like Murder* (F)	
	Everything is Strange (V)	
	MacLaverty, *Walking the Dog* (F)	
	McWilliam, *Debatable Land* (F)	
	Crumey, *Music in a Foreign Language* (F)	
	Greig, *Western Swing* (V)	
	Jamie, *The Queen of Sheba* (V)	
	Herbert, *Forked Tongue* (V)	
	Kinloch, *Paris-Forfar* (V)	
	A. P. Campbell, *One Road* (V)	
	Montgomery, *The Length of the Night* (V)	
1995	Welsh, *Marabou Stork Nightmares* (F)	Seamus Heaney awarded Nobel Prize
	Kennedy, *So I Am Glad* (F)	Peace process begins in Northern
	Smith, *Free Love and other Stories* (F)	Ireland
	Dillon, *Me and Ma Gal* (F)	Film *Braveheart*
	Warner, *Morvern Callar* (F)	
	Crumey, *Pfitz* (F)	
	Cambridge, *The Shell House* (V)	
	Clanchy, *Slattern* (V)	
	Frater, *Under the Shell* (V)	
	Boyle (dir.), *Trainspotting* (C)	
1996	Morgan, *Collected Poems* (V)	EU ban on British beef
	Galloway, *Where You Find It* (F)	Dolly the Sheep successfully cloned at
	MacNeacail, *A Proper Schooling* (V)	the Roslin Institute
	Gorman, *Fax and other poems* (V)	'Dunblane massacre' changes gun law
	Herbert, *Cabaret McGonagall* (V)	in UK
1997	Hird, *Nail* (F)	Blair and 'New Labour' come to power
	Massie, *Shadows of Empire* (F)	In referendum 74% say 'yes' to Scottish
	Kennedy, *Original Bliss* (F)	parliament
	MacLaverty, *Grace Notes* (F)	Rebellion in Albania
	McLean, *Bunker Man* (F)	Hale-Bopp Comet
	Butlin, *The Sound of My Voice* (F)	Hong Kong returned to China
	Burnside, *The Dumb House* (F)	
	Warner, *These Demented Lands* (F)	
	Rowling, *Harry Potter and the Philosopher's Stone* (F)	
	Paterson, *God's Gift to Women* (V)	
	Bateman, *Lightness* (V)	
1998	Welsh, *Filth* (F)	Scotland Act passed
	Kay, *Trumpet* (F)	

Date	Author	Event

1998 cont
Spence, *Way to Go* (F)
Rose, *War Dolls* (F)
Warner, *The Sopranos* (F)
McCall Smith, *The No. 1 Ladies' Detective Agency* (F)

1999
Hird, *Born Free* (F)
Greig, *When They Lay Bare* (F)
Kennedy, *Everything You Need* (F)
Smith, *Other Stories and other stories* (F)
Jamie, *Jizzen* (V)
Crawford, *Spirit Machines* (V)
Duffy, *The World's Wife* (V)
Clanchy, *Samarkand* (V)
McCabe, *Body Parts* (V)

Clinton impeachment defeated
Scottish Parliament opens in Edinburgh on Mound
War in Kosovo

2000
Burnside, *The Asylum Dance* (V)
Faber, *Under the Skin* (F)
Crumey, *Mr Mee* (F)
Elphinstone, *The Sea Road* (F)
Robertson, *The Fanatic* (F)
Dunn, *The Donkey's Ears* (V)
Burnside, *The Asylum Dance* (V)

Roth, *The Human Stain*
Human Genome project completed in 10 years
Controversy over US presidential election process

2001
Kelman, *Translated Accounts* (F)
Welsh, *Glue* (F)
Jenkins, *Childish Things* (F)
Smith, *Hotel World* (F)
Frame, *The Lantern Bearers* (F)
McCabe, *A Date with My Wife* (F)
Burnside, *The Locust Room* (F)
Bruce, *Today Tomorrow: Collected Poems* (V)
MacNeil, *Love and Zen in the Outer Hebrides* (V)

World Trade Centre destroyed in NY
US invasion of Afghanistan
George W. Bush declares 'War on Terror'

2002
Warner, *The Man Who Walks* (F)
Galloway, *Clara* (F)
Faber, *The Crimson Petal and the White* (F)
Dunn, *New Selected Poems* (V)
Morgan, *Cathures* (V)
Gibson, *Wild Women of a Certain Age* (V)

Introduction of Euro notes and coins as legal tender in 12 European countries

2003
Smith, *Whole Story and other stories* (F)
Donovan, *Buddha Da* (F)
Robertson, *Joseph Knight* (F)

Invasion of Iraq
Space Shuttle Columbia disintegrates on re-entry

Date	Author	Event
2003 cont	Lochhead, *The Colour of Black and White* (V) Crawford, *The Tip of my Tongue* (V)	
2004	Saadi, *Psychoraag* (F) Greig, *In Another Light* (F) Jamie, *The Tree House* (V) Kennedy, *Paradise* (F) Kelman, *You Have to be Careful in the Land of the Free* (F) Leonard, *Access to the Silence* (V) Clancy, *Newborn* (V)	Opening of new Scottish Parliament building at Holyrood Tsunami in Indonesia Train bombing in Madrid
2005	Butlin, *Without a Backward Glance* (V) Kay, *Life Mask* (V) Paterson, *The Book of Shadows* (aphorisms) Kinloch, *In My Father's House* (V) Bissett, *The Incredible Adam Spark* (F) Meek, *The People's Act of Love* (F)	G8 Summit at Gleneagles Terrorist bombs in London Earthquake in Kashmir Scottish Parliament listed as 'best' and also 'worst' building of year Pinter wins Nobel Prize

Select Bibliography and Further Reading

Literary History

Craig, Cairns: (General Editor), *The History of Scottish Literature* (Aberdeen: Aberdeen University Press, 1987–8):
  Volume One, *Origins to 1660*, ed. R. D. S. Jack (1988).
  Volume Two, *1660–1800*, ed. Andrew Hook (1987).
  Volume Three, *Nineteenth Century*, ed. Douglas Gifford (1988).
  Volume Four, *Twentieth Century*, ed. Cairns Craig (1987).
Craig, David, *Scottish Literature and the Scottish People, 1680–1830* (London: Chatto & Windus, 1961).
Daiches, David (ed.), *A Companion to Scottish Culture* (London: Edward Arnold, 1981).
Findlay, Bill (ed.), *A History of Scottish Theatre* (Edinburgh: Polygon, 1998).
Gifford, Douglas and McMillan, Dorothy (eds), *A History of Scottish Women's Writing* (Edinburgh: Edinburgh University Press, 1997).
Gifford, Douglas, Dunnigan, Sarah and MacGillivray, Alan (eds), *Scottish Literature in English and Scots* (Edinburgh: Edinburgh University Press, 2002). Contains over 200 pages of an outstandingly extensive and detailed bibliography of primary and secondary texts and further reading.
Hart, Francis, *The Scottish Novel* (London: John Murray, 1978).
Henderson, T. F., *Scottish Vernacular Literature*, 3rd rev. edn (Edinburgh: John Grant, 1910).
Lindsay, Maurice, *History of Scottish Literature* (London: Robert Hale, 1977; 1992).
Maclean, Magnus, *The Literature of the Highlands* (London and Glasgow: Blackie, 1925).
Millar, J. H., *A Literary History of Scotland* (London: Fisher Unwin, 1903).
Royle, Trevor, *The Mainstream Companion to Scottish Literature* (Edinburgh: Mainstream, 1993).
Smith, G. Gregory, *Scottish Literature, Character and Influence* (London: Macmillan, 1919).
Speirs, John, *The Scots Literary Tradition* (1940), revised edn (London: Faber, 1962).
Thomson, Derick, *An Introduction to Gaelic Poetry* (London: Gollancz, 1974).
—— (ed.), *A Companion to Gaelic Scotland* (Oxford: Blackwell, 1983).
Walker, Marshall, *Scottish Literature Since 1707* (London: Longman, 1996).
Wittig, Kurt, *The Scottish Tradition in Literature* (Edinburgh: Oliver & Boyd, 1958).

Literary and Cultural Criticism

Asherson, Neal, *Stone Voices: The Search for Scotland* (London: Granta Books, 2002).

Ash, Marinell, *The Strange Death of Scottish History* (Edinburgh: Ramsay Head Press, 1980).

Bell, Eleanor and Miller, Gavin (eds), *Scotland in Theory: Reflections on Culture and Literature* (Amsterdam: Rodopi, 2004).

Beveridge, Craig and Turnbull, Ronald, *The Eclipse of Scottish Culture* (Edinburgh: Polygon, 1989).

Brown, Terence (ed.), *Celticism* (Amsterdam: Rodopi, 1996).

Carruthers, Gerald, Goldie, David and Renfrew, Alastair (eds), *Beyond Scotland: New Contexts for Twentieth-Century Scottish Literature* (Amsterdam: Rodopi, 2004).

Chapman, Michael, *The Celts: The Construction of a Myth* (New York: St Martin's Press, 1992).

Crawford, Robert, *Devolving English Literature* (Oxford: Clarendon Press, 1992).

Craig, Cairns, *Out of History: Narrative Paradigms in Scottish and British Culture* (Edinburgh: Polygon, 1996).

——, *The Modern Scottish Novel: Narrative and the National Imagination* (Edinburgh: Edinburgh University Press, 1999).

Davie, George Elder, *The Democratic Intellect* (Edinburgh: Edinburgh University Press, 1964).

——, *The Crisis of the Democratic Intellect* (Edinburgh: Polygon, 1986).

Devine, T. M. and Finlay, R. J. (eds), *Scotland in the 20th Century* (Edinburgh: Edinburgh University Press, 1996).

Donnachy, Ian and Whatley, Christopher (eds), *The Manufacture of Scottish History* (Edinburgh: Polygon, 1992).

Ferguson, William, *The Identity of the Scottish Nation* (Edinburgh: Edinburgh University Press, 1998).

Fielding, Penny, *Writing and Orality: Nationality, Culture and Nineteenth-Century Scottish Fiction* (Oxford: Clarendon Press, 1996).

Gonda, Caroline (ed.), *Tea and Leg-Irons: New Feminist Readings from Scotland* (London: Open Letters, 1992).

Hook, Andrew, *From Goosecreek to Gandercleugh: Studies in Scottish-American Literary and Cultural History* (East Linton: Tuckwell Press, 1999).

Hunter, James, *A Dance Called America: The Scottish Highlands, the United States and Canada* (Edinburgh: Mainstream, 1994).

McCrone, David, *Understanding Scotland: The Sociology of a Stateless Nation* (London: Routledge, 1992).

McCrone, David, Morris, Angela and Kiely, Richard, *Scotland – The Brand: The Making of Scottish Heritage* (Edinburgh: Edinburgh University Press, 1995).

MacDougall, Carl, *Painting the Forth Bridge: A Search for Scottish Identity* (London: Aurum Press, 2001).

——, *Writing Scotland: How Scottish Writers Shaped the Nation* (Edinburgh: Birlinn, 2004).

Manlove, Colin, *Scottish Fantasy Literature: A Critical Survey* (Edinburgh: Canongate Academic, 1994).

Muir, Edwin, *Scott and Scotland: The Predicament of the Scottish Writer* (London: Routledge, 1936).

Pick, J. B., *The Great Shadow House: Essays on the Metaphysical Tradition in Scottish Fiction* (Edinburgh: Polygon, 1993).

Pittock, Murray H., *The Invention of Scotland: The Stuart Myth and the Scottish Identity, 1638 to the Present* (London: Routledge, 1991).

Scott, Paul H., *Scotland: A Concise Cultural History* (Edinburgh: Mainstream, 1993).

Whyte, Christopher (ed.), *Gendering the Nation: Studies in Modern Scottish Literature* (Edinburgh: Edinburgh University Press, 1995).

Bibliography

Aitken, William R., *Scottish Literature in English and Scots* (Detroit: Gale Research, 1982).

Burgess, Moira, *The Glasgow Novel: A Survey and Bibliography*, 3rd edn (Glasgow: Scottish Library Association, 1999).

Crawford, Robert, *Literature in Twentieth-Century Scotland: A Select Bibliography* (London: British Council, 1995).

Scheps, Walter and Looney, Anna J., *Middle Scots Poets: A Reference Guide to James I of Scotland, Robert Henryson, William Dunbar and Gavin Douglas* (Boston, MA: G. K. Hall, 1986).

General History

Campbell, R. H., *Scotland since 1707* (Oxford: Blackwell, 1965).

Dickinson, W. C., *Scotland from the Earliest Times to 1603* (Edinburgh: Edinburgh University Press, 1965).

Devine, T. M., *The Scottish Nation, 1700–2000* (London: Allan Lane, 1999).

——, *Scotland's Empire 1600–1815* (London: Allan Lane, 2003).

Donaldson, Gordon (General Editor), *The Edinburgh History of Scotland* (Edinburgh: Oliver & Boyd, 1978):

> Volume 1, *Scotland: The Making of the Kingdom*, ed. Archibald A. M. Duncan (1978).
>
> Volume 2, *Scotland: The Later Middle Ages*, ed. Ranald Nicholson (1978).
>
> Volume 3, *Scotland: James V–James VII*, ed. Gordon Donaldson (1978).
>
> Volume 4, *Scotland: 1689 to the Present*, ed. William Ferguson (1978).

Fry, Michael, *The Scottish Empire* (Edinburgh: Birlinn, 2001).

Harvie, Christopher, *Scotland and Nationalism: Scottish Society and Politics, 1707–1994* (London: Routledge, 1994).

——, *Fool's Gold: The Story of North Sea Oil* (London: Allan Lane, 1994).

——, *No Gods and Precious Few Heroes: Twentieth-Century Scotland* (Edinburgh: Edinburgh University Press, 1998).

Hechter, Michael, *Internal Colonialism: The Celtic Fringe in British National Development with a new introduction and a new appendix by the author* (New Brunswick and London: Transaction Publishers, 1999).

Kermack, W. R., *The Scottish Highlands: A Short History, 1300–1746* (Edinburgh: Johnston & Bacon, 1957).

Lenman, Bruce, *An Economic History of Modern Scotland, 1660–1976* (London: Batsford, 1977).

Lynch, Michael, *Scotland: A New History* (London: Century, 1991).

Marr, Andrew, *The Battle for Scotland* (London: Allan Lane, 1992).

Nairn, Tom, *The Break-Up of Britain: Crisis and Neo-Nationalism* (London: New Left Books, 1977).

Smout, T. C., *A History of the Scottish People, 1560–1830* (London: Collins, 1969).

——, *A Century of the Scottish People, 1830–1950* (London: Collins, 1986).

Scottish Culture

Cameron, David Kerr, *The Ballad and the Plough: A Portrait of the Life of the Old Scottish Farmtouns* (London: Gollancz, 1978).

——, *Willie Gavin, Crofter Man: Portrait of a Vanished Lifestyle* (London: Gollancz, 1980).

Carter, Ian, *Farm Life in North-East Scotland: The Poor Man's Country* (Edinburgh: Birlinn, 2003).

Carter, Jennifer and Withrington, Donald (eds), *Scottish Universities: Distinctiveness and Diversity* (Edinburgh: John Donald, 1992).

Collinson, F. M., *The Traditional and National Music of Scotland* (London: Routledge & Kegan Paul, 1966).

Dick, Eddie (ed.), *From Limelight to Satellite: A Scottish Film Book* (London: Scottish Film Council, BFI, 1990).

Douglas, Sheila (ed.), *The Sang's the Thing: Voices from Lowland Scotland* (Edinburgh: Polygon, 1992).

Dunbar, John Telfer, *Highland Costume* (Edinburgh: William Blackwood, 1977).

Fyfe, J. G. (ed.), *Scottish Diaries and Memoirs, 1550–1746* (Stirling: Eneas Mackay, 1928).

——, *Scottish Diaries and Memoirs, 1746–1843* (Stirling: Eneas Mackay, 1942).

Gardiner, Michael, *Modern Scottish Culture* (Edinburgh: Edinburgh University Press, 2005).

Graham, Henry G., *The Social Life of Scotland in the Eighteenth Century* (London: A. & C. Black, 1909).

Hay, George, *Architecture of Scotland* (Stocksfield, Northumberland: Oriel Press, 1977).

Keay, John and Julia (eds), *Collins Encyclopaedia of Scotland* (London: HarperCollins, 1994).

McArthur, Colin (ed.), *Scotch Reels: Scotland in Cinema and Television* (London: British Film Institute, 1982).

MacLean, Calum I., *The Highlands*, foreword by Sorley MacLean (Edinburgh: Mainstream, 1990; 1st edition 1959).

Macmillan, Duncan, *Scottish Art, 1460–2000* (Edinburgh: Mainstream, 2000).

McNeill, F. Marian, *The Silver Bough*, 4 vols (Glasgow: William Maclellan, 1957–68).

MacNeill, Seumas, *Piobaireachd* (Edinburgh: BBC, 1968).

Millman, R. N., *The Making of the Scottish Landscape* (London: Batsford, 1975).

Purser, John, *Scotland's Music* (Edinburgh: Mainstream, 1992).

Ross, Anne, *Folklore of the Scottish Highlands* (London: Batsford, 1976).

West, T. M., *A History of Architecture in Scotland* (London: University of London Press, 1967).

Scots and Gaelic

Aitken, A. J. and McArthur, T. (eds), *Languages of Scotland* (Edinburgh: Chambers, 1979).

Corbett, John, *Language and Scottish Literature* (Edinburgh: Edinburgh University Press, 1997).

Kay, Billy, *Scots: the Mither Tongue* (Edinburgh: Mainstream, 1986).

McClure, J. Derrick, *Language Poetry and Nationhood: Scots as a Poetic Language from 1878 to the Present* (East Linton: Tuckwell Press, 2000).

McClure, J. Derrick (ed.), *Scotland and the Lowland Tongue: Studies in the Language and Literature of Lowland Scotland* (Aberdeen: Aberdeen University Press, 1983).

MacKinnon, Kenneth, *Gaelic: A Past and Future Prospect* (Edinburgh: Saltire Society, 1991).

MacLennan, Malcolm, *A Pronouncing and Etymological Dictionary of the Gaelic Language: Gaelic–English, English–Gaelic* (Edinburgh: Acair & Mercat Press, 1995).

Murison, David, *The Guid Scots Tongue* (Edinburgh: William Blackwood, 1977).

Robinson, Mairi (ed.), *The Concise Scots Dictionary* (Aberdeen: Aberdeen University Press, 1985).

Anthologies

Bateman, Meg and Crawford, Robert (eds), *Scottish Religious Poetry: An Anthology* (Edinburgh: St Andrews Press, 2000).

Black, Ronald (ed.), *An Tuil* (Edinburgh: Polygon, 1999). 20th-century Scottish Gaelic verse.

Burgess, Moira (ed.), *The Other Voice: Scottish Women's Writing since 1808* (Edinburgh: Polygon, 1987).

Clancy, Thomas (ed.), *The Triumph Tree: Scotland's Earliest Poetry, AD 530–1350* (Edinburgh: Canongate Classics, 1998).

Craig, Cairns and Stevenson, Randall (eds), *Twentieth-Century Scottish Drama* (Edinburgh: Canongate Classics, 2001).

Crawford, Robert and Imlah, Mick (eds), *The New Penguin Book of Scottish Verse* (London: Allan Lane, 2000).

Dunn, Douglas (ed.), *The Faber Book of Twentieth-Century Scottish Poetry* (London: Faber, 1993).

Kerrigan, Catherine (ed.), *Scottish Women Poets* (Edinburgh: Edinburgh University Press, 1991).

Leonard, Tom (ed.), *Radical Renfrew: Poetry from the French Revolution to the First World War* (Edinburgh: Polygon, 1990).

MacAulay, Donald (ed.), *Modern Scottish Gaelic Poems* (Edinburgh: Canongate Classics, 1995).

McCordrick, David (ed.), *Scottish Literature: An Anthology*, 3 vols (New York: Peter Lang, 1996; 2002).

MacDougall, Carl (ed.), *The Devil and the Giro: Two Centuries of Scottish Stories* (Edinburgh: Canongate Classics, 1991).

MacLaine, Allan H. (ed.), *The Christis Kirk Tradition: Scots Poems of Folk Festivity* (Glasgow: Association for Scottish Literary Studies, 1996).

McMillan, Dorothy and Byrne, Michel (eds.), *Modern Scottish Women Poets* (Edinburgh: Canongate Classics, 2003).

Meek, Donald (ed.), *The Wiles of the World / Caran An T-Saoghail* (West Lothian: Barbour Books, 2003). 19th-century Scottish Gaelic poetry.

O Baoill, Colm (ed.), *The Harp's Cry / Gàir nan Clàrsach* (Edinburgh: Birlinn, 1994). 17th-century Gaelic poems.

O'Rourke, Daniel (ed.), *Dream State: The New Scottish Poets* (Edinburgh: Polygon, 1994; 2002).

O'Rourke, Daniel and Whyte, Hamish (eds), *Across the Water: Irishness in Modern Scottish Writing* (Glendaruel: Argyll, 2000).

Tasioulas, J. (ed.), *The Makars: The Poems of Henryson, Dunbar and Douglas* (Edinburgh: Canongate Classics, 1999).

Thomson, Derick (ed.), *Gaelic Poetry in the Eighteenth Century* (Aberdeen: Association of Scottish Literary Studies, 1993).

Watson, Roderick (ed.), *The Poetry of Scotland: Gaelic, Scots, English, 1380–1980* (Edinburgh: Edinburgh University Press, 1995).

Watson, W. J. (ed.), *Bàrdachd Ghàidhlig: Specimens of Gaelic Poetry, 1550–1900* (Glasgow: An Comunn Gaidhealach, 1959).

Scottish Texts Society: Most of the major older Scottish poets and MS collections are available in these often multi-volume scholarly editions.

Scottish Gaelic Texts Society: The works of almost all the older Gaelic poets, usually with translations and helpful introductions, can be found in this series.

Scotnotes

For school and college teaching, *Teaching Scottish Literature: Curriculum and Classroom Applications*, ed. Alan MacGillivray (Edinburgh: Edinburgh University Press, 1997) is a detailed professional package, while the ASLS *Scotnotes* series offers a useful collection of student study-guides to individual authors and texts.

Baird, Gerald, *The Poems of Robert Henryson*.

Blackburn, John, *The Poetry of Iain Crichton Smith*.

Burgess, Moira, *Naomi Mitchison's 'Early in Orcadia', 'The Big House', 'Travel Light'*.

Carruthers, Gerard, *Robert Louis Stevenson's 'Dr Jekyll and Mr Hyde', 'The Master of Ballantrae' and 'The Ebb-Tide'*.

Dickson, Beth, *William McIlvanney's 'Laidlaw'*.

Jack, Ronald D. S., *The Poetry of William Dunbar*.

McCulloch, Margery Palmer, *Liz Lochhead's 'Mary Queen of Scots Got Her Head Chopped Off'*.

MacGillivray, Alan, *Iain Banks' 'The Wasp Factory', 'The Crow Road' and 'Whit'*.

MacGillivray, Alan, *George Mackay Brown's 'Greenvoe'*.

MacLachlan, Christopher, *John Buchan's 'Witch Wood', 'Huntingtower' and 'The Thirty-Nine Steps'*.

Petrie, Elaine, *James Hogg's 'The Private Memoirs and Confessions of a Justified Sinner'*.

Riach, Alan, *The Poetry of Hugh MacDiarmid*.

Robb, David S., *Muriel Spark's 'The Prime of Miss Jean Brodie'*.

Simpson, Kenneth, *Robert Burns*.

Smith, Iain Crichton, *Robin Jenkins' 'The Cone-Gatherers'*.

Smith, Iain Crichton, *George Douglas Brown's 'The House with the Green Shutters'*.
Thomson, Geddes, *The Poetry of Edwin Morgan*.
Watson, Roderick, *The Poetry of Norman MacCaig*.
Young, Douglas, *Lewis Grassic Gibbon's 'Sunset Song'*.

1   The twentieth century: the Scottish Literary Renaissance

Abrioux, Yves, *Ian Hamilton Finlay: A Visual Primer with Introductory Notes and Commentaries by Stephen Bann*, 2nd edn (London: Reaktion, 1992).

Anderson, Carol and Christianson, Aileen (eds), *Scottish Women's Fiction, 1920s to 1960s: Journeys into Being* (East Linton: Tuckwell Press, 2000).

Bold, Alan, *Modern Scottish Literature* (London: Longman, 1983).

——, *MacDiarmid: A Critical Biography* (London: John Murray, 1988).

——, *George Mackay Brown* (Edinburgh: Oliver & Boyd, 1978).

——, *Muriel Spark* (London: Methuen, 1986).

Bold, Valentina (ed.), *Smeddum: A Lewis Grassic Gibbon Anthology* (Edinburgh: Canongate Classics, 2001).

Burns, John, *A Celebration of the Light: Zen in the Novels of Neil Gunn* (Edinburgh: Canongate, 1988).

Butter, Peter, *Edwin Muir: Man and Poet* (Edinburgh: Oliver & Boyd, 1966).

—— (ed.), *The Complete Poems of Edwin Muir* (Aberdeen: Association for Scottish Literary Studies, 1991).

Carswell, Catherine, *Lying Awake: An Unfinished Autobiography* (Edinburgh: Canongate Classics, 1997).

Craig, Cairns; Stevenson, Randall (eds), *Twentieth-Century Scottish Drama* (Edinburgh: Canongate Classics, 2001).

Crawford, Tom (ed.), Lewis Grassic Gibbon, *'A Scots Quair'* (Edinburgh: Canongate Classics, 1995).

D'Arcy, Julian, *Scottish Skalds and Sagamen: Old Norse Influence on Modern Scottish Literature* (East Linton: Tuckwell Press, 1996).

Finlay, Alec (ed.), *Wood Notes Wild: Essays on the Poetry and Art of Ian Hamilton Finlay* (Edinburgh: Polygon, 1995).

Fulton, Robin, *Contemporary Scottish Poetry: Individuals and Contexts* (Edinburgh: Macdonald, 1974).

Gillies, William (ed.), *Ris `a Bhruthaich: the Criticism and Prose Writings of Sorley MacLean* (Stornoway: Acair, 1985).

Glen, Duncan, *Hugh MacDiarmid and the Scottish Renaissance* (Edinburgh: Chambers, 1964).

—— (ed.), *Hugh MacDiarmid, a Critical Survey* (Edinburgh: Scottish Academic Press, 1972).

Gold, Eric, *Sydney Goodsir Smith's Under the Eildon Tree* (Preston: Akros, 1975).

Grieve, Michael and Aitken, W. R., *Hugh MacDiarmid: Complete Poems*, 2 vols (Manchester: Carcanet, 1993).

Gunn, Neil M., *The Atom of Delight* (Edinburgh: Polygon, 1986).

Hart, F. R. and Pick, J. B., *Neil M. Gunn: A Highland Life* (London: John Murray, 1981).

Henderson, Hamish, *Alias MacAlias: Writings on Songs, Folk and Literature* (Edinburgh: Polygon, 1992).

Hendry, Joy and Ross, Raymond J. (eds.), *Norman MacCaig: Critical Essays* (Edinburgh: Edinburgh University Press, 1990).

Hutchison, David, *The Modern Scottish Theatre* (Glasgow: Molendinar Press, 1977).

Kerrigan, Catherine, *Whaur Extremes Meet: The Poetry of Hugh MacDiarmid, 1920–1934* (Edinburgh: Mercat Press, 1983).

Lindsay, Maurice, *Francis George Scott and the Scottish Renaissance* (Edinburgh: Paul Harris, 1980).

—— (ed.), *As I Remember: Ten Scottish Authors Recall How Writing Began for Them* (London: Hale, 1979).

Lopez, Tony, *The Poetry of W. S. Graham* (Edinburgh: Edinburgh University Press, 1989).

McCulloch, Margery Palmer, *Edwin Muir: Poet, Critic and Novelist* (Edinburgh: Edinburgh University Press, 1988).

——, *The Novels of Neil Gunn: A Critical Study* (Edinburgh: Scottish Academic Press, 1987).

—— (ed.), *Modernism and Nationalism, Literature and Society in Scotland, 1918–1939: Source Documents for the Scottish Renaissance* (Glasgow: Association for Scottish Literary Studies, 2004).

MacDiarmid, Hugh, *Lucky Poet: A Self-Study in Literature and Political Ideas* (Manchester: Carcanet, 1994).

McNeill, Marjory, *Norman MacCaig: A Study of his Life and Work* (Edinburgh: Mercat Press, 1996).

Malcolm, William, *A Blasphemer and Reformer: A Study of James Leslie Mitchell / Lewis Grassic Gibbon* (Aberdeen: Aberdeen University Press, 1984).

Massie, Allan, *Muriel Spark: A New Assessment* (Edinburgh: Ramsay Head Press, 1979).

Miller, Karl (ed.), *Memoirs of a Modern Scotland* (London: Faber & Faber, 1970).

Muir, Edwin, *Scottish Journey*, intro. T. C. Smout (London: Fontana, 1985).

——, *Scott and Scotland: The Predicament of the Scottish Writer*, intro. Allan Massie (Edinburgh: Polygon, 1982; 1st pub. 1936).

——, *An Autobiography*, intro. Peter Butter (Edinburgh: Canongate Classics, 1993).

Muir Willa, *Belonging: A Memoir* (London: Hogarth Press, 1968).

Munro, Ian S., *Leslie Mitchell: Lewis Grassic Gibbon* (Edinburgh: Oliver & Boyd, 1966).

Murray, Isobel, *Jessie Kesson: Writing Her Life* (Edinburgh: Canongate, 2000).

—— (ed.), *Scottish Writers Talking* (East Linton: Tuckwell Press, 2002). Mackay Brown; Kesson; MacCaig; McIlvanney; Toulmin.

Murray, Isobel and Tait, Bob, *Ten Modern Scottish Novels* (Aberdeen: Aberdeen University Press, 1984).

Nicholson, Colin (ed.), *Iain Crichton Smith: Critical Essays* (Edinburgh: Edinburgh University Press, 1992).

Pick, J. B., *Neil M. Gunn* (Tavistock: Northcote House, British Council, 2004).

Price, Richard, *The Fabulous Matter of Fact: The Poetics of Neil Gunn* (Edinburgh: Edinburgh University Press, 1991).

Riach, Alan, *Hugh MacDiarmid's Epic Poetry* (Edinburgh: Edinburgh University Press, 1991).

Ross, Raymond. J. and Hendry, Joy (eds), *Sorley MacLean: Critical Essays* (Edinburgh: Scottish Academic Press, 1986).

Scott, Alex (ed.), *William Soutar, 'Diaries of a Dying Man'* (Edinburgh: Canongate Classics, 1991).

Spark, Muriel, *Curriculum Vitae* (London: Constable, 1992). Autobiography.

Watson, Roderick, *Hugh MacDiarmid* (Milton Keynes: Open University Press, 1985).

—— (ed.), Nan Shepherd, *'The Grampian Quartet'* (Edinburgh: Canongate Classics, 1996).

Whyte, Christopher, *Modern Scottish Poetry* (Edinburgh: Edinburgh University Press, 1996).

—— (ed.), *Sorley MacLean, 'Poems to Eimhir'* (Glasgow: Association for Scottish Literary Studies, 2002).

2 The twentieth century: Beyond the Renaissance – old themes, new blood, new voices

Christianson, Aileen and Lumsden, Alison (eds), *Contemporary Scottish Women Writers* (Edinburgh: Edinburgh University Press, 2000).

Crawford, Robert and Kinloch, David (eds), *Reading Douglas Dunn* (Edinburgh: Edinburgh University Press, 1992).

Crawford, Robert and Nairn Thom (eds), *The Arts of Alasdair Gray* (Edinburgh: Edinburgh University Press, 1991).

Crawford, Robert and Varty, Anne (eds), *Liz Lochhead's Voices* (Edinburgh: Edinburgh University Press, 1993).

Crawford, Robert and Whyte, Hamish (eds), *About Edwin Morgan* (Edinburgh: Edinburgh University Press, 1990).

Gray, Alasdair, *Alasdair Gray* (Edinburgh: Saltire Society, 1988).

Kelman, James, *Some Recent Attacks* (Stirling: AK Press, 1992).

McNeill, Kirsty, 'Interview with James Kelman', *Chapman*, 57 (Edinburgh: Chapman Publications, 1989).

March, Cristie L., *Rewriting Scotland: Welsh, McLean, Warner, Banks, Galloway and Kennedy* (Manchester: Manchester University Press, 2002).

Morgan, Edwin, *Crossing the Border: Essays on Scottish Literature* (Manchester: Carcanet, 1990).

——, *Nothing Not Giving Messages: Reflections on his Work and Life*, ed. Hamish Whyte (Edinburgh: Polygon, 1990).

——, *Collected Poems* (Manchester: Carcanet, 1996).

Murray, Isobel (ed.), *Scottish Writers Talking, 2* (East Linton: Tuckwell Press, 2002). Banks; MacLaverty; Mitchison; Crichton Smith; Spence.

Nicholson, Colin, *Poem, Purpose and Place: Shaping Identity in Contemporary Scottish Verse* (Edinburgh: Polygon, 1992). MacLean; Mitchison; MacCaig; Morgan; Bruce; Mackay Brown; Crichton Smith; Henderson; Neill; Ransford; Dunn; Lochhead; Butlin; Abbot.

Petrie, Duncan, *Contemporary Scottish Fictions: Film, Television and the Novel* (Edinburgh: Edinburgh University Press, 2004).

Royle, Trevor, *James and Jim: A Biography of James Kennaway* (Edinburgh: Mainstream, 1983).

Smith, Iain Crichton, *Towards the Human: Selected Essays* (Edinburgh: Macdonald, 1986).

——, *Collected Poems* (Manchester: Carcanet: 1995).

Somerville-Arjat, Gillean and Wilson, Rebecca E. (eds), *Sleeping with Monsters: Conversations with Scottish and Irish Women Poets* (Edinburgh: Polygon, 1989).

Spring, Ian, *Phantom Village: The Myth of the New Glasgow* (Edinburgh: Polygon, 1990).

Stevenson, Randall and Wallace, Gavin (eds), *The Scottish Novel since the Seventies* (Edinburgh: Edinburgh University Press, 1993).

——, *Scottish Theatre since the Seventies*, (Edinburgh: Edinburgh University Press, 1996).

Witschi, Beat, *Glasgow Urban Writing and Post-Modernism: A Study of Alasdair Gray's Fiction* (Frankfurt: Peter Lang, 1991).

Index